Abstracts of Philadelphia County Pennsylvania

1810-1815

F. Edward Wright

HERITAGE BOOKS
2007

HERITAGE BOOKS
AN IMPRINT OF HERITAGE BOOKS, INC.

Books, CDs, and more—Worldwide

For our listing of thousands of titles see our website
at
www.HeritageBooks.com

Published 2007 by
HERITAGE BOOKS, INC.
Publishing Division
65 East Main Street
Westminster, Maryland 21157-5026

Originally published 1998 F. Edward Wright

All rights reserved. No part of this book may be reproduced or transmitted in any form or by any means, electronic or mechanical, including photocopying, recording or by any information storage and retrieval system without written permission from the author, except for the inclusion of brief quotations in a review.

International Standard Book Number: 978-1-58549-461-3

CONTENTS

Introduction v

Book 3 1

Book 4 70

Book 5 123

Index 187

INTRODUCTION

These wills were abstracted under the auspices of the Historical Society of Pennsylvania in the early 1900s. Copies of these abstracts were made available to various libraries in Pennsylvania and microfilm copies made by the Genealogical Society of Utah (LDS). Recently bound photostat copies of the abstracts were offered for sale by the Genealogical Society of Pennsylvania.

We extend our appreciation to the staffs of the Historical Society of Pennsylvania (1300 Locust Street, Philadelphia, PA 19107) and encourage use and support of its facilities and to the Genealogical Society of Pennsylvania whose collections are housed in the Historical Society Library. We also encourage membership in the Genealogical Society of Pennsylvania (1305 Locust Street, Philadelphia, PA 19107-5699).

F. Edward Wright
Westminster, Maryland
1998

ABBREVIATIONS

&c.	etc.
adj.	adjoining
admin.	administration
afsd.	aforesaid
bro(s).	brother(s)
Co.	County
dau(s).	daughter(s)
dec'd	deceased
Esq.	Esquire
exec(s).	executor(s)
extx.	executrix
Revd.	Reverend
sd.	said
Twp.	Township

U.S. Postal Service State Abbreviations

ABSTRACTS OF PHILADELPHIA COUNTY WILLS, 1810-1815

BOOK 3

BARTRAM, MOSES. Phila. Druggist. March 29, 1809. Jan 4, 1810. 3.51.
Sons: George W. Bartram, William Bartram, late son Archibald Bartram. Daus.: Rebecca, Elizabeth , Ann and Rachel. Granddaus.: Eliza, dau. of late son Thomas Say. Leaves his property in Philadelphia and that on Wissahickon or Ridge Road adj. Isaac Bartram's land to his said children.
Execs: Son George W. Bartram, daus. Rebecca and Ann, friend Peter Thompson of Philadelphia, Conveyancer.
Wit: Joseph Ridgway, Thomas Dugdale, Jr.

JERVIS, ELIZABETH. Phila. Oct 6, 1808. Jan 5, 1810. 3.56.
Estate to niece Sarah Jervis. Friends: William Drinker, Samuel Shoemaker in connection with her real estate.
Exec: Niece Sarah Jervis.
Wit: George Bringhurst, John Phillips.

BIEGLER, PHILIP. Phila. Vichualler. Jan 30, 1809. Jan 5, 1810. 3.57.
Mother Ann Biegler, nephew Samuel P. Beigler, niece Juliana Biegler, sister Mary Beigler. All his property in Phila. he bequeaths to wife Ann Biegler and dau. Elizabeth. Property adj. that of Samuel Wetherill.
Execs: Wife Ann, father-in-law Benjamin Severn, Phila.
Wit: William Severne, Henry W. Pugh.

GRASSLER, ANNA SOPHIA. Phila. Widow. April 30, 1809. Jan 9, 1810. 3.60.
Bequeaths all estate to friend Godfrey Smith, Phila.
Exec: Godfrey Smith.
Wit: Daniel Vanderslice, Stacy Madden.

SMITH, VALENTINE. Roxborough Twp. Phila. Co. Cooper. Feb 14, 1807. Jan 10, 1810. 3.60.
Nephew Valentine Smith, son of bro. Frederick Smith. To wife Susanna, use, rents, &c., of all estate, real and personal, during her life. After her death to be converted into money and proceeds to bro. John Smith, children of bro. Geo. Smith, dec'd, sister Elizabeth Good (wife of Jacob Good), bro. Jacob Smith, bro. Frederick Smith, bro.-in-law Daniel Barndollar, sister-in-law Elizabeth Smith (wife of bro. John Smith), bro.-

in-law John Barndollar, sister-in-law Mary Mitchel (wife of James Mitchel), bro.-in-law Christopher Barndollar.
Exec: Wife Susanna, bro. Frederick Smith, and bro.-in-law John Barndollar.
Wit: Godfrey Bockius and Robert Alloway.

PARRY, JONATHAN. Byberry Twp. Phila. Co. April 6, 1809. Codicil Sept 6, 1809. March 1, 1810. 3.63.
Provides for wife Rebecca Parry. Bequeaths to his son Jonathan Parry the plantation on which he lives, also his lot of woodland in Richilieu, Bucks Co. Legacies to dau. Susanna Stackhous. Grandchildren: Jonathan Marshall son of Nathan Marshall, Thomas Stackhous son of Joseph Stackhous dec'd and Phebe Comly dau. of Joseph Comly.
Execs: Son Jonathan Parry, friend Ezra Townsend.
Proved March 1, 1810.
Wit: Silas, Walton, Thomas Knight, Jesse Wilson.

FRANCIS, THOMAS. Dec 25, 1808. Oct 30, 1810. 3.66.
Provides for wife Sarah Francis. After her decease he desires all real estate to be sold, proceeds he bequeaths to his dau. Elizabeth wife of Elisha Gordon. Two grandchildren: Margaret, wife of Dr. Dale, and Catharine Fitzgerald, children of his eldest dau. Catharine, dec'd. Five grandchildren: Thomas, Robert, Sarah, Clarise and David, children of dau. Elizabeth Gordon.
Exec: Sole exec. sd. wife Sarah Francis during her life. After her decease he appoints his two sons-in-law Thomas Fitzgerland, Elisha Gordon.
Wit: Nathan Chapin, Jacob Thomas, Thomas Amies. Thomas Fitzgerald renounced.
Letters granted to Elisha Gordon.

HANSELL, JACOB. Phila. Blacksmith. May 3, 1807. Jan 15, 1810. 3.68.
All estate to wife: Mary during widowhood, if she marries, to have one third. Residue to his children (names not given). Wife to be guardian of children. Mentions property in Kingsessing Twp. on Darby Road.
Execs: Wife Mary, bro.-in-law Peter Lex, Phila.
Wit: Jacob Painter, Frederick Beates.

RICE, MARIA. Phila. Dec 13, 1809. Jan 16, 1810. 3.69.
Bequeaths to her husband John Rice her house in Dublin, Ireland, with all personal property &c. left in care of Mrs. Eloner Byrne.

Exec: James Byrne, Merchant of Wilmington, DE. Mentions John Betler her attorney in Dublin.
Wit: Paul Houston, Mary McGuire, Thomas Washington.

DUCHè, JOHN. Southwark. Phila. Co. March 12, 1802. Feb 28, 1810. 3.70.
Wife Jane to whom he leaves all estate, which consists chiefly in houses and lots in Phila. purchased of John Smith and wife, extending back to ground late of Edward Tew, land granted to William Robinson the younger, house in tenure of William Workman extending back to John Murray's ground, lots part of same granted to John Conrade bounded by ground of Charles Wharton's by land belonging to heirs of Joseph Wharton, dec'd, and by Thomas Penrose's ground. Lot in Moyamensing Twp. reaching ground late of widow Parham. Also ground rents payable by Isaac Wharton agent for Mr. Alsop of NY out of lot late in possession of Lucy Brown, now of John Turner. Lot granted to Joseph Richardson. Ground rents payable by following persons namely: James Hendricks, Jemima Berrimin, late payable by Mr. Cramond now by John Flowers. By William Robinson the elder, by Samuel Piles, by Edward Stiles, by Andrew Summers, late by Gerard Vogels now by John Arnell, by John Simpson and James Simpson, Rebecca Barker and Joseph Conrade. Ground late the estate of George Griffith, dec'd, subject to annuity payable to his son George.
Exec: Wife Jane.
Wit: William Robinson, Jr., Isaac Hozey, Gibbs Jones.

JONES, MARY. Southwark. Phila. Widow of Blathwaite Jones, late of sd. city. April 1, 1799. Jan 16, 1810. 3.73.
To grandson Samuel Lieberhichn Shober her bible which her aunt Deborah Morris left her. All estate to dau. Susanna Budd Shober widow of Dr. Samuel Shober, whom she appoints sole executrix.
Exec: Dau. Susanna Budd Shober.
Wit: Caleb Bickham, Samuel Law, Isaac Morris.

BICKLEY, JACOB. Northern Liberties Twp. Phila. Co. Yeoman. Feb 8, 1807. Jan 18, 1810. 3.74.
Provides for wife Mary Bickley and their six children namely: Mary, Margaret, Abigail, Henry, Jacob and Eliza Bickley.
Exec: Sd. wife Mary so long as she remains his widow and his bro. Daniel Bickley.
Wit: Benjamin Sutton, Sebastian Hoffman, Robert Whitehead.

McKOWEN, GRACE. Phila. Widow. Sept 10, 1809. Jan 22, 1810. 3.75. Bequeaths her property in Phila. to son Robt. McKowen now of Port Royal in the Island of Jamaica and to her dau. Mary McFall wife of Daniel McFall. Annuity to Isaac W. Morris of sd. city.
Execs: Sd. son Robert, son-in-law Joseph Campbell of Phila.
Wit: Isaac W. Morris, Joseph Caskey.
Letters granted to Joseph Campbell.

RUTTER, JOHN. Southwark. Cordwainer. Dec 13, 1809. March 30, 1810. 3.76.
All estate real and personal to wife Sarah Rutter during widowhood, if she marries, he gives same to his children: Jane, Elizabeth, John, Maria, William, Robert and child with which wife is now pregnant. Sd. wife to be guardian of children, after her decease or second marriage appoints his trustees Wm. T. Donaldson of Southwark sheriff and Jacob Kean of Northern Liberties, tanner as guardians.
Execs: Sd. wife Sarah Rutter, friends Sd. William T. Donaldson, Jacob Kean.
Wit: Samuel Barclay, Benjamin Morton, Rich. Renshaw.

SNOWDEN, ISAAC. At present residing in Phila., but lately of Cranberry in Middlesex Co., NJ, Esq. April 11, 1809. Jan 25, 1810. 3.78. Sons: Isaac, Samuel F., Nathaniel R., Charles and William, sd. William living in Bucks Co. and incapable of attending to his affairs, his share to be in Trust. Grandchildren: Mary, Sarah, Gilbert T., William Snowden (children of dec'd son Gilbert T. Snowden).
Execs: Son: Nathaniel R. Snowden and Charles Snowden.
Wit: Daniel Jaudon, John Huffnagle, Frederick Beates. Charles Snowden renounces.
Wit: George Miller, George A. Baker, Jr.

RICE, JOHN. Phila. Dec 23, 1809. Jan 31, 1810. 3.81. (Nuncupative.) Wife Maria Rice, dec'd. Bequeaths his house in Dublin, Ireland and all other property to his adopted son Robert Rice during his life, at his death to James Bryin.
Exec: James Bryin.
Wit: Thomas Washington Houston, Mary McGuire.

DUTILH, STEPHEN. Phila. Merchant. Jan 4, 1810. Jan 29, 1810. 3.83. Provides for wife Catharine Magdalen Dutilh and children (names not given). Legacies to Mary Stevens and Rachel Biegel born Rachel Burke.

Marriage articles attached to will mentions Catharine Magdalen Dutilh as dau. of Catharine Martin widow of Abel Peter Dutilh.
Execs: Sd. wife Catharine Magdalen, Leopold Nottnagel, Lewis Clapier, Augustin Bousquet and Charles Graff, all of Phila., merchants.
Wit: Fournier Vostain, Peter S. DuPonceau.

CHEW, BENJAMIN. Phila. April 1, 1806. Feb 13, 1810. 3.86.
Provides for wife Elizabeth Chew. All Plate marked with first wife's Family Coat of Arms quartered with his own he gives to his three surviving daus. of sd. first wife. Property in Phila. purchased of John Penn, Esq., and his country place near Germantown which he purchased of Blair McClenachan, called Cliveden, he leaves to his wife and his only son Benjamin. Sold to James Gallaghar a house in Phila., built by himself on lot belonging to his wife. Appoints sons-in-law Edward Tilghman and Philip Nicklin execs. in case of death of son Benjamin. Unmarried daus. Anna Maria Chew, Henrietta Chew, Maria Chew and Catherine Chew. Married daus. Sarah Galloway wife of John, Margaret Howard wife of John Eager Howard, Juliana Nicklin and Sophia Philips. Negroes George, Jesse, Harry, Sarah and David. Son-in-law Charles Carroll, Jr., husband of dau. Harriet. Children of dec'd dau. Marry Wilcocks.
Codicil alters legacies to his daus. to provide more fully for dau. Juliana Nicklin who has been left a widow with six children. Legacy to granddau. Mary Tilghman dau. of sd. dau. Elizabeth Tilghman, names of sd. Elizabeth's other children not given, Aug 8, 1809.
Execs: Sd. wife Elizabeth Chew and son Benjamin.
Wit: William Tilghman, Edward Burd, James Gibson.

WRIGHT, HANNAH. Phila. Gentlewoman. Jan 13, 1810. Feb 5, 1810. 3.94.
All estate to son Charles Lukens now living with her, he to maintain her mother Sarah Wright, if sd. son dies under age or without issue, estate shall go to children of bro. John Wright, Cooper, of Louden Co., Old VA.
Execs: Friends Alexander Whitesides, Plaisterer and Adam Ecfeldt, Smith both of sd. city.
Wit: R. Whitehead, James Flanegan, William Smith.

HUMPHREYS, JAMES. Phila. Bookseller. Oct 12, 1807. Feb 6, 1810. 3.95.
All estate to children: Susanna Y. Humphreys, James Y. Humphreys, Mary Yorke Humphreys, Thomas Y. Humphreys, Assheton Y. Humphreys, Andrew Y. Humphreys, Lodowick Sprogell Humphreys and

Martha Y. Humphreys. Mentions John Vaughan having share in his books.
Execs: Friend Samuel Yorke and daus. Susanna Y. Humphreys and Mary Yorke Humphreys.
Wit: Benjamin Tanner, William W. Potter.
Letters granted Feb 20, 1810 to daus.

BOYLE, ALEXANDER. Phila. Jan 13, 1810. Feb 8, 1810. 3.96.
Bequeaths to wife Catharine Boyle alias Catharine Matthias all property real and personal, appointing the sd. Catharine Boyle or Matthias executrix. Revokes will and Power of Attorney to Daniel Suter, Jr.
Exec: Sd. Catharine Boyle or Matthias.
Wit: Thomas Breintnall, George Schively or Shively.

GORDON, JOHN. Willow Grove, Montgomery Co. Grocer. Sept 6, 1809. Feb 10, 1810. 3.96.
Provides for wife Ann and daus. Ann and Catharine Gordon. If daus. die in minority or without issue, bequeaths same to children of late sister Jane Steward and to children of bros. James and Henry Gordon. Legacies to bro.-in-law Daniel McMullin and Catharine McMullin.
Execs: Robert Fleming and bros. Henry Gordon and William Graham.
Wit: George C. Potts, John Floyd, William Graham, Thomas Algeo of Phila., merchant, affirmed.
Letters granted Oct 4, 1811 to Robt. Fleming.

GEORGE, MARY. Phila. Jan 24, 1810. Feb 12, 1810. 3.99.
Bequeaths to William H. Tod, Esq., and George Campbell, Jr., of sd. city her frame house and lot in Northern Liberties, Phila. in trust, they to receive rents &c. and pay same to niece Margaret George, after her decease, sd. property to John Donnaldson, Esq., and to his son George Donnaldson. Legacy to Sarah Donnaldson dau. of sd. John Donnaldson. To John Donnaldson, Jr., share in Germantown and Perkiomen Turnpike Co. To aforesd. George Donnaldson also share in sd. Turnpike Co. Legacies to Mrs. Sarah Donnaldson wife of sd. John Donnaldson, to Edward M. Donnaldson, to Mary Tod dau. of sd. William H. Tod, to Philip Stock, Jr., her looking glass now at Mrs. Keats, to niece Elizabeth Sweeny, to Catharine Smith dau. of Frederick Smith of Germantown, to Rachel Baynard now living at Mrs. Donnaldsons, to sd. William H. Tod and George Campbell, Jr., to Helen and Eliza Donnaldson, to Richard M. Donnaldson, to Hugh Donnaldson, to Mary Shed, to Mrs. Mary

Donnaldson, to Susan M. Donnaldson, to Mrs. Helen Campbell, to aforesd. Margaret George.
Exec: Sd. George Campbell, Jr.
Wit: George Campbell, Samuel P. Griffitts.

BETTON, SAMUEL. Market Street, Phila. March 14, 1809. Feb 15, 1810. 3.104.
Wife Catherine Betton. Sons Samuel and John Price Betton and dau. Mary Ann Betton.
Codicil Bequeathes to sd. sons all estate real and personal in Island of Jamaica, providing for wife and dau. Legacy to sister Martha Williams, to be paid her in Shrewsbery, England. April 5, 1809.
Execs: Sd. wife Catherine Betton, Thomas Forrest, Thomas Leiper, sons Samuel and John Price Betton.
Wit: William Truxton, George Crower, James G. S. Leiper, John Barney, Vichualer.
(Superceded by later will see page 293.)

LESHER, ANNA MARIA. Frankford. Phila. Co. Dec 2, 1809. Feb 16, 1810. 3.104.
All estate to dau. Catherine and her heirs, appointing sd. Catherine sole executrix.
Exec: Dau. Catherine.
Wit: Watson Atkinson, Jesse Roberts of Phila.
Letters granted to extx. March 2, 1810.

NORQUE or NORKEY, JOHN. Southwark. Rigger. May 12, 1803. Feb 16, 1810. 3.105.
Leaves all estate to wife during life or widowhood, at her death or marriage he leaves one half his property to dau. Mary Porter and the other half to his two grandchildren Eliza and Mary Norque, requesting his wife and dau. to have an oversight of sd. children.
Wit: Joseph Huddell, Jr., John K. Drummond.

STIER, MARIA (widow of Jacob STIER). Phila. Inn Keeper. June 3, 1807. Feb 17 & 28, 1810. 3.105.
Leaves estate to her five children (by her three husbands, all dec'd), namely: John Wentz, Maria Wentz, Catharine Thunn, Elizabeth Thunn and Jacob Stier.

Codicil Jan 19, 1810 bequeaths to Sabina Kursus the possession of Tavern desiring her son Jacob Stier to be under her guardianship. Mentions Landlord Steinmetz.
Wit: Jacob Timmel, Samuel Mecklin.
Execs: Charles W. Westphal and Samuel White.
Wit: Francis Tremner, Lewis Harmer, Samuel Mecklin.

RASER, MARY. Phila. Widow of Bernard RASER of same city, Mariner. Feb 7, 1810. Feb 23, 1810. 3.107.
All estate to her children: William, Thomas, John, George and Mary Raser.
Exec: Bro. John Heyl.
Wit: Catharine Raser, Isaac Wampole.

HENDERSON, ANN. Northern Liberties. Phila. Co. Feb 24, 1810. Feb 27, 1810. 3.108.
All estate to Peter Fenton, David Fenton, Margeret Wevers and Mary Page.
Exec: Friend William Eshers.
Wit: Jacob Vanderslice, James Cummons, William Sides.

EMRY, JOHN. Phila. April 7, 1808. March 2, 1810. 3.109.
All estate to wife Sarah during life or widowhood, at her death or intermarriage, to his six children: Sally, Hannah, Julian, John, William and Hetty Emery.
Execs: Wife Sally, dau. Sally and son John.
Wit: Benjamin Johnson.
Letters granted to the two exec.

BAUGIER DELA BRUYER, MARGARET. Phila. Milliner. Aug 17, 1809. March 5, 1810. 3.110.
Appoints her husband Anthony Baugier Dela Bruyer exec. to whom she leaves 3/4 of her estate, real and personal, the other 1/4 she leaves to Alexis Prosper Riber. Mentions indenture of property recorded in Phila. Office for recording Deeds in Book E. F. No 50, page 251.
Exec: Husband Anthony Baugier Dela Bruyer.
Wit: Ths. Pintard, P. S. Barbear Du Plessis.

BENNINGHOVE, JACOB. Phila. Tobacconist. Feb 16, 1810. March 6, 1810. 3.111.

Provides for wife Elizabeth. Dau. Susanna wife of Daniel Dick. five grandchildren: Catharine, Elizabeth, Sarah, Susanna and John Benninghove. Mentions house in Church Alley, Phila. where he lives and mills, plantation &c. in Nether Providence Twp., Delaware Co.
Execs: Sd. wife Elizabeth, son-in-law Daniel Dick and friend William Nassau of Phila., tobacconist, also to be guardians of said grandchildren.
Wit: Samuel Gilbert, Isaac Wampole.

JACOBS, JAMES. Phila. Mariner. Feb 28, 1807. March 12, 1810. 3.114.
Mentions two estates in NY to be sold proceeds to be used for education of his three sons Joseph Dwight Jacobs, Chapman Jacobs and James Jacobs.
Exec: And Guardian of sd. children, Stephen Paterson, Phila., merchant.
Wit: Richard Renshaw, Christopher Wetherill, James Marison.

GROVER, MARTHA. Lower Dublin Twp. Phila. Co. Spinster. March 26, 1807. March 7, 1810. 3.115.
All estate to Mary Roberts and her son Grover Roberts.
Exec: Friend John Fryhoffer.
Wit: John Guyon, Isaiah Ships, Abraham Engard.

CLEMENT, ADELAIDE. Phila. Single woman. Aug 20, 1808. March 20, 1810. 3.116.
Mentions property in Phila. which she and her mother Lucy Ducasse Clement purchased of John Cream, Deed recorded in Deed Book E. F., No. 22, page 70.
Exec: Sd. mother Lucy Ducasse Clement to whom she leaves all estate.
Wit: Abraham Shoemaker, John M. Souldier.

ORLANDY, MARY. Widow of Paul ORLANDY, sometimes known as Mary or Madam Paul, maiden name Mary Eustack dau. of Margaret Eustack (sometimes known as Margaret Boiren) and Daniel Eustache. Feb 10, 1810. March 19, 1810. 3.117.
John Jaudrau, native of Cambe in Department of La Gironne, to be exec. and guardian of her son John, to whom the sd. John Jaudrau is the father. Leaves all estate to sd. exec.
Exec: John Jaudrau.
Wit: John Fournier, Simon Augustin Sabal.

BLAIR, WILLIAM. Phila. Lumber Merchant. Feb 17, 1810. March 19, 1810. 3.118.

All estate to wife Hannah Blair and children Robert and Elizabeth Blair. Execs: James Stewart, grocer, and William Dalzell of sd. city. Member of Firm of Blair & Workman. Unsettled account in his favor from Joseph Donath & Co.
Wit: Lawrence Sink, J. Workman.

WORRILL, HANNAH. Phila. Spinster. March 26, 1795. April 10, 1810. 3.119.
Legacies to Nathan Yarnall, Jr., son of sister Rachel, to Jane Sermon dau. of Joseph Sermon, dec'd, to Rachel, Mary and Rebecca Budd children of sister Rebecca Budd, dec'd.
Codicil Dec 17, 1805. Legacies to friend Hannah Johnson and to Sarah Davids dau. of Joseph Davids, dec'd.
Execs: Bro.-in-law Joseph Budd and Ellis Yarnall.
Wit: To will and codicil, Nicholas Waln, William Waln, Garland Davies and Nicholas Burns.

HAINES, MARGARET. Aug 8, 1809. April 5, 1810. 3.121.
Estate to her dau. Mary Yorke and children (names not given).
Execs: Sd. dau. Mary and nephew John Taylor, Jr.
Wit: Thomas Stewart and Eden Haydock.

BUCHANNEN, RACHEL. Northern Liberties, Phila. Widow. Jan 22, 1808. March 29, 1810. 3.122.
Estate to her three grandchildren: Ann Lawson, Lavinia Lawson and Elizabeth Lawson, children of Capt. John Lawson and her dau. Rachel, his wife, they to be execs. and guardians of sd. grandchildren.
Execs: Capt. John Lawson and her dau. Rachel his wife.
Wit: John Long, David Wilson, R. Whitehead, John Lawson sworn Oct 1, 1810.

MARKER, ANDREW. Moyamensing Twp. Phila. Co. Yeoman. March 22, 1810. April 3, 1810. 3.124.
Estate to wife Elizabeth Marker and his children (names not given), sd. wife to educate and support children during minority.
Execs: Friends Benjamin Jones, the elder, John Lesher of Moyamensing Twp. and said wife Elizabeth.
Wit: Jacob Heinissen, T. Mitchell.

HAINES, ANNA CATHARINE. Phila. Widow. March 16, 1810. April 2, 1810. 3.125.

Estate to daus. Catharine and Margaret, daus.-in-law Margaret and Ann Haines, last named wife of son John. Relation Catharine Wagner. Releases dau. Margaret or her husband (name not given) from payment of certain note. Legacy to granddau. Matilda Sharpneck.
Exec: Son-in-law Christian Danacker.
Wit: Catharine Dannaker, Isaac Wampole.

JONES, JESSE. Northern Liberties, House Carpenter. Feb 10, 1810. April 3, 1810. 3.126.
Estate to wife Caroline, she to board, school &c. all his children during minority, namely: Jacob Comly Jones, Emly, Kitte Ann and Mary.
Execs: Sd. wife Caroline and friend George Knor of Northern Liberties.
Wit: Joshua Comly, Franklin Comly.

ROBERTSON, ANN. Phila. Widow of John ROBERTSON. Jan 27, 1809. April 11, 1810. 3.128.
Estate to her three children: Ann Dawson, wife of George B. Dawson, Jane Edwards, wife of David Edwards and James Robertson. Granddau. Margaretta Jane Robertson dau. of son Robert, dec'd. Bond from Margaret Grant.
Execs: Son James Robertson, friends Samuel Price and Ebenezer Ferguson.
Wit: T. Mitchell, Augustus Hey.
Letters granted to Samuel Price and Ebenezer Ferguson.

CAMPBELL, JAMES. Phila. June 29, 1809. April 24, 1810. 3.130.
All estate consisting of several houses in Phila. to wife Susanna, she to support and educate his children. Son I. James Campbell being of weakly condition desires he shall have a reasonable allowance. Son David Campbell, dau. Elizabeth and Hannah Campbell.
Exec: Sd. wife Susanna.
Wit: George Rutter, Moses Stewart.

MAXWELL, WILLIAM. Kensington, Northern Liberties. Phila. Shipwright. May 11, 1809. April 12, 1810. 3.131.
Estate to wife Sarah Maxwell, whom he appoints extx.
Exec: Wife Sarah Maxwell.
Wit: Henry Lott, Thomas Timings.

DUFFY, PATRICK. Late of Ireland now of Phila. Dealer. April 5, 1810. April 16, 1810. 3.132.

All estate to sister Catharine Duffy. Land in Co. of Miskdown, Twp. of Deptford and in Ezenswell, both in OH, U.S.A. Legacy to sister Mary wife of James Brady, Co. of Cavan, Town of Rusky, Ireland.
Execs: Catharine Duffy and John Logue.
Wit: Daniel Hitchcock, Cornelius Havlind.

LAUCK, DAVID. Phila. Cooper. Feb 12, 1810. April 18, 1810. 3.133.
Provides for wife Anna Martha. After decease of wife property to be sold and proceeds to dau. Hannah and her two daus. Margaret Snyder and Mary Keyser. To grandsons Joseph and William Lauck sons of son John, dec'd. To grandson Joseph D. Lauck son of son Joseph, dec'd.
Execs: Sd. wife Anna Martha and friend John Smith of Germantown Twp., Blacksmith and Abraham Keyser of Germantown, Cordwainer (son of John).
Wit: Christian Snyder, Isaac Wampole.
Letters granted to John Smith and Abraham Keyser.

HILL, MOSES. Northern Liberties. Phila. Lumber Merchant. Dec 29, 1809. April 21, 1810. 3.135.
All estate to wife Elizabeth Hill and his six children: Jonathan, Catharine, Mary, Rachel, Hannah and Elizabeth Hill.
Execs: Sd. wife Elizabeth Hill and friends Jesse Cleaver and Henry Miller, Jr., all of Phila.
Wit: Thomas Dugdale, Jr., Peter Thomson.

COLHOUN, THOMAS. Phila. Mariner. Nov 14, 1806. April 23, 1810. 3.138.
Intending to depart for Calcutta, East Indies. All estate to bro. Gustavus Colhoun of Phila., Merchant, whom he appoints exec.
Exec: Bro. Gustavus Colhoun.
Wit: Peter Lohra, H. P. Borrekens, And. Sheals. Daniel Kuhn of Phila., accomptant and Margaret Kuhn of sd. city affirmed.

KUHL, CONRAD. Phila. Gentleman. Oct 23, 1809. April 26, 1810. 3.140.
Exec. is bro. Henry Kuhl to whom he leaves all estate.
Exec: Bro. Henry Kuhl.
Wit: R. Whitehead, John Dowe

EVANS, MARY. Phila. Spinster (dau. of Robert Evans late of sd. city dec'd). April 4, 1810. April 25, 1810. 3.140.

Nieces Jane Evans and Rachel Evans daus. of bro. John Evans. Money due late father's estate from cousin Stephen Schotten and others, her share of which she relinquishes. To cousin Jane Roberts (sister of sd. Stephen Schotten) in trust so not to be liable for husband's debts. To cousin Mary McVeaugh and her two sisters Alice and Rachel. To cousin Eleanor McVeaugh (another sister of sd. Mary McVeaugh). To Ruth Rowland (sister of sd. Mary McVeaugh) not subject to control of her husband. To cousin Ruth Harrison, widow of Robert Harrison. To friend Jane Lownes. To bro. John Evans property in Northern Liberties now in Penn Twp., Phila. Co., which her late father Robert Evans purchased from William Ward Burrowes and wife. Residue of estate to aforesd. nieces Jane Evans and Rachel Evans daus. of sd. bro. John Evans. If either should die under age and without issue, share of them so dying shall go to her bros.: David, Robert, Joseph, John and William Evans, sons of sd. bro. John Evans. Property in Northern Liberties which her late father Robert Evans purchased from William Sansom and wife to be sold.
Execs: Bro. John Evans and friend William Yardley. Friends Clement Remington and Charles C. French to be guardians of estate bequeathed to his residuary devisees and also overseers and trustees to see that will is correctly executed &c.
Wit: Daniel Thomas, Peter Thomson.

RUSH, WILLIAM. Phila. Glazier. Nov 23, 1809. May 4, 1810. 3.144.
Provides for wife Mary Rush. To dau. Barbara his tenement in which he now dwells on Sassafras Street in Phila., bounded on east by ground formerly ---- Hodge----. After death of wife all estate to his two daus. the sd. Barbara and Ann Roush.
Execs: Wife Mary, dau. Ann and Frederick Beates of Phila., Scrivener.
Wit: Abraham Stein, Tobias Schoenheit.
Letters granted to Mary Rush and to Ann Rush now Ann Nisbet wife of John Nisbet, House Carpenter.

GORDON, REBECCA. Phila. May 10, 1804. May 16, 1810. 3.146.
To Rebecca Oliver dau. of John Oliver of Bordentown, NJ. To Harriot Prentice dau. of sister Elizabeth, dec'd. Residue of estate to Enoch Walton son of sister Patience, dec'd.
Execs: John Cox of Phila., carpenter and Nathan Chapin of sd. city.
Wit: Mary Oliver, John Oliver, Maria Oliver ---- Elisha Gordon and Enoch Walton affirmed.

STINE, CATHARINE. Phila. Widow. Aug 14, 1797. June 6, 1810. 3.147. Late husband John Stine. Mother Barbara Marquedant to have all estate, at her decease to sd. bro. and sister.
Execs: Bro. Charles Marquedant of Phila. and her sister Margaret Beard, widow, now of North Carolina, about moving to sd. city.
Wit: Jacob Thomson, Peter Thomson. George Burns of Phila., storekeeper, affirmed.

HUBLEY, BERNARD. Phila. Co. Gentleman. Dec 19, 1809. May 10, 1810. 3.149.
Provides sd. wife Elizabeth and his seven children namely: Eve, Mary Magdalen, Elizabeth Rich, Geo. Washington, John Adams, Tamar Sarah Ann and James Sample Hubley.
Execs: Wife Elizabeth Hubley and friends William Mann of Northern Liberties, grocer and George Breidenhart of Phila., upholsterer.
Wit: Frederick Beates, Peter Wagner, Jr., Tobias Schoenheit.
Letters granted to Elizabeth Hubley and William Mann. George Breidenhart renounced.

SHINCKLE, FREDERICK. Phila. Skindresser. Jan 20, 1809. May 18, 1810. 3.152.
Leaves to wife Salome his dwelling house in which he now lives on Mulberry Street, with provision for her support. Legacies to sd. grandson Frederick Graff. To granddau. Susanna Black. To dau. Elizabeth Hall, not to be liable for husbands debts. To John, Maria and Perie Shinckle, children of dec'd son Frederick Shinckle. To grandchildren Frederick Graff and Charles Graff, children of dec'd dau. Mary Graff wife of Jacob Graff. Mary Shinckle dau. of dec'd son William Shinckle. Susan and Jacob Shinckle children of dec'd son Jacob. Mentions yearly ground rents assigned to him by Benjamin Shoemaker. Desires property to be sold excepting that devised for benefit of his wife, grandsons Frederick Graff and Charles Graff shall have preference of purchasing or taking sd. property at valuation.
Codicil alters some the division of legacies, signed Nov 17,1809.
Wit: As above.
Letters granted to Charles Graff.
Execs: Grandsons Frederick Graff and Charles Graff and friend Frederick Beates of Phila., serivener.
Wit: Yost Hollabush, John A. Coleman.

SHITZ, JACOB. Germantown Twp., Phila. Co. House Carpenter. Nov 30, 1809. May 12, 1810. 3.158.
Leaves to wife Elizabeth the use of house in Germantown wherein he dwells with provision for her support. Son Jacob Shitz to have one shilling only. To children: Michael, Ulrick, John, Daniel, George, Henry, Margaret, Elizabeth, Barbara, Susanna, Ann, Catharine and Mary Shitz. Execs. to convert into money all his real estate excepting that bequeathed to his wife. Children of son Michael namely: Jacob, Elizabeth and Sarah.
Execs: Sd. wife Elizabeth, sons-in-law Christopher Grafely and Jacob Holgate.
Wit: John Huston, William Huston.

BRINGHURST, JAMES. Phila. Gentleman. June 14, 1805. June 6, 1810. 3.162.
Provides for wife Ruth Bringhurst, sons: James Bringhurst, Joseph Bringhurst, Jr., and Jonathan Bringhurst. $80.00 to Dr. Jonathan Easton of Newport, Rhode Island for his attendance on grandson John Bringhurst. To grandchildren the children of sons James and Joseph. Legacy to Westtown boarding school. To overseers of Friends black school in Phila. for use of sd. school. In trust to friends Robert Wharton, Samuel Coates and John Biddle, his property in Phila., in Passyunk Twp. on Grays Ferry Road extending to George Gray's land, also land bounded by land late of William Shipley, dec'd, and by land of Daniel Dupuy, land joining that of Frederick Deshong's. House and lot in Wilmington, DE, lately purchased of bro. Joseph Bringhurst, they to pay rents &c. to sd. wife and sons: James, Joseph and Jonathan, wives of James and Joseph to receive an interest. Property in Phila., next to Francis Gurney's and land now or late in Bedford Co., PA, to be sold. Legacy to John Hoyland of Great Britain with whom his late son John had some dealings.
Wit: Nicholas Waln, Emmor Kimber and Joshua Kimber.
Codicil May --, 1806. Mentions grandsons Joseph and James Bringhurst (sons of son James) directs that John C. Evans of Spruce Street, house carpenter be united with Robert Wharton, Samuel Coates and John Biddle as Trustees. Revokes appointment of son James as exec.
Codicil March 20, 1807. Property in Southwark in tenure of George Hess and lands in Chester Co., PA, farms and plantations in tenure of Ames and Grant. Appoints wife Ruth Bringhurst, son Joseph Bringhurst and friends Samuel Coates and John C. Evans, execs.
Wit: Samuel R. Fisher, Mary Davis, Peter Thomson.
Letters granted to John C. Evans and Joseph Bringhurst, Jr.

Execs: Sd. wife Ruth Bringhurst, sons James and Joseph and friend Samuel Coates.

JACOBS, ISRAEL. Phila. Gentleman. Dec 15, 1807. May 18, 1810. 3.177. Legacies to two step daus. Rebecca Phillips widow of James Phillips, late of Phila. and Sarah Moses wife of Philip Moses of Charlestown, SC. To Margaret Dowell who lives in his family. All residue of estate to his dau. Rachel Cohen wife of Jacob J. Cohen of Richmond, VA, at her death to go to his sd. two step daus.
Exec: Sd. dau. Rachel Cohen.
Wit: Jno. Chri., Baker, George A. Baker, Jr., George A. Baker.

YEAKLE, CHRISTOPHER. Germantown Twp. Phila. Co. June 24, 1794. May 19, 1810. 3.178.
Wife Mary and six children, namely: Abraham, Christopher, Susanna wife of Abraham Heydrick, Mary wife of George Dresher, Regina wife of Abraham Shultz and Anna wife of Casper Yeakle.
Execs: Son Christopher and son-in-law George Dresher.
Wit: Michael Conrad, Conrad Schultz, John Roop.

COBB, MARY. Phila. Widow. March 22, 1810. May 24, 1810. 3.179. Legacies to Elizabeth Burd, Sarah Lea, Mary McIlvaine and Elizabeth Shippen widow of Dr. Edward Shippen of Burlington. To her Landlady Mary Wolfe. Legacy to the Female Association of Phila. for relief of women and children in reduced circumstances.
Exec: Edward Burd of Phila.
Wit: Anthony Fannen, John Wright.

HARRISON, WILLIAM. Phila. Mariner. Dec 29, 1806. May 22, 1810. 3.180.
Paul Freno of Phila., Vichealler, sole legatee and exec.
Exec: Paul Freno.
Wit: John Spencer, Robert Stewart.

WILLIAMS, PETER. Phila. Co. Northern Liberties Twp. Baker. May 3, 1809. May 23, 1810. 3.181.
Leaves to his wife Margareta his house on Chesnut Hill Road and contigious to John Tutviler's Estate also garden now in possession of Jacob Haas as long as she remains his widow. To grandson John Williams stone house on Chesnut Hill Road adj. estate of Peter Plecker's, he to pay an annuity to sd. wife Margareta. To grandson Solomon Williams,

estate on Chesnut Hill Road adj. Andrew Ardman's estate, he also to pay an annuity to said wife. Grandson Benjamin Williams to have possession of wife's estate after her death or marriage.
Execs: Jacob Lentz and Christopher Yagel.
Wit: John Adolph, George Riche.

DAHETZE, MARTIN. Saint Thomas Island. About returning to Samana. March 7, 1810. April 28, 1810. 3.183.
Messrs. Andre Sacaze and Seillard execs. for all property in Colonies as well as in America. Andre Sacaze universal heir. Legacy to Miss Agnes Mauge at present on his estate in Samana. Mentions James Yard of Phila., Julien Duharst and Thomas Taggart of Phila. ---- Francois Sallet and Jean Baptiste Duvignan affirmed. Francis Melizet and John Wonter a Seafaring Captain and the sailor Timothy Logue declared that Martin Dahetze was on board the British Schooner *Two Bro.s* at the time she was lost on her passage to Samana Commanded by Jacob Wonters and that he was drowned off coast of Samana.
Execs: Messrs. Andre Sacaze and Seillard.

BURKET, JACOB. Northern Liberties. Phila. Co. Fence Maker. March 19, 1804. May 25, 1810. 3.190.
Provides for wife Margaret Burkert. His property in Northern Liberties to his four children: Jacob Burket or Burkert, Mary wife of William Wilson, Elizabeth wife of John Segar and Margaret Burket.
Exec: Friend, Frederick Frickes of Northern Liberties, Cabinet Maker.
Wit: John Reakirt, John Bender and Frederick Wolbert.

KENNEDY, DAVID. Phila. Gentleman. March 26, 1809. June 2, 1810. 3.191.
Legacy to Hannah Wills. Directs execs. to apply sum for education of Geo. Washington Kennedy son of late bro. Francis by Elizabeth Harris now or late of Bucks Co., to also give him a legcy to start in business, if sd. Elizabeth Harris shall refuse to commit her son to care of execs. provision before named and legacy shall be void. Residue of estate to bros. Robert and James.
Execs: Bros. Robert Kennedy and James Kennedy.
Wit: Benjamin Jones and Frederick Beates.

KARR or KERR, JAMES. Phila. Mariner. March 8, 1809. June 1, 1810. 3.192.
Wife Rachel sole legatee and extx.

Exec: Wife Rachel.
Wit: George Chard, Micahol Hulings. Peter A. Browne affirmed.

BALL, WILLIAM. Phila. Esq. Sept 4, 1809. June 2, 1810. 3.193.
Legacy to nephew Joseph Ball son of late bro. Samuel Ball. To each of the daus. of Ann Stout dau. of cousin David Hall. To negro man Robert. To sister Ann Gibson and to her children a piece of land in Northern Liberties marked in plan of the division of his father's land no. 18. Mary Ball late in tenure of Henry Funk. All lands, tenements &c. in City and Co. of Phila. to children of sd. nephew Joseph Ball, namely William Whyte Ball, Joseph Ingles Ball, Benjamin Ball (lots before devised excepted). All other estate in Wilmington and Counties of New Castle and Kent or elsewhere in DE and in Counties of Berks, Northumberland, Luzerne, Huntingdon, Westmoreland and elsewhere in PA, in Hampshire Co., VA, or any other part of the world he gives to sd. nephew Joseph Ball during his life, at his death to his children.
Execs: Sd. nephew Joseph Ball and his father-in-law John Hewson and Joseph L. Inglis of Phila., Clerk, in case of death of sd. John Hewson, he appoints his son John Hewson, Jr.
Letters granted to John Hewson and Joseph L. Inglis. Joseph Ball affirmed Oct 22, 1821. John Hewson Sept 8, 1825.

HOUGH, THOMAS. Phila. April 30, 1810. June 4, 1810. 3.196.
Provides for wife Mary Hough, leaving to her free use and rents of his dwelling house, stables, stores in Pine Street, Phila. His granddaus. Mary Hough Oldden and Elizabeth Oldden to be under care of sd. wife and niece Ann Bunting. Property in Phila. to sd. granddaus. bounded by lot lately sold to John Folwell. After decease of wife Mary he gives to dau. Jane Jackson his property before devised to his wife. To nieces Ann Bunting and Margaret Bunting. To friend Samuel Sansom in trust for benefit of Friends Free Schools in Phila. for negro and mulatto children. To friend Jonathan Willis. To grandson Thomas Hough Oldden. To sons-in-law James Oldden and Holliday Jackson. Meetinghouse of Friends of Phila., Southern District to have free liberty of opening its windows over his grounds in Pine Street. Legacy to be distributed amongst poor men, women and children of sd. city. Property lately purchased of John Dorsey, after death of dau. Jane Jackson he bequeaths to her children.
Execs: Sd. wife Mary Hough and friend Jonathan Willis.
Wit: Clayton Earl, Charles Roberts.

FITE, RICHARD. Germantown Twp. Phila. Co. May 29, 1810. June 12, 1810. 3.200.
All estate to wife Anna so long as she remains his widow. After her death leaves legacies to Sally Boock and George Fite Boock, rem. of estate to the children of Christopher Osius and to George Swarz a single man.
Execs: Sd. wife Anna and Christopher Osius.
Wit: Jacob Meyers, George Berger.

HILL, RICHARD. Northern Liberties. Phila. April 30, 1810. June 12, 1810. 3.201.
Directs execs. to sell estate in Callowhill Street where he dwells, residue of estate to his wife and minor children (no names given).
Exec: Sister Margaret Hill.
Wit: Joseph Wilson, Joshua Comly, John Blight.

JONES, DAVID. Blockley Twp. Phila. Co. Husbandman. Jan 4, 1808. June 13, 1810. 3.201.
Provides for wife Jane Jones during widowhood. To children: Lewis, Ann, Catharine and Nathan Jones, property in Blockley Twp. adj. lands of James Jones, William West and others, his grist mill in Blockley aforesd. known as Schuylkill Mill and all lands thereunto belonging. Legacy to sister Ann Jones. Whereas he has contracted to sell to George Holston his part of land held with James Jones in Upper Merion, Montgomery Co. &c. Bequeaths to son Thomas Jones $300.
Execs: Two sons Lewis Jones and Nathan Jones.
Wit: Abram Heston, Joseph George.

HOGAN, DENIS. Phila. Gentleman. Dec 15, 1809. June 16, 1810. 3.205.
All estate to two nephews Michael Neale and John Neale and to Miss Elizabeth Bowers, his adopted dau.
Execs: Nephews Michael and John Neale and Eliza Bowers now of New York City.
Wit: John Horner, 261 Market Street, Joseph Hemphill, 261 Market Street.

TOMKINS, JACOB. Phila. Late Shopkeeper. Sept 30, 1803. June 20, 1810. 3.206.
Legacy to son Isaac Tomkins. To wife Sarah his houses bought of Peter Swarts in Vine Street, his house at the billet bought of Joshua Potts where his son Isaac now dwells he orders execs. to sell. Legacy to grandson Joseph Y. Tomkins. Dau.-in-law Hannah Y. Lukens. Legacy to

Northern District Monthly Meeting for use of poor widows and orphans. Residue to his six daus. namely: Susanna Austin, Lydia Jarrett, Elizabeth Bunting, Hannah Williams, Mary Jarrett and Martha Lukens.
Execs: Son Isaac Tomkins and sons-in-law Philip S. Bunting and Thomas William.
Wit: Leonard Snowden, Thomas Smith, Samuel Garrigues, Jr.
Codicil May 24, 1806. Estate stands bound to Samuel Shoemaker, Taner for about £33 borrowed of him by Joseph Naylor, execs. to settle and deduct amount from dau. Lydia Jarrett's share. Dau.-in-law Hannah Lukens, dec'd, her share to son Isaac.
Wit: As to will.
Letters granted to Philip S. Bunting and Thomas William.

ROBERTSON, JAMES. Moyamensing Twp. Phila. Co. June 3, 1810. June 21, 1810. 3.209.
Estate to wife, she to maintain and educate his son and dau. When of age estate to be divided. If wife marries before sd. children are of age, he directs other exec. to have property and management thereof in his own hands.
Execs: Sd. wife Margaretta and his bro.-in-law Daniel Bussier, Esq., also to be guardians of sd. children.
Wit: Dr. John A. Monges, Charles Schultz, Daniel Bussier, Hannah McCabe, Susanna Dubuy. (Nuncupative.)

BARKER, GEORGE. Moyamensing Twp. Phila. Co. Yeoman. June 25, 1808. June 25, 1810. 3.210.
Land in Moyamensing bounded by land of Samuel Wheeler and by Daniel Norbeck, dec'd, to be used for Family burying ground, his descendents forever to have a right to be interred therein free from any charge. Bequeaths to dau. Mary Baker and her heirs his frame house (now in tenure of John Walters) and lot on which sd. house is erected extending to land late of John Bartholomew's, dec'd, along line fence between his land and Gardner's land to land late of Daniel Norbeck, dec'd. Lane mentioned in Deed from Casper Heiley and wife to him recorded in Deed Book No. 18, Page 59. If sd. dau. should die without issue, he give sd. property to son George Barker, wife Mary Barker to have free use and income of all rest of land and tenements &c. She to educate his six children: George, Catharine, Elizabeth, Thomas, Ann and John.
Execs: Sd. wife Mary Barker during widowhood and sd. son George Barker.
Wit: George Sheer, John Walter.

Letters granted to Mary Barker.

MOORE, SAMUEL. Mariner. Aug 19, 1809. June 21, 1810. 3.213.
All estate to friend Rebecca Bean, wife of Joseph Bean of Phila., appointing sd. Rebecca Bean execs.
Exec: Rebecca Bean.
Wit: John White, Joseph Wissinbanks.

TODD, ELISHA. Carter of Northern Liberties. Phila. May 8, 1810. June 29, 1810. 3.213.
All property in Northern Liberties to wife Feby. At marriage or decease of sd. Feby he bequeaths legacy to Affracan Benavelent Asoseaation of Bethell Church wharein he is a member, to mother Philes Tood, to neffu Elisha Todd son of Hester Todd. Property left to wife he bequeaths at her marriage or death to the A Methodeth Opiscople Church called Bethell in Phila.
Execs: Sd. wife Feby Todd, Jonathan Trusty, Robert Green and Prince Pruance.
Wit: Jacob Tapsico, Jesse Brown.
Letters granted to Jonathan Trusty and Robert Green.

CUNNINGHAM, MARY. Southwark. Widow of Thomas Cunningham of Phila. June 22, 1810. July 5, 1810. 3.215.
All estate to bro. Robert Wallace with exception of a few articles to friend Rebecca Brown.
Exec: Friend James Hamill of Phila., House Carpenter.
Wit: B. Drum, Moses McIlhenney.

PEMBER, EDWARD. Southwark. Dealer. Oct 31, 1809. July 11, 1810. 3.215.
All estate to wife Margaret Pember.
Execs: Sd. wife Margaret and his friend Robert Grant of sd. District, grocer.
Wit: Richard Renshaw, Luis Roberts.

SHEWELL, ELIZABETH. Phila. April 11, 1810. June 15, 1810. 3.216.
Legacy to her nephew Samuel Beddome Smith son of Joseph B. Smith and her sister Frances. If sd. nephew should die without issue, the legacy to be divided amongst his bros. and sisters (names not given). All residue of estate she bequeaths to niece Elizabeth Shewell Lorain oldest dau. of

John Lorain, Jr., and her sister Lydia. At death of sd. niece to her bros. and sisters.
Wit: John Morrell, Garret Newkirk.
Codicil May 4, 1810. Legacy to niece Rachel Smith dau. of Joseph B. Smith.
Wit: Elizabeth Hodgdon, John Lorain, Jr., Lydia Lorain. Joseph B. Smith affirmed July 18th and John Lorain, Jr. July 20, 1810.
Execs: Bros.-in-law John Lorain, Jr., and Joseph B. Smith.

HERTZOG, EVE. Southwark. Widow. April 24, 1804. July 14, 1810. 3.218.
Legacy to her grandson William Orr son of James Orr by her dau. Mary, his wife. All residue of estate she bequeaths to her three children to wit: Sibella Fox wife of William Fox, Walter Hertzog and Mary Orr.
Exec: Friend Philip Peltz.
Wit: Abraham Shoemaker and Edward Bonsall.

KIRKHAM, CHARLES. Phila. April 10, 1804. July 23, 1810. 3.219.
Estate to wife Deborah during her life, at her decease to his children (names not given).
Exec: Sd. wife Deborah.
Wit: Francis McShane, Philip I. Claridge, James Cameron, Isaac Bartram.

JONES, JAMES. Phila. Labourer. Nov 26, 1799. July 25, 1810. 3.220.
Wife Sebina Jones to have his stone house with land in Lancaster Co. adj. Adam Rinehart. Legacy to sister-in-law Phebe Sanders.
Execs: Friends William Jackson and sd. wife Sebina Jones.
Wit: John Hemery, Absalom Jones.
Codicil Nov 26, 1799. Property bequeathed to wife, he bequeaths at her death to neufue James Jackson son of sister Ann Jackson.
Wit: Same as to Will.
Sarah Emery of Phila., spinster affirmed that she was acquainted with signature of her father John Hemery, dec'd.

VREDENBURGH, ESTHER. Phila. Feme Sole Trader. Wife of Capt. Isaac Vredenburgh. April 4, 1810. July 28, 1810. 3.221.
Stock to be sold, money from sale to son Lewis Robinson, dau. Sarah B. Murray wife of James S. Murray of Cambden, South Carolina, to son John S. Willett, dau. Rachael Willett. Money in trust for sd. husband Isaac Vredenburgh. Bequeaths to daus. Sarah B. Murray and Rachael

Willett each a butter boat bequeathed to her by Johanna Young as expressed in the bottom of sd. boats. Legacy to sister Abigail Gordon widow of Enoch Gordon, at her decease to son Mordecai L. Gordon.
Codicil. Mentions former husband Capt. Robinson.
Wit: Same as to will.
Execs. and Trustees: Lewis Robinson and John S. Willett.
Wit: Samuel Anderson, John Riley.

SCHNEIDER, GEORGE. Bristol Twp. Phila. Co. Farmer. May 13, 1806. July 31, 1810. 3.224.
Wife Catharine Schneider to have use, interest &c. of all estate during life or widowhood, she to support his younger children. Older children: John, George, Mary (dec'd) and Elizabeth. Younger children: Catharine, Margaret, Daniel and Susanna. Grandchildren: Elizabeth, Catherine and Matilda Etris children of dau. Mary Etris, dec'd.
Codicil May 17, 1810. Mentions estate of William Hulby, dec'd.
Wit: R. Whitehead, John Clark, Hannah Eyre.
Execs: Sd. wife Catharine, son John and son-in-law Thomas Hewson of Phila. Sadler. Sd. exec. Thomas Hewson to be guardian of sd. three grandchildren.
Wit: Joseph Peters, Robert Whitehead, Hannah Eyre.
Letters granted to Catharine Schneider, Aug 6, 1810.

RIGHTER, GEORGE. Roxborough, Phila. Co. Farmer. March 29, 1810. Aug 13, 1810. 3.226.
Wife Christina to have free use, occupancy &c. of all his property during widowhood, at her death or marriage, estate to be divided between his two sons George and John.
Execs: Sd. wife and sons George and John.
Wit: John K. Day, Stephen Davis.

SCHWARTZ, PHILIP. Germantown Twp. Phila. July 9, 1810. Aug 15, 1810. 3.227.
Desires his ground adj. Peter Bechtel's land which her purchased of Hezekiah Huntsman be sold. Wife Susanna Schwartz to have use of all estate, after her decease to be sold and proceeds to his children viz: Daniel, George, Joseph, Ann, Susan and Sarah Schwartz.
Execs: Sd. wife and sons Daniel and George Schwartz.
Wit: Jacob Myer, John Gorgas.

HARR, ELIZABETH. Phila. Widow. Oct 9, 1809. Aug 15, 1810. 3.228.

Legacies to son Ezekiel E. Maddock, at his decease to his sons William and Ezekiel. Four prints presented to her by her bro. Ezekiel Edwards she bequeaths to sd. William and Ezekiel Maddock. Legacies to granddaus.: Caroline Maddock, Jane Maddock, Emma Maddock, Elizabeth Harr Maddock (dau. of son William L. Maddock, dec'd) and her sister Sarah. Legacies to William McDowell. To friend Charles Evans. To granddau. Sarah Moore Maddock. To grandson Randall Malon Maddock. To bro. Griffith Edwards, at his death, to his children. To sister Ann McDowell. To sister Sarah E. Evans. To sister Mary Rowlett. To dau.-in-law Phoebe Maddock. To sister-in-law Sarah Edwards. To niece Elizabeth Harr Abbott. To niece Sarah Evans McDowell. To Sarah Ann Rowlett, Louisa Rowlett, sister Jane Haines.
Execs: Joseph Moore and sd. son Ezekiel Maddock, both of Phila.
Wit: Charles Evans, Sarah E. Evans. Griffith Edwards of Phila., grocer and Mary Rowlett wife of John Rowlett of sd city, accomptant affirmed.

DICKINSON, JOSEPH. Northern Liberties. Phila. Yeoman. July 24, 1810. Aug 15, 1810. 3.230.
Provides for wife Mary and three children: Charles, Tabitha and infant dau. yet unnamed. If wife should die or marry before sd. youngest child attains age of sixteen years, he nominates his execs. as guardians.
Execs: Bro. Jesse Dickinson and friend Andrew Thatcher.
Wit: R. Whitehead, Jacob Keen, Philip Halzel.

FALCONER, WILLIAM. Phila. Aug 4, 1810. Aug 16, 1810. 3.231.
Wife Mary Falconer to have interest of all estate during life, at her decease to the Trustees of General Assembly of Presbyterian Church of America to be applied to use of Theological Seminary. Property consist s of following viz: house in Union Street, four shares in Bank of PA, mortgate from Clement Biddle, bond from George Dorland of Chester Co., and a bond from John Heveland and Stephen Heveland.
Execs: Wife Mary Falconer and friends Robert Ralston and David Mandeville of Phila.
Wit: Ashbel Green, Christopher Marshall.
Letters granted to Mary Falconer Aug 18, 1810.

McCURDY, JOHN. Radnor Twp. Phila. Co. April 18, 1807. Aug 6, 1810. 3.233.
Provides for wife Mary McCurdy. Son Robert to be educated and fitted for a store at discretion of son Hugh, whom he appoints his guardian. At decease of wife, estate to his children.

Execs: Nephew John McCurdy of Phila. and John McCreales.
Wit: Robert Martin, John Elliott. John McCurdy sworn Sept 3rd. and John McCreals sworn Oct 2, 1810.

LASHER, JACOB. Northern Liberties. Phila. Grocer. June 7, 1810. July 6, 1810. 3.234.
Annuity to mother Barbara Lasher and sister Maria Young. Residue of estate to bro. Francis Lasher.
Exec: Friend Peter Hertzog.
Wit: Robert Whitehead, George Gorgas, Davis Ozum(?) Admin. granted with will annexed see Admin. File for 1811, No. 141.

MURGATROYD, MARY. Late of Phila. Now of Trenton, NJ. Jan 15, 1810. Sept 11, 1810. 3.235.
Richard Rundle of Blockley Twp., Phila. Co., John Perot, merchant and James S. Smith, Counsellor at Law both of Phila., to collect Rents, Issues, &c. of all estate, real and personal and to pay same to her parents Thomas Murgatroyd and Sarah P. Murgatroyd.
Execs: Sd. Richard Rundle, John Perot and James S. Smith.
Wit: N. Belleville, Molly Rhea(?), Thomas F. Leaming. Anna Cliffords and Sarah Clifford of Phila., spinsters affirmed.

TAYLOR, JOHN, Jr. Native of Phila. and resident of that city, son of John Taylor, dec'd, and Jane of same place, now living. At Havanna Aug 3, 1810. Aug 17, 1810. 3.237.
Wife Maria Taylor and children: James and Jane, minors. Dn. Juan Reynolds, merchant residing in Havanna to have charge of property there, that in Phila., Europe or elsewhere to be under care of Matthew Semple, his attorney, residing in sd. city.
Had contracted for sale of Schooner, his property named the Comet, with Joaquin Riva, which writing he had not formally finished &c., in case he should die before to completion desires that sd. Dn. Juan Reynolds should act as his exec. in this place for that purpose.
Wit: John Taylor, Jr., Joseph M. Ferrety, and before Joseph De Salinas.
Execs: Sd. Dn. Juan Reynolds and Matthew Semple. Wife and two children his universal heirs.
Wit: Dn. Mariano Josep Canelas, Dn. Andre Bernal and Dn. Francisco Valerio of this place.
Letters granted to Matthew Semple Sept 24, 1810.
(Translation)

LIDDON, ABRAHAM. Phila. Formerly Merchant. Dec 8, 1808. Sept 11, 1810. 3.239.
Legacy in trust to friends Ellis Yarnell and Thomas Wistar both of sd. city, merchants, the interest of sd. fund for use of Elizabeth Cox (widow of James Cox) during life, after her decease to assistance of poor Inhabitants of Phila. under care of Society of Friends. Residue of estate to wife Isabella Liddon, at her decease to his grandson Abraham Lidddon Pennock.
Execs: Sd. wife Isabella and grandson Abraham Liddon Pennock.
Wit: Thomas Sheppard, Isaac Bartram.
Letters granted to Abraham Liddon Pennock.

STUART, SARAH. Phila. April 13, 1810. Sept 12, 1810. 3.241.
All estate to sister Elizabeth Stuart. To niece Sarah Moody dau. of sister Margaret one bond due with interest by John Martin, Dr. of Medicine (now absent at sea) in case of her death, it reverts to sd. sister Elizabeth. To Rebecca Read and Margaret Read dau. of Dr. Read and to Maria Wilson her nieces each a mourning ring. Legacy to niece Anna Jennings, after death to sister Elizabeth Stuart.
Exec: Sd. sister Elizabeth.
Wit: George C. Potts, Andrew Browne.

LAWERSWYLER, JACOB W. Phila. Merchant. Nov 10, 1809. Sept 14, 1810. 3.242.
Legacy to sister Frances Cuthbert. Legacy in trust to sd. execs. to be invested and income to sd. sister Frances, at her decease to her children, if any. Legacy to John and Jacob Peter, children of dec'd uncle Jacob Peter. To James S. Cuthbert his gold watch and gold headed cane given to him by Jacob Winey, Esq., dec'd. To John Cuthbert, to Joseph Peter, to Sybilla Wilson. All residue of estate to mother Eliza Lawerswyler.
Execs: Mother Eliza Lawerswyler and uncle John Maybin of Phila.
Wit: Thomas Morris, Charles Schaffer.
Letters granted to Eliza Sawerswyler.

RIFFERT, PHILIP. Phila. Innkeeper. Sept 9, 1810. Sept 17, 1810. 3.243.
Estate to wife Ursula Riffert and children.
Execs: Sd. wife Ursula and Andrew Leinau of sd. city, hatter.
Wit: Michl. Bright, Lewis Rush, Isaac Wampole.

BASON, ELIZABETH. Phila. Co. July 2, 1810. Aug 17, 1810. 3.244.

Legacy to sister Elizabeth now wife of Samuel Stall of Baltimore, at her death sd. legacy to her children. Legacy to sister Ann Collins of Fawn Twp., York Co. Legacy to niece Hannah, now wife of Samuel Fisher, to be left in hands of Nathan Sellers, overplus at her decease, to her children. Legacy to niece Ann Keichler, now wife of George Kiechler and her nephew James Elkins. To William Elkin and Mary Elkin son and dau. of Joseph and Ann Elkin late of Baltimore, dec'd. To Sarah Roberts dau. of James and Abby Roberts. To children of niece Sarah Ruall(?) viz: Joseph, Mary, John and Hannah. Residue of estate to sd. Sarah Roberts and her young bro. whose name she does not recollect.
Exec: Friend George Knorr of Northern Liberties, Board Merchant.
Wit: Michael Hartley, John Dreprefontaine.
Letters granted to exec. Nov 22, 1810.

ROSSETER, JOHN CAPT. Sept 6, 1810. Sept 21, 1810. 3.246.
We, Dr. Benjamin Rush, John Meany and John Smith being at the house of Capt. John Rosseter Sept 6, 1810 heard the sd. John Rosseter declare his will to be one half to his wife Eliza and one half to his natural son John Rosseter.
Execs: Lewis Clapier, John Ashley and James Sawer.
Wit: James Cooper, Mary Smith.

HOW, JEFFERY. Phila. Coachmaker. Aug 15, 1807. Sept 21, 1810. 3.246.
All estate to friend Joseph Randolph of sd. city, painter and glazier, as he knows of no relatives. Sd. Joseph Randolph to be exec.
Exec: Joseph Randolph.
Wit: Abraham Shoemaker, George Willard.

ELLIOTT, JOHN. Phila. Druggist. Aug 26, 1810. Sept 22, 1810. 3.247.
To Alice Harlan who now lives in his family he leaves an annuity to be paid out of his estate on Grays Alley purchased of the Ramsay family. Legacies to nieces Elizabeth and Mary Elliott. To dau. Hannah Elliott in trust, interest there of for use of Aimwell School, if sd. Society should be dissolved the sd. sum to be given to friends Ellis Yarnall and Caleb Peirce, to be paid to Treasurer for time being of the Institution under care of Religious Society of Friends for PA, NJ, &c., the interest to be used for education young women unable to attain the benefits of that Institution. Residue of estate to dau. Hannah Elliott, to son John Elliott, Jr., to son Daniel Elliott, the remaining full share to friends Joseph Cruckshank and Isaac Wistar Morris in trust for son Harvey Elliott.

Desires that the Southern Farm on his tract of land in Oxford Twp., called Glenfield be not sold but remain for mutual accommodation of his children.
Execs: Sons John Elliott, Jr., and Daniel Elliott and friends Joseph Cruckshank and Isaac Wistar Morris.
Wit: John Wilson, Stephen Taylor.

JACKSON, JOSEPH. Late of Gloucester Co., NJ, now of Northern Liberties, Phila. Sept 6, 1810. Sept 26, 1810. 3.249.
To son John Jackson one half of place purchased of Shippen, also a piece of land off sd. tract to be run off in same manner it was by Nelson. Execs. to sell the other half of sd. place. The monies there from to be placed at interest for benefit of son Isaac, at his death to his children. Sold part of sd. lot to Jeptha Abbott near the Meeting House. To son Thomas plantation purchased of Samuel Tomlin on which Henry now lives. To son Henry the place he purchased of Samuel Nicholson, also land adj. land purchased of Quinton, also land adj. that which he purchased of Benjamin Whitall, Sheriff, adj. that purchased of Thomas Wilson, all above lands are in Gloucester Co., NJ. To grandchildren Robert Sparks and Elizabeth Sparks, children of dau. Sarah, place where he lives in N. L., Phila. To dau. Sarah estate which formerly belonged to her as the widow of Job West and which he (Joseph Jackson) purchased of Charles French. Provides for wife Lydia. Legacies to daus.: Nancy, Edith, Mary and Hannah. Residue of personal estate to his four sons: John, Isaac, Thomas and Henry and to his last mentioned four daus.
Execs: Son John Jackson and friend Josiah Herritage.
Wit: Francis Turner, Isaiah West, Christian F. Fackman.
Codicil Sept 7, 1810. Alters legacies, mentions Joseph and Ann West children of dau. Edith.
Wit: Same as to will.

McCURDY, JAMES. Phila. Grocer. Sept 25, 1810. Oct 4, 1810. 3.251.
Estate to wife Mary McCurdy so long as she remains his widow. Legacy to stepdau. Martha Scoles. To stepson Francis Scoles. At decease of wife all estate to sd. stepson subject to the bequeath before mentioned to his sister Martha Scoles.
Execs: Sd. wife Mary and friend John Cunningham.
Wit: Samuel H. Jacobs, B. Newcomb, Jr.

MILLER, HESTER ANN. Phila. Co. Widow. June 24, 1808. Sept 24, 1810. 3.252.

Legacy to Hester Ann Dick dau. of sister Mary Dick. Remainder of furniture to be sold, money placed at interest and used for support and education of sd. Hester Ann Dick, when she arrives at twenty one years or gets married, all residue to be divided amongst the following: sd. Hester Ann Dick, Richard P. Thomas son of sister Elizabeth Thomas, William Thomas Palmer son of bro. William, dec'd, Elizabeth Palmer dau. of Richard Palmer, Phoebe Jones Palmer dau. of John Jones Palmer and Francis Dickinson son of Phoebe Dickinson, if sd. Hester Ann Dick departs this life in her minority without issue, her share to her sd. Hester Ann Dick's sisters.
Execs: Bro. Richard Palmer and friend James Engle.
Wit: Justinian Fox, Heronimus Warner, Robt. Whitehead, Benjamin Brown, W. - James Engle renounced.

WALLACE, WILLIAM, DR. Southwark. Phila. Co. Sept 18, 1810. Oct 6, 1810. 3.253.
All estate to wife Margaret Wallace and son Wesley William Wallace.
Execs: Wife Margaret Wallace and bro.-in-law John Tittermary, Senr.
Wit: John D. Armstrong, John Riddle, Peter Hortz.

BERGENDOLLAR, CATHARINE. Northern Liberties. Phila. Widow. May 14, 1810. Oct 10, 1810. 3.254.
Legacy to granddau. Eliza dau. of son Frederick. Desires her messuage and lot of ground where she dwells shall be sold, monies from sd. sale to son Daniel. To dau. Nancy and to Eliza, John and Anne children of son Frederick. Residue of estate to her three children: Daniel, Frederick and Nancy.
Execs: Sd. son Daniel and friend Joseph Fricker.
Wit: Robt. Whitehead, Henry Burckhart, Hannah Eyre. Joseph Fricker renounced.

ACKLEY, DAVID. Phila. Shopkeeper. Feb 12, 1808. Oct 15, 1810. 3.256.
All estate to be converted into money, income of sd. estate to his parents Thomas Ackley and Elizabeth his wife, at decease of parents, legacy to bro. John B. Ackley, at his death to his two daus. Mercy Ackley and Elizabeth Ackley and their children. Mary Ackley late Mary Miller, wife of sd. John B. Ackley. Annuity to sister Hannah Johnson, at her death to her children, if any, if not to Magdalen Society of Phila. To sister Sarah Watson. To sister Martha Coughling. To children of William Watson and sister Sarah his wife, namely: Joseph, Thomas, David, Hannah, Elizabeth, Mary, Sarah, John, Josiah, Martha, Washington and Tolbert

Watson. To children of late bro. Thomas Ackley and Rachel his wife, namely: Martha, Sarah, John and Thomas Ackley. To David and Mary Ackley children of bro. Mordecai Ackley and Rebecca his wife, both dec'd. To children of Thomas Coughling and sister Martha, his wife namely Lydia, Samuel, Elizabeth and Rebecca Coughling. To John Tolbert son of sister Hannah. to Mercy and Elizabeth Ackley daus. of bro. John Ackley. To Society for the institution and support of First day or Sunday Schools in Phila. and Districts of Southwark and Northern Liberties, to Phila. Dispensary and to Overseers of Publick Schools in Phila.
Execs: Bro. sd. John B. Ackley, Josiah Johnson and Gilbert Gaw, Windsor chairmaker all of Phila.
Wit: Peter Thomson, Silas E. Weir. Gilbert Gaw renounced.

HITNER, SARAH. Now or late of Phila. Formerly wife of Daniel Hitner but now a feme sole. Aug 15, 1810. Oct 19, 1810. 3.261.
To children by sd. Hitner namely: Mary, Elizabeth, Isabella, Sarah and George. Robt. Kennedy and James McCawley trustees for her and her sd. children.
Execs: Bros. John McCalla, Northern Liberties, William McCalla of Jenkin Town and Alexander McCalla of Phila.
Wit: Richard F. Leech, Clement Sheppard.
Codicil Sept 10, 1810. to Harriott Lora who now lives with her.
Wit: James Dewey, Christiana Kenderdine.

WARNER, FREDERICK, Germantown. Phila. Co. Sept 7, 1810. Oct 22, 1810. 3.263.
To wife Margarett Warner the house in which he lives with ground, all household goods &c. at her decease to all his children (names not given).
Execs: Sd. wife Margarett and son John Warner.
Wit: Isaac Bringhurst, Woolery Fryhoffer, Jacob Ashmead.

FISHER, THOMAS. Phila. Gentleman. Dec 19, 1806. Oct 24, 1810. 3.263.
Bequeaths his property to children: William Logan Fisher, James Logan Fisher, Hannah Logan Fisher and Esther Fisher. Eldest son Joshua Fisher lately died leaving wife Elizabeth Powell Fisher, enciente. Property in Phila. purchased from Peter Reeve and wife, property devised to him by his father Joshua Fisher, dec'd, Meadow in Passyunk Twp. Phila. Co., devised to him by sd. father. Property in Southwark held with bro. Miers Fisher, land now or late in Twp. of Chemung, State of NY, purchased of Richard Harrison and wife, half of which he sold to

William Cooper of Coopertown. Property originally in Westmorland Co., PA, by division of that co. thrown into several counties. Bros. Samuel R. Fisher and Miers Fisher and nephews Joshua and Thomas Gilpin interested is sd. property. Property in Bristol Twp., Phila. Co., now annexed to Country Seat Wakefield, formerly the estate of his late wife Sarah Logan under the will of her father William Logan. Property in Bristol Twp., Phila. Co., purchased from William Dagnie and wife and from Assignees of John Mayo. Brew house, malt house &c. in Phila., purchased from John Baker, Esq., administrators of William Van Phul, Esq. Property in Phila. purchased from trustees of William Peters. Property in Baltimore, MD, which John Brown and Jane his wife conveyed to George Emlen who conveyed the same to him according to leases made to Abraham France, Henry Hartman, Tinker & Stiles and James Davidson, all which sd. George Emlen conveyed to him and he has leased to Michael Peters, rents received by friend John McKim of Baltimore. Ground in Southwark, Phila. Co. held with bro. Miers Fisher by devise from sd. father. Land in Canaan Twp., Wayne Co., sometime called the Proprietors Garden and afterwards Elk Forrest bought of William Cooper now held in common with sister Lydia Gilpin and bros. Samuel and Miers Fisher. Purchased form Samuel Emlen, Jr., and wife, land in or near Otsego Co., NY State being part of tract since called Bloomfield. Lands in Otsego Co., N. Y. formerly property of Henry Hill who conveyed them to John Holker, he to Thomas Fitzimons &c. Legacy to yearly Mtg. of Friends, Indian Natives who received our first Proprietary William Penn to derive benefit thereof. Legacies to PA Hospital, Monthly Mtg. of Woman Friends Southern District, Phila. To friends Rebecca Jones and Benjamin Mason. To Elizabeth Scott who served her time in his family. To Mary Kirkpatrick. To Priamus Stanton. Entered into partnership with his father, later taking in bros. Samuel R. and Jabez Maud Fisher. Entered into lumber business with bro. Miers, Thomas Hough and Caleb Bickham about 1784. Connected with Paper Mills at Brandywine. Partnership with Leonard Snowden in 1800 in Brewery Business. To grandchildren Thomas Fisher and Sarah Logan Fisher children of son William and to nephew Thomas Fisher son of bro. Samuel R. Fisher. To expected grandchild, child of son Joshua.
Execs: Sons William Logan Fisher and James Logan Fisher, also to be guardians of dau. Esther Fisher and of expected grandchild.
Wit: Charles Wharton, Redwood Fisher, Owen Jones, Robert Waln, John Roberts.
Codicil. Sister Lydia Gilpin since deceased, son born to dau.-in-law Elizabeth Powell Fisher named for her husband Joshua, dec'd.

Wit: Robert Waln, John B. Wallace, Jno. Roberts. Signed Jan 18, 1809.

BAIRD, WILLIAM. Southwark. Phila. Co. Mariner. Feb 17, 1810. Oct 24, 1810. 3.274.
Provides for wife Sarah. To sister Martha, wife of Christopher Cunningham of this state. At decease of sd. wife execs. to sell property, money from such sale to his bros. and sisters namely: Mark Baird, Ann wife of William Ferguson, Susannah wife of Patrick Rankin all of Ireland and Martha wife of Christopher Cunningham of PA.
Execs: Sd. wife Sarah Baird and friends Joseph Snowden and James Sawer of Phila., merchants.
Wit: Samuel S. Veacock, H. H. Kennedy.

ANDREWS, JOHN. Phila. Oct 22, 1810. Oct 26, 1810. 3.276.
All estate in U. S. or in Denmark or elsewhere to daus. Elizabeth and Sophia. Estate left to him by uncle in Denmark.
Execs: Friends George Reed and William Mann of Phila.
Wit: William Way, John Allison.

GARDNER, JOHN JACOB. Germantown. Phila. Co. Sept 17, 1810. Oct 27, 1810. 3.277.
All property to be sold, monies to be invested for support of wife Rachael during life, at her decease to his five children namely: Valentine Gardner, Jacob Gardner, Henry Gardner, Nancy Brown and Catharine Zerns.
Execs: Sd. sons Valentine and Jacob.
Wit: Henry Sorber, Frederick Youngkorth, Elias Sorber.

PRITCHETT or PRICHETT, ABRAHAM KINTZING. Phila. House Carpenter. Oct 8, 1810. Oct 30, 1810. 3.278.
Provides for wife, three children: Anna Elizabeth Prichett, Josephine Prichett and Abraham Kintzing Prichett.
Execs: And guardians bro. John Prichett and relation William Thackara, they to consult with Mrs. Goodwin wife of Thomas Goodwin. Peter Thomson to be overseer.
Wit: Jonathan Evans, Peter Thomson.

FRANCIS, SARAH. Oct 6, 1810. Oct 29, 1810. 3.279.
Property in Radnor Twp., Delaware Co. bequeathed to her by her father David Cornogg to be sold. Monies from sale to grandchildren according to

her husband Thomas Francis' last will. To son-in-law Thomas Fitzgerald, to dau. Elizabeth Gordon.
Execs: Sd. son-in-law Thomas Fitzgerald and dau. Elizabeth wife of Elisha Gordon.
Wit: Nathan Chapin, John Hellings. Thomas Fitzgerald renounced.

KESLER, FREDERICK. Northern Liberties. Phila. Co. Cordwainer. Aug 27, 1810. Nov 5, 1810. 3.280.
Estate to be sold. Provides for wife Catharine Kesler. Residue of estate to eight children namely: Mary Stork, Martin Kesler, Eve Kesler, Frederick Kesler, Adam Kesler, Catharine Kesler, Daniel Kesler and Susan Kesler.
Codicil Sept 13, 1810.
Exec: Friend and neighbour William Binder, Northern Liberties, hatter.
Wit: Samuel Lehman, blacksmith, John Palmer.

SPENCER, JOHN. Southwark. Phila. Co. Grocer. Oct 19, 1810. Nov 5, 1810. 3.281.
To dau. Jane Spencer by Sarah Sapley in Parish of Kilmore, Co. of Armaugh and Kingdom of Ireland, in case of decease of sd. dau. leaving no issue, estate to be divided amongst the children of bro. Thomas Spencer, dec'd, living in co. above named.
Execs: Con. O. Donel and Christopher Armstrong.
Wit: James Eccles, Henery McCully.

HAMMITT, FRANCES. Phila. Co. Widow. Dec 16, 1808. Nov 9, 1810. 3.282.
All estate to friend John C. Otto of Phila., Physician, whom she appoints exec.
Execs: John C. Otto.
Wit: William Stevenson, William Allibone.

WILLIAMS, MARY. Northern Liberties. Phila. Widow. Sept 18, 1810. Nov 13, 1810. 3.283.
Estate to children namely: Sarah Boyd (wife of William Boyd), John, Eliza and Mary Williams.
Exec: Bro.-in-law James Stokes, he to be guardian of her three minor children: John, Eliza, Mary.
Wit: George Ireland, Peter Thomson.

EWING, WILLIAM. Bristol Borough. Bucks Co. June 10, 1810. Nov 17, 1810. 3.285.
Bequeaths to Samuel Ewing and William Davidson one seventh part of George Tavern at Second and Arch Streets, Phila. in trust for use of children: William Elliott Ewing and Amelia Ewing, other children: Elizabeth, Thomas, John and Hannah. Also bequeaths to sd. trustees his share of KY Lands he is entitled to from his father's estate in trust for sd. William Elliott Ewing and Amelia Ewing. Appoints sd. trustees Samuel Ewing and William Davidson his execs. and guardians for sd. minor children.
Execs: Samuel Ewing and William Davidson.
Wit: George Klingel. Thomas Ross and Thomas Sergeant, Attornies at Law affirmed. William Davidson renounced.

LOWNES, DAVID. Phila. Watchmaker. Oct 26, 1810. Nov 19, 1810. 3.285.
Legacies to nephew John Lownes (son of bro. Caleb Lownes and Margaret his wife). To nephew Edward Lownes, to nephew George Lownes both sons of sd. bro. Caleb and Margaret his wife also bequeaths to sd. nephews his two Patent Rights, one for insuring the Schuylkill water clear and cold in all seasons as the pump water, the other for insuring Hydrants from the effects of frost in coldest weather. To Mary Livingston, ground in Moyamensing Twp., Phila. Co., adj. estate of the late John Lownes along line of George Goodwins Rope walk. All residue of estate to sd. three nephews.
Execs: Friends Peter Robeson of Phila. Co., miller and Samuel Pancoast of sd. city, iron monger.
Wit: Francis Mallet, William Andrews.
Letters granted to Samuel Pancoast Nov 29, 1810.

COLLINS, CHALKLEY. Phila. Biscuit Baker. Nov 1, 1810. Nov 26, 1810. 3.287.
All estate to wife Elizabeth Collins, she to support and educate his three children namely Thomas B., Caroline and Joshua Collins. At her decease or marriage, estate to sd. three children. If sd. wife should die during minority of dau. Caroline, he commits her to guardianship of his sister Mary Collins.
Codicil Nov 1, 1810.
Wit: Same as will.
Execs: Friends William Yardley, Timothy Paxson and Joseph Beale, all of Phila.

Wit: Benjamin Collins, Peter Thomson.

LARGE, EBENEZER. Phila. Merchant. July 5, 1810. Nov 28, 1810. 3.289.
Annuity to wife Dorothy Large. To dau. Sarah Mifflin, not liable for debts of her husband. To sons John Baldwin Large and James Large.
Execs: Wife Dorothy Large and sons John Baldwin Large and James Large.
Wit: James B. Thompson, Thomas W. Morgan, Wharton Lewis.

NACE, JACOB. Germantown Twp. Phila. Co. Farmer. July 18, 1807. Dec 3, 1810. 3.290.
Provides for wife Alice Nace. to sons Peter and John, land in Germantown Twp. To a line between his (Jacob Nace) land and Donaldson's in a line of Charles Nice's land &c. To place of beginning (as may more clearly appear by Deed of Release in his possission, Jacob Van Winkel and others to Sebastian Miller) and by Widow Mason's land. To children of son Martin, dec'd.
Execs: Sd. wife Alice and sons Peter and John Nace
Wit: Casper Guyer, John Burnheter.
Letters granted to Alice Nace and John Nace the surviving execs.

HEFFERNAN or HIFFERNAN, JOHN. Southwark. Phila. Co. Cordwainer. Dec 17, 1804. Dec 3, 1810. 3.292.
Estate to wife Mary Heffernan whom he appoints extx.
Exec: Wife Mary Heffernan.
Wit: William Allison, William McCall.

CUBIN, JOHN. Southwark. Phila. Co. Rigger. July 13, 1810. Dec 10, 1810. 3.292.
To stepson Nicholas Armstrong a silver watch &c. which belonged to his father, all residue of estate to wife Sarah and son William.
Execs: Friends Alexander Urquhart of Southwark, gentleman and Daniel Coates of Northern Liberties, tanner.
Wit: John Curtis, James Moffett.

BETTON, SAMUEL. Of the Parish of Saint Ann's Middlesex Co., Jamaica. (Liber 82 Folio 168). Dec 16, 1809. March 3, 1810. 3.294.
All estate to wife Catharine Betton, sons Samuel and John Betton and dau. Mary Anne Betton.

Execs: Wife Catharine Betton and sd. sons Samuel Betton and John Price Betton.
Wit: James Newby, John Wallis, Charles Campbell.

MASSEY, CHARLES. Phila. Oct 13, 1809. Dec 13, 1810. 3.295.
All estate to sons John and Thomas Massey. To dau. Ann Brown and granddau. Margaret Duncan.
Codicil June 30, 1810 . Alters legacies mentions William Brown, husband of dau. Ann.
Wit: Same as to will.
Exec: Friend John Greiner of Phila., merchant.
Wit: William Leedom, Jonathan Percival.

ALLEN, JOHN. Co. of Dutchess and State of NY. Gentleman. Nov 14, 1808. April 19, 1809. 3.296.
Estate to wife Christina Livingston Allen, after her death to his children (names not given). All real estate in PA, NJ, NY, and elsewhere to be sold.
Execs: John Johnston, Esq., of Dutchess Co., NY, bro. William Allen of same co. and state and wife Christina Livingston Allen.
Wit: Robert Taylor, Joseph Bird, David J. Johnston.

SULLENDER, JACOB. Northern Liberties. Phila. Blacksmith. July 6, 1810. Dec 13, 1810. 3.299.
Wife Wilhelmina Sullender to have all rents, incomes &c. of estate. Son Peter Sullender and granddau. Sarah Ann Sheppard child of late dau. Elizabeth. Appoints wife guardian of sd. granddau. and extx. of will so long as she remains his widow.
Execs: Wife, George Kline, Charles Yetter.
Wit: R. Whitehead, Peter Grim, Adam Schaffer.

KLING, JOHN. Phila. Gentleman. Nov 18, 1808. Dec 20, 1810. 3.301.
All estate to wife Mary Ann Kling, after death or marriage to be divided as folows viz: to dau. Catharine Baker wife of George Baker, Esq, to son Dr. John Kling, York Co., PA, to dau. Rachel Keslor's (dec'd) children, to dau. Susannah Raybold, to dau. Elizabeth Kling, to son George Philip Kling, shoemaker, to son George A. Kling, Mariner, to dau. Sopha Charlotte Kling.
Execs: Friends John Long and Isaac Wampole.
Wit: Jacob Painter, Samuel Young.

Codicil Sept 5, 1810. Wife Mary Ann Kling to sell house in which they live if she desires.
Wit: William Porter, Samuel Young, Joseph Norman. Isaac Wampole renounced.

RHOADS, SARAH. Phila. Relict of Samuel Rhoads late of same place, merchant. Sept 21, 1810. Dec 21, 1810. 3.303.
Legacies to grandsons Coleman Fisher and Samuel Rhoads Fisher, to be paid out of a Pasture Lot in Passyunk Twp. in tenure of the heirs of Robert Erwin. All residue of estate to son-in-law Samuel W. Fisher and friend Dr. Thomas Parke (except what is disposed of in a memorandum dated April 24, 1809) in trust for benefit of grandchildren: Samuel Rhoads, Sarah Rhoads Jr., Elizabeth Rhoads and Mary Rhoads. Memorandum. Legacies to son-in-law Samuel W. Fisher. To sister Mary Pleasants. To granddaus.: Sarah, Elizabeth and Mary Rhoads (a set of tea table plates which S. W. Fisher returned to her on his second marriage). To grandsons Coleman and S. Rhoads Fisher. To Jane McLeod. To Hannah Chamberlain. To Betty Porter (formerly Randolph). To Frank her little waiting man. Signed April 26, 1809.
Execs: Sd. Samuel W. Fisher and Thomas Parke.
Wit: John Townsend, Isaac T. Hopper.

OVERINGTON, JOHN. Belmont Place near Vaux Hall in Parish of Saint Mary Lambeth in Co. of Surry. Gentleman. Aug 10, 1807. March 21, 1811. 3.307.
All estate in England or America to his wife Sarah Overington, after her decease, to his son William Overington, in case of death of sd. son, bequeaths whole estate to bro.-in-law Thomas Ffogden of parish of Troten in Sussex Co., yeoman, to his (Thomas Ffogden's) dau. Elizabeth Upton wife of Thomas Upton of Colworth, sd. Co. of Sussex, farmer, and to his son Thomas Ffogdon. To wife Sarah Overington's aunt Mary Ffeachon wife of William Ffeachen parish of East Dean of Sussex Co., husbandman, to William Todman of Wool Lavington in sd. co., husbandman. To first cousins both of his father Thomas Overington and his mother Mary Overington.
Execs: Sd. wife Sarah Overington, if wife and sons die, he appoints friends Thomas Fogdon of Troton and Thomas Smith of Parish of Creatham, Co. of Sussex, husbandman.
Wit: William Gifford, G. Kerwood, Daniel Fryett, Millbank St. Westmn.

LIPPINCOTT, NATHANIEL. Waterford, Gloucester Co. NJ. Farmer. Aug 30, 1787. Aug 16, 1790. 3.310.
Provides for wife Mary Lippincott during widowhood. To son Caleb Lippincott part of land bought of Richard Haines, adj. lands of Amos Haines and Samuel Stokes, also part of his home place adj. lands of sd. Samuel Stokes, John Matlack, meadow in tenure of John Griffith. To grandson Wallace Lippincott, plantation on which he (Nathaniel Lippincott) now lives including land in tenure of William Bell. To grandsons John Lippincott and Jesse Lippincott. To son Seth's daus. Grandson Jesse Lippincott to have that part of land and Cedar Swamp before given to his father, at his death to his bro. Joshua Lippincott. to grandson Aquilla Lippincott property in Moores Town descended to him (Nathaniel Lippincott) from his father, he paying to granddaus. Abigail and Martha Borton and to niece Phebe Burr's dau. Sarah &c. at his death to his eldest son. To niece Martha Borton. To grandson Nathaniel Busby, son of dau. Martha Busby. To granddaus. Ann and Mary Busby house in Arch Street, Phila., purchased of Lazarus Pine. To survivors of dau. Grace's children and appoints their father Jabez Busby trustee for his sd. children. To granddau. Mary Haines. To grandsons Benjamin and Nathaniel Busby sons of dau. Grace, should they both die, the whole shall go to their sisters. To Treasurer of Preparative Meeting of Haddonfield.
Execs: Sons Caleb Lippincott and Joshua Borton.
Wit: Thomas Stokes, Samuel Allinson, William Allinson.
Codicil July 22, 1788. Since making will has exchanged meadow property with Samuel Allinson, bequeaths to grandson Wallace Lippincott.
Wit: Samuel Allinson, Jane Siddons, Mary Allinson.

EVERHART, CHARLOTTE. Phila. Dau. of John Everhart. Dec 10, 1810. Dec 26, 1810. 3.317.
All estate to friend Aaron Wolff of Phila. Sister Johanna Thauworth. Martin Reesse administrator to the estate of her father.
Exec: Sd. Aaron Wolff.
Wit: George Sees, Samuel Weeks, Thomas Stewart.

BROWNE, PETER. Northern Liberties. Phila. Blacksmith. April 13, 1799. Dec 31, 1810. 3.318.
To sons John Coats Browne and William Johnson Browne and dau. Sarah Browne. All residue of estate to his wife Sarah Browne. Exec. and guardian of minor children William and Sarah, sd. wife Sarah and his son

John Coats Browne, exec. Money advanced for good will of lease purchased of execs. of Robert Magie's estate &c.
Execs: Sd. wife Sarah and his son John Coats Browne.
Wit: Jos. Cowperthwait, Ab. M. Garrigues.
Codicil March 17, 1804. Directs that no rent shall be charged to son John Coats Browne for use of his estate in Kensington and that his son William J. Browne and his friends Abraham M. Garrigues be execs. instead of Joseph Cowperthwait and John W. Vancleve, whose names he has erased out of above Testament. William McFaden of Phila., merchant and John Welsh of sd. city, merchatn, affirmed.
Letters granted to William J. Browne and John Coats Brown.

BOOKCHOP, JOHN GEORGE. Northern Liberties. Phila. Sept 21, 1810. Jan 3, 1811. 3.320.
Appoints John Lowe, organ builder of Northern Liberties, Phila., exec. he to forward all money to bro.-in-law in Germany (name not given).
Exec: John Lowe.
Wit: James Brearley, Mary Brearley.

DAVISSON, JOHN. Mariner of Phila. and late Master of Ship Mount Vernon of that place. June 1, 1808. Oct 15, 1810. 3.321.
Legacies to Mrs. Rebecca Wilkinson, widow of ---- Wilkinson and dau. of Rebecca Rice, wid. of John Rice, late of Phila. and formerly ship carpenter of Kensington. to Charlotte Rice another dau. of sd. Rebecca Rice wid. of John. Remainder of estate to sd. Rebecca Rice, at her death to her children: Rebecca Wilkinson, Charlotte Rice, John Rice and Thomas Rice.
Execs: Thomas Beale, Esq., of ---- in Great Britain and James Smith Wilcocks of Phila., both now residing in China.
Wit: Dom. Jose Gomes, Alex. Vearson, John Budwell, Manuel Anto. du Silva, Matthew Vandenberg.

SCOTTEN, SAMUEL. Borough of Bristol, Co. of Bucks, PA. Nov 30, 1805. Jan 3, 1811. 3.323.
Provides for wife Jane Scotten. To bro. William Scotten, a rent charge payable out of lot in Southwark in tenure of James McKinley, at his death to his children, except his son Samuel. To sisters Sarah and Lucy rent charges payable out of property in southwark in tenure of Robert Maffett and a Tavern called Ewe and Lamb in Northern Liberties Phila., in tenure of William Brown. Annuity to Mary DeNormandie. To half sister Elizabeth Jones payable out of lot in Southwark in tenure of

Margaret Coulton, at her death to First day or Sunday School Society of Phila. for education of poor children. To Philadelphia Society for support of Charity Schools and to African Episcopal Church of Phila. To nephew Samuel Scotten son of bro. William, at his death to his children, if he dies without issue, to his (the sd. Samuel's) bros. and sisters. Nieces Hannah Johnson, Sarah Hartshorne and Ann Brown. Nephew Isaac Wilson. to friends Robert Haydock, his wife Susan Haydock, Eden Haydock, Samuel Haydock and his mother and Ann Haydock. To James Wills, Jr. Execs. to pay to Thomas Hall a legacy for use of Samuel Scotten Hall (who bears his name). To Elizabeth Stackhouse. Property in tenure of Adam Trip. To Major, Aldermen and Citizens of Phila. a rent charge payable out of property in tenure of John Long, they to pay on the 23rd of Feb each year (it being his birthday) twelve dollars worth of bread to the poor of Phila. and Southwark. To nephew Samuel Scotten Street. to contributors of PA Hospital. To Bristol Preparative Meeting in Bucks Co. to be used for free school for blacks founded by Anthony Benezet.
Codicil April 11, 1806. Ann Scotten dau. of sd. bro. William, property in Borough of Bristol purchased of James Harrison.
Wit: James Dunlap, Robert Frazer.
Codicil June 15, 1808.
Wit: John Bonsall, Joseph Beale, Robert Frazer.
Codicil Oct 2, 1810. Leaves Sundry articles of personal property to those mentioned in his will and to Sarah Hartshorne his wife's niece.
Wit: James Wills and John Bonsall.
Execs: Friends Eden Haydock, Samuel Haydock and James Wills, Jr.
Wit: James Wills, Robert Frazer.

LASKEY, CATHARINE. Northern Liberties. Phila. Widow. Dec 14, 1810. Jan 4, 1811. 3.333.
To children: Mary Gardner, Elizabeth Fraley, Sarah Stokes, John Laskey, Rebecca Aldenburgh, Harriet Laskey and Edward Laskey. Grandchildren Francis and Edward Boyd, children of dec'd dau. Catharine. Son-in-law John W. Fraley.
Exec: Isaac Wampole of Phila., Scrivener.
Wit: Enoch Wheeler, Charles Wheeler.

HEYL, PHILIP. Phila. Baker. Jan 31, 1810. Jan 5, 1811. 3.334.
Children: Mary Raser, Philip Heyl, Jr., John Heyl and Elizabeth Heyl. Nephew John Heyl son of late bro. John. Mary Heyl wife of sd. son Philip Heyl, Jr. Property in Phila. purchased of the late widow Meser.

Messuage, tenement, Bake House &c. purchased of George Peters in Germantown, Phila.
Codicil March 7, 1810. Dau. Mary Raser, dec'd, leaves her share to her five children namely: William, Thomas, John B., George and Mary Raser.
Wit: Thomas Dugdale, Jr., Peter Thomson.
Execs: Son John and nephew John Heyl.
Wit: Thomas Dugdale, Jr., Peter Thomson.

CAMPBELL, GEORGE. Esq. Phila. Oct 22, 1810. Jan 5, 1811. 3.339.
Estate to wife Helen Campbell.
Exec: Son George Campbell, Jr.
Wit: John C. Otto, Thomas I. Hewson.

BURROWS, JOHN. Phila. Mariner. Nov 16, 1808. Jan 3, 1811. 3.339.
Estate to friend Amos Marshall of Phila., wafer maker, if not living to Mary Marshall, his wife.
Execs: Sd. friend Amos Marshall or his wife Mary.
Wit: Benjamin R. Morgan, Samuel Walker.

BEATES, CONRAD. Phila. Tobacconist. Sept 16, 1793. Jan 11, 1811. 3.340.
Income of estate to wife Barbara during widowhood. Children: Frederick, Henry, William, Catharine and Mary. to sd. execs. in trust for son Peter and dau. Barbara, wife of Frederick Schutz.
Execs: Sons Frederick, Henry and William.
Wit: George Dannacher, Josannen Gierdor(?), George F. Alberti, Adam Kuhn.
Letters granted to Frederick Beates.

SMALLWOOD, ISAAC. Phila. Innkeeper. Oct 16, 1809. Jan 14, 1811. 3.343.
Estate to be sold, monies from sale to wife Priscilla, at her decease to Robert Sparks, Jr. (son of half bro. Robert Sparks). To Isaac Smallwood Porch (son of nephew John Porch). To Isaac Smallwood Ashton (son of George Ashton). To Isaac Smallwood Clark. To Isaac Smallwood (son of Peter Smallwood). To Isaac Smallwood (son of Manlie Smallwood) and to Priscilla Smallwood (dau. of sd. Manlie Smallwood) now Priscilla Hampton.
Execs: Wife Priscilla Smallwood and friend Samuel C. Champion of Gloucester Co., NJ.
Wit: Thomas Dugdale, Jr., Peter Thomson.

MUMFORD, THOMAS. Phila. Feb 21, 1811. Feb 26, 1811. 3.345.
All estate to mother (name not given). Bro. John Mumford.
Execs: Friends Samuel Logan and John Murry.
Wit: John Treas, Samuel Hammett, John Collman.

GAMBER, MARY. Blockley Twp. Phila. Co. Widow. Nov 2, 1809. Jan 30, 1811. 3.345.
All estate to son John Gamber, whom she appoints exec.
Exec: Son John Gamber.
Wit: Frederick Beates, Peter Wagner, Jr.

CROSBY, SAMPSON. Southwark. Phila. Co. Innkeeper. Sept 5, 1805. Feb 2, 1811. 3.346.
All personal estate to wife Elizabeth Crosby, also property in Phila., purchased of Jonathan Penrose, Esq., Sheriff. Property where he lives purchased of John Cassin. Stepdau. Elizabeth Werebrook. George Snyder, son of Philip Snyder. Sister Lucy Kitteridge wife of Dr. Francis Kitteridge of Mass.
Execs: Sd. wife Elizabeth and friends George Dougherty and George Barclay.
Wit: Abraham Shoemaker, Daniel Addis.
Letters granted to Elizabeth Crosby and Geo. Barclay Feb 8, 1811.

WOODWARD, JACOB. Phila. House Carpenter. Feb 27, 1794. Feb 5, 1811. 3.347.
All estate to wife Mary, at her decease to her children: Mary, Elizabeth, Sarah and Deborah.
Exec: Sd. wife Mary.
Wit: John Yeager, Adam May.

BURKIT, JOHN. Phila. Carter. Jan 27, 1811. Feb 6, 1811. 3.348.
Provides for wife (name not given). Mentions several children, but gives no names excepting Moses and Harriet.
Execs: Friends Samuel Curtes and John Bowers, requesting them to consult friends John B. Wallace and Thomas Bradford, Jr., debt due him by Philip Anderson.
Wit: Thomas Bradford, John H. Smith, Samuel Colhoun, M.D.

DIETERICK, JOSEPH. Phila. Gentleman. July 18, 1810. Feb 11, 1811. 3.350.
Estate to wife Catharine Dieterick whom he appoints extx.

Execs: Wife Catharine Dieterick.
Wit: Michel Hertzog, Robert Whitehead, Andrew Seguin.

TAWS, JAMES. Passyunk. Phila. Co. Dec 9, 1801. ----. 3.350.
Estate to wife Cathrine Taws, formerly Cathrine Kier.
Execs: Sd. wife and James Gibson, distiller and Thomas Mackie, merchant.
Wit: William Mitchell, James Cooper, T. Lowry Mackie.

ALBERTSON, SUSANNAH. Abington Twp., Montgomery Co. Widow. Sept 25, 1809. Aug 22, 1810. 3.351.
To daus. Sarah Webster and Susannah Beans and to Benjamin Albertson and Jonathan Albertson. To children of Thomas Albertson and to Susan and Thomas Albertson, children of Benjamin Albertson. Directs Nicholas Waln to sell land bought of son Benjamin. Legacies to Benjamin Webster and Benjamin Beans.
Execs: Sons Jacob and Benjamin Albertson.
Wit: Nicholas Waln and Nicholas Waln, Jr.
Letters granted Feb 16, 1811.

SALTAR, JOHN, Phila. Co. Sept 27, 1808. Sept 12, 1810. 3.352.
Provides for wife Elizabeth Saltar. Six children viz: Margret, Maria, Lucy, John, George and Francis. Execs. to sell real estate in NJ. Deducts from shares of daus. Margret and Maria, amount lent their husbands (names not given).
Codicil July 2, 1810. Mentions derangement of dau. Maria's husband's affairs. Son George, dec'd, appoints grandson Lynford Lardner exec. in his place.
Wit: Ann McMurtrie, Anna Maria Tilghman, Henry McMurtrie.
John Saltar sworn Feb 16, 1811, Elizabeth Saltar Feb 27, 1811.
Execs: Sd. wife Elizabeth and sons John and George G. Saltar.
Wit to will: John Wilkinson, Thomas Chappell, William Ashton.

McCURRACH, JAMES. Phila. Broker. Feb 19, 1811. March 2, 1811. 3.354.
Legacies to sister Isabella McCurach, Deskford, near Cullen, North Britain. To niece Margaret McCurach Sharp. To friend John Baker of Phila., Alderman. Residue of estate to wife Ann Isabella and son James Grant McCurrach, a minor.
Execs: And guardians sd. wife Ann Isabella McCurrach, friend Thomas Orr of Phila. and Edward Sharp of NJ.

Wit: John Francis, Isaac Wampole.
Letters granted to Thomas Orr and Edward Sharp.

KEEN, JACOB. Northern Liberties. Phila. Tanner. Jan 5, 1811. March 4, 1811. 3.355.
Legacies to Jacob Keen Cresson son of Richard C. Cresson. To Eleanor Cresson sister of sd. Jacob. To wife Eleanor and children Mercy and John a rent charge out of ground granted to Philip Halzell, his messuage where he dwells also Tan Yard and other buildings. If both children die without issue, sd. property to trustees of Second Baptist Church in Northern Liberties, Phila. Land formerly the estate of Martin Thomas. Rebecca wife of sd. Martin Thomas and her children.
Wit: Robert Whitehead, Philip Halzel, Richard C. Cresson.
Codicil Jan 27, 1811. If children die in minority &c. bequeaths to Moses Esty, Unice Brarman, Lucy Matthews and Rebecca Thomas the bro. and sister of sd. wife. John Prentice, teacher to be paid for teaching children of sd. Martin Thomas.
Wit: Robert Whitehead, Samuel Bowers and Hannah Tyson.
Execs: Sd. wife Eleanor Keen and friends Jesse Cleaver and Thomas Timings of N. L.

NORTH, JOSEPH. Phila. Shopkeeper. Aug 27, 1801. March 4, 1811. 3.359.
Estate to children: Joseph, Jane and Lydia North, at their death to his grandchildren, the children of son Joseph by his present wife Mary.
Execs: Sd. son Joseph and daus. Jane and Lydia North.
Wit: John Roush, Samuel Taylor, Peter Thomson, Joseph North the exec., dec'd.
Letters granted to Jane and Lucy North.

McGANDY, HENRY. Moyamensing Twp. Phila. Co. Labourer. Jan 30, 1811. March 4, 1811. 3.361.
To wife Margaret Gandy*[sic]* the rents &c. from property in Moyamensing Twp. and Southwark, at her decease to his bros. Daniel and Patrick McGandy of Donegal Co., Ireland.
Execs: John Maitland of Moyamensing Twp., grocer and James Farron of Phila., tallow chandler.
Wit: Thomas Hoskin, James McGowan.
Letters granted to James Fearon.

KIRK, ROBERT W. Germantown. Phila. Co. Tanner. Feb 20, 1811. March 11, 1811. 3.362.
All property consisting of houses, lots and wharf in Alexandria, District of Columbia and elsewhere to wife Sarah Kirk. Wharf in tenure of William Hartshorn or Mordecai Miller. Son James to have sd. wharf at wife's decease. Legacy to sister Harriot Jackson.
Execs: Sd. wife Sarah and father-in-law William Keyser of Germantown.
Wit: Jacob Good, Joachim Lange, William Hiseler.

HARE, ROBERT. Phila. Porter Brewer. May 1, 1806. March 14, 1811. 3.363.
Annuity to wife Margaret Hare with property in Germantown,his household goods &c. Children; Charles Willing Hare, Robert Hare, Jr., Martha Hare, Jr., and John Powel Hare. To Mrs. Ann Hare wife of son Charles Willing Hare. To bros. and sisters Richard and James Hare, the widow of Charles Hare, Martha and Charlotte Hare all of England, Great Britain.
Codicil Feb 23, 1807. As sons Charles W. and Robert Hare are of age, he appoints them execs. in place of friends Edward Burd and Thomas M. Willing.
Wit: Jacob Smith, Samuel McClurg.
Execs: Messrs. Edward Burd, Barrister at Law and Thomas Mayne Willing, merchant, both of Phila. with his wife Margaret Hare.

ROWAN, JOSEPH. Phila. Laborer. Feb 7, 1811. March 19, 1811. 3.365.
Legacy to friend James Rowan of Chichester Twp., Delaware Co.
Residue of estate to friend William Lindsay of Phila., whom he appoints exec.
Execs: William Lindsay.
Wit: Richard Renshaw, James Robb.

PRESTON, JAMES. Southwark, PA. Mariner. Sept 15, 1810. March 15, 1811. 3 366.
Estate to wife Sarah Preston, appointing her sole extx.
Execs: Wife Sarah Preston.
Wit: Samuel Barclay, Henry McEuen.

WHITTLE, ROBERT. Leicester in Co. of Leicester, Framesmith, about to depart on a voyage to North America. Dec 4, 1794. March 25, 1811. 3.367.
All estate to wife Ann Whittle, whom he appoints extx.

Execs: Wife Ann Whittle.
Wit: Stephen Johnson, Thomas Coombe, M. Johnson. William Y. Birch and Abraham Small both of Phila., booksellers affirmed.

LONG, BRIDGET. Phila. Widow. March 6, 1811. April 2, 1811. 3.368.
Legacies to Mary Magner, to niece Maria O'Connor. All residue of estate to son James Long, if sd. son die leaving no issue, she leaves sd. residue to her three nephews: James, William and Christopher children of sister Mary O'Connor.
Execs: Friends Francis Higgins and Cornelius Tiers, they to be guardians of sd. son during minority.
Wit: James Brady, William Wood.

ROBINEAU DE BOUGON, JOHN VINCENT MARIE. Born in St. Domingo, domiciliated at Nantz and now on account of business in Phila. U.S.A. April 20, 1802. April 3, 1811. 3.370.
Legacy to Moran his servant, if he is still with him at his decease. His estate to be divided according to the law to his natural heirs, excepting the legacies menitoned. Appoints Monsieur Le Marquis de Caxaux the only trustee of his estate in the island of St. Domingo.
Exec: Mr. Marie Dominick James D'Orlie of St. Domingo, now in Phila., he to remit proceeds to Commerical house of Mr. Lincoln at Nantz and he to place it at disposal of M. de Caxaux.
Wit: Peter Stephen Du Ponceau, of Phila., Attorney at Law and Nicholas Amous of sd. city. exchange broker.

RILEY, ELIZABETH. Phila. Widow. Feb 21, 1811. March 27, 1811. 3.372.
Estate to children: William Riley, Margaret Boat, John Riely, Catharine Brady and Mary Winton.
Execs: Friends John Greiner and Daniel Groves of Phila.
Wit: Lawrence Ford, Isaac Wampole.

STUNTZ, FREDERICK. Phila. Baker. Jan 25, 1811. April 4, 1811. 3.374.
Leaves to bro. Heinrich Philip Stuntz in Weiblingen-Wunderberg (son of Henrich Philip Stuntz) a legacy with his Hereditary Claim in Germany. All residue of estate to wife Catharine. Sister Sabina Curfis.
Execs: Friends Jacob Chur and Frederick Schaber.
Wit: Frederick Shaber, Jacob Chur, Samuel Mechlin. Jacob Chur renounced.

ELLING, WILLIAM. Phila. Clergyman, late Pastor of Trinity Church. March 31, 1811. April 5, 1811. 3.375.
To nephew Ludwig Goelhardt of City Bamberg between Wertzberg and Nierenberg, once in the Circle of Franconia all estate.
Execs: Friends Louis Hammer and Matthias James O. Conway, both of Phila.
Wit: N. LeFavre, Joseph A. Wigmore.

STRONG, MATTHEW. Phila. Mariner. April 6, 1793. March 21, 1811. 3.376.
All estate to wife Agness Strong whom he appoints extx.
Exec: Wife Agness Strong.
Wit: Joseph Harker, Robert Whitehead and Richard Whitehead.

BICKHAM, CALEB. Southwark. Merchant. April 15, 1806. March 29, 1811. 3.376.
All estate to wife Mary and children: Ann, Mary, Joshua, George and Elizabeth. Sons Thomas and Abia by a former marriage, each to have a legacy. Legacy to his sister Margaret. Legacy to grandson Caleb Bickham Henry. Wife and friend Alexander Wilson to be guardians of minor children.
Execs: Sd. wife Mary and friends Miers Fisher and Jonathan Willis.
Wit: Wm. Jones Williams, Jacob S. Waln, Jr. Miers Fisher and Jonathan Willis renounce.

SHAW, MARY. Phila. Single Woman. May 23, 1804. April 9, 1811. 3.378.
Only dau. a Devisee, Trustee and sole extx. named in last will of late father Samuel Shaw of sd. city, merchant. Exec. bro. Thomas Shaw whom she directs to sell all estate, monies to bro. Samuel Burgess Shaw, Spence Shaw, John Auldham Shaw and Thomas Shaw. The Trust vested in her by her father's will shall be vested in Sarah McCulloch.
Exec: Samuel Shaw.
Wit: Thomas Shaw, Sarah McCulloch. Rachel Allen wife of Chamless Allen of Phila., merchant affirmed.

CLIFTON, ANNA MARIA. April 11, 1811. April 17, 1811. 3.380.
Legacies to Mrs. Tacey Lenox, Miss Sarah Keene, Mrs. Rebecca Sterret for her dau. Augusta Sterret, Mrs. Hannah Biddle for her dau. Ann, Mr. Thomas Ketland and Mrs. Elizabeth Ketland in trust for their niece Kitty Ketland, if she dies under age, for their own benefit. To Miriam Warder. To Thomas H. White and William S. Biddle in trust to teach

boys to sing as a choir in the Orchestra of Christ Church. To her black boy Robert she gives his freedom. Her diamond mourning ring inscribed with names of father, mother and sister Elizabeth and a Cornelian Seal with a Crest of the Clifton Arms she gives to Alfred Wharton Clifton. Annuities to niece Elizabeth Tucker and to niece Frances Clifton. All residue of estate to Alfred Wharton Clifton son of Col. Franklin Wharton, if he should die under age or cease to bear the name of Clifton, she directs that sd. estate shall descent to Washington Wharton, another son of Col. Wharton on condition that he assumes the name of Clifton, on failure thereof or death without issue, to the other sons of Col. Wharton, the income thereof to be received by Col. Wharton for benefit of his children.
Exec: William S. Biddle. the person who shall take the sd. estate devised to children of Col. Wharton shall previously be baptized according to the Episcopal Church.
Wit: Benjamin Rush, John Syng Dorsey.

BARDON, MOSES. Essequibo. Oct 12, 1800. 3.381.
His bros. John and Luke Bardon with his surviving sisters to inherit his estate. Bro. Luke to take his mulatto son named Moses under his care as if he was his own son, also to take his slaves &c.
Execs: Bro. Luke Bardon and Richard Nugent both of aforesd. Colony.
Wit: William Waters, Charles Par J Da Haza, H. E. Lemmire, Charles Parsons, Thomas Bourke, Laurce. Kelly. Deposited in Sur: Office at Demerary April 8, 1805.

BARDON, LUKE. Now residing in Essequibo. Aug 7, 1802. 3.382.
Legacy to the poor of sd. Colony. To mulatto boy Moses Bardon, in case of his death to his (Luke's) Br. and sisters in Ireland. To bro. John Bardon. Cousin Thomas Bardon. Residue to bro. John and surviving sisters in Ireland.
Execs: Richard Nugent, Esq., and Mr. Charles Parsons both planters of Essequibo. Uncle Stephen Bardon in Phila. in America.
Wit: Thomas Moore, Thomas Gavin, Lawr. Kelly, John Wells, Henry L. Burton, George Wells. Deposited in Secretary's Office of Demarara April 8, 1805.

TRAQUAIR, JAMES. Phila. Stonecutter. Oct 16, 1810. April 18, 1811. 3.383.

All estate to wife Ann Traquair whom he appoints extx. at her death to his two sons Adam and James, they to pay a legacy to his son. Son Thomas. Mary Ann Scott, his wife's niece.
Exec: Wife Ann Traquair.
Wit: Charles Blain, David Scott.

NEWMAN, MARY. Northern Liberties. Phila. Widow. Aug 1, 1810. April 19, 1811. 3.384.
To dau. Mary Newman property in Northern Liberties, Phila. purchased of ---- Mitchell. Bro.-in-law Daniel Brautigam of N. L. Granddau. Mary Newman dau. of son Daniel to have property in Frankford, Phila. Co. purchased of Michael Krafft and others, if she dies without issue, sd. property to her bros. and sisters. To son Daniel and his wife Lucy. All residue of estate to dau. Mary whom she appoints extx.
Execs: Dau. Mary.
Wit: Abraham Stein, Frederick Beates.

JOHNS, MATTHEW. Southwark. Phila. Cordwainer. May 18, 1809. April 19, 1811. 3.386.
Bro. Thomas Johns. Estate to mother Mary Allen now the wife of Matthew Allen of Southwark aforesd. gentleman.
Execs: Sd. Mary Allen and Thomas Johns.
Wit: James Buchanan, Thomas Blackson, Mary Barry.

SMALLWOOD, THOMAS. Phila. Cordwainer. Jan 20, 1803. April 3, 1811. 3.387.
All estate to wife Elizabeth Smallwood whom he appoints extx.
Exec: Wife Elizabeth Smallwood.
Wit: Benjamin Brown W., Robert Whitehead. George Heyl, Jr., of Phila., Attorney at Law affirmed. April 23, 1811.

THUM, GEORGE. Southwark. Phila. Co. Baker. July 31, 1810. April 29, 1811. 3.387.
Property in Southwark and Phila. to dau. Elizabeth Rees and to son John Thum. Legacy to three children of son Jacob, to wit: Sarah, Charles and Jacob. Grandsons George Rees, Charles Rees and George Thum. Granddaus. Sarah Rees, Mary Ann Thum and Eliza Thum. All residue of estate to sd. dau. Elizabeth sd. son John.
Execs: Son John and son-in-law George Rees.
Wit: John M. Hartly, Isaac Wampole.

SAUNDERS, FRANCIS. Moyamensing Twp. Phila. Co. Grocer. March 26, 1811. April 29, 1811. 3.399.
Estate to Thomas Devis, a minor at this time living with him. If he dies under age to bro. John Devis and his sister Sarah Devis, both minors. Desires his new cloathing to be returned to his taylor John Culine.
Execs: Thomas Smith (a clerk in the late Bank of U.S.) and Edward Rowler (storekeeper).
Wit: Rebecca Hastings, G. Kempe.

SIMPSON, JAMES. Bucks Co., PA. Warminster Twp. ----. April 29, 1811. 3.400.
Income of estate to wife (not named) after her decease to her children (not named). Legacies to David Simpson, John Simpson, Ruth Hilborn and James Simpson is bro. John Simpson's children. To wifes bro. Peter's son John Shoemaker. to Hannah Carethorn(?) granddau. of sister Hannah. Remainder of estate between Margret Newbould and Isaac and Jonathan Shoemaker.
Codicil May 20, 1809.
Wit: James Melone, Mary Melone.
Execs: Mikel Newbould and Isaac Shoemaker.
Wit: David Jarrett, Rebecca Jarrett.

McDOUGAL, JOHN. Phila. Co. Mariner. April 28, 1811. May 6, 1811. 3.401.
Estate to be sold, monies to wife Eliza McDougall and sons Samuel McDougall and John McDougall, minors.
Execs: Francis Gurney, George Ludlam and John S. Smith, all of Phila.
Wit: Richard Renshaw, John Barclay, Simon Kingston.

SHIRLEY, THOMAS. April 29, 1811. May 9, 1811. 3.402.
Legacies to African Episcopal Church of Saint Thomas. To Trustees of Mr. Allen's Church 6th Street. To school in Willings Alley, African School of St. Thomas. To friend Russell Perot. Moses Bunton, Revd. Robert Blackwell. To Myra Long now in service of Mr. Robert Murdock. To female charitable society. To friend Mary Moore now residing as cook at Major Moores in Pine Street.
Execs: Absalom Jones, Richard Allen.
Wit: Thomas Mitchell of Phila., conveyancer and Revd. Robert Blackwell.

COX, WILLIAM. Phila. Wind[s]or Chair Maker. Aug 18, 1810. May 9, 1811. 3.404.

To wife Ruth Cox his household goods, kitchen furniture, wearing apparel &c. Annuity to wife's sister Priscilla Lloyd. To wife's sister Sarah Bristol (now widow of Jacob Bristol). To Jacob Kennard and Mary his wife, cousin of sd. William Cox. Late son John D. or John G. Cox has left a natural son born July 11, 1802 and named Charles English, real name of mother of sd. child Emily Corcey, but having adopted sirname given to child she is known as Emily English. To friend Isaac Harvey. Legacies to nephews William, Thomas, David and Benjamin Cox (children of bro. Nicholas Cox of MD). To Christopher Dilts (son of Henry Dilts and wife Martha his (William Cox) niece. Property in tenure of Isaac Norris. Property late in tenure of William Shufflebottom, now in tenure of James L. Dunn, property purchased of Capt. Keith, income of sd. property to wife Ruth Cox. To friends Isaac Harvey, Thomas Norton and George Williams in trust for educating poor children belonging to the Society of Friends in Phila.
Codicil Oct 6, 1810. Mentions Job Harvey, father of Isaac Harvey.
Wit: James Allinson, Peter Thomson.
Execs: Sd. Isaac Harvey, Thomas Norton and George Williams.
Wit: Thomas Dugdale, Jr., Peter Thomson.

CORYELL, JOSEPH. Bristol Twp. Phila. Co. Miller. April 9, 1811. May 11, 1811. 3.408.
Provides for wife Susanna Coryell and children: Deborah, Sarah and Ann Eliza.
Execs: Wife Susanna and friend Samuel Mechlin, Jr.
Wit: Isaac Kulp, John Deprefontaine.
Letters granted to Susanna Coryell and Samuel Mechlin.

DENCKLA, CHRISTIAN H. Phila. Merchant. Dec 29, 1810. May 11, 1811. 3.409.
Legacy to Ministers, Vestrymen and Church Wardens of the German Lutheran Congregation in and near Phila. To Trustees of Evangelical Lutheran Congregation of St. John's Church in Phila. and vicinity. To John Long. To PA Hospital. Children: Henry Augustus, Christian Christopher, Maria Magdalen, Sarah and Paul, all minors. Sister Magdalen Elizabeth Roland wife of George William Roland of Hamburgh and to each of her children Henry and William. Property in Phila. purchased of James Ash and Joshua Maddox Wallace, of Thomas Stewardson, of Richard Wilcocks and other execs. of John Wilcocks, of Benjamin Johnson, Francis Dumas and Charles Biddle, Edward Bartholomew, Ann Giles, George Wescott, Jacob Hansell, Jesse Oat and

Israel Roberts execs. of Martha Roberts, of Frederick Kuhl, Jeremiah Warder, of Israel Israel, Sheriff. Spread Eagle Tavern and Store purchased of Richard Tunis and Hunt Downing administrators of John Dunwoody, James Milnor exec. of Matthew Huston, Miliah Martha Moore, Robert Waln and Dr. [of] Physick. Apppoints friends John Long, Charles Eberle, Henry Lehr, John K. Helmuth and Isaac Wampole guardians of his children.
Execs: Wife Anna Maria and friends Abraham Piesch, John Jordan, Jacob Ritter, Jr., and Frederick Beates all of Phila.
Wit: Charles Bitters, Isaac T. Longstreth.

HUTT, JONATHAN. Phila. Labourer. Oct 24, 1810. May 15, 1811. 3.415.
Estate to wife Tabitha and children: Elijah, Mary, Rebecca and Lucy.
Exec: Friend Jonathan Trusty.
Wit: Thomas Savery, John D. Smith.

WEAVER, HENRY. Northern Liberties. Phila. Bricklayer. March 22, 1808. May 16, 1811. 3.415.
Income of estate to wife Hannah Weaver, she to support and educate his minor children. Seven children namely: Mary, David, Henry, Catharine, Wilhelmina, John and Thomas Weaver.
Exec: Sd. wife Hannah.
Wit: David Pearson, John Adolph.

WELSH, LYDIA. Phila. Widow. Sept 25, 1808. May 23, 1811. 3.416.
To grandsons Eli and Amos Yarnall and to granddau. Matilda Yarnall, to be at interest until they are of age. Residue to son John Welsh.
Exec: Friend Jesse Williams.
Wit: Mord. Churchman, John Hutchinson.

LYMAN, WILLIAM. Formerly of Northampton in Hampshire Co., MA, and late consul of United States at London but at Cheltenham, Gloucester Co., Esq., dec'd. Sept 17, 1811. Oct 12, 1811. 3.417.
To son William Lyman and five daus.: Jerushia, Frances, Anna, Martha and Helen Maria all estate in England, America or elsewhere. Desires to be interred in the Cathedral Church of Gloucester.
Exec: Dau. Jerushia Lyman, spinster.
Wit: Edward Jenner, M.D., Joseph Eaden, Richard Pruen Soln. Cheltenham. Given at London as to time of search and sealing Oct 12, 1811. Reuben Gacent Beasly, Consul of U.S.A. for London &c. do certify that George Gostling, Nathaniel Gostling and R. C. Cresswell whose

names are subscribed to will of William Lyman, Esq., dec'd, are Deputy Registers of the Prerogative Court of Archbishop of Canterbury &c.

PRICE, EDWARD. Late of Phila. Now of Fort Wilkerson in the Creek Nation. Jan 14, 1799. ----. 3.421.
Sarah the dau. of Susan Baker of Phila. reputed to be his natural child and to the male child of Rachel (sd. child was named Lennephy by the Tussices Mico Warren King of the Casset-ah), the dau. of Thomas Giles, late of Buffaloe Settlement, Hancock Co., to have all his estate, reserving for support of the mothers of sd. two children.
Execs: Mr. John Wilson of the Bank of U. S., Accountant, bro. Joseph Price of Montgomery Co., PA, and friend Richard Tunis, merchant of Phila.
Wit: Matthew Hopkins, William Carson, State of Georgia, Hancock Co. Myles Greene Clerk of the Court of Ordinary of Hancock Co. and William Chandler a Justice of Inferior Court of sd. Co. affirmed. John Wilson affirmed June 8 and Joseph Price Aug 8, 1812.

HOULTON, MARY. Phila. Maiden. Feb 13, 1805. May 25, 1811. 3.423.
Bro. David Houlton now residing in Baltimore. To sd. bro.'s dau. Jemima Medcalf, wife of Abraham Medcalf also of Baltimore. To bro.'s son Thomas Houlton. To niece Mary late the widow of Huson Langstroth, dec'd. To niece Sarah Dexter wife of Richard Dexter of Phila. To Mary Gardner dau. of niece Elizabeth Meredith. To Sarah Houlton wife of nephew John Houlton. To George Norris, her sisters son. To George Langstroth, son of Huson Langstroth, dec'd and Mary his wife. To Mary Houlton Scott dau. of nephew George Scott. To John and George Scott sons of sd. nephew George Scott. To Hannah Logan Fisher dau. of Thomas Fisher. To sister Lydia Wells, widow, of Baltimore. To niece Jehosheba Brown wife of Josiah Brown of Baltimore. To relation Elizabeth Harden, wife of Charles Harden. To relation Alice Wenner. To Margaret Porter. To Hannah Townsend, wife of John Townsend, residue to her half sister Sarah Leech and niece Sarah Dexter.
Codicil. Sarah Houlton died since making will her share to Mary Houlton dau. of William Houlton, late of Baltimore, dec'd, revokes legacy given to John Scott, his share to bro. Joseph Scott. To Mary, Anna, Lydia, Fanny and Jane Scott. To relation Allis Warner.
Wit: George Scott, John Scott.
Execs: Sd. friends John Townsend, Hannah his wife and relation Alice Warner all of Phila.
Wit: Charles Townsend, Mordecai Churchman.

TILLY, PETER. Phila. Merchant. May 1, 1809. May 27, 1811. 3.427.
All estate to wife Mary Tilly and his children (names not given).
Execs: Andrew Kennedy of Phila., Tallow Chandler and Dockeray Smith of same place, merchants.
Wit: William Oliver, John F. Holdernesse, John G. Oliver.

LIESZ, HENRY. Phila. Victualler. Nov 6, 1809. May 29, 1811. 3.428.
All estate to wife Elizabeth, at her decease, to his children namely: Catharine the wife of Noah Davis, Dorothea, Conrad Weaver's wife, John Elizabeth*[sic]* the wife of Lewis Frank, Susanna Curry the wife of William Curry, Henry, George, Maria and Jacob Liesz.
Execs: Friend Noah Davis and wife Elizabeth Liesz.
Wit: Jacob Mechlin, Samuel Mechlin.

CASTER, GEORGE. Oxford Twp. Phila. Co. May 3, 1811. May 30, 1811. 3.429.
Income of all estate to wife Margaret Caster, at her decease the following legacies to be paid to son Mathias Caster, granddau. Susannah Jender. Should she die under age or without issue, to her surviving bros. and sisters. To granddau. Margaret Caster dau. of Mathias Caster. To granddaus. Maria Johnson and Susannah Johnson. All residue of estate to sons Mathias and William Caster. To dau. Maria Johnson and Susannah Jenders, at their decease, to their children. To children of son George Caster, dec'd.
Execs: Wife Margaret and sons Mathias and William and William Caster.
Wit: Thomas Eringer, Henry Vandike, Andrew Doner(?). Margaret Caster renounced.

ROBESON, RUDEMAN. Phila. Hatter. Oct 25, 1790. June 6, 1811. 3.431.
All estate to William Lawrence of sd. city, hatter, whom he apppoints exec.
Execs: William Lawrence.
Wit: John Alexander, Samuel Taylor, John Pinkerton, Jr.

MURRAY, ANN. Phila. Widow of Rev. Alexander Murray, late of Phila. May 10, 1808. May 30, 1811. 3.432.
Legacies to Joseph Clark. To Rector, Church Wardens &c. of Christ and St. Peters Churches in Phila. for benefit of charity schools belonging to sd. churches. To sd. Joseph Clark for female Association of Phila., for Sunday Charity schools and for Phila. Dispensary. To Rebecca Patrick if

living, if not to her children. To Sarah Jones her bro. Joseph's granddau. To friend Jane Harrison. To friend Marcia Ross wife of Capt. David Ross. To Johanna Armstrong, widow, (niece of John Ross, Attorney at Law) now living at Wilmington. To Catharine Bird. To Gertrude Vangesil of New Castle. To Elizabeth Car. To Jamima Berryman. To Mary Lafferty. To Mrs. Newport, widow of James Newport. To Sophia who lives with her. All residue of estate to William Burrows, Sarah Thomson and Harriet Burrows children of Col. William Burrows, dec'd.
Exec: Friend Joseph Clark.
Wit: Catharine Clark ----, Peter Lohra affirmed.

PHIPPS, ISAAC. Northern Liberties. Phila. Oct 29, 1809. June 8, 1811. 3.434.
Property in sd. Liberties to son Llewellyn Phipps. Property in Phila. to friend Daniel Thomas, Jr., in trust for dau. Hannah Carmalt wife of Jonathan Carmalt, Jr, at her decease to her children whether by her former or present husband. To granddau. Susanna Carmalt. All residue of estate to the children of dau. Hannah Carmalt by her present husband Jonathan Carmalt.
Execs: Dau. Hannah Carmalt and nephews Thomas Phipps and Joseph Bird.
Wit: Anthony Johnson, Justus Johnson, Samuel Deavs.

PELTZ, MARY. Phila. Single Woman. Jan 15, 1811. June 14, 1811. 3.435.
Legacy to aunt Mary Maag. All residue of estate to sister Elizabeth Lyle, to sister Catherine Boehm, at her decease to her children.
Execs: Uncle Philip Peltz and her bro.-in-law William Lyle.
Wit: Willm. Dalzell, John Steel, Stephen C. Fotterall.

DESCAMPS, JOHN. A native of Bordeaux in France, now of the city of Phila. Merchant. May 25, 1811. June 19, 1811. 3.437.
Bequeaths to Mrs. Fyan, wife of John Fyan, shoemaker, residing in Northern Liberties in trust for his wife Sarah Descamps from whom he has long since been separated by mutual consent. To Anna Fletcher. To contributors of PA Hospital. To Peter Barriere of Phila., baker. To John Saulmier of Phila., merchant. To Christopher Lindmuth, baker. To John Lindmuth, son of sd. Christopher. All residue of personal estate to his father Dominique Descamps who formerly lived at Bordeaux, if he is not living, to his (John Descamps) sister or her children if any. To the CurÕ

for time being of the parish of St. Seuvin at Bordeaux for poor of sd. parish.
Execs: Peter Lambert, Claudius Bernanos, both of Phila.
Wit: James Ham, J. R. Malenfant.

DALLEY, MARY. Phila. Single Woman. May 4, 1811. June 26, 1811. 3.439.
Legacies to sister Catherine Simmons. To niece Catherine C. McDaniel. To grandniece Catherine O. Simmons. To grandniece Catherine S. Raguet. To grandnephew John B. Simmons. To grandnephew William S. Simmons. To grandniece Mary Dalley Murdock. To niece Mary Price. To grandnephew William Annely. To her bound girl Sarah Speer. All residue to niece Mary Murdock.
Exec: Nephew William Murdock of Phila., merchant.
Wit: Thomas Firth, Isaac Bonsal.

BERT, CLAUDIUS MEDARDUS FELIX. Now residing in Charleston, South Carolina. June 10, 1811. June 24, 1811. 3.440.
Having transferred to Phila. part of his property, appoints as execs. Thomas W. Bacot, Esq., of Charleston, and Charles Marquedant, Esq., of Phila. Bequeaths to four children of friend George Reid of this city namely: George Bert Reid (his godson), Isabella Eliza Reid, William Moultrie Reid and to Anne Reid, the youngest dau. of his dec'd friend. To bro. Allexis Caspard Michael Bert residing at present in France he leaves all his property in Europe.
Execs: Thomas W. Bacot, Esq, Charles Marquedant, Esq.
Wit: Henry H. Bacot, Pat. Fol Forer, T. W. Bacot, Jr. Jacob Houpt of Phila., grocer, and Joseph Solms of Phila., merchant, affirmed.

LOGAN, THOMAS. Phila. Shipwright. March 16, 1811. June 27, 1811. 3.445.
All estate to wife Elizabeth, whom he appoints extx.
Exec: Wife Elizabeth.
Wit: Samuel Barclay, Jame McLenehey.

SMITH, THOMAS. Northern Liberties. Phila. Co., Lumber Merchant. May 4, 1811. June 28, 1811. 3.445.
Provides for wife Griszell Smith. To eleven children namely: Charles E. Smith, Margaret Smith, Margery Smith, Deborah Parker, (wife of Joseph Parker), Thomas Smith, Jr., Mary W. Smith, Hugh Smith, Jr.,

Newberry Smith, Jr., Ann Smith, Susanna Smith and William Allen Smith.
Execs: Sd. wife Griszell, his two sons Charles E. Smith and Thomas Smith, Jr., and bro. Newberry Smith.
Wit: Nathan A. Smith, William Andrews.
Letters granted to Newberry Smith and Charles E. Smith.

CARMALT, THOMAS SAY. Northern Liberties. Phila. Co. Taylor. April 17, 1811. July 1, 1811. 3.448.
All estate to wife Sarah, at her decease to her dau. Mary Mitchell and her children.
Execs: Sd. wife Sarah and friend James Howell.
Wit: Thomas Millard, John Uhlen.

KEYSER, CATHERINE. Widow of Michael Keyser of Germantown. Phila. Co. June 7, 1811. June 24, 1811. 3.449.
All estate to her three children namely: Andrew Keyser, Daniel Keyser and Ann Peebles, (wife of John Peebles), at death of dau. Ann, to her children.
Exec: Sd. son Andrew Keyser of Germantown.
Wit: Ennion Williams, John Nutz.

GRAY, WILLIAM. Phila. March 19, 1811. July 6, 1811. 3.450.
Provides for wife Elizabeth Gray. Daus. Sarah and Kitty Gray.
Execs: Friends the Revd. Absalom Jones, Joseph Randolph and Cyrus Porter, also wife Elizabeth Gray.
Wit: Thomas D. Pee, George McFarland. Absalom Jones and Joseph Randolph renounced.

WALTMAN, MICHAEL. Phila. Inn Keeper. ----, 1811. July 9, 1811. 3.451.
In trust to son William Waltman and friend Francis Higgins for wife Eve Waltman and such of his other children as shall reside with her until the youngest comes of age, at the time estate to be sold and divided.
Children: William, Mary Ann, Margaret, Catharine and Samuel.
Execs: Sd. William Waltman and Francis Higgins in conjunction with his wife Eve Waltman guardians of his minor children.
Wit: James Skerrett, Jacob Walahan.

TUCKER, ABNER. Phila. Inn Keeper. Sept 13, 1807. July 10, 1811. 3.454.

All estate to wife Johanna Maria Tucker, whom he appoints extx. and his friend Samuel Mechlin of sd. city exec.
Execs: Wife Johanna Maria Tucker, Samuel Mechlin.
Wit: Richard Folwell, Thomas Swann.

RITTENHOUSE, JACOB. Roxborough Twp. Phila. Co. Paper Maker. Dec 23, 1797. July 15, 1811. 3.455.
Woodland adj. land of Jacob Rinker in Roxborough Twp. he bequeaths to niece Susanna Trout. To Martin and William Rittenhouse sons of bro. Nicholas Rittenhouse. To bro. Abraham Rittenhouse. To children of bro. Henry Rittenhouse. To children of bro. William Rittenhouse. To children of bro. Isaac Rittenhouse. To Margaret Rittenhouse, widow of late bro. John Rittenhouse during widowhood, at her marriage or death her share to sd. John's children. To children of sister Mary Hook the wife of John Hook. To sister Susanna Bright wife of Jacob Bright. To sister Margaret Smith wife of Peter Smith. To sister Barbara Kolp wife of Isaac Kolp, at decease of sd. sisters, to their children. All residue of estate to Enoch and Samuel Rittenhouse, sons of bro. Abraham Rittenhouse.
Execs: Enoch and Samuel Rittenhouse and Susanna Trout.
Wit: William Huston, Jacob Markle, Daniel Rittenhouse.

HERTZOG, ANDREW. Phila. Co. Taylor. Sept 9, 1803. July 15, 1811. 3.458.
Wife Barbara to have income of all estate during life, at her decease to his children namely: Susan Suter, Rebecca Miltman, Joseph and Peter Hertzog and to grandchildren: Christian, Andrew, Rachel, Rebecca and Juliana Wilt. children of late dau. Rachel Wilt.
Execs: Sd. wife Barbara Hertzog and sd. two sons Joseph and Peter Hertzog.
Wit: Israel Roberts, Nathan Roberts.
Letters granted to Joseph and Peter Hertzog.

NERBACK, JACOB. July 10, 1811. July 27, 1811. 3.460.
All estate to wife Mary Nerback, at her decease, to his eight children, seven girls and one boy (names not given).
Execs: Frederick Vollmer and Francis Austin.
Wit: Frederick Vollmer, Francis Austin and Edward Pole, Jr. Francis Austin renounced.

PEMBERTON, HANNAH. Phila. April 27, 1809. July 29, 1811. 3.461.

To sister Sarah Zane property in Moyamensing Twp. on road leading from Phila. to Gloucester Point devised to her (Hannah Pemberton) by her late father Isaac Zane. To nephew John Zane. To niece Sarah Zane house and grounds in Phila. purchased of Thomas J. Ridgway. Ground rent payable out of ground conveyed by William Garrigues and wife to Samuel Ashton. To Hannah and Mary, daus. of sd. nephew John Zane. To Mary Pleasants, widow of Samuel Pleasants. To her (Mary Pleasants) sister Sarah Rhoads. To Dr. Thomas Parke. To his son James. to his sister Hannah Parke. To committee of Yearly Mtg. of Friends for relief of Indians. Late husband John Pemberton bequeathed a legacy to John Wilson. All residue of estate to sister Sarah Zane.
Execs: Relation Dr. Thomas Parke and friends Elliston Perot and John Wilson.
Wit: Joseph Clark, Nathan Sellers, Joseph Roberts.
Codicil ----, 1811. Mentions in addition to those in the will, Isaac Zane son of nephew John Zane and Sarah Pancoast of Alexandria in VA widow of David Pancoast.
Execs: James Pemberton Parke in addition to those in will.

DICK, ALEXANDER. Phila. Tanner and Courier by trade and Grocer. Aug 15, 1810. July 25, 1811. 3.466.
To his wife Nancy Dick all his real estate in Phila., Camden, NJ, and in VA. Bro. James Dick.
Exec: Sd. wife Nancy Dick.
Wit: James Jno. Namie, Robert Ralston.

BIDDIS, SAMUEL. Germantown. Phila. July 20, 1811. Aug 1, 1811. 3.467.
To nephews George Biddis and John Biddis. To nieces Catharine Ross, Sarah Barton and Margaret Windergast.
Execs: Sd. niece Margaret Windergast and Samuel Fleckinstine.
Wit: Jacob Ashmead, Lewis Lehman.

BACHE, RICHARD. Settle in Bucks Co., PA. Jan 2, 1810. Aug 2, 1811. 3.468.
Mentions his ancestor Dr. Benjamin Franklin. To Major David Lenox, President of Bank of U. S. Son Louis Bache of Bucks Co. and son Richard Bache of Phila. in trust for children of his late son Benjamin Franklin Bache. To sd. trustees for son William Bache and Catharine his wife and their children. To sd. trustees for dau. Elizabeth Franklin Harwood and her children. To dau. Deborah Duane. To sd. trustees for

dau. Sarah Bache. Gives son Louis the privilege of taking the farm at Settle at valuation. Mentions house in Franklin Court. To sisters Martha Bache and Anna Maria Bache (now he hopes living at Preston in Lancashire England).
Execs: Sd. David Lenox, Louis Bache and Richard Bache.
Wit: Isaac Johnson, Lawrence Johnson, Robert M. Green. David Lenox renounced.

CARVER, RACHEL. Byberry Twp. Phila. Co. March 30, 1796. Aug 6, 1811. 3.476.
Dau. Rachel Carver, son John Carver, grandson John Carver son of sd. John, dau. Mary Samms and her two sons Thomas and John Samms.
Exec: Dau. Rachel Carver.
Wit: Jesse Tomlinson, Sarah Tomlinson and Jemima Tomlinson.

UNSWORTH, JOHN. Phila. Mariner. June 9, 1807. Aug 6, 1811. 3.478.
All estate to wife Mary Unsworth whom he appoints extx.
Exec: Wife Mary Unsworth.
Wit: Richard Palmer, Thomas Story.

HOLAHAN, DAVID. Phila. Blacksmith. May 22, 1810. Aug 8, 1811. 3.479.
Erxs. wife Hannah Holahan and bro. Amos Holahan. Estate to wife Hannah and dau. Phoebe Holahan.
Execs: Wife Hannah Holahan and bro. Amos Holahan.
Wit: G. Ehrenzeller, Alexr. Hampton.

HALL, MARTHA. Phila. Widow. Aug 20, 1810. Aug 15, 1811. 3.480.
Legacies to Rev. Joseph Turner, his dau. Eliza Turner and to Mrs. Ann Hutton wife of John Hutton. To bro. John Bradford living in Wilmington, DE, after his death to nephew William Bradford son of Joseph Bradford, dec'd. If nephew is not living at death of his uncle John, sd. sum to Trustees of General Assembly of Presbyterian Church in America for support of a Theological Seminary.
Execs: Joseph Turner and Robert Ralston, Esq.
Wit: Robert S. Green, William McIlhenney.

ALLINSON, JAMES. Phila. June 14, 1811. Aug 19, 1811. 3.482.
Provides for wife Bernice Allinson. Legacy to Benjamin Tucker, Charles Townsend and Benjamin Ferris, they to pay to Thomas Stewardson,

Treasurer of the boarding school at Westtown under care of Yearly Meeting of Friends. Residue of estate to his children (name not given).
Exec: And guardian of children bro. William Allinson.
Wit: Newberry Smith, Wm. Widdifield, Evan Davis.

LONG, RACHEL. Phila. Bonnetmaker. July 6, 1811. Aug 21, 1811. 3.484.
Legacies to mother Anne Long, bro. Alexander Long, sisters Lettice Wallen and Kezia Long, bro. William Long, bro. Silas Long and to his son William Long, niece Kezia Wallen, niece Lydia Long, niece Ann Long dau. of Silas Long. To niece Rachel Long a looking glass formerly sister Ruth's. Aunt Martha Hilyard, cousins Margaret Estlack and Kezia Hilyard. All residue of estate to nieces Kizen Wallen, Hope Wallen, Sarah Wallen and Rachel Wallen.
Exec: Abraham Hilyard.
Wit: Nathan Hatfield, Pamela Ives.

MEREDITH, JONATHAN. Phila. Gentleman. Aug 18, 1811. Aug 27, 1811. 3.486.
To four of his children namely: Elizabeth Ogden, Mary Hawthorn, William and Jonathan Meredith a suit of new wearing apparel each. All residue of estate to son David Meredith whom he appoints exec.
Exec: Son David Meredith.
Wit: William McCalla, Charles Stewart.

CLINE, JOSEPH. Northern Liberties. Phila. Cooper. Aug 2, 1811. Aug 28, 1811. 3.487.
Provides for wife Mary she to educate his children: Joseph, Barbara, Mary, Anne and Rebekah Cline.
Execs: Sd. wife Mary and friend Henry Brunner of Germantown, Phila. Co.
Wit: Thomas Timings, Francis Pflaume.

LAFORCADE, AUGUSTE. June 28, 1811. Aug 28, 1811. 3.489.
Exec. Augustin LeMoine, authorizing him to dispose of everything as he thinks proper.
Exec: Augustin LeMoine.
Peter Gaudiehand, Phila., goldsmith and Peter Lamesiere of sd. city, goldsmith affirmed.

SCHNEIDER, LUDWICK. Northern Liberties. Phila. Yeoman. July 23, 1796. Aug 30, 1811. 3.490.
Provides for wife Catherine Schneider and children: George and Ludwick Schneider, Margaret Shaffer late Kensel and David Schneider.
Execs: Sd. wife Catherine and friend Peter Gravenstine.
Wit: Thomas Masters, Robert Whitehead, T. L. W. Frank, R. Whitehead.
Codicil May 15, 1801.
Wit: R. Whitehead, Benjamin Brown, W. ----. Robert Whitehead the surviving witness to will and codicil affirmed.

BRINGHURST, JOSEPH. Phila. Gentleman. Now sojourning in Wilmington, DE. May 8, 1810. Sept 3, 1811. 3.493.
To friends Thomas Stewardson, John Morton, Jr., and John C. Evans all of Phila. in trust for nephew James Bringhurst and his family. For nephew Joseph Bringhurst, Jr., and his family. Nieces Elizabeth Foulke and Deborah Tyson. Mary Pearson dau. of sd. Deborah by her former husband William Pearson, dec'd. Children of late nephew Dr. John Foulke. Ann Bringhurst wife of nephew James Bringhurst, Eleanor Foulke widow of late nephew Dr. John Foulke and to his three children namely: Richard, Mary and Eleanor Foulke. Deborah Bringhurst wife of nephew Joseph Bringhurst, Jr. Grandnephews Joseph Bringhurst and James Bringhurst, Jr., sons of nephew James. Harry a black man whom he formerly set free. Late sister Mary Foulke, niece Mary Foulke, dec'd.
Execs: Thomas Stewardson, John Morton, Jr., John C. Evans and nephew Joseph Bringhurst, Jr.
Wit: James Allinson, Thomas Dugdale, Peter Thomson.
Codicil May 8, 1811.
Wit: Isaac Bonsall, Clement Biddle, Jr.
Memorandum. Great aunt Deborah Claypoole, dec'd. Late sister Elizabeth Bringhurst. Joseph son of nephew Joseph Bringhurst. Grandnieces Sarah Anne Bringhurst, Elizabeth Bringhurst and Mary Bringhurst daus. of nephew James. To grandnephew William Bringhurst, grandniece Mary Bringhurst, grandnephews Joseph Bringhurst and Edward Bringhurst children of nephew Joseph. Dr. Thomas Chalkley James of Phila., grandson of Thomas Chalkley. Signed Aug 5, 1810. Grandnephew John Bringhurst son of nephew James born since writing the above May 8, 1811. Samuel Bettle affirmed. Joseph Bringhurst, Jr., one of the execs. affirmed April 20, 1812.
Letters granted to the other execs. Nov 13, 1811.

ANDERSON, THOMAS. Phila. Mariner. July 22, 1797. Sept 3, 1811. 3.509.
To his natural son Esker Anderson, brought up by him. Wife Elizabeth to have income of estate until youngest child is of age if she remains his widow. To all children by sd. wife Elizabeth (names not given) she to be sole extx.
Exec: Wife Elizabeth.
Wit: Clement Biddle, Geo. Biddle, Francis Marshall.

LAWRENCE, THOMAS. Northern Liberties. Phila. Co. Cooper and Guager. Aug 18, 1811. Sept 5, 1811. 3.512.
Provides for wife Elizabeth. Bros. John and Samuel Lawrence.
Execs: Sd. wife Elizabeth Lawrence and father-in-law Thomas Barnes.
Wit: William Moore Smith, Catharine Sheppard.

CLARE, WILLIAM. Phila. Aug 3, 1811. Sept 6, 1811. 3.514. (Nuncupative.)
All estate to wife Rebecca Clare, making her the extx.
Exec: Wife Rebecca Clare.
Wit: Mary McClan of Phila., widow, Henry Wood of sd. city, taylor.

COX, THOMAS R. Germantown, Phila. Co. Coachmaker. July 9, 1811. Sept 10, 1811. 3.515.
Provides for wife Barbary Cox, at her decease to children of sister Lytia Simpers and sister Margaret Cox also children of bro.-in-law Casper Moyt(?)*[sic]*.
Execs: Wife Barbary Cox, John Fry, Jr., and Samuel Fleckenstine.
Wit: Jacob Ashmead, John Street.

GALLAGHER, ANNA M. Phila. Spinster. Aug 8, 1811. Aug 14, 1811. 3.516.
Aunts Mary Gallagher and Catharine Gallagher. Bros. Thomas and John P. Gallagher.
Execs: Joseph Donath and sd. bro. John P. Gallagher.
Wit: James Gallaher*[sic]*, J. A. Monges.

PICKANDS or PICHANDS, THOMAS. Sept 18, 1809. Sept 12, 1811. 3.518.
Provides for wife Rebecca and sons James and Samuel.
Execs: Charles Clayton, coachmaker and John Warnock, nail manufacturer, both of this city and sd. wife Rebecca Pickands.

Wit: Mrs. Arcadia Senix, John Train and William Lee.

POYNTELL, WILLIAM. Phila. Gentleman. June 29, 1811. Sept 16, 1811. 3.519.
Provides for wife Ann Poyntell. His servant Isaac to be educated if he continues in ther service of the family. Bro. John E. Poyntell now living in London. Uncle William Tayler, Esq. Son George Poyntell residing in London. Friend Thomas Newton. Children of late sister Ann Reider, to wit: Ann, William and Elizabeth. Cousin Elizabeth Crane dau. of his mother's sister. Eldest son George, youngest William a minor. Dau. Sarah Relf wife of Samuel Relf. Dau. Rebecca, dau. Ann both married. Desires one of his sons to take his farm at Auburn hill in Northern Liberties, Phila. at valuation. Son William Poyntell and sons-in-law Robert A. Caldcleugh and Alexander Johnston to have charge of all his lands twenty miles from Phila.
Execs: Son-in-law Robert A. Caldcleugh, friend Paul Beck of Phila., merchant and son William. Wit: John Wagner, Thomas Astley.

FRAZIER, NALBRO. Phila. Merchant. Sept 17, 1811. Sept 19, 1811. 3.532.
All estate to wife Ann Frazier appointing her sole extx.
Exec: Wife Ann Frazier.
Wit: William H. Tod, Francis West.

JANNEY, LEWIS. Ridley Twp., Delaware Co. Dec 25, 1810. Sept 20, 1811. 3.533.
Provides for wife Mary Janney. Dau. Elizabeth Janney and sons: Benjamin Janney, Israel Pennock Janney, George Fox Janney and friend Say Janney. Property in Baltimore purchased of John Stricker with all real estate in MD and elsewhere he leaves to his sons.
Execs: Wife Mary Janney and friend John McIlvaine.
Wit: William Worrall, John McIlvain. John McIlvain renounced.

CROCKER, THOMAS. Phila. Barber. Jan 13, 1810. Sept 24, 1811. 3.534.
All estate to wife Charlotta Crocker, if no children estate shall go to Mary Boon.
Execs: Wife Charlotta Crocker and Edith Boon.
Wit: Blathwaite I. Shober, George Feinoue(?)*[sic]*.

DEDECKER, CHARLES. Northern Liberties. Phila. Co. Farmer. Sept 16, 1811. Sept 25, 1811. 3.536.

Income of estate to wife Mary, at her decease to his children (names not given).
Execs: John Simons of Northern Liberties and sd. wife Mary Dedecker.
Wit: John McAllister, Robert Sherard.

KENNEDY, ANDREW. Phila. Manufacturer. Jan 31, 1811. Sept 28, 1811. 3.537.
Provides for wife Elizabeth Kennedy. Sons Robert and Andrew Kennedy and daus. Susan Leib, Mary Tilly, Eliza Long and Eleanor Schott. Sd. trustees to pay to son Geo. Washington Kennedy.
Execs and Trustees: Friends William Richards of Phila., merchant, Dockeray Smith of same city, merchant and Kennedy Long of Baltimore, gentleman, they to sell all estate &c.
Wit: Benjamin Richards, Matthew Carey.
Codicil Jan 31, 1811.
Wit: Same as to will.
Codicil May 4, 1811. Appoints James McAlpin of Phila., merchant taylor, exec. and trustee in conjunction with those in will.
Wit: As above.

STRAHAN, GREGORY. Phila. Porter. Aug --, 1805. Oct 2, 1811. 3.542.
Estate to wife Margaret Strahan and his four sons and dau. to wit: Joseph, John, Paul, Charles and Mary.
Execs: Sons Joseph and John Strahan.
Wit: I. N. Gravenstine, James C. Kenton, Daniel Addis.

PILE, SAMUEL. Phila. Mariner. June 1, 1807. Oct 7, 1811. 3.544.
All his property for benefit of his wife Rebecca Pile and their children (names not given).
Execs: Rebecca Pile, Abel Saterthwait and Caleb Earle, New Orleans.
Wit: Benjamin Morgan, Elisha G. Price, George W. Morgan. In the room of Thomas Morgan he has appointed Abel Saterthwait July 6, 1811.

WHITBY, WILLIAM. Phila. Plasterer. Oct 1, 1811. Oct 9, 1811. 3.545.
To sons George and Robert and dau. Jane he leaves all his real estate at Locust and Tenth Streets bounded on south by William McAnnall's estate.
Execs: Charles Blair and Robert Orr.
Wit: I. Rolph, Henry O'Neill.

BANTOM, MOSES. Phila. Sept 1, 1811. Oct 9, 1811. 3.546.

Provides for wife Sarah Bantom. To Richard Willing, Esq, in trust, money lately bequeathed to him (Moses Bantom) by Thomas Shirley, interest for support of wife and children (no names given).
Exec: Sd. wife Sarah.
Wit: Samuel Watt, William Lyle.

GREBLE, GEORGE. Phila. House Carpenter. May 10, 1811. Oct 9, 1811. 3.547.
Wife Rebecca to have income of all estate supporting his younger children &c. To son William and other children.
Execs: Wife Rebecca, bro. Jacob Greble and bro.-in-law Joseph Rapine.
Wit: Michael Sager, John George Frederick.

HOFFNER, HENRY. Northern Liberties. Phila. Bricklayer. Jan 25, 1810. ----. 3.549.
Wife Anna Maria to have use, interest &c. of all estate, at her decease to Henry and Maria, children of dec'd son William and to Eliza dau. of son George. To children of dau. Susan Dietz. Residue of estate to dau. Susan Dietz.
Execs: Sd. wife Anna Maria and friend Nicholas Armbruster of Northern Liberties.
Wit: Christian Peiffer, Frederick Beates.

SHELL, JACOB. Northern Liberties. Phila. Yeoman. March 1, 1811. Oct 14, 1811. 3.551.
Estate in trust to sd. exec. for wife Rosanna Shell, at her decease to sd. John George Kehr.
Exec: His friend John George Kehr, baker.
Wit: R. Whitehead, Nicholas Schweppenhieser.

EISENRING, GEORGE. Oct 8, 1811. Oct 15, 1811. 3.552.
Estate to be sold and divided amongst his children Andrew his son and Christian Smith his dau. and sons Lawrence and John, last two minors.
Execs: Friends Adam Brunner and Frederick Haas.
Wit: John Ricker and Christian Fox.

FOX, JOSEPH. Phila. Gentleman. July 3, 1809. Oct 14, 1811. 3.553.
Income, rents &c. to wife Frances Fox until youngest dau. Frances attains age of twenty one years, at that time estate to be divided.
Execs: Sd. wife Frances and friend Samuel Wheeler, Esq.
Wit: Robert Whitehead, Philip Scheetz, Justinian Fox.

Letters granted to Frances Fox.

BEIDEMAN, DANIEL. Kensington. Phila. Co. Fisherman. Oct 8, 1811. Oct 16, 1811. 3.554.
Lot on green woods lane and Frankford road purchased by him and his bro. Jacob of Thomas Eyre to be sold. Monies from sale to son Daniel and daus. Mary and Margaret. Income of remainder of estate to wife Elizabeth, at her death his land and farm in Waterford Twp., NJ, ground purchased of heirs of Dr. Shippen with wharf &c. ground purchased of Michael Peck, ground at Point no Point adj. Esterly's ground &c. to his sd. children.
Execs: Bro. Jacob Beideman and friend Michael Collard, wife Elizabeth to be extx. so long as she remains his widow.
Wit: Robert Whitehead, Johannes Christ and Jacob Moser.

HYDE, CATHARINE. Phila. Widow. Sept 10, 1811. Oct 2, 1811. 3.557.
Legacy to grandson John Shinkle, residue to granddau. Maria Shinkle.
Exec: Friend Thomas Norton, he to be guardian of estate devised to sd. granddau.
Wit: Robert Whitehead, Thomas Conaroe.
Letters granted to exec. Oct 18, 1811.

GREINER, SARAH. Phila. Co. Widow of George Greiner, late of Bristol Twp. July 30, 1811. Oct 21, 1811. 3.559.
To sister Ann Pugh. To nieces Sarah and Susan Pugh. To nephew Edward Pugh.
Execs: Edward Gough and Jesse Gouge, Bristol.
Wit: James McVaugh, Hector McCravey and Ella Skillan.
Letters granted to Edward Gouge.

COHEN, JACOB. Phila. Reader to the Portuguese Congregation of sd. city. Dec 4, 1810. Oct 23, 1811. 3.559.
Desires to be interred in burying ground of sd. congregation. All estate to wife Rebecca Cohen and his two single daus. Deborah and Richea or Richey. At wife's death to all his children. Married daus. Goodhous Phillips, Esther Hart and Rachel Lyons and son Abraham.
Execs: Wife Rebecca Cohen, son Abraham Cohen and Levy Philips of Lancaster.
Wit: Samuel D. Hart, Isaac B. Phillips.
Codicil Feb 25, 1811. Dau. Deborah has since married (husband's name not given).

Wit: Isaac B. Phillips of Phila., merchant and Abraham Forst of sd. city, merchant.

LAWRENCE, MARY. Widow of William Lawrence late of Phila. Co., Penn Twp. Oct 7, 1811. Oct 24, 1811. 3.562.
To children namely: Mary Lewis (wife of Joseph Lewis), Lawrence Lawrence, Anna Coulston (wife of Barney Coulston) and George Washington Lawrence. Mentions estate of the Penns in Penn Twp., late Northern Liberties.
Exec: Friend John Trout of sd. Liberties.
Wit: Valentine Gavaner, Rudolph Neff.

SUMMERS, MARTIN. Phila. Blacksmith. Oct 1, 1811. Oct 24, 1811. 3.566.
Desires to be buried in the family burying ground under the inspection of the Philanthropic Society. All estate to wife Mary Summers, at her decease to his children (names not given).
Execs: Wife Mary and his friend Jeremiah Linton.
Wit: William Griffiths, James Truman and John Buttam(?).

CROZET, J.B.M. Phila. Sept 24, 1811. Oct 29, 1811. 3.568.
Estate to wife Christiana Crozet, whom he appoints extx.
Exec: Wife Christiana Crozet.
Wit: T. T. Eberlin, John P. Ripley.

BETZ, CHRISTIAN. Phila. Baker. Aug 20, 1808. Oct 31, 1811. 3.568.
To granddau. Catharine Betz. To grandchildren Samuel and Catharine Mervin, children of late dau. Catharine. To dau. Hannah Flanagan. Late son John Betz.
Execs: Sd. dau. Hannah Flanagan and friends Godfrey Haga and John Jordan of sd. city, merchants.
Wit: Jacob Sulger, Isaac Wampole.
Letter granted to Hannah Long formerly Hannah Flanagan.

WERTMULLER, ADOLPH ULRICK. Portrait Painter. Dec 25, 1802. Nov 5, 1811. 3.571.
His share in legacy left by Mr. Joachim Wrotman, merchant at Amsterdam to his father's children and to his half bro.'s children to be divided between the two families after the death of Joachim Lyringren(?) and his sister, he leaves with all his other estate to his wife Elizabeth Wertmuller, whom he appoints extx.

Execs: Wife Elizabeth Wertmuller.
Wit: Peter Thomson, Adam May, Gust. Risberger.
Codicil July 3, 1811. Since date of will he has purchased of John Warder of Phila. and Ann his wife the plantation where he now resides on Naamans Creek in New Castle Co., DE, which he bequeaths to his wife Elizabeth Wertmuller.
Wit: Isaac Elliott, Benjamin Chew Burden, Peter Thomson.

JOHNSON, MOSES. Phila. A free black man. Oct 22, 1811. Nov 7, 1811. 3.575.
All estate to wife Eleanor, at her decease one half to niece Jane Johnson who now lives in his family. The other half to friends Joseph Keen of sd. city, currier, Levi Garrett, tobacconist, and Joseph S. Walter, bricklayer, in trust for support of poor widows and others, white or black belonging to the First Baptist Church at Second and Mulberry Streets.
Execs: Sd. Joseph Keen, Levi Garrett and Joseph S. Walter.
Wit: Peter Thomson, Benjamin C. Burden.

MILLER, FREDERICK. Norther Liberties. Phila. House Carpenter. Oct 24, 1811. Nov 11, 1811. 3.578.
Income, rents &c. of his property in Northern Liberties to wife Ann and his mother Barbara Miller. Bro. John Miller. John Long and George Bastian, Jr., trustees. To wife's bro. and sisters (names not given). To bro. Andrew Miller, bro. Henry Miller.
Execs: Wife Ann Miller, friends John Long and George Bastian, Jr.
Wit: Isaac Parry, Frederick Beates.

WHITE, SARAH. Northern Liberties. Phila. Co. Jan 10, 1811. Nov 12, 1811. 3.582.
To dau. Mary White the contents of house where she lives in Northern Liberties.
Wit: Peter Heisler, Michael Brody, Nicholas Fricker.

BAKER, RICHARD. District of Southwark. Mariner. Aug 6, 1808. Jan 16, 1811. 3.584.
All estate to friend Sarah Hendry wife of James Hendry of sd. District, boarding house keeper.
Exec: Sd. Sarah Hendry.
Wit: Samuel Barclay, Richard Renshaw.

BOOK 4

WOODROW, SUSANNAH. Town of Jonesborough, Washington Co., TN.
May 5, 1810. Feb 3, 1812. 4.1.
To dau. Elizabeth Jackson (wife of Samuel Jackson). Children of sd. Samuel and Elizabeth to wit: Eliza, Caroline, Harriet and Alfred E. Jackson. To David Draidreich of Jonesborough, Henry Jackson her grandson of Davidson Co. and James C. Anderson of Jonesborough, Washington Co. all of TN in trust &c. Extx. sd. dau. Elizabeth Jackson, property in PA and NJ.
Exec: Sd. dau. Elizabeth Jackson.
Wit: John Adams, Joseph Brown and Hugh Brown.

Extracted from Prerogative Court of Canterbury.
PRATCHETT, ANN. Beaumont St. Parish of Saint Mary LeBone of Middlesex Co. Spinster. Aug 10, 1806. Oct 3, 1806. 4.3.
To William Lewthwait of sd. Parish, surgeon and Thomas Trivitt of sd. Parish, coachmaker in trust. Nephew Mr. John Mort. To servant Ann Shorman if she is still living with her. To Alice Wilson (wife of Mr. David Wilson at Great Chesterfield Street, baker). Goddau. Ann Pratchett Wilson, dau. of sd. Alice. Nephew Joseph Mort now of Phila. North America, his wife and children.
Execs: Sd. William Lewthwaite and Thomas Trivitt.
Wit: Edward George Adams, Mary LeBone, and Archer Brumell Aldermanbury.

WILLING, JAMES. Haverford Twp. Phila. March 5, 1795. Nov 18, 1811. 4.8.
Requests his bro. Richard Willing and Thomas Wg. Francis to see his will executed. Lands in PA and West FL to be sold. To sister Byrd, sister Hare and to sister Eliza Powell. To a child called Elizabeth by Mary Ruth of the Natchez supposed to be his. Property in Natchez District West FL bought of Collingwood. Residue to sister Frances, Thomas Wg. Francis, Thos. Wg. Willing and bro. Richard Willing.
Exec: Thos. W. Francis.
Wit: Patima Gray, Sarah Greenay. John Donaldson of Phila., broker, affirmed.
Letters granted to surviving exec. Thos. W. Francis.

ASH, ABIGAIL. District of Southwark. Widow. Aug 31, 1810. Nov 21, 1811. 4.9.
To daus. Alice Pearson and Ann Evans Sellers. To son-in-law George Sellers in trust for support of son Joshua Ash. To sons Samuel Evans Ash and Charles Ash. Son-in-law Benjamin Pearson.
Execs: Son-in-law George Sellers and friend Alexander Elmslie of Phila., merchant.
Wit: Caleb Ash, Richard Renshaw. George Sellers renounced.

CAUFFMAN, CHARLOTTE. Phila. Widow of Jacob Cauffman. Aug 31, 1807. Nov 22, 1811. 4.11
To son John Smith son of her late husband Frederick Smith, dec'd. Property left her by her late father John Haffline. Children by her late husband Jacob Cauffman viz: Samuel, Eliza and Catharine Cauffman.
Execs: Isaac Wampole and George Lybrand both of Phila. Sd. Geo. Lybrand to be guardian of her minor children.
Wit: Johan G. Kehr, Peter Wagner, Jr.
Letters granted to George Lybrand.

SCHNEIDER, HANNES. Germantown Twp. Phila. Co. Yeoman. Dec 28, 1802. Nov 26, 1811. 4.14
To wife Catharine and son Jacob Schneider. Land purchased of Christian Schneider of Germantown Twp.
Execs: Sd. son Jacob and friend Joseph Alderffer.
Wit: John Heiling, Saml. Johnson.

PINKERTON, LYDIA. Phila. Widow. Sept 28, 1811. Nov 26, 1811. 4.16
Granddaus. Lydia and Eliza, daus. of son John. Daus. Rebecca Carnes and Sarah McGreggor.
Execs: Friend Charles Widdis and sd. dau. Rebecca Carnes.
Wit: Charles Widdis, John Ashmead.

WATSON, ISAAC. Phila. Late Lumber Merchant, about 62 years of age. July 17, 1809. Nov 27, 1811. 4.17
To wife Anne Watson the following real estate: property in Phila. occupied by Samuel McCutcheon, property in tenure of Alexander Dean, ground rent belonging to George Shea &c. Granddau. Anne Watson. Sons Charles & Joseph Watson. House and lot in village of Attlebury in Middlesex Twp., Bucks Co. in which Mary Parker now a pauper on sd. township hath a right by paying him &c.
Execs: Sons Charles and Joseph Watson.

Wit: Samuel Shinn, John Warner.

OTTO, DANIEL B. Phila. Mariner. June 12, 1811. Nov 28, 1811. 4.20
Estate to bro. John C. Otto of sd. city, Dr. of Physick, whom he appoints exec.
Execs: Bro. John C. Otto.
Wit: William King, Isaac Wampole.

WISLEY, MARGARET. ----. Nov 13, 1811. 4.21.
Extx. dau. Hannah Bell. Grandson James Forder Bell to have all estate when of age.
Exec: Dau. Hannah Bell.
Wit: Samuel Burkloe, Michael Durney.

WILLIAMS, THOMAS D. Seaman of Southwark shortly going to sea. Nov 10, 1810. Dec 2, 1811. 4.21.
All estate to wife Christiana Williams whom he appoints extx. Inventory of clothing was left on schooner Ranger commanded by Capt. David Wilson bound for Portorico, when sd. Williams was sent in company with McFagerty the mate and two other seamen on the brig Angelina &c.
Exec: Wife Christiana Williams.
Wit: Ebenezer Ferguson, George McGlathery.

BOWERS, JACOB. Northern Liberties. Phila. Co. Cordwainer and Brickmaker. Nov 26, 1811. Dec 8, 1811. 4.24.
Estate to wife Mary Bowers, she to keep his minor children. At death of wife, to all his children namely: George, John, Samuel, Susannah, William, Joseph Thorne, Jacob Lowns(?) Bowers.
Execs: John Thorne, Jesse Shoemaker.
Wit: Samuel Havenstrite, Andrew Owlson and Jacob Havenstrite.

MALONE, PATRICK. Phila. Upholsterer. Sept 21, 1807. Dec 9, 1811. 4.26.
Estate to wife Mary Malone. Sons John S. Malone and William H. Malone and their children. Granddau. Mari Ann Malone.
Execs: Sd. wife Mary Malone if she survives him, if not he appoints his friend Moses Stewart, grocer of Phila. and dau.-in-law Rebecca Malone execs.
Wit: Nicholas McHenry, Felix McCarty, Abraham Jones. John Lisle of Phila., merchant and William Turner of Northern Liberties, accoumptant, affirmed.

BROWN, JAMES. Phila. Shop Keeper. Jan 23, 1810. Dec 11, 1811. 4.28. Bequeaths tortoise shell case watch made by B. Duhamel of London to bro. William Brown. Silver watch made by Bray and son, London to nephew John Browne son of sd. William. To nephew James Laird, son of sister Margaret Laird. Deceased daus. Margaret and Elizabeth. Property to be sold proceeds to sister-in-law Margaret Peters, bro. William Brown of Loughbrick land in Ireland and sister Margaret Laird near Londonderry in Ireland.
Execs: Friends Caleb Shreeve, merchant and Benjamin Williams, tanner and currier.
Execs: Jesse Thomas, Thomas S. Field.

SHETTSLINE, JOHN. Northern Liberties. Phila. Co. Farmer. Nov 17, 1810. Dec 20, 1811. 4.30.
Estate to wife Barbara Shettsline and his six children namely: George, John. Elizabeth, Catharine, Michael and Samuel.
Execs: Wife Barbara and son John Shettsline.
Wit: Thomas Mitchell, Caleb Carmalt, Jr.

BARCLAY, JAMES. Phila. Merchant. April 16, 1803. Dec 25, 1811. 4.31. To mother Mary Barclay of Ireland. Residue to wife Ann and child or children which he has or may have.
Execs: Wife Ann, John Wm. Barclay at school in sd. city under care of Mrs. George.
Wit: Clement Biddle, Thos. Wright, Jr.

McKINZEY, MARY. Phila. Widow. Dec 6, 1811. Dec 26, 1811. 4.32. To son John Robeson. To son Thomas McKenzey. To dau. Elizabeth Wiley. To dau. Margaret Bingham. To sons James and Alexander McKenzey.
Exec: Thomas Montgomery of Phila. Gentleman.
Wit: Lawrence Sink, Joseph Huckel.

SCHREINER, JACOB. Phila. Iron Monger. Dec 2, 1811. Dec 30, 1811. 4.33.
Provides for wife Elizabeth Schreiner. To niece Catharine Schreiner dau. of late bro. Christopher. Residue of estate to his children namely: Joseph H., Maria, Jacob, Elizabeth, Harriet, William and Amelia Schreiner.
Execs: Sd. wife Elizabeth Schreiner, son Joseph H. Schreiner and friend Philip Peltz of Phila. Esq.
Wit: William Spohn, Christian Bosby.

HANSMAN, CHRISTOPHER. Phila. Taylor. April 26, 1811. Dec 30, 1811. 4.35.
Property in Northern Liberties, Phila. To grandson Peter Lees and Maria Fowler his wife and their children. Received by mortgage from son-in-law Peter Schreiber's estate which by death of her (Mary Edenborn's) bro. Jacob now belongs to granddau. Mary Edenborn or her children. to grandson-in-law George Beckel, now married to granddau. Maria Magdalen Lees with whom he (Christopher Hansman) now dwells.
Execs: Grandsons-in-law George Beckel and Jacob Erdman and friend John Swain.
Wit: John McHartly, D. H. Miller, Samuel Etris, Samuel Young.

WINEMORE or WINNEMORE, PHILIP. District of Southwark. Phila. Co. Porter.
Oct 15, 1811. Jan 4, 1812. 4.38.
To wife Elizabeth Winemore, son Philip Winemore, dau. Elizabeth Cope, sons Henry, Jacob and John Winemore. Money in hands of John Warner.
Execs: Wife Elizabeth Winnemore, sons Philip and Henry Winemore.
Wit: James James, William Bishop, Daniel Hansman.

PORTER, CATHARINE. Phila. Co. Widow. March 5, 1811. Jan 6, 1812. 4.39.
To grandchild Eliza Catharine Carter. Residue of estate to son Thomas Clarke Porter.
Exec: Friend Richard Renshaw, Phila. Co., Esq.
Wit: David Coombs, Jonathan French.

FRANCIS, ANN. Phila. Widow. Nov 6, 1810. Jan 6, 1812. 4.40.
To dau. Elizabeth Powell Fisher. To dau.-in-law Abby Francis. To each of his grandchildren. To niece Ann Morris. To cousins Catharine Wallen and Elizabeth Shippen. Silver &c. to son Thomas Willing Francis. To niece and dau.-in-law Dorothy Francis. To son-in-law George Harrison. To dau. Sophia Harrison. To son Charles Francis. To grandson John Brown Francis. All residue to dau. Elizabeth Powell Fisher. Property to be sold, proceeds to his four children: Thomas Willing Francis, Sophia Harrison, Charles Francis and Elizabeth Powell Fisher.
Execs: Son Thomas Willing Francis and friend and relation William Tilghman, Esq.
Wit: Benjamin Say, Elizabeth Mifflin, John Willis.

SPARKS, SIMON. Phila. Co. July 7, 1809. Jan 6, 1812. 4.43.

Estate to step son Atcheson Thomson whom he appoints exec.
Exec: Step son Atcheson Thomson.
Wit: Phillip Duffy, Richard Palmer, Robert McMullen.
Codicil Nov 22, 1809. Denies every part of will and testimony in preferance to a will dated Nov 22, 1809. Attest Philip Duffy, Robert McMullin, Richard Palmer.
Wit: George Hire, Samuel B. Ellis, John Kissick.

ISRAEL, WILLIAM HEWITT. July 7, 1811. Jan 7, 1812. 4.44.
To grandson Joseph Israel, he to be educated as wife Mary Reading Israel, son-in-law George Breck and son Charles Hutchinson Israel shall think proper. All property in Jamaica to be sold, proceeds to wife Mary Reading Israel, dau. Catharine Douce Breck and dau. Mary Cammack McKenzie. At her death, to her (Mary Cammack McKenzie's) children.
Execs: And trustees Mary Reading Israel, George Breck and Charles Hutchinson Israel.
Wit: Edward Swift, James Hepburn, Eliza Burils.

LOYD, MARY. Phila. Spinster. Nov 5, 1810. Jan 9, 1812. 4.46.
To Mary Loyd and Rebecca Loyd, daus. of bro. John Loyd. To bros.: John Loyd, William Loyd, Phillip Loyd, also to Joseph Loyd, at his death to his (sd. Joseph's) children. To nephew George Morris, bookbinder of Phila. All residue of estate to sisters Martha Smallwood and Rebecca Loyd, both of Phila.
Execs: Sd. sisters Martha and Rebecca.
Wit: Daniel Shoemaker, Anthony Steel.

KILBY, TURPIN. Phila. Oct 19, 1811. Jan 9, 1812. 4.48.
All estate to wife Jennet Kilby whom he appoints extx.
Exec: Wife Jennet Kilby.
Wit: Samuel Carpenter, Otto James, Joseph Huddell, Jr.

COUPER, BELFOUR. District of Southwark. Phila. Co. Mariner. Oct 24, 1807. Jan 8, 1812. 4.49.
All estate to wife Bridget Couper whom he appoints extx.
Exec: Wife Bridget Couper.
Wit: Thomas Mitchell, Caleb Carmalt.

SCHLATTER, ESTHER. Germantown Twp. Phila. Co. Aug 9, 1809. Jan 11, 1812. 4.50.

To sisters Elizabeth and Rachel Schlatter, at death of sd. sisters to William Schlatter, at present in Phila.
Execs: Sd. two sisters Elizabeth and Rachel and aforesd. William Schlatter.
Wit: John Huston, John Huston, Jr.

MERVINE, GEORGE. Southwark. Phila. Co. Dec 23, 1811. Jan 22, 1812. 4.51.
To wife Hannah Mervine and children: Samuel and Catharine Mervine.
Execs: George Sheeds of Southwark (plaister) and Benjamin Lyndal of Phila. (cabinet maker).
Wit: David Coombs, Daniel Sutherland and John Odenheimer.

YOUNG, SAMUEL, SR. Phila. Harbour Master. Dec 20, 1811. Jan 22, 1812. 4.53.
All estate to sd. wife, at her death to son Samuel Young. To granddau. Eliza Young Atcheson. Property in Phila. in tenure of Capt. Caleb Hathaway. To Mary Clarkson wife of John Clarkson.
Execs: Wife Elizabeth Young and David Atcheson of sd. city, merchant.
Wit: Niel Mathison, James McCulloch, William Wilson.
Letters granted to David Atcheson.

MOORE, HANNAH. Phila. Widow. Dec 13, 1811. Jan 24, 1812. 4.55.
All estate to dau. Elizabeth Moore, interest to be used during her minority. To bro.-in-law Absolom Gustis. Should sd. dau. die in minority property bequeathed to her, she bequeaths to the African Female Society of First African Presbyterian Church, Rev. John Gloucester, present Pastor.
Execs: Friend John Morris and Andrew Moore, both of sd. city. Rev. John Gloucester to be guardian of sd. dau. Elizabeth.
Wit: John McCulloch, Charles Crooke, John Mades Elliott.

RUMSEY, RACHEL. Northern Liberties. Phila. Co. Widow. Jan 23, 1812. Jan 29, 1812. 4.56.
All estate to dau. Hannah Golden and her children: David and John.
Execs: Sd. dau. Hannah Golden and nephew Shepard Ayars.
Wit: Joseph Barton, Hambleton Ayars.

CLOUD, CHARLES F. Northern Liberties. Phila. Parchment Manufacturer. Sept 23, 1811. Jan 29, 1812. 4.57.

Income of estate to wife Susan Cloud, she to support and educate his minor children. At her decease to children: Anne, Caroline, Helen and Susan.
Execs: Friends William Stevenson, Northern Liberties, currier, George Halberstadt and sd. wife. Susan Cloud.
Wit: R. Whitehead, John Limeburner, John Rightly, Henry Schracks.
Letters granted to William Stevenson and Susan Cloud.

PARRISH, SAMUEL. Phila. Merchant. Jan 24, 1812. Feb 1, 1812. 4.59.
All estate to parents Isaac and Sarah Parrish.
Execs: Bro. Joseph Parrish, bro.-in-law William Wright and friend Joseph S. Lewis, desires sd. Joseph S. Lewis to be acting exec.
Wit: Eliza Davis, Coleman Sellers.

JOHNSON, MARY. Phila. Spinster. May 24, 1811. Feb 5, 1812. 4.60.
To aunts Rachel and Ruth Morgan. To nephews John, Joseph and Edward Ewing (children of sister ----). To nephew Joseph Morris Johnson (son of bro. Joseph). To nieces Mary Johnson and Elizabeth Jones Johnson daus. of sd. bro. Joseph Johnson. Mentions property in Phila. in which Richard Tittermary, Joseph Johns, Magdaglen Johnson and herself (Mary Johnson) were interested, bounded by ground now or late of Joseph Sims, river Delaware &c. Also property in Moyamensing Twp. bounded by lands belonging to Enock Flower, by land of Isaac Zane's &c., also in Southwark adj. land allotted to bro. Joseph and to sister Magdalen Johnson &c, land in Moyamensing Twp. aforesd. adj. lands of Abraham Johnson. Joseph Wharton, Alexander Parker &c.
Exec: Bro. Jos. Johnson.
Wit: Thomas Mitchell, Caleb Carmalt, Jr.

BRANHAM, EBENEZER. Phila. Gentleman. Oct 28, 1809. Feb 6, 1812. 4.65.
To mother Mary Branham of Orange Co., VA. To son John Branham. To bros. Ludlow and Marmaduke Branham. To Susan Kinneman. All residue of estate to sons Henry and John Branham. To dau. Mary Dolby and granddau. Elizabeth Noble child of late dau. Christiana.
Execs: Sons-in-law William Noble and John Dolby and friend John McFarlane of the firm of Park and McFarlane of Phila., merchants.
Desires to be buried in the grave with his wife Elizabeth Branham.
Wit: Robert Whitehead, John Clark, Henry Schell.

SHALLCROSS, JOHN. Lower Dublin. Phila. Co. Yeoman. May 14, 1806. Jan 8, 1812. 4.67.
Estate to wife Mary Shallcross, she to educate their four children, at her death to sd. children: Joseph, Priscilla, John and Ann Shallcross.
Execs: Kinsman John Livezey and sd. wife Mary, also guardians of sd. children.
Wit: Anthony Livezey, Nathan Livezey, Jr., and John Livezey.

BICKHAM, GEORGE. Phila. Merchant. Dec 19, 1811. Feb 10, 1812. 4.69.
Whereas he has made a disposition of part of his property in favour of step children Jacob and Mary Reese, Mary since dec'd, sd. property to Jacob solely. Signed Mar 9, 1808. Wits. Frederick Beates, Philip T. Dunn. To son-in-law Lewis Neill and friends James Whitehill of Strasburg, Lancaster Co. and Alexander Henry of sd. city, merchant in trust for sister Ann Quigley (wife of James Quigley). To dau. Christiana Finney. To sd. trustees for daus. Ann Neill (wife of sd. Lewis Neill) and Susanna Brown (wife of Lewis R. Brown).
Execs: Sons-in-law Lewis Neill, James Whitehill and Alexander Henry.
Wit: Benjamin Rush, Samuel Pancoast, Jr.

BECKER, JOHN. Northern Liberties. Phila. Co. Shopkeeper. Jan 19, 1812. Feb 14, 1812. 4.74.
Estate to wife Elizabeth and his ten children namely Martin, Mary, Elizabeth, Sarah, John, William, Jacob, Joseph, Samuel and George.
Execs: Joseph Slingloff and Charles Yetter of Northern Liberties.
Wit: Thomas W. Pryor, John Chr. Warner.

MYER, GEORGE. Nov 10, 1812. Nov 16, 1812. 4.75.
Legacy to William Clement, farmer at Pittsburgh. To George Schlintz, labourer of the Sugar house, Phila. To Jacob Chur. Remainder to his sisters in Germany, if not living, to their children.
Wit: Dav. Graham, George Dawson, Frederick Felgentreff.
Letters granted to execs. Feb 15, 1813.

HOFFMAN, VALENTINE. Phila. Smith. Jan 20, 1812. Feb 10, 1812. 4.76.
To Daniel Hoffman now in his employ. To Christian Jackson. All residue of estate to wife Susanna Hoffman, at her decease to his seven children to wit: Susanna Lockman, Catharine Brown, Ann Wynard, Mary, Frederick, John and Valentine Hoffman.

Execs: Sd. wife Susanna and friend Mark Rodes of sd. city.
Wit: John Hanchman, Isaac Wampole.

MOYLAN, JASPER. Phila. Feb 11, 1812. Feb 17, 1812. 4.78.
To dau. Anna Maria Walsh and her husband Robert Walsh, Jr. Remaider to wife Isabella. Annuity to sister Julia Moylan of Cork, Ireland.
Execs: Son-in-law Robert Walsh, Jr., and sd. wife Isabella Moylan.
Wit: John Syng Dorsey, Elizabeth Van Trump.

WILKINS, THOMAS. Nov 24, 1811. Feb 14, 1812. 4.79.
Estate to wife Jane Wilkins, at her decease, to be sold and proceeds as follows: eldest son Thomas Wilkins, to son John Wilkins, to Thomas Maknew. To granddau. Elizabeth Wilkins 1/8 part when divided as aforesd. To Thomas Wilkins. To Solomon Slone. To Mary Slone. To Elizabeth Slone his dau. and Elijah Slone her husband.
Execs: Thomas Harper and James Harper, Jr., his bro.
Wit: James Cuthbertson, John Hindsillwood and William Lee.

DRAPER, MARY. Phila. Oct 28, 1811. Feb 18, 1812. 4.81.
To father-in-law Jonathan Draper, Sr., of Phila., cordwainer, appointing him sole exec.
Execs: Father Jonathan Draper, Sr.
Wit: Jacob Hugg, William Millard.

SUTTON, MARY. Phila. Widow of Wollman Sutton, late of sd. city, Mariner. Oct 9, 1810. Feb 21, 1812. 4.82.
All property to niece Elizabeth Mary Douglass wife of Abraham Douglass, now residing at Richmond, VA, and to her issue, she or they paying to sister Margaret Quirk an annuity. To Elizabeth Mary Douglass dau. of sd. niece Elizabeth Mary and to Gustavus Douglass also son of sd. niece.
Execs: John Coulter, merchant, and John Douglass, Jr., cabinet maker, both of Phila.
Wit: Stephen Russel, Alexander Stewart, John Coulter, John Douglass, Elizabeth Caldwell.

REAVER, HENRY. Northern Liberties. Phila. Co. Laceweaver. Feb 26, 1812. Mar 2, 1812. 4.84.
To wife Margaret Reaver. To grandchildren, children of late son Philip Reaver namely Henry Reaver and Catharine Beiderman. To family of his bro. Jacob Reaver. To family of bro. Ulrich Reaver. To family of dec'd

bro. Bastian Reaver. To family of sister Margaret who married John Adolph.
Exec: Sd. John Adolph of Northern Liberties, house carpenter.
Wit: John Bleyler, Isaac Stricker.

SMITH, WILLIAM T. Phila. Merchant. May 31, 1810. May 2, 1812. 4.86. Children: Anthony Smith, Elizabeth Elder, Mary Richards, Ann McKean, Rebecca Smith, Richard E. Smith and Wm. T. Smith, Jr. Thos. Elder, husband of dau. Elizabeth. Samuel Richards, husband of dau. Mary. Robert McKean late husband of dau. Ann. Granddau. Ann wife of Peter Wager, dau. of Stafford Smith, dec'd. Grandson William L. Smith son of sd. Stafford. Trustees and execs. Joseph Ball of sd. city, Esq., and son-in-law Samuel Richards. Property in Phila. adj. Jacob Downing's ground, sugar plantation on Island of St. Martins, debt due him by Hanson and Smith of sd. Island &c. Also other property in Phila. adj. Boyer Brooks, land purchased of ---- Goodman, wharf on estate purchased of sd. Goodman with dock adj. Jacob Downing's line. Boyer Brooks &c. Land in New Castle Co., DE, purchased of Thomas Montgomery, Esq., also farm in sd. state. Land in Eustatia in Saba and in Bermuda all of which he bequeaths to children and grandchildren.
Execs: Joseph Ball, Esq., and son-in-law Samuel Richards.
Wit: Lambert Wilmer, George DB. Keim and William Hirebone(?), Jr.

PALMER, THOMAS. Phila. Gunsmith. Nov 7, 1811. March 4, 1812. 4.96. Legacy to bro. Jonathan Palmer. To wife Ann Palmer, at her decease to his four children viz: Asher, William and John Palmer and Elizabeth Shaw.
Execs: Sd. sons William and John.
Wit: William Fox, Daniel Brodhead.

SMITH, JONATHAN BAYARD. Phila. June 1, 1812. June 20, 1812. 4.97. Trustees Robert Ralston, Abraham Kintzing and William Rush. Estate to sd. trustees for use of his children: John R. Smith, Samuel H. Smith, Susan Bayard Smith, Ann Caroline Smith and Jonathan Smith.
Execs: His three sons John R., Samuel H., and Jonathan Smith.
Wit: Jared Ingersoll, James Glen and Thomas Williams.

GALBRAITH, ANDREW. Phila. Oct 23, 1811. March 5, 1812. 4.98.
To Andrew and Hugh Galbraith sons of bro. Samuel Galbraith of Ireland, money to pay their passage to America and expences until they are put to trade. Bro. Hugh Galbraith. To dau. Betsey Galbraith for her own and

her mother's support. Residue to son John Galbraith, to be kept at interest until he is of age.
Execs: Thomas Donagan and John Johnson.
Wit: John Rayfield, Thomas Entrikin.

COX, JACOB. Phila. June 27, 1806. March 6, 1812. 4.99.
All estate to wife Kitty Cox. Children to pay no board until of age.
Exec: Sd. wife Kitty.
Wit: Samuel H. Williams, James Whitaker, Francis Johnson, Esq., affirmed.

NORTHROP, MARY. Lower Dublin Twp. Phila. Widow. Sept 1, 1808. March 9, 1812. 4.100.
To son John Northrop. To grandchildren: Elizabeth, John and Jacob Shearer (children of dau. Sarah Shearer, dec'd). All residue of estate to her four daus. namely: Rachel Duffield, Eleoner Wright, Elizabeth Wright and Phebe Taylor.
Execs: Friend Joseph Wright of Lower Dublin township and son-in-law William Wright.
Wit: Thomas Miles, Daniel McVeaugh.

EMERICK, DEWALT. Kensington. Northern Liberties. Phila. Physician. Sept 16, 1804. March 10, 1812. 4.101.
To wife Maria Catharina and children: Henry, Frederick, Dewalt and Maria Magdalena. Sd. execs. to be guardians of children.
Execs: Christian Sheets of Kensington, Jacob Brown, blacksmith and Frederick Haas, cordwainer of Phila.
Wit: Frederick Beates, Peter Wagner, Jr.
Letters granted to Christian Sheets and Frederick Haas.

WETHERHEAD, ESTER. Phila. Spinster. Oct 24, 1811. March 10, 1812. 4.103.
To niece Ester Banks. All residue to her three children namely: Alexander, Catharine and Margaret Wetherhead.
Execs: Friends Joseph Randolph of Phila., painter and glazier, Revd. Absolom Jones of St. Thomas African Episcopal Church of sd. city.
Wit: Hannah Quinter, Nathan Gray.

BAKER, JACOB. Northern Liberties. Phila. Farmer. Feb 14, 1812. March 14, 1812. 4.104.

Estate to wife Eleanor, at her decease to dau. Susanna wife of James Jasper, at her death, to her children.
Execs: Sd. wife Eleanor and dau. Susanna.
Wit: Enoch Thomas, Anthony Kennedy, John McAllister.

BLODGET, WILLIAM HENRY. Phila. Aug 10, 1810. May 16, 1812. 4.105.
To sister Maria Louisa West of Baltimore all property of which he now is on may be possessed.
Execs: Friends Robert Hare, Jr., Richard McCall of Phila.
Wit: Elihu Chauncey, Edward Earle, Samuel G. Blodget.
Letters granted to Robert Hare, Jr.

BOYD, ANDREW. Phila. Feb 27, 1812. March 16, 1812. 4.105.
All estate to dau. Sarah Boyd and grandson Andrew Boyd Kitchen.
Execs: Sarah Boyd and friend John Hall of Phila., watch maker. Sd. Sarah to be guardian of grandson.
Wit: William Newell and Nathan Eyre.

BODENSTINE or BODENSTEIN, ANDREW. Southwark. Farmer. Jan 7, 1808. March 18, 1812. 4.106.
Estate to wife Hannah Bodenstein.
Execs: Friend Henry Ross of sd. District and sd. wife Hannah.
Wit: Malcom McNevan, Peter Lovell, Hannah Garritson.
Letters granted to surviving exec. Hannah Cavilson, late Hannah Bodenstein. March 23, 1812.

WALLACE, ROBERT. Phila. Labourer. Sept 10, 1811. March 24, 1812. 4.107.
Estate to friend John Dillon, he to recover from James Hammel the exec. of estate of Mary Cunningham the estate left to him by her, he to appropriate same for his own use.
Exec: Friend Andrew Scott.
Wit: Rodiah Dillon, Nathan R. Potts.

DEFORREST, HENRY. Phila. Cabinet Maker. March 12, 1812. March 25, 1812. 4.108.
All estate to wife Mary Deforrest, at her decease, to his four children: Peter, George, Sophia and John.
Execs: Sd. wife Mary, son Peter and friend Joseph Morris.
Wit: John De La Mater, Anthony A. Palmer.

PEARCE, MARGARET. Phila. March 12, 1812. May 30, 1812. 4.109. Sister Mrs. Mary Levy. Niece Anna Gertrude Pearce. Bro.-in-law Moses Levy. Martha Levy dau. of sd. Moses. Cousin Dr. Edward Earle. Legacy to Manus Capelle and Joseph Capelle, his bro., to be paid out of legacy devised to her by her bro. Henry Pearce. Cousin Mary Pearce of Cecil Co., now lodging in house of Michael Hague. All residue of her estate to her four nieces: Anna G. Pearce, Emma Pearce, Henrietta Maria Levy and Martha Mary Ann Levy. To Alice an old servant of the family.
Execs: Friends James and John Read of Phila., sister-in-law Mary Pearce, Susan R. Eckard, bro. Mathew Pearce.
Wit: Rachel Levy, Susan R. Eckard.

DECATUR, ANN. Phila. Widow of Capt. Stephen Decatur of Phila., dec'd. March 5, 1812. April 3, 1812. 4.111.
She bequeaths to dau. Ann Hurst. To sons Stephen and John V. Decatur. To grandchildren Stephen D. McKnight, Mary McKnight, Anna McKnight and Priscilla McKnight. To Mary Cooper who has resided with her for many years. To Mrs. Mary Gurney wife of General Francis Gurney. To Mrs. Eliza Josiah wife of Capt. James Josiah. To godchild Ann Peart dau. of William Peart of Frankford.
Execs: Sd. James Josiah and Capt. Arthur Stotesbury.
Wit: William Montgomery, Thomas Mitchell.
Codicil March 17, 1812.
Wit: Same as to will.

HULSECAMP, GARRET. Phila. Pilot. April 4, 1808. April 6, 1812. 4.113.
To dau. Mary (who is unmarried). At her death to dau. Catharine Rushman and grandson William Roland.
Exec: Sd. dau. Mary Hulsecamp.
Wit: Jehu Hollingsworth, Jr., Robert Clinton.

PARRENNE, ELIZABETH. Phila. Jan 31, 1811. April 7, 1812. 4.115.
Estate to friend James Oellers, whom she appoints exec.
Exec: Friend James Oellers.
Wit: I. M. Connelly, W. Spickennagel.

GEYER, ELIZABETH. Phila. Widow of Caspar Geyer late of sd. city, Stone Cutter. Nov 26, 1808. April 8, 1812. 4.116.
She bequeaths to bro. Lewis Smith, nieces Catharine Fritz and Sarah Harland, nephew Caspar Greaves, niece Elizabeth Steel, Mary Steel dau. of sd. niece Elizabeth, niece Mary Greaves, nephew Jacob Fritz, nieces

Catharine Smeck and Elizabeth Nailer, godchild Elizabeth Ford, Elizabeth Fritz dau. of nephew John Fritz and to sd. nephews dau. Catharine. To German Reformed Church of Germantown, Phila. Co. To German Reformed Church of Phila. for support of poor widows of both congregations. Sd. nephew John Fritz to have her dwelling house in Phila. and in Frankford, Phila. Co. At his death to his two daus. Elizabeth and Catharine.
Execs: Sd. nephew John Fritz and Thomas Savery of Phila., house carpenter.
Wit: Frederick Beates, John Brown.

CLARK, MARY. Aug 5, 1808. April 11, 1812. 4.119.
To son Thomas Clark as soon as information can be obtained of him, if not heard of in ten years, she bequeaths to the Society of St. Joseph for educating poor orphan children. To Revd. Michael Eagen. To Julia Ann Matthews and Nancy McClakin. To Henry Byne Carrell. To Elizabeth Byne*[sic]*. All residue to James M. Byrne, Eleanor Maher, Ann Byrne, Patrick Byrne, Eleanor Ann Carrell, Maria Eleanor Carrell, Ferdinand Flavell(?) and Edwin Carrell.
Exec: Edward Carrell.
Wit: Mary Cakrin or Corkrin, Eliza M. Carrell.

KLING, ELIZABETH. March 8, 1812. April 15, 1812. 4.119.
Bequeaths to Ann Maria Raybold. To bro. John Kling. All remainder including whatever is coming from her father John Kling, either from property in town or from the place near Schoolkile she bequeaths to her bro.-in-law Thomas Raybold and to his children.
Exec: Sd. bro.-in-law Thomas Raybold.
Wit: Jacob Raybold, Sarah Raybold.

KEAN, JOHN. May 25, 1810. April 15, 1812. 4.120.
To wife Sarah Kean, at her death, to his bro. Daniel Kean of the Co. of Londonderry, Parish of Glendarmont, Kingdom of Ireland, and to Eliza Kean of Bucks Co., PA, dau. of dec'd bro. Neal Kean, late of Bucks Co.
Exec: Sd. wife Sarah Kean, John Steel, storekeeper, and Alexander Campbell, cordwainer.
Wit: Andrew McConnell, John Johnston.

BROWN, JOHN. Southwark. Phila. Co. Shipwright. April 26, 1800. April 21, 1812. 4.121.
All estate to friend and relation David Allen of sd. District, cordwainer.

Exec: Sd. David Allen.
Wit: Alexander Lee, Daniel Hawthorn. William Middleton of sd. District, taylor, and Thomas P. Hawthorn, mariner, affirmed. Wits. dec'd.

PORTER, THOMAS C. Southwark, Phila. Co. Printer. Feb 6, 1812. April 21, 1812. 4.121.
Legacies to niece Eliza Catherine Carter and to cousin Jane Allen Middleton when of age and all remainder to friend and cousin Joseph Middleton of sd. District, tailor. Desires to be buried by the side of his mother Catherine Porter.
Exec: Sd. Joseph Middleton.
Wit: David Allen, James Gamble.

BECKER, JOSEPH. Germantown. Phila. Co. Labourer. April 14, 1812. April 25, 1812. 4.122.
Estate to wife Elizabeth Becker including that bequeathed to him by his father John Becker.
Execs: Sd. wife Elizabeth and Jonathan Scott.
Wit: Jacob Myers, George Berger.

LYONS, SOLOMON. Frankford. Phila. Co. Gentleman. Sept 15, 1806. April 28, 1812. 4.122.
Appoints wife Sarah formerly called Rebecca and his friends Simon Gratz, merchant and Frederick Beates, scrivener of that city execs. To Watson Atkinson of Frankford aforesd., storekeeper in trust for his wife Sarah. To his four children by sd. wife namely: Benjamin, Rachel, Moses and Zaligman and such other child or children that may be born.
Execs: Wife Sarah, Simon Gratz, Frederick Beates.
Wit: Abraham Stein, William Montelius.

DENNIS, HANNAH. Greenwich Twp. Cumberland Co., NJ. Widow. Feb 2, 1799. May 8, 1805. 4.123.
To daus. Deborah Newbold and Sarah Dennis. To nephew Samuel Newbold.
Exec: Bro.-in-law Thomas Daniel.
Wit: Nathaniel Rulon, Abel Rulon, Joshua Newbold.

WICKAM, JAMES. Phila. Taylor. May 28, 1811. May 4, 1812. 4.124.
Execs. to sell his property in Northern Liberties of sd. city bounded by lot granted or intended to be granted to Edward Cutbush, by ground of Frederick Kuhl's, by lot formerly of Isaac Bartram's, also other property

in sd. Liberties bounded by lot granted or intended to be granted to John Satterbach, by land which Miles Evans and Hannah his wife by Indenture granted and conveyed to him (James Wickam) also his real estate in Washington, District of Columbia &c., wife Eleanor Wickam to have all estate until youngest child is of age. To daus. Margaretta and Anastacia Wickam property in Phila. bounded by lot late of William Rush, dec'd, by lot formerly of Brian Wilkinson and by land which Jane Vansise and others conveyed to him, subject to disposition to their mother. To his father Michael Wickam and mother Anastacia of Ireland, if not living, to his bros. and sisters in Ireland. All residue to sons Michael and Nicholas Wickam.
Execs: Sd. wife Eleanor Wickam and friends Michael Doran and Philip Smith.
Wit: Patrick Harper, Nicholas Molloy, Patrick Barny.

EASTBURN, ESTHER. Phila. March 28, 1812. May 7, 1812. 4.125.
To James Young of Phila., store keeper, he to secure a tract of land in Monongalia Co., VA, sd. land to her daus. Rachel Hunter, Elouisa and Caroline. To grandchildren Samuel, John and Hester Eastburn.
Exec: Sd. James Young.
Wit: Joshua Buffington, Robert E. Nuttle.

TUSTON, WILLIAM. Twp. of Northern Liberties. Phila. Co. April 4, 1812. May 9, 1812. 4.126.
Estate to wife Susannah Tuston, at her death to his four children to wit: Thos., Septimus, Joseph and Eliza Tuston.
Execs: Sd. wife Susannah and bro. Israel Tuston.
Wit: Joseph Barton, Adam Barton.

ROE, URIAH. Kingsessing Twp. Phila. Co. Cordwainer. Dec 26, 1811. April 25, 1812. 4.127.
Property to his children viz. to: David Roe, Samuel Roe, Elias Humphries Roe, Joanna Turner, Anna McNemea and Hannah McColloh.
Execs: Friend Benjamin Pearson of Darby, Delaware Co., and son David Roe of Kingsessing.
Wit: Richard Cribs, James Makemson.

HOOK, JOHN, SR. Phila. Co. Potter. Jan 3, 1807. May 16, 1812. 4.127.
All estate to wife Elizabeth, after her decease, to his four children by his former wife, namely: John, Elizabeth, Mary and Hester and to son

William and daus. Catharina, Margaret, Christina Susannah. Dau. Catharina to have only the interest during her present husband's life.
Execs: Sd. wife Elizabeth Hook and friends Heronimus Warner and John Adolph.
Wit: Peter Fritz, Jacob Marny(?), Thomas Eickands.

ALLEN, JANE. Phila. Widow. Nov 29, 1810. May 18, 1812. 4.129.
To dau. Mary McClintuck, at death of sd. dau. to her three children namely: Joseph, Thomas and Eliza McClintuck. To dau. Jane Thompson*[sic]*, (wife of Charles Thomson) at her death to her children. To children of late dau. Elizabeth Needles. To three children of late dau. Hanna Sawyer namely: Joseph Allen Sawyer, Margaret Sawyer and Jane Allen Sawyer. To sons Joseph and Charles Allen, at death of sd. sons, to their children. Sons Joseph and Charles to be execs.
Execs: Sons Joseph and Charles.
Wit: John Townsend, Jane Ashbridge, Peter Thomson.

SHEETZ, DANIEL. Kensington, Phila. Co. Yeoman. Feb 23, 1812. May 18, 1812. 4.130.
Wife Catharine to have rents, income &c. of estate, she to educate his minor children. Sons John, Daniel and Samuel to learn a trade. At wife's death estate to his five children namely George, Mary, John, Daniel and Samuel.
Execs: Sd. wife Catharine and friend Jacob Taylor.
Wit: Robert Whitehead, Michael Day, Johannes Geise(?).

THOMAS, ROBERT. Phila. Taylor. July 16, 1812. Aug 7, 1812. 4.131.
Interest &c. of estate to wife Jane Thomas, she to educate and maintain his minor children. Extx. sd. wife Jane, desiring her to consult with his friend John Stite of Northern Liberties, lumber merchant. After death of sd. wife, to dau. Letitia Thomas, step son Joseph E. Bowen, daus. Hannah A., Barbara A. and Jane Thomas and sons Robert, Richard S., Isachar, Ezekiel C. and Edward A. Thomas.
Exec: Sd. wife Jane.
Wit: Robert Whitehead, John Hewson, Sr., and John Hewson, Jr.

BIDDLE, GEORGE WASHINGTON. Phila. Merchant. May 6, 1809. May 22, 1812. 4.132.
Bequeaths to bro. Thomas Biddle and bro.-in-law Thomas Cadwalader, both of Phila. in trust. Parents Clement Biddle, Esq, and Rebecca Biddle,

at death of sd. parents, to all his bros. and sisters. Sd. trustees to be execs.
Execs: Bro. Thomas Biddle and bro.-in-law Thomas Cadwalader.
Wit: James Crawford, Jr., Nicholas Biddle, Thomas Biddle, affirmed. May 25, 1812. Thomas Cadwalader Oct 17, 1812.

RIEGER, JACOB. Germantown. April 25, 1788. June 8, 1812. 4.132.
Legacy to Charles, son of Rudy, this to be his share of the estate in his father's place and that neither from his mother nor child any demand what ever shall be allowed or accepted. Remainder of the children shall be heirs alike. Provides for wife Margaretha Rieger.
Execs: Sd. wife and son Leonhard Rieger.
Wit: Johann Zeller, Charles Colladay.

McCLENACHAN, BLAIR. Phila. April 4, 1811. May 19, 1812. 4.133.
Estate to his two daus. Mary and Anne McClenachan.
Execs: Dau. Mary McClenachan and Henry Tolland.
Wit: Robert McClenachan. Edward Lane of Phila., accomptant, affirmed., Henry Toland sworn May 25 and Mary McClenachan Aug 17, 1812.

MORRELL, JOHN. July 28, 1812. Aug 11, 1812. 4.134.
Bequeaths to wife (name not given) his property in Phila., his shares in Rancocus Toll bridge &c. To sons: Richard, James, Thomas, Abraham and Benjamin.
Execs: John W. Morrell, Robert Morrell and Richard Morrell.
Wit: John Hutchinson, Charles King.

MATTHEWS, JAMES. Phila. Hair Dresser. May 1, 1805. July 21, 1812. 4.135.
All estate to wife Mary Matthews.
Execs: Sd. wife Mary and John Parry.
Wit: To will, Samson Levy, John Hall, B. Ashmead.
Codicil Jan 8, 1807. Declares that sd. John shall not be exec. but tht sd. wife Mary shall be sole extx.
Wit: Moses Levy, R. Ashmead.

EWING, AMELIA. Lamberton, NJ. Sept 3, 1811. June 11, 1812. 4.136.
Bequeaths to Samuel Ewing of Phila., Attorney at Law, in trust. Annuity to Sarah Hall, wife of John Hall now of Phila. To Catharine Hannah dau. of sd. John Hall and Sarah his wife. To Catharine Ewing wife of bro. James S. Ewing and to their children.

Exec: Sd. Samuel Ewing.
Wit: Mary Wood, John Fox.
Codicil Dec 22, 1811.
Wit: John Ewing, Margaret C. Ashton.

HELM, ELIZABETH. Phila. Dec 11, 1805. July 2, 1812. 4.137.
To sister Martha Jones, at her death to Elizabeth Helm Rees dau. of nephew George Rees. To niece Ann Rees. To nephew George Rees. To sister's dau. Hannah Butler, at her death to her five children viz: Martha, George, Sarah, William and Ann. To nephew Alexander Rees. To Christian Helm, bro. of her late husband. To John and Ann Helm, children of sd. Christian. To Elizabeth Hughes dau. of Derick Cooper and sister's dau. of late husband. To godchild Juliana Elizabeth Wager, dau. of Philip Wager. To Elizabeth Burrows dau. of Eden Burrows of Northampton Co. To Frederick Baker son of John Baker. To Elizabeth Baker. To Maria Kirkham, dau. of Charles Kirkham of Phila., shopkeeper. Mourning rings to Mrs. Haga, wife of Godfrey Haga. Mrs. Wager, wife of Philip Wager, Mary Reigart dau. of sd. Philip Wager, Mrs. Febiger wife of late Christian Febiger, Mrs. Baker wife of John Baker, Esq., and Ann Johnston wife Capt. Johnston of Baltimore. To Mary Rohr (wife of Henry Rohr) who lived with her many years. Wearing apparel to sister Martha Jones and her two daus.
Execs: Friends John Jordan, Isaac Wampole and Frederick Beates.
Wit: John Boller, Frederick Haga, Godfrey Haga, surviving wits. affirmed. Benjamin Woglom of Phila., accomptant affirmed. John Jordan renounced.

WILSON, PHILIP, JR. Phila. Ship Master. June 29, 1811. Aug 3, 1812. 4.139.
To wife Elizabeth Wilson all estate, at her decease, if they have no children, he bequeaths to his bros. and sisters children.
Execs: Sd. wife Elizabeth and his bro. David Wilson.
Wit: John R. Alexander, Samuel Jamison. William Meredith of Phila., Attorney at Law and Dominick T. Rosseter affirmed.

DOWNHEIM, JOHN. Northern Liberties. Phila. Weaver. Feb 12, 1812. June 9, 1812. 4.140.
Wife Maria Magdalen Downheim to have income of all estate. To daus. Margaret Coleman and Catharine Smith. To children of dau. Mary Whitehead, dec'd.

Execs: Sd. wife Maria Magdalen, dau. Margaret Coleman and grandson Jacob Coleman.
Wit: John J. Huiges, William Anderson.
Letters granted to Jacob Coleman. Maria Magdalen Downheim is stated to be deceased and Margaret Coleman it is stated has declined to act.

DAVIS, ISRAEL. Phila. Innkeeper. May 19, 1808. July 28, 1812. 4.141.
Bequeaths to Frances Roberts, wife of ---- Roberts and dau. of Jacob Summers, if not living to her children. To Ann Brown. To James Steward and Mary his wife to be used by them for instruction of their children. To Charity Schools belonging to St. Pauls Church in Phila.
Execs: Adam Eckfeldt and James Stewart of Phila.
Wit: James Flanagan, Francis Reynolds.
Letters granted to Adam Edkfeldt.

JORDAN, JOSEPH. Phila. Plasterer. July 6, 1812. Aug 11, 1812. 4.143.
Mentions in connection with his property in Phila., John Stoddart and Peter Mac Gaulley (?). Estate to wife Mary Jordan and his seven children namely: John, Jeremiah, Samuel, Hannah, Ann, William Ross and Lydia Cooper Jordan. Money to be kept at interest until sd. children are of age. To dau. Isabella wife of Benjamin Baker. Wife to be guardina of dau. Lydia Cooper Jordan, if wife should die before sd. dau. is of age, appoints wife's sister Susan Shinn as guardian.
Execs: Samuel Richards (silver smith) and Jonathan Knight (lumber merchant) of Phila.
Wit: Robert Ross, Mary Ann Ralston, Rebecca C. Ralston.

EVANS, SARAH. Phila. Jan 14, 1808. July 22, 1812. 4.145.
To mother Sarah Evans all her estate.
Execs: Bros. Robert and Issachar Evans and Jenkin Evans.
Wit: Eliza Locke, Eliza Evans. Jenkin Evans, Twp. of New Britain, Co. of Burks, miller, affirmed.
Letters granted to Robert T. Evans.

WATERMAN, THOMAS. Germantown. Phila. Co. March 16, 1812. June 8, 1812. 4.146.
Estate to wife Hannah Waterman, at her death to his children (names not mentioned).
Execs: Sd. wife Hannah and friends George Ingels of United Arsenal and John Conard of Germantown, Esq.
Wit: Christopher Bockius, Wollery Fryhoffer.

SMITH, HUGH. Phila. House Carpenter. May 22, 1812. July 17, 1812. 4.147.
To wife's sons Joseph and Samuel Miller. All property in Phila. and Burlington, NJ, to his wife Mary Smith, dau. Margery Abbott, son Ralph H. Smith and dau. Mary Smith. children of dau. Margery namely Mary Ann Abbott, Eliza Wood Abbott, Juliann Abbott, William Smith Abbott and Charlotta Clarissa Abbott.
Execs: Sd. wife Mary Smith, dau. Margery Abbott and son Ralph H. Smith.
Wit: Ralph Smith, Samuel Bainitt.
Letters granted to Ralph H. Smith.

LEIBERT, PETER. Germantown. Publishes Codicil. July 4, 1810. June 17, 1812. 4.148.
To grandsons: Peter Leibert, William Keyser and Libert Keyser. To Mary Miller, widow of George Miller, dec'd. To Lidia Ox, widow. To Catharina Gramer, single woman. To Dorothy Stebbry, single woman. To Charlotta Neufferin, single woman. To Dorrothy Kies. To Maria Steigerin, last two living in Blomery of Lycoming Co. All above sums to be paid to his son William Leibert, who shall pay to the above named.
Wit: Christopher Mason. Francis Bailey, affirmed.

LEIBERT, PETER. Germantown. Phila. Printer. Sept 4, 1802. June 17, 1812. 4.149. (Will.)
Provides for wife Mary. Sons William and John, daus. Mary Billmeyer and Barbara Keyser. Mentions in connection with his property Christian Mason and Conrad Good.
Execs: Son John Leibert and son-in-law William Keyser.
Wit: Johannes I. Heber, Christopher Mason.

MORRIS, SAMUEL. Phila. Gentleman. Jan 8, 1810. July 15, 1812. 4.152.
As he has advanced to sons Benjamin W. Morris and Anthony Morris, he leaves residue of estate to his other children: Sarah Wistar, Casper W. Morris, Luke W. Morris, Isaac W. Morris, Catharine W. Morris and Israel W. Morris.
Execs: Sons Caspar W. Morris, Luke W. Morris, Isaac W. Morris and Israel W. Morris.
Wit: Nath'l. Holland, Thomas Young.

ROBERTS, JONATHAN. Bristol Twp. Phila. Co. March 24, 1812. July 25, 1812. 4.155.

Estate to his children viz: Robert, Jonathan, Eliza, Morris and Samuel. David Hillis, Sr., of Frankford to be guardian.
Execs: Bro. Jesse Roberts and Nathan Harper of Frankford.
Wit: John Roberts, Rachael Roberts.

WOOD, ANDREW. Roxborough Twp. Phila. June 24, 1801. June 13, 1812. 4.156.
Provides for wife Elizabeth. Children: Hannah, (wife of James Lane), George, Michael, Elizabeth, John and Ann and children of young son Andrew, dec'd, namely: George, Mary, Elizabeth and Andrew.
Execs: Bro. George Wood, son-in-law Michael Wills and sd. son John Wood.
Wit: Michael Lippard, Samuel Johnson and Jacob Knorr. Desires that the family buring place shall remain where it now is on his property. Surviving witness Michael Lippard and Samuel Johnson affirmed.

LEVERING, NATHAN. Twp. of Roxborough. Phila. Co. May 19, 1812. June 20, 1812. 4.157.
To trustees of Bastist*[sic]* Meeting in Roxborough. To nephews Thomas, Aaron, Nathan and Charles Levering. To wife Sarah Levering property in Roxborough bought of bro.-in-law Peter Kiser or Riser &c. To daus. Deborah (wife of Horatis Gates Jones) and Susanna. Land bought of Burket. Sd. wife to be guardian of dau. Susanna.
Execs: Wife Sarah, son-in-law Horatis Gates Jones and nephew Nathan Levering of Roxborough and friend Algeron Roberts.
Wit: John Holget, John Wood.
Codicil May --, 1812. His island in Schuylkill called Num-hill fall with its fisheries, to be rented during wife's life, at her decease to dau. Susanna Levering.
Wit: Same as to will.

RÜHLE, JOHN SIGMUND. Phila. Co. Tobacconist. March 29, 1808. May 28, 1812. 4.161.
Provides for wife Margaret Rühle, residue of his estate to his three children: William Rühle, Susanna Reed and Catharine Rühle.
Execs: Sd. wife and children William, Susanna and Catharine Rühle.
Wit: Lewis Walker, John Morris. Lewis Walker surviving witness affirmed.
Letters granted to William Rühle.

DAVIS, ELIZABETH. Wife of Richard Davis of Phila. Gentleman. July 4, 1812. Aug 11, 1812. 4.163.
Legacies to friend Catharine McCall and maid Dorcas Derrcham. All residue to her husband Richard Davis, at his death, to their children. To children of deceased bro. Clifford Smith. To children of sister Anna Philips to wit: John, Elizabeth, William, Emmeline, Clement and Anna.
Exec: Sd. husband Richard Davis.
Wit: Harriet Church, Thomas C. James.

CALDWELL, JAMES. Northern Liberties. Phila. Co. Blacksmith. Oct 14, 1810. July 8, 1812. 4.164.
To sons James and Andrew and daus. Rosanna, Mary and Elianor Caldwell. To son Robert, he to live with his mother. Provides for wife Elizabeth Caldwell whom he appoints exec. with his bros. George Alcorn, lashmaker and John Johnson, boxmaker.
Execs: Wife Elizabeth Caldwell, friends George Alcorn, lashmaker and John Johnson, boxmaker.
Wit: Spencer Maffat, James McGrath, Chas. S. Stewart.

LOLLER, ALEXANDER. Northern Liberties. Phila. Co. Sept 22, 1804. Aug 18, 1812. 4.165.
To wife Hannah. To son Peter and youngest dau. Mary. Bequeaths to his two eldest (natural) children Maria Loller and Thomas Loller all his real estate.
Execs: Friends Samuel Thomas, Jacob Fillar and John Jones.
Wit: Charles Souder, James Harrison, Joseph Norman.

LIKENS, NEWBERY. Phila. Sept 23, 1811. June 23, 1812. 4.166.
All estate to wife Sarah Likens whom he appoints extx.
Exec: Wife Sarah Likens.
Wit: Enoch Thomas, John H. Fry.

GRIFFITHS, ELIZABETH. March 14, 1811. May 26, 1812. 4.167.
Memorandum for execs. - for will see Will Book No. 6 - Folio 629.
To friends Rebecca Ashbridge, to Sidney E. Hutchinson and Frances Lewis.
Execs: Samuel Powel Griffiths, physician and Joseph S. Lewis.
Wit: R. Hutchinson. William Master of Phila., cordwainer, affirmed.
Letters granted to execs. Samuel Powel Griffiths, physician and Joseph S. Lewis.

ROTHENWALDER, NICHOLAS. Phila. Potter. July 27, 1809. May 26, 1812. 4.168.
To wife Esther all estate, appointing her extx.
Exec: Wife Esther.
Wit: Catharine Baker, Susanna Louisa Baker, George A. Baker.

SCHMIDT, JOHN FREDERICK. Phila. Minister of the Gospel. Feb 6, 1812. June 1, 1813. 4.168.
To Elizabeth Meyers, his house keeper. To Margaret Rittenhouse, of Germantown, (sister of his dec'd wife) if not living, to her children. To Barbara Rush dau. of Castharine Rush, dec'd (the other sister of dec'd wife). To son Frederick. To son Godfrey. To son Jacob Schmidt. To dau.-in-law Caty Smith, dau.-in-law Sally Smith, dau.-in-law Hetty Smith.
Execs: Sons Frederick, Godfrey and Jacob.
Wit: Ernst Christian Bethusen, Christian G. Keck, George Gosner.

FRYBURG, JOHN. Phila. Victualler. May 4, 1811. June 25, 1812. 4.170.
Interest of all estate to wife Susanna Fryburg, at her decease to his children namely: Catharine (wife of Joseph Merot), Elizabeth, Jacob, Mary, Sarah, Hannah and Joseph and grandson John L. Fryburg.
Execs: Sd. wife Susanna and son Jacob Fryburg.
Wit: R. Whitehead, Robert Bayne, John Gamble.

HOOPER, SARAH. Southwark. Phila. Co. Jan 16, 1812. Aug 24, 1812. 4.172.
Estate to her three children viz: John Burks, Henry Hooper and Luveazer Wilkes.
Exec: Josuah Raybold of Moyamensing Twp., constable.
Wit: John Heren, George E. Leckler.
Codicil July 25, 1812.
Wit: Michael Cooper, Stephen Burwell.

KAMMERER, JOSEPH R. Phila. Printer. Oct 1, 1811. Aug 25, 1812. 4.173.
Bequeaths all estate to his partner in business, William Fry, in trust for following purposes: for support of wife Mary Kammerer and his father (name not mentioned).
Execs: Sd. William Fry, Samuel V. Anderson and Isaac Wampole.
Wit: Joshua Collins, Eliza Laetitia Collins.

NUNGESSER, JOHN. Germantown. Phila. Blacksmith. Aug 14, 1812. Sept 9, 1812. 4.174.
All estate to wife Catharine Nungesser whom he appoints extx.
Exec: Wife Catharine Nungesser.
Wit: Frederick Smith, Joseph Buckius.

COTTMAN, BENJAMIN. Lower Dublin Twp. Yeoman. Dec 31, 1811. Sept 11, 1812. 4.175.
Land bought of Isaac Leech in Oxford Twp., joining land of John Meyer, except the house rented to Cesar Penrose, (of African descent) to be sold. Provides for wife Susanna Cottman. To Elizabeth Miles (wife of Joseph Miles). To grandson Benjamin Cottman Harbeson (son of dau. Susanna dec'd). All residue of estate in Oxford and Lower Dublin he bequeaths to his four granddaus. namely Susanna Waterman (wife of Jesse Waterman), Elizabeth Thomas and Sarah Thomas (these three are daus. of dau. Rebecca and Joseph Thomas, both dec'd) and Mary Nightingale (dau. of dau. Hannah, dec'd). To great grandson Benjamin Cottman Waterman (son of granddau. Susannah Waterman). To Lydia Thompson (of African Race) wife of Nevil Thomson*[sic]*, land joining William Hallowell's land. His black woman Fenders to be cared for. His father Benjamin Cottman, his sons Benjamin, Joseph and William and daus. Mary, Susannah, Rebecca and Sarah Cottman are buried in Oxford Church Yard. Son-in-law Thomas Nightingale.
Execs: Friend James Ross of New Castle Co. and Jesse Waterman of Lower Dublin Twp.
Wit: John Trump, Abednego T. Whitton, Joshua Lonstreth.

REX, WILLIAM. Roxborough Twp. Phila. Co. Yeoman. March 20, 1812. Sept 15, 1812. 4.178.
To son Daniel Rex. To wife Catharine, property adj. John Streeper's land, at her death, to his children.
Exec: Sd. wife Catharine.
Wit: John Bicking, George Martin.

MORTON, JOHN, JR. Phila. Merchant. July 1, 1812. Sept 21, 1812. 4.178.
To wife Margaret, the rents, income &c. of all estate, she to maintain and educate his minor children, at her death to his children.
Execs: Friend Alexander Wilson, bro.-in-law Samuel Canby, Jr.
Guardians of sd. children his friends Alexr. Wilson and Emmers Kimber.
Wit: Joshua Claibborn, James Morton.

FISHER, JOHN. July 11, 1808. Oct 3, 1812. 4.179.
All property to wife Elizabeth, she to pay for schooling of his minor children.
Exec: Sd. wife Elizabeth.
Wit: Christian Sheetz and Peter Sheetz.

LOLLER, ALEXANDER. Northern Liberties. Phila. Co. Sept 22, 1804. Aug 18, 1812. 4.180.
Wife Hannah, son Peter. Two eldest (natural) children Maria Loller and Thomas Loller.
Execs: Samuel Thomas, Jacob Fillar and John Jones.
Wit: Charles Souder, Jos. Harrison, Joseph Norman.
Letters granted to Samuel Thomas and John Jones.

SIBADAY, JOHN. Boatswain of ship Atalanta. Aug 14, 1810. Sept 15, 1812. 4.181.
Mother Mary Sibaday to have all estate. Money to be invested in Canton by William Heyl and Francis G. Smith, to be delivered to Capt. Loyd Jones in trust for sd. mother Mary Sibaday. Money in his possession belonging to Peggy Hardy, Conrad Rigger and Mrs. Curlet.
Wit: William Heyl, Francis Gurney Smith.

SPROUL, GEORGE. Southwark. Phila. Mariner. Aug 31, 1812. Sept 15, 1812. 4.181.
Property in Southwark (late the property of his father John Sproul) to friend Capt. John Brice of Northern Liberties, mariner. Late sister Sarah Brice.
Exec: Sd. John Brice.
Wit: Thomas Mitchell, Frederick Shear.

PEMBERTON, PHEBE. Widow of James Pemberton of Phila. Former husband Samuel Morton. Oct 10, 1811. Aug 31, 1812. 4.183.
To niece Esther Eddy, widow of George Eddy and her ten children viz: Lewis, George, Charles, James, Mary Ann, Esther, Catharine, Phebe, Lucy and Frances Eddy, their uncle David Lewis to manage their share during minority. To niece Ann Wharton wife of Thomas Wharton and her sister Sarah Green. To niece Sarah wife of nephew Robert Lewis and their children, dau. Phebe only one named. To Mary Mifflin widow, and to her dau. Lydia Husband. To friend Sarah Harrison. To friends Rebecca Jones, Rebecca Price and Sarah Matthews. To aunt Ruth Lewis widow of uncle Ellis. To cousin Mary Dickinson sister of Cyrus Newlan.

To Hannah Elliott and Sarah Parrish, Jr., in trust for Monthly Meeting of Phila. To nephew David Lewis and his wife Mary Lewis. To niece Phebe Waln. To nephew Robert Murdock. To three nephews, Robert, Lawrance and Nathaniel Lewis. To niece Mary Lewis, Jr. To niece Sarah Green. To niece Emeline Murdock. To nieces Esther Eddy, Elizabeth Higbee and Mary Glen. To sister-in-law Lucy Jervis. To sister-in-law Francis*[sic]* Lewis, widow. To nephews Robert, John and Lawrence Lewis and their sister Mary Lewis, Jr. To great nieces viz: Ann Wharton, Mary Ann Eddy, Mary Porcol, Virginia Higbee, Mary Lewis, Phebe Lewis, Frances Glen and Harriot Murdock. Mentions children of bro. Lewis, dec'd. All residue to nephews and nieces, viz: Robert Murdock, Mary Glen, her bro. Nathaniel Lewis, Elizabeth Higbee and her bros. Robert, John and Lawrence Lewis.
Wit: Eden Haydock, Catharine Roberts, Hannah Haines.
Codicil April 4, 1812.
Wit: Catharine Roberts, Esther M. Roberts.
Codicil May 20, 1812. To Catharine Cammal and Sarah Stafford who now live with her. To Rachel Downing who lived with her many years. To Essex a coloured man, if still in her service &c.
Execs: Nephews Robert Waln, David Lewis, Robert Murdock and Lawrence Lewis.

GOETZ, MICHAEL. Moyamensing. Phila. Co. Yeoman. May 9, 1809. Oct 12, 1812. 4.186.
To wife Barbara, at her death to his five children to wit: Catharina married to George Bruner of Phila., Andrew Goetz, George Goetz, Apollonia Seyman, widow and Johannes Goetz.
Execs: Sd. wife Barbara and son Johannes.
Wit: Charles Erdman, Adam Shetzline, James Martin.
Letters granted to John Goetz.

HORNKETH, JEREMIAH. Oct 2, 1812. Oct 15, 1812. 4.187.
All estate to wife and children (no names mentioned).
Execs: Michael Fox and Adam Eckfeldt.
Wit: Michael Fox, Isaac Wampole.

LOTT, HENRY. Phila. House Carpenter. July 13, 1812. Oct 15, 1812. 4.188.
To wife Elizabeth Lott and four children namely: Samuel, Elizabeth, Mary and Henry. To son Samuel and to Henry Euskile all his carpenter tools.

Execs: Friends Matthew Weaver and Alphonso Ireland.
Wit: John Wright, John McKinley.

KNORR, JACOB K. Germantown. Phila. Co. Cabinet Maker. Sept 11, 1812. Oct 19, 1812. 4.189.
All income &c. of estate to wife Elizabeth Knorr for benefit of herself and children namely: Susanna, Ann and Francis whilst in their minority.
Execs: Bro. George Knorr of Phila., lumber merchant and Abraham Keyser of Germantown, Phila. Co. cordwainer.
Wit: Samuel Johnson, John Eagle.

WELSH, EPHRAIM. Late of Savannah, Georgia. Now in Phila. Merchant. Oct 15, 1812. Oct 20, 1812. 4.190.
To bro. John A. Welsh and sisters Abagail Brunard, Sarah Cutteridge, Mary Welsh and Rachael Welsh.
Execs: Thomas Coffin and James Mott of Phila., merchants.
Wit: Daniel McMullen, Anna Swaine, Sarah Howell.

SIMON, JOHN BERNARD. Phila. Taylor. June 13, 1812. Oct 22, 1812. 4.192.
Estate to wife Maria Margaret, at her death to his children: David, Elizabeth and Mary.
Execs: Sd. wife Maria Margaret and friends Revd. George Lockman and George Krebs.
Wit: John Brown, Isaac Wampole.
Letters granted to Maria Margaret Simon and George Krebs.

MENG, MELCHOIR. Germantown. Phila. Co. Sept 4, 1812. Oct 21, 1812. 4.193.
Provides for wife Elizabeth, at her death, her children to have the goods she brought with her at her marriage. Mentions estate he sold to James Matthews.
Codicil Oct 10, 1812. Mentions son Jacob, dec'd, and his heirs.
Execs: Son Christopher Meng, dau. Mary Davis Meng, eldest grandson Jesse Ogden and John Smith.
Wit: Conrad Carpenter, Benjamin Carpenter.

MEAD, MARY. Northern Liberties. Phila. Co. Widow, July 16, 1812. Oct 23, 1812. 4.194.
Estate to her dau. Mary Greenman. To Barsheba and Anna Greenman, daus. of son Thomas Greenman, dec'd, by his first wife. To Jolianna

Greenman, dau. of son David Greenman. To William son of James Greenman. To granddau. Eliza, dau. of Jonathan and Ann Flagg.
Execs: Friends Robert Ralston and Joseph Abbott.
Wit: Jonathan Collom, Samuel Bacon. Robert Ralston renounced.

KNOX, ELIZABETH. Southwark. Phila. Co. Widow of John Knox, late of Lumberton, Burlington Co., NJ. Jan 7, 1812. Oct 3, 1812. 4.195.
To mother Jemima Higgins. To Elizabeth Knox Nelson, dau. of George and Acksah Nelson. To John Knox Esler, son of friend George Esler of Southwark, house carpenter and to Elizabeth Knox Elser, dau. of sd. George Esler. Mentions Samuel Penrose, merchant of Southwark and Jonathan Penrose, Esq. To cousin Sarah Parkinson. Residue to sd. George Esler and wife Rebecca, at their death to above named John Knox Esler and Elizabeth Knox Esler.
Execs: Sd. George Esler and friend Jesse Williamson of Southwark, house carpenter.
Wit: Joseph Williamson, Thomas Mitchell.

KENNARD, GEORGE. Phila. Merchant. Oct 17, 1812. Oct 26, 1812. 4.197.
To son Richard Tilghman Kennard. Estate to children namely: William, Asbury, John Westly, George, Henry and Mary. Mentions real estate in Delaware known by general name of White Hall and other property adj. White Hall, purchased from John Goldsmith.
Execs: Son William Kennard and friend John Cummings of Smyrna in Delaware. John Cummins to be guardian of three youngest children and son William to be guardian of sons Asbury and John Westly.
Wit: James Gallaher, David Cummins and Ch: Chauncey.

VANDIKE, ELENOR. Jan 1, 1801. Sept 7, 1812. 4.199.
To dau. Christena Vandike. Legacy left by her (Christena Vandike) father Cristoff Longstreth now in estate of Aron Vandike. Late husband Dirrick Van Dyke. To granddau. Nelley Vandike. To sons William and David Vandike and to William V. Griffith if he lives to twenty one years.
Execs: Sons William and David Vandike and friend John Shaleroff.
Wit: Samuel Grifith, Alexander Lyle, Catharine Wile.

CLARK, JANE. Phila. Widow. Jan 11, 1812. Oct 30, 1812. 4.199.
To her three bros. Robert, David and Adam Hoop and to sisters Mary Barclay and Margaret Walker. To four children of nephew Robert Barclay, dec'd, son of sd. sister Mary Barclay viz: Mary, Elizabeth,

Thomas, James and Maria Barclay. To nieces Jane Isabella Swan and Martha Hoop Syme. To niece Elizabeth Finney Walker. To niece Maria Isabella Coulter and dau. Mary Jane Coulter. To nephew Daniel Clark of New Orleans the minature picture of his uncle Daniel Clark, dec'd. To sister-in-law Mary Clark. To sister Mary Clark, to be sent to her dau. Jane Green of Liverpool. To friend Mrs. Hulings. To friend Ellen Campbell. Releases John Barclay. To Mrs. Sarah Barclay, widow of sd. nephew Robert Barclay. To bro. David Hoops. Money due from John S. Wells and Col. Massey of OH. To her emancipated yellow girl Mary Menbrun. Mentions claim on land in OH.
Execs: William H. Tod, Esq., and William E. Hulings.
Wit: John Morrison, George Cambell.
Codicil. Claim to lands in KY which she bequeaths to Peyton Harrison of Bunkerville, KY, and to sd. bro. David Hoops and sister Mary Barclay.
Wit: Same as will.
Codicil Oct 14, 1812.
Wit: Geo. Campbell and Anne Frazier.
Codicil. Bequeaths to servant girl Elizabeth Orange and to sd. Mary Mumbrun. Francis Markoe of Phila., merchant to be trustee and guardian of sd. Mary and Elizabeth.
Wit: William E. Hulings, Isabella Moylan.

FOLWELL, RUTH. Widdow of John Folwell, late of Southampton, Burks Co., at present living in Phila. Aug 24, 1811. Nov 3, 1812. 4.203. To dau. Mary Weed Folwell. To niece Frances Dean, wife of John Dean and to her children Ruthy Ann, Mary, William and Elizabeth Dean. To Pamella Vanhorn, dau. of Barnard Vanhorn. To setpdau. Margaret Rue, wife of Richard Rue in Chester Co. Desires to be buried in Southampton Grave Yard.
Execs: Bro. William Mitchell and nephew John Dean.
Wit: William Mitchell, John Dean. John Bray, Jr., affirmed.

SMITH, JOHN. Roxborough. Phila. Co. Wheelwright. Oct 10, 1812. Nov 10, 1812. 4.204.
Bequeaths to wife Elizabeth use &c. of estate until dau. is of age. Children Jacob and Susan Smith. Bro. Frederick Smith.
Execs: Wife Elizabeth, son Jacob and bro. Frederick Smith.
Wit: John K. Day, Daniel Fibler.

ROGERS, ELIZABETH. Phila. Widow. March 18, 1809. Nov 11, 1812. 4.204.

Legacy to Olivia Williams who has lived with her family many years. To Elizabeth Rogers Williams, dau. of sd. Olivia property in Northern Liberties purchased of late bro. Andrew Craig, dec'd. To son Thomas Rogers. Residue in trust to Caleb Pierce of Phila., merchant and Peter Thompson, of sd. city, conveyancer, for son Thomas Rogers, at his death, if no issue, bequeaths to Elizabeth Walker of Burlington, NJ, and dau. of bro. Joseph Craig and Elizabeth Rogers Cummings and Mary Ann Cummings, daus. of nephew William Cummings of Hanover Twp., Burlington Co., NJ.
Execs: Sd. Caleb Peirce and Peter Thomson.
Wit: Joseph Moore, Nathan Dunn, Isaac Tyson.

CARSON, CHARLES. July 7, 1808. Nov 19, 1812. 4.208.
To bro. Patrick Carson all his estate appointing him sole exec.
Exec: Bro. Patrick Carson.
Wit: John Connelly, John Burten(?), George Holmes.

DE LA ROCHE, JOHN GOYAUX. Native of France, residing in PA since his arrival from Cape Francis, Island of St. Domingo in the year 1792, Merchant and Exchange Broker of Phila. Aug 8, 1811. Nov 25, 1812. 4.208.
Estate to wife Mary G. De La Roche during life. Desires to be buried with remains of his two daus. Isabella and Louisa at Abington Church Yard. Property sold to Dr. C. Caldwell. To Celia, his black woman, servant and to Margaret Broton to be paid by his wife Mary White, the last two legacies crossed out.
Execs: Wife Mary G. De La Roche and friends Lewis D. Carpenter and Thomas Hale, the husband of his wife's niece.
Wit: Thomas Hale, L. Desauque, William Bourke, J. A. Monges.
Letters granted to wife Mary G. De La Roche.

TAYLOR, MARY ANN. Phila. Widow of Ezekiel Taylor. ----. Nov 26, 1812. 4.210.
Mother Catharine Herenstad. Daus. Ann Loxley Taylor, Elizabeth Williams Taylor and Mary Ann Taylor.
Execs: Mother Catharine Herenstead, bro. Joseph Hernstad and friends George Wilson and Mary his wife. Bond and Judgment on Presbyterian Church at Frankford and Bond and mortgage on property of John Donaldson, book binder near Frankford.
Wit: James Williams, Charles L. Smith, G. W. Loxley.
Letters granted to Joseph Hernstead and George Wilson.

HARE, MARY. Phila. Widow. Feb 24, 1812. Nov 26, 1813. 4.210.
Bequeaths to daus. Hannah Hand, widow of Nathan Hand, Sidney Pancass, wife of Jonathan Pancass, Jane Thornton, wife of Joseph Thornton, Ann Murphy, wife of William Murphy and Mary Elton, wife of Anthony Elton. To sons William and George Hare in trust for dau. Elizabeth Hare. To sd. sons Wm. and Geo. share in capital stock in Bank of Potomac and Bank of Alexandria in trust for Robert Hare son of sd. George Hare and Ann his wife.
Codicil Nov --, 1812. Bequeaths to Robert Winters of Delaware.
Execs: Sons William and George Hare.
Wit: James M. Shaw, William Andrews.

BRANNON, ANN. (formerly widow Jones). Aug 25, 1812. Nov 19, 1812. 4.211.
To children John and Elizabeth Jones residing in Great Britain or elsewhere, at death of sd. children bequeaths all estate to her sister Marthat*[sic]* Philips.
Exec: Arthur Blayney of Phila., physician.
Wit: Alexander McAllister, William Faries.

HERNEISEN, JACOB. Phila. Yeoman. May 8, 1812. Nov 30, 1812. 4.212.
Interest of estate to wife Anna Maria, at her death to dau. Ann Margaret Blake (wife of George E. Blake) at her death to children of sd. dau. Ann Margaret and the two children of dec'd son George.
Execs: Sd. wife Ann Maria Herneisen and son-in-law sd. Geo. E. Blake.
Wit: Conrad Weckerly, Isaac Wampole.

CLOVET, JOSEPH. Phila. Mariner. July 6, 1812. Dec 1, 1812. 4.213.
Estate to wife Anne Clovet, whom he appoints extx.
Exec: Wife Anne Clovet.
Wit: Jh. Morely, Peter S. DuPonceau.

GARRET, ANDREW. Northern Liberties. Phila. Co. Sept 2, 1809. Dec 5, 1812. 4.213.
Bequeaths estate to nephew Samuel Garret and to relation Prudence Warner. Legacy to relation Nelly Kewtan.
Codicil May 10, 1812. Desires plantation on which he lives to be divided between his nephew Samuel Garret, Morton Garret and Prudence Warner. Samuel Biddis having since died appoints as exec. friend Frederick Rednor in his place.
Execs: Friends Samuel Biddis and Jacob Ashmead.

BROWN, WILLIAM. Late of Phila. Merchant. Now residing at Sharow, Parish of Ripon, Co. of York. May 18, 1812. Dec 4, 1812. 4.214.
Bequeaths to Miss Margaret Brogden Duncan (niece of late wife Ann Brown). To father William Brown of Markington, York Co., gentleman and cousin James Brown the younger, of Leeds, sd. co., merchant, in trust for sd. father. All real estate in Phila. to friend John Greiner of Phila., merchant in trust, &c.
Execs: For estate in England sd. father and cousin William Brown and James Brown. And for America his friend sd. John Greiner.
Wit: Isabella Woodhouse of Bridge Hewnick, spinster, Elizabeth Woodhouse of Sharow, spinster, John Howard, solicitor. Ripon Edward Thomson of Phila., merchant and William H. Todd of sd. city, Attorney at Law, affirmed.

VANDUSEN, MATTHEW. Kensington, Northern Liberties. Phila. Co. Blacksmith. Nov 6, 1812. Dec 5, 1812. 4.217.
Income of all estate to wife Lydia Vandusen, at her death to his eight children namely: Nicholas, Andrew, Matthew, Eliza, Lydia, John, Mary and Washington Vandusen.
Execs: Sd. wife Lydia, son Matthew Vandusen and nephew Samuel Bonnell.
Wit: George Eyre, Franklin Eyre, Peter Thomson.

BURNS, HUGH. Phila. Watch Maker. Nov 24, 1812. Dec 9, 1812. 4.218.
All estate to aunt-in-law Johanna Dobbie now residing in Glasgow, Great Britain, in case of her death, to her dau. Margret Dobbie. Residue to Walter Roble Weaver, Gallow Gate sd. city Glasgow, in trust for his (Hugh Burns) step bros. and step sisters now or lately residing in Renton near Dunbarton.
Execs: Thomas Dobson and Adam Ramage, both of Phila.
Wit: Robert Adams, James Hamilton.

ASHTON, WILLIAM. Phila. Oct 14, 1810. Dec 16, 1812. 4.219.
Provides for wife Susan Ashton, at her death to his bros. and sisters viz: George and John Ashton, Mary Keller, wife of Adam Keller, Sarah Hutchinson, wife of James Hutchinson, Elizabeth Scarot, wife of James Scarot, and Rachael Mynick.
Exec: Sd. wife Susan Ashton.
Wit: John A. Collman, Adam Stoll.

BARTRAM, JOHN. Kensington. Phila. Co. Nov 15, 1809. Dec 14, 1812. 4.219.
Estate to his three children viz: Mary Jones (wife of Nathan Jones), Ann M. Carr*[sic]* (wife of Robert Barr), and James Bartram.
Execs: Sons-in-law Nathan Jones and Robert Carr and sd. son James Bartram.
Wit: Jacob Mattson, Anna Bartram, Rachel C. Bartram.

WEBB, SAMUEL P. Phila. Mariner. Dec 17, 1812. Dec 22, 1812. 4.220.
Estate to father Reynold Webb of Saybrook, Connecticut.
Exec: Friend William H. Dillingham.
Wit: Henry Bickley, Michael Allen.

COLLINS, SARAH. Phila. Widow. Dec 4, 1812. Dec 21, 1812. 4.221.
Property in Germantown, Phila. Co. purchased of Robert Street, also in Village of Hamilton, Blockley Twp., Phila. Co. (except that on York Street devised to step son Benjamin Collins) to be sold. Property in Phila. To her dau. Mary Kammerer and to son Joshua Collins. To Hannah Hart her demand against her.
Execs: Sd. dau. Mary Kammerer and friend Thomas Parker of Phila., watch maker.
Wit: Elizabeth Marshall, Jos. Parrish, Mordecai L. Gordon.

MARSHALL, ISAAC R. Phila. Attorney at Law. March 17, 1812. Dec 30, 1812. 4.223.
Legacies to nephew Mathias M. Bush, William M. Currie, Marshall C. Slocum and Charles M. Slocum and nieces Cornelia Currie, Ann Collins, Isabella Currie, Emiline Slocum and Margaretta Currie. To uncle Charles Marshall. To cousin Hannah Pool of NY. Directs bro.-in-law William Currie to sell his land in Sussex Co., Delaware, being part of lands which belonged to Deep Creek Furnace and Nanticoke Forge and which Humprey*[sic]* Atherton, Esq., conveyed to him. To sister Ann Currie, property in Borough of Lancaster, also in Northern Liberties joining land formerly said to be of John Doyles. Bequeaths to wife Sarah Hutchins Marshall, property in Phila. in tenure of Rebecca Wharton &c. To mother Margaret Marshall and wife Sarah all residue of personal estate. To son Edmund Marshall, wife to educate him until of age. Sister Elizabeth F. Slocum.
Codicil July 8, 1812. Mentions Jonathan Petit and Samuel Woolsey.

Execs: Wife Sarah H. Marshall, mother Margaret Marshall, son Edmund Marshall, bro.-in-law Dr. William Currie and friend Humphrey Atherton, Esq.
Wit: Bayse Newcomb, Jr., Andrew A. Stevenson.

EAKIN, SAMUEL. Phila. Clerk. Sept 21, 1812. Dec 29, 1812. 4.226.
To dau. Henrietta Bankson Eakin, land in New Castle Co., Delaware on Red Lion Creek, known by name of Red Lyon Marsh, at present occupied by his mother Ann Eakin and his bro. Alexander, bounded by land of Daniel Turner, Alexander Porter, by lands of the late William Eakin, Jr., dec'd. Provides for wife Eliza Eakin. Mother-in-law Mrs. Henrietta Bankson.
Exec: Quintin Campbell.
Wit: William Dunlap, William Crabb, Michael Whiteman.

DUNLAP, JOHN. Phila. Late Printer. Oct 1, 1807. Dec 14, 1812. 4.227.
To son John Dunlap, property in Phila. and in KY. Annuity to wife Elizabeth Dunlap. Residue of estate to his seven children namely: Sarah, Elizabeth, Mary, Ann, Harriott, John and Charlotte.
Codicil Oct 14, 1809. To son John property in Phila. bounded by Broad, Juniper, Walnut and George Streets.
Execs: Dau. Sarah, son John and friend Joseph Crukshank, George Fox, Samuel Coats and William Poyntell.
Wit: John Elliott Cresson, William Andrews.

SCHOLFIELD, JONATHAN. Moorland. Phila. Co. Dec 23, 1812. Jan 4, 1813. 4.229.
Provides for wife Rebecca Scholfied. To son Abraham he bequeaths his plantation where sd. now dwells partly in Lower Dublin and partly in Mooreland, Phila. Co. which he (Jonathan Scholfield) bought of Abraham Duffield. To dau. Sarah Leedom the farm where he now lives, which he bought of Jacob Comly, also land bought of Lukins and Spencer in Southampton, Bucks Co.
Execs: Son Abraham and friend Jacob Sommer, Esq.
Wit: Joshua Comly, Jonathan Comly and James Yeates.

DUTTON, JAMES. Northern Liberties. Phila. Co. Gentleman. Nov 26, 1812. Jan 13, 1813. 4.230.
Legacies to Newberry Witman, Stephen Witman, Nathan Witman, Jr., Joseph Morhaine. To his house keeper Amelia Wasley. To John C. Browne, blacksmith and Franklin Eyre, shipwright, both of Northern

Liberties in trust for keeping in repair the wall around Coates burial ground in Northern Liberties where his father James Dutton, mother Hannah Dutton, bro. John Dutton and aunt Sarah Evans are interred, he requests to be buried in same ground. Residue of estate to corporation "The Guardians of the Poor of Phila., District of Southwark and Northern Liberties."
Codicil Dec 29, 1812.
Wit: Amelia Wasley and Peter Thomson.
Execs: Thomas Norton and Casper Snider.
Wit: John Thomas, Peter Thomson.

SPEEL, JOHN. Phila. Baker. June 7, 1808. Jan 19, 1813. 4.233.
All rents, interest &c. of estate to wife Elizabeth, she to support his children until they are of age. Property in tenure of John Freeman bounded by land late of George Taylor, dec'd. Residue to his seven children namely: John L. Speel, Elizabeth, Catharine, Sophia, Maria, Julianna and Thos. Jefferson M. Speel.
Execs: Wife Elizabeth Speel and Isaac Wampole of Phila., scrivener.
Wit: Valenten Unbehert, Frederick Beates.
Letters granted to Elizabeth Speel.

JOHNSON, WENYFRED. Northern Liberties. Phila. Dec 28, 1812. Jan 21, 1813. 4.234.
Friend Samuel McClary*[sic]*, Sr., to be guardian of only child John Johnson. Sister Catharine Cramneer.
Execs: Sd. friend Samuel McClury, Sr., and friend William E. Cooper.
Wit: Samuel McClury, Jr., Jacob Clapper.

PAGE, DAVID. Northern Liberties. Phila. Co. Yeoman. Feb 6, 1810. June 20, 1813. 4.235.
Provides for wife Hannah Page. Son John Page and dau. Elizabeth, wife of Godfrey Felton.
Execs: Son John Page and son-in-law Godfrey Felton.
Wit: Philip Limeburner, James Howey, Robert Johnson, R. Whitehead, John Shipley.

MANNA, SARAH. Whitpain Twp., Montgomery Co. April 1, 1812. Jan 30, 1813. 4.236.
To Sary Megergey, lately married to Jacob Megerey all her estate.
Exec: Sd. Jacob Megergey.
Wit: Christopher Loeser, Job Roberts.

CLYMER, GEORGE. Phila. Esq. Jan 5, 1813. ----. 4.236.
Provides for wife Elizabeth Clymer. Trustees, sons Henry and George Clymer and friends John Read and James Gibson. Grandchildren George Clymer McCall and William Coleman McCall.
Execs: Sd. John Read and James Gibson.
Wit: Lambert Cadwalader, Maria Meredith and Ann Howell.
Codicil Jan 18, 1813. Adds friend Dr. Caspar Wistar to his Trustees.
Wit: Same as to will.
Codicil Jan 22, 1813.
Wit: Lambert Cadwalader, Samuel Meredith, Ann Howell.

CONCHY, JAMES. Southwark. Phila. Co. Storekeeper. Oct 29, 1812. Feb 6, 1813. 4.238.
Provides for wife Janet Conchy and dau. Margaret Conchy. Legacies to Alexander Withersip(?) who was married to dau. Agnes and to Adam Johnston who was married to dau. Eleanor. To Associate Synod of North America and the Associate Congregation of Phila.
Execs: Friend John McAra and John McColloch or McCulloch.
Wit: W. C. Brownlee, David Hogan, Alexander Towar.

SNELL, MATTHIAS. Phila. Co. Mariner. March 12, 1812. Jan 30, 1813. 4.239.
Legacy to Catharine Richerts of Northern Liberties, Phila., widow. Residue to his three children (names not given).
Exec: Friend Peter Keyser of Northern Liberties.
Wit: Robert Whitehead, Ralph Smith.

MURPHY, JOHN. Phila. Yeoman. Dec 23, 1812. Feb 8, 1813. 4.239.
Wife Sarah, Sister Laetitia, daus., Eleanor, Sarah and Rebecca Murphy, property in Phila. adj. that now or late of William King. Son John Murphy.
Execs: John Snider, flour merchant and Peter Bennert, brick maker, also to be guardians of sd. children.
Wit: Thomas Armstrong, Thomas Armstrong, Joseph Taylor.

PULLINGER, JACOB. Roxborough. Phila. Co. Yeoman. Jan 8, 1813. Feb 15, 1813. 4.241.
Provides for wife and children (not named).
Exec: Son-in-law Sebastian Wunder.
Wit: John K. Day, James B. or R. Smith.

HIGGINS, FRANCIS. Phila. Gentleman. Now residing in Dublin, Ireland. Sept 14, 1805. Feb 12, 1813. 4.242.
To friends Richard Wistar, merchant and John Crone, builder, both of Phila. in trust for wife Hannah Higgins, at her decease for benefit of sister Margaret Doran, wife of Patrick Doran of Ireland. Cousin Francis Higgins of Ballynea in Co. of Down. Mrs. Susanna Norman wife of friend John Norman of Dublin. Nephew John McCartar.
Execs: Sd. wife Hannah Higgins, in America and Mrs. Susanna Norman in Ireland.
Wit: John Allen, Alex. Montgomery, David Ashmead.

GRIFFING, JOSEPH CARSON. Citizen of U. S. but now in Calcutta. Aug 4, 1811. Feb 16, 1813. 4.244.
Wife A. Griffing.
Execs: Father-in-law Daniel Beckley and Walter Sims.
Wit: R. D. Carson, George Foulke.

DAVIS, NOAH. Northern Liberties. Phila. Bricklayer. Jan 6, 1813. Feb 19, 1813. 4.245.
Provides for wife Elizabeth. To Union Methodist Church of which he is amember. Wife to be guardian of child with which she is ensient.
Execs: Bro. Stephen Davis and friend Abel Matthias.
Wit: David Paul, Frederick Beates.

NIPPES, ABRAHAM. Northern Liberties. Phila. Gunsmith. Dec 7, 1812. Feb 18, 1813. 4.247.
Interest of estate to wife Anna Maria Nippes, she to educate his children viz: Abraham, Louisa and Charles Nippes, during minority.
Execs: Sd. wife Anna Maria Nippes, her son Daniel Henkels or Hinckles and his bro. Daniel Nippes.
Wit: Robert Whitehead, George Heiberger and Henry Afflerback.

BELL, MARY. Phila. Widow. Aug 24, 1808. Feb 16, 1813. 4.248.
To Mary Land who resides in her service. Property in possession of Neil McGinnis. To Rachael Gardner, at her death to Thomas Bell, nephew of her (Mary Bell) late husband and son of James Bell of New Garden, DE. Emancipates her black man Syrus and indentured servant Ezekiel Morris. Property now or late of Patrick Travis. To Mary Sloan. To Ann Dorsey, widow of Dr. Dorsey. To Mary Ann Lawson. To Elizabeth Lawson. To Charles Steward and Hannah, his wife. To Mary Rogers. To Mary Ann Truxton. To niece Fanny Morton. To sister Sarah Worth. To

niece Mary Ann Morton. To nephew Richard Marshall. To Thomas Marshall. To niece Mary Worth. To Mary Forrest. To poor and distressed Masters of Ships, their widows and children in memory of late husband, Capt. Thomas Bell, dec'd. To Debby Logan, wife of Dr. Logan. To nephew Armitt Marshall, nephew Benjamin Martin, nephew John Morton, Elizabeth Ackerman, Dr. William Currie. To children of late niece Margaret Marshall. To children of Fanny Morton and Sarah Worth.
Execs: Thomas Forrest, William McKinzie and Thomas Mitchell, conveyancer.
Wit: James Sawer, John V. Cawell or Crowell.

EVANS, ELIZABETH. Germantown. Phila. Feb 1, 1813. Feb 20, 1813. 4.250.
To sister Sarah Foster. To aunt Rebecca Fraley. To cousin Agnes Hallowell. To friend Jane Street. To cousins Luke and Daniel Williams. To aunt Ann Williams.
Codicil Feb 1, 1813. To cousin Elizabeth Fraley.
Wit: Same as to wills.
Execs: Joseph Rapp of Germantown, preceptor.
Wit: Christian Van Lashet, Richard Pitt.

AXLEY, JOHN. Parish called St. Michael in Barbados. April 10, 1743. June 27, 1743. 4.252.
To wife Sarah Axley, interest of all his estate in Barbados, PA, or elsewhere, at her death to his three children: John and Henry Axley and Ann Callender.
Execs: Sd. wife and son John ----, negro woman named Sary and two sons Primus and Peter.
Wit: Jemmy Lilly, James Butler.
True copy from Secretarys office attested this day Aug 18, 1791. Valentine Jones, D. Secy. [Deputy Secretary].

CALLENDER, ANN. Town and Parish of St. Michael and Island of Barbados. Widow. Feb 4, 1768. July 21, 1768. 4.253.
To children: Hannah Callender, Ann Calender, Edward Callender and William Pitt Callender, her negroes Mary, Sabinet, her rights in negro man Primus, Prince, Mary Lemon, Philenah and her children viz: Lemon and Betty (girls) Newton and Sammy (boys) Phebe and Betty Grace, (women) Kitty and Tom (men) and Joe, a boy, Sarah Lemon (woman) Joanna and Violet (girls) and John a boy. Negroes Peter and Lucy to be

sold. House in which Jacob Joseph now lives to dau. Ann Callender. Deceased father John Oxley.
Execs: And guardians James Hendy, nephew John Jackson and friends James Polgreen and John Carter, Attorney at Law.
Wit: John Phillips, John Sutton, taylor, John K. Lunhoff.

OXLEY, JOHN. Parish of St. Michael and Island of Barbados. ----. ----. 4.256.
To wife Jane Oxley, all estate, she paying to sons Nathaniel and William Oxley &c. Slaves, viz: Aubah, Rose, Bob, York, Tibbat Rose and Castledose. Geo. Moody Reed and Elizabeth, his wife.
Execs: Wife Jane Oxley, Samson Wood, Philip Gibbes and James Hendy.
Wit: George Hartle, Robert Reed, Benjamin Duce. Pilgrim March 18, 1867.*[sic]*

OXLEY, WILLIAM. Parish of St. Michael and Island of Barbados. Practitioner in Physic. Oct 21, 1784. Jan 31, 1785. 4.257.
Mentions Samuel Robinson, William Moore, Francis Brittain, exec. of William Shuge, dec'd. Land and buildings in possession of Dowding Thornhill Bonnitt, Parish of Christ Church and St. Michael in Island of Barbados. To wife Ann Oxley, she to educate his sons William and John.
Execs: Sd. wife Ann, Dr. Jas. Hendy, Daniel Wiles, Samuel Laraque Bruce and William Read.
Wit: Henry Walter Punnett, John Ulysses Thorne.

MAGUIRE, PHILIP. Jan 30, 1813. March 2, 1813. 4.259.
Bequeaths to his father, each of his bros. and to his sisters children (no names given) if bro. Hugh is dead, his share to his children. To Margaret Irwin. To Mitchal McBarson.
Execs: William Wray, I. Parke and Bernard Conway.
Wit: Luke Reilly. Henry Monaghan of Phila., blacksmith, affirmed.

BICKLEY, MARY. Phila. Widow. Feb 2, 1791. March 4, 1813. 4.260.
Estate to her seven children namely: Margaret, Elizabeth, Abraham, Robert, Hannah, Lydia and Isaac, property in Phila. in tenure of bro. Stephen Shewell. Father Robert Shewell and mother Elizabeth Shewell, both dec'd. Late husband and Abraham Bickley.
Execs: Two sons Abraham and Robert Bickley and dau. Margaret Bickley.
Wit: Peter Thomson, Nath'n. Falconer, Peter Thomson, Jr.
Letters granted to Robert Bickley.

COCHRAN, ELIZABETH. Phila. Gentlewoman. Feb 20, 1813. March 5, 1813. 4.263.
To niece Sarah Donnell. To each of the seven youngest children of Nathaniel and Sarah Donnell and to Sarah Donnell the dau. To John Mitchell, her nephew and to his dau. Mary Wilcox. To Catharine Keppele, wife of Michael Keppele, and to each of their five eldest children and to Mary Ann their youngest dau. To Elizabeth Caldwell, sister of Mrs. Keppele. To nephew Francis Feariss and to his two sisters (not named). To Mary Smith, her niece and to Eleanor Smith. To the two daus. of John and Mary Greener and their five sons. To the four granddaus. of Randal Mitchel. To Susan Jours(?). To Rachel Gardner. To widow January. To widow MacPherson. To Hannah Johnston. To Elizabeth Redman. To Margaret Pinyard. To Mrs. Esther Pepper. To Mrs. Elizabeth Greener.
Exec: Friend John Greener.
Wit: W. W. Woodward, James Darrach, William Major. Letters granted to John Greiner.

HARVEY, MARGARET. Phila. Widow. Dec 29, 1812. March 2, 1813. 4.264.
To son Thomas Harvey. To dau. Margaret, wife of Joseph Shankland of Phila., taylor. Residue to grandchildren William and Charles Shankland.
Exec: Sd. Joseph Shankland.
Wit: Anna Thomas, Emma Wilson.

MODE, HENRY. Laberer. Feb 23, 1813. March 10, 1813. 4.265.
Interest of estate to wife Mary Mode, at her death to his daus. Pachens and Elizabeth.
Execs: Friend Jas. Champean and Jesse Brown.
Wit: Jonathan Trusty, Saml. Cock.

BAISCH, JACOB. Germantown. Phila. Cedar Cooper. June 28, 1809. March 10, 1813. 4.266.
Estate to wife Catharine Baisch. Legacy to son George Baisch, and at death of wife estate to son Joseph Baisch and dau. Margaret Engle (formerly Margaret Baisch).
Execs: Sd. wife Catharine and son Joseph Baisch.
Wit: Woolery Fryhoffer, Thomas Waterman, Peter Buckius or Backius.

COMING or CUMMINGS, JOHN. Phila. April 11, 1810. March 9, 1813. 4.267.

Bequeaths all estate to wife Catharine Comings, appointing her sole extx.
Exec: Wife Catharine Comings.
Wit: Zane W. Thomson, Sidney Jane Houston, Rachel Somers, Johannes Killeher.

KILLHOWER, MARTIN. Passyunk Twp. Phila. Co. Farmer. May 3, 1812. March 13, 1813. 4.268.
Estate to wife Sarah Kilhower, at her death, to his seven children viz: Catharine, Michael, Elizabeth, Adam, Martin, Nancy and Sarah.
Execs: Wife Sarah and son Michael.
Wit: Frederick Vollmer, Edward Pole, Jr.
Codicil May 29, 1812. Legacy to Elizabeth Marshall out of her mother Catharine Stineman's estate.
Wit: Same as to will.

UNROD, JACOB. Germantown. Phila. Co. Collar Maker. Feb 22, 1813. March 16, 1813. 4.269.
Legacy to daus. Ann and Elizabeth, also property where he dwells adj. Peter Keyser's lot so long as they remain single. To sons Jacob and Frederick Unrod. To German Reformed Presbyterian Church in Germantown, opposite the Market House. Residue of estate to daus.: Ann, Elizabeth, Catharine, Sarah, Susan and Mary and to son Frederick Unrod. Sd. daus. Catharine, Sarah, Mary and Susan to be charged with the sums lent to them or their husbands. No charge to be made for support of grandchildren who lived with him.
Execs: Sd. dau. Elizabeth Unrod, friend Seth Craig of Phila., sadler, and Charles Backius (his son-in-law).
Wit: John Conrad, William Keyser, Jacob Clemens.

HARRIS, HANNAH. Phila. Single Woman. Dec 31, 1812. March 19, 1813. 4.272.
Discharges bro. Jesse from payment of debts. Bequeaths to bro. Samuel and to his wife. To bro. George. To bro. Thomas. To sisters Mary Harris, Abigail Harris, Sarah Bonsley. To sister-in-law Elizabeth Harris (widow). To niece Sidney Wells. To niece Hannah Harris, dau. of Jesse. To sister Mary's dau. Hannah. To sister's dau. Jane Boyce. Chairs in care of Samuel Grub to sister-in-law sd. Elizth. Harris. To niece Hannah Harris, dau. of sister Mary. To Rebecca Harris, dau. of bro. Joseph Harris. To Mary, wife of Samuel Richards of Phila., silver smith. To Sarah Hoops and her mother Mary Hoops.

Execs: Friends Joseph Townsend of Phila., shoe dealer and Benjamin Mears of same place, brush maker.
Wit: Samuel Richards, S. S., John Warrington.

MITCHELL, MARY. Phila. Jan 28, 1813. March 25, 1813. 4.274.
Bequeaths to Mrs. Sarah Bunner and Mrs. Rebecca Leaming, her property in Phila., owned in common with Mrs. Elizabeth Brown. To Mrs. Elizabeth Caldwell and Mrs. Lydia Smith, property also held with Mrs. Elizabeth Brown. To Elisha Pierson of NJ, ground near Trenton. To Clarissa Pierson, dau. of Daniel Pierson. To Daniel Pierson of Morristown, NJ. To Mrs. Mary Austin. To Thomas L. Smith and Elizabeth Smith, children of James S. Smith. To Mrs. Margaret Stocker. To Thomas F. Leaming. To Mrs. Roberts. To Thomas Bradford, Jr. To Dr. Pierson of Morristown, NJ, nephew of Daniel Pierson. To Sarah Pierson, dau. of Dr. Pierson. To Dr. Charles Pierson, son of Daniel Pierson. To Mrs. Jones, niece of Daniel Pierson, a ring inscribed with names of John and Ann Pierson. To negro servant Chloe. Minature picture of Mrs. Fuller to Mrs. Leaming, at her death to Mrs. Berry. To John C. Stocker and to James S. Smith.
Execs: Sd. John C. Stocker and James S. Smith.
Wit: Samuel Shoemaker, John Twaddell, Joseph Steel.

EDWARDS, MARGARET. Phila. School Keeper. Feb 16, 1797. March 26, 1813. 4.277.
To Christ Church. To sister Mary Hilbourn. To Mrs. Mary Conner. Picture of Rev. Jacob Duche to James Sawer. To Betsy Sawer, dau. of James. To Nancy Redman, dau. of Dr. John Redman. To Mrs. Catharine Smith, wife of Capt. Samuel Smith. to Mrs. Catharine Keple, wife of Adam Kepple. To Rebecca Howard, Jr. To niece Betsy West. To Mrs. Mary White, the Bishop's wife. To Mrs. Sarah Govett. To Mrs. Elizabeth Finney. To niece Rachel Roberts. To each of Betsy West's children, to her son James West and to her dau. Eliza West.
Execs: Friend James Sawer and nephew William West.
Wit: James Sawer, Michael Connor and Mary Connor.

CAMPBELL, MARY. Phila. Widow. Feb 2, 1811. Jan 21, 1813. 4.278.
All estate to dau. Sarah Campbell, appointing her sole extx.
Exec: Dau. Sarah Campbell.
Wit: John Gilliard, Isaac Wampole.

SHALLCROSS. LEONARD. Oxford Twp. Phila. Co. Jan 4, 1808. April 1, 1813. 4.279.
To son John, plantation bought of John Hall &c. To sons Leonard, William, Thomas and Benjamin, each the house they now occupy. Houses in Laetitia Court and Water Street, lot in Phila., to be sold, proceeds to daus. Hannah Paul, Mary Kirkner, Martha Knight and Rachel Johnson. To dau.-in-law Sarah, wife of son Benjamin. To Mary Yeates.
Execs: Sons Leonard and Benjamin and sons-in-law Thos. Paul and Joseph Kirkner.
Wit: John Barndollar, Wm. Yeates, Watson Atkinson.

ATTMORE, ANNE. Phila. Widow. May 5, 1812. April 3, 1813. 4.280.
To granddau. Anne Robinson, who now lives with her. To children of dau. Mary Robinson (including sd. granddau. Anne Robinson). To friends Isaac W. Morris of Phila., brewer and Samuel Bettle of same city, merchant in trust for dau. sd. Mary Robinson (wife of James Robinson, Jr., of Washington Co., Rhode Island). Mentions bond given to him by John Biddle.
Codicil May 9, 1812. Mentions late husband Caleb Attmore &c.
Wit: William Willson, Richard Smith and Peter Thomson.
Execs: Sd. Isaac W. Morris and Samuel Bettle, also to be guardians of children of sd. dau. Mary.
Wit: James Lynd, Peter Thomson.

ABINGTON, SUSANNA PENEOPE. Phila. Widow in her 77th year. Nov 4, 1812. April 6, 1813. 4.286.
To Rebecca Love now living with her. Shares in Farmers and Mechanics Bank to friend Patience Marshall, wife to Charles Marshall, Sr. To PA Hospital also her fathers likeness drawn by Mr. Pine. To Phineas Bond and his sister Miss R. Bond.
Exec: Sd. Rebecca Love.
Wit: Joseph S. Lewis, Henry Kuhl.

WORTHINGTON, BENJAMIN. Byberry Twp. Phila. Co. March 24, 1813. April 7, 1813. 4.287.
Land bounded by that of John Larrew and John Stevens. To sons Asa and Enos Worthington. To son Joshua Worthington, he to pay to sons John, James, Mahlon, Benjamin, dau. Martha Worthington Tomlinson, wife of John Tomlinson and to son Asa Worthington. To dau. Hannah Walton.
Execs: Sons John, James and Joshua Worthington.

Wit: George H. Pawling of Moreland Twp., Phila. Co., accomptant and James Worthington.

HILL, MARGARET. Northern Liberties. Phila. Spinster. Feb 7, 1813. April 13, 1813. 4.290.
To sister Elizabeth Wilson, at her death, to her children. To children of dec'd bros. Richard Hill and John Hill. To niece Elizabeth Wilson, Jr. To nephew Joseph Wilson. To niece Margaret Hill.
Execs: Sister Elizabeth Wilson and nephew Joseph Wilson.
Wit: John Evans, Robert W. or H. Graham, John Lare.
Letters granted to Jos. Wilson.

SMITH, JOSEPH B. Northern Liberties. Phila. Late one of the bookkeepers in the Bank of N. America. Oct 3, 1812. April 10, 1813. 4.291.
Provides for wife Frances Smith. Son Samuel, daus. Rachel, Frances and Mary.
Execs: Also guardians of minor children, sd. wife Francs Smith and friends Thomas Norton of Northern Liberties and Thomas Wistar of sd. city.
Wit: James Mitchell, William Andrews.

SELICK or SILECK, JOHN. Southwark. Phila. Co. Sept 29, 1805. April 15, 1813. 4.293.
To wife Elizabeth Selick. To children: John, Sarah, Joseph, Hannah and Louisa Selick.
Wit: Same as will.,
Execs: Wife Elizabeth Selick, if wife should die during minority of children, appoints nephew John Selick of Lunenburg, Nova Scotia as guardian.
Wit: Francis Daymon, Philip Tear, Edward Hay.
Codicil Sept 29, 1805. Since signing will, wife is in state of pregnancy.

ORR, ROBERT. Moyamensing Twp. Phila. Co. Plaisterer. Dec 12, 1811. April 13, 1813. 4.295.
To grandsons and children of son James and his wife Mary, viz: William and James Orr.
Exec: George McKnight, grocer of Southwark.
Wit: James Robinson, David Williams and John League.

TOWNSEND, NOE. Northern Liberties. Phila. Dealer in Grain. Sept 22, 1810. Dec 21, 1812. 4.296.
Wife Elizabeth Townsend to have use of estate, at her death, to dau. Sarah Smith.
Execs: Son-in-law, Joseph Smith and sd. wife Elizabeth Townsend.
Wit: Robert Whitehead, Casper Sybert.

WIRTZ, CHRISTIAN. Phila. Gentleman. Feb 19, 1813. April 26, 1813. 4.297.
Provides for wife Mary Wirtz. Mentions Agreement between himself and James Irwin of Cumberland Co., PA. To dau. Hannah Wager, wife of Philip Wager.
Exec: Grandson Peter Wager of Phila., merchant.
Wit: Samuel Macferran, Michael W. Ash.

BISHOPHBERGER, JACOB. Northern Liberties. Phila. Co. Yeoman. Feb 8, 1813. April 20, 1813. 4.299.
Provides for wife Susannah Bishophberger. To son Jacob and dau. Christina Bishophberger. To grandsons Jacob and George Bishophberger.
Execs: Friends John L. Shaffer, Northern Liberties, house carpenter and Joseph Slingloff, Jr., bricklayer, of sd. Liberties.
Wit: Jacob Long, John Springer. Jacob Belsterling, affirmed.

YATES, ANN. Phila. Jan 10, 1813. April 26, 1813. 4.300.
To daus. Harriot Conway and Catharine Ligers or Legers and their children. To son John Yates of Baltimore.
Exec: Bro. Thomas Armat.
Wit: Christopher Fest, Thomas Armat, Eliza Fest.

SHEED, ISABELLA. Southwark. Phila. Widow of William Sheed, late of Phila. Sept 19, 1803. April 26, 1813. 4.301.
Bequeaths to William Sheed, the younger, son of William and Mary Sheed, and great grandson of her late husband, should he die under age, to his bro. or sister. To Abi Kite, dau. of Benjamin and Rebecca Kite.
Execs: John Hutchinson and Benjamin Kite.
Wit: Jeremiah Paul, Jacob Thomas, Michael Wightinburg.
Codicil March 5, 1808, June 22, 1810, April 18, 1813. Provides for Mary Sheed widow of late husband Wm. Sheed's grandson Wm.
Wit: Hannah Thomson, Jeremiah Paul, Rebecca Kite, Ann Wood, Jacob Thomas.

WEGMAN, MARGARET. Formerly of Phila., now residing in Borough of Lancaster. Widow. Aug 5, 1811. April 26, 1813. 4.305.
To daus. of bro. Philip Wager, viz: Margaret, the wife of William I. Baker, Sarah Wager, Elizabeth, Henrietta, Julianna and Sophia Maria Wager. To friend Elizabeth Mannon. Bond from John Hinkle. To niece Mary Seelig. To John William Wager, son of nephew John Wager. To nephew Peter Wager, son of bro. Philip. To Maria C. Reigart son of the daus. of late niece Mary Reigart. To Mary Seelig, Peggy Williamson, Hannah Humphries and Elizabeth Wager, daus. of late bro. John Wager. All residue to nephews and nieces, to wit: Peter, Geo., William Stein Wager, Philip Stein Wager, Margaret Baker, Sarah, Elizabeth, Henrietta, Juliana, Hannah and Sophia Maria, sons and daus. of sd. bro. Philip Wager.
Execs: Bro. Philip and nephew Peter Wager.
Wit: George Graff, Em Reigart, Philip Gloninger. Mary Lawrence of Phila., widow and William Gertrard of Phila., hatter, affirmed.

WRIGHT, WILLIAM. Lower Dublin Twp. Phila. Co. Mason. April 3, 1813. April 24, 1813. 4.307.
Provides for wife Elenor and children namely: Mary, Sarah, Enoch, George, Elizabeth, Rachel, Morgan, Phebe and Hiram.
Execs: Wife Elenor, son Enoch and son-in-law Daniel McVeaugh.
Wit: Amos Dungan, Mary Hamilton.

DAVIS, CALEB. Kingsessing. Phila. Co. Esq. March 24, 1813. April 28, 1813. 4.308.
Bequeaths to wife Lydia, ground in Phila., bought of James Jones with all buildings &c. Property devised to servant boy George Gesner. After decease of sd. wife, to Caleb Davis West, son of Thomas West, dec'd, and to children of bro. George Davis. To Elders and Overseers of Springfield Meeting of Friends, Delaware Co., for repairing grave yard &c. To servant girl Maria Gesner. To late servants namely Emericus Bender and Mary, his sister and to Catharine Colin. To sister Sarah West. To Joel West, son of sister Sarah. To niece Esther, dau. of sister Sarah West. To Rebecca, dau. of sister Sarah West. To Susanah Thomas. To nephew George Thomas. To niece Rebecca Thomas. To Patience, wife of John Vactor and to Mary, wife of Job Helms.
Execs: Wife Lydia Davis and friend Joseph Bunting of Darby, Delaware Co., and William Hill of Kingsessing, they also to be guardians of sd. George Gesner.
Wit: Edward Garrigues, George Donehower, John Hill.

WRIGHT, REBECCA. Lower Dublin Twp. Phila. Co. Spinster. June 16, 1807. April 24, 1813. 4.313.
To sisters Rachel Wright and Sarah Potts. To nieces Rebecca Potts, Sarah Wright and Esther Wright. To Trustees of Baptist Church at Penepack. To her bros. Joseph, John, William, Thomas and Enoch.
Exec: Bro. Joseph Wright.
Wit: John Watts, Margaret Watts.

BOUGHMAN, AARON. Southwark. Phila. Co. Windsor Chair Maker. April 31*[sic]*, 1813. April 26, 1813. 4.314.
To bro. Peter Boughman. All residue to mother Ann Boughman &c. to sister Ann Boughman, Jr., of Wilmington, DE.
Execs: Friend James Stuart of Phila., grocer, and aunt Rebecca Brevard of same city, widow.
Wit: Reuben Stevens, Sarah Hendry.

WALTER, PETER. Northern Liberties. Phila. Biscuit Maker. Aug 12, 1809. April 29, 1813. 4.315.
To dau. Sophia Dixon. Residue to wife Hannah Walter, at her death to son Peter and dau. Hannah Walter.
Exec: Sd. wife Hannah.
Wit: Robert Whitehead, Hannah Eyre. Signed John Peter Walter.

LLOYD, ROBERT. Northern Liberties. Phila. Co. House Carpenter. March 18, 1811. April 9, 1814. 4.317.
To father, William Lloyd, his property in Northern Liberties, bounded by ground now or late of John Coburn.
Exec: Sd. father, William Lloyd.
Wit: Jacob Miller, William Levis and George Sterr.

WALKER, JOSEPH. Phila. Merchant. Nov 5, 1812. May 3, 1813. 4.318.
To wife Beulah Walker, dau. of George Vanlier, Esq. To son John V. L. Walker, property in Phila. conveyed to him (Joseph Walker) by owners of estate of Benjamin and Elizabeth Shoemaker, dec'd, also ground devised to him by his late father Emanuel Walker, purchased by him of Henry Gurney bounded by ground of Mahlon Hutchinson and William Craig, dec'd, also ground granted on ground rent by him to Benajah A. Farquhar, being part of lot, which John, William, Frances and Hannah Laraner conveyed to bro. Samuel Walker. Lot conveyed by him to Edward Mott. Property in Burlington, NJ, purchased of execs. of Manuel Eyre, dec'd. Lot in sd. city purchased of Joseph McIlvaine, Esq., also that

purchaed of Thomas P. Cope, assignee of Barker and Ansley, now rented to Caleb Gaskill, property formerly of George Painter, property bought of Brazilla Deaton. Land purchased in company with uncle Joseph Walker, dec'd, as the property of Adam Mendinhall, Co. of Gloucester, NJ, conveyed to him by William Borden and Mahlon Budd, High Sheriff. To bro. Samuel Walker, cousin William Blakey, Jr., and bro.-in-law Thomas Hutchinson in trust, for dau. Elizabeth, property in Phila., granted to Michael Murray, property in Phila. purchased of Robert Coltman, property formerly estate of John Fairpoux, property purchased of Daniel Burnett, of John Brown, exec. of George Michael Goodman, dec'd. Property in Burlington purchaesd of Jesse Thomas and others, assignees of Smith and Jones, now rented to Lemuel Howell for a Tavern, other property in Burlington purchased of George West, of Miriam Cochell and of Anna Redman, dec'd, at death of sd. dau. Elizabeth, to her children. Legacy to sister Sarah Paxson and to her children. To nephew Joseph W. Paxson, son of sd. sister Sarah Paxson, property in Burlington, purchased of widow of John Lar Zelere. To Mahlon Paxson, husband of sister Sarah. Bond given by sd. Mahlon Paxson to William Blakey, Jr., &c. Annuity to sister Nancy C. Hutchinson. To niece Ann Eliza Minnick, dau. of sister Beulah Minnick, property in Phila., purchased of Jonathan Carmalt, Jr. To bro. Samuel Walker, property in Kensington &c.
Execs: Bro., Samuel Walker, cousin, William Blakey, Jr., son of Joshua Blakey of Middletown, Bucks Co. and bro.-in-law Thomas Hutchinson of Bucks Co., husband of sister Nancy. Son when of age to be co-exec. Samuel Walker, guardian of son John V. L. Walker and dau. Elizabeth Walker.
Wit: Abraham Stein, Frederick Beates and Tobias Schoenheit.

ST. JOHN, CATHARINE. Wife of Thomas St. John, Bordentown, NJ. April 15, 1811. May 12, 1813. 4.327.
Late father, Frederick Kuhl, late of Phila., gentleman. To sd. husband Thomas St. John, all estate left her by her sd. father.
Wit: Abraham Stein, Frederick Beates.

SIMES, SAMUEL. Phila. Accomptant. April 9, 1813. April 28, 1813. 4.328.
Bro. James Simes. All estate to wife Jane R. Simes.
Execs: Sd. wife, Jane and friend Thomas Mitchell, of Phila., conveyancer.
Wit: John Morris, James Peale, Jr.
Letters granted to Thomas Mitchell.

RUSH, BENJAMIN, M.D. and Profesor of Medicine in University of PA Jan 18, 1812. April 30, 1813. 4.330.
Leaves to his wife Julia Rush, his farm called Lydenham near Phila., to receive income &c. for support of herself, her minor sons and dau. Julia Rush, at her death to his children. Son John's share in trust while in his present insane state. Great great grandfather, John Rush formerly an officer in Oliver Cromwell's Army. Sons: Dr. James Rush, Richard Rush, Benjamin Rush, Samuel Rush and William Rush. Legacy to servant William Bowen.
Execs: Sd. wife Julia Rush and sons Dr. James Rush and Benjamin Rush.
Wit: Philip Syng, Physick, and John S. Dorsey.
Letters granted to Benjamin Rush.

COX, JOHN T. Phila. House Carpenter. April 4, 1813. May 8, 1813. 4.332.
To wife Mary Cox. If she marries, to his children.
Execs: Sd. wife Mary Cox and friends John Hutchinson and Samson Davis.
Wit: Sarah Ogden, Thomas Hoskin.

IVES, JOHN. Phila. House Carpenter. May 5, 1813. May 18, 1813. 4.333.
Estate to wife Pamelia Ives, at her death to the heirs of his bro.
Exec: Sd. wife Pamelia Ives.
Wit: Mary Clifford, Kezia Long.

MIFFLIN, JOHN. Phila. Oct 24, 1812. May 20, 1813. 4.334.
To Dr. Caspar Wistar and Edward Burd, Esquires in trust. To wife Clementina, children: Sarah, John, Elizabeth and Charles Mifflin, last two named are minors.
Execs: Dr. Casper Wistar and Edward Burd.
Wit: Timothy Blake, James Sawer.

MILLER, JOHN GEORGE. Formerly of Rommelspack in Wurtenburg in Germany, now of Northern Liberties. Phila. Baker. Feb 26, 1805. May 20, 1813. 4.336.
Interest of all estate to wife Catharine Miller, at her death to his bro. John Jacob Miller and two sisters Anna Barbara and Barbara, now or late of Wurtenberg and to his wife's bros. and sisters (names not given).
Execs: Wife Catharine and friends John Adolph and John Diffenback of sd. Liberties.
Wit: John Jordan, Isaac Wampole.

WAGER, PHILIP. Phila. Merchant. Feb 21, 1813. May 19, 1813. 4.337.
Provides for wife Hannah Wager. Residue to his children viz: Peter and George Wager, Margaretta Baker, Sarah, Elizabeth, William S., Juliana, Philip S., Hannah S. and Sophia Wager and to his six grandchildren (children of dec'd dau. Maria) to wit: Maria, Ann, Henrietta, Philip Wager, Margaretta and Susanna Reigart and James and Hannah W. Smith (children of dec'd dau. Amy).
Execs: Son Peter Wager and sons-in-law Adam Reigart, Jr., and Wm. I. Baker.
Wit: Plunket F. Glentworth, John Perkin.

KEYSER, JOHN. Germantown. Phila. Cordwainer. Feb 10, 1803. May 15, 1813. 4.341.
Wife Elizabeth to have use and profits of estate, at her death to children viz: Jacob and Abraham Keyser, Anna Weaver, Charles Keyser and Mary Heisler, the wife of William Heisler.
Execs: Sons Jacob, Abraham and Charles Keyser.
Wit: William Keyser, Joseph Gorgas.

MARPLE, JESSE. Lower Dublin Twp. Phila. Co. Carpenter. March 22, 1813. May 19, 1813. 4.343.
To his father and mother Edward and Christena Marple, at decease of both parents, to his bros. and sisters: Joseph Marple, Phebe Gibeson, Sarah Roberts, Joshua Marple, John Marple, Thomas and Ann Marple.
Execs: Bro. John Marple and Joshua Jones, Esq.
Wit: Richard Burke, Amos Dungan.

HUGHES, DANIEL. Phila. Lumber Merchant. April 16, 1813. May 25, 1813. 4.345.
Annuity to bro. William Hughes of Northampton Co., at his death to friend Jonathan Knight of Northern Liberties, lumber merchant. Provides for wife Mary, at her death to Charity School of Phila. and the Adelphi Charity School, Northern Liberties.
Exec: Friend Jonathan Knight.
Wit: Peter A. Browne, John Bonsall.

LINNINGTON, MARIA. Phila. Widow. Feb 26, 1813. May 31, 1813. 4.346.
To daus.: Esther Linnington, Sarah Shewell, wife of Thomas Shewell and Mary Linnington. Dau. Esther to have income of house and lot in

Northern Liberties, so long as she remains single, residue to sd. daus. Sarah and Mary. Legacy to grandchild Mary Shewell.
Execs: Son-in-law Thomas Shewell and her bro. Dr. George De Benneville.
Wit: Robert Barnhill, Samuel Jones.

DELAUNAY, PETER. Phila. May 28, 1813. May 31, 1813. 4.348.
To wife Josephine Verrier. To son Peter Delaunay. To children of son John Delaunay. To child of late son Robert Delaunay, called Julia Delaunay. To son John Delaunay.
Execs: Friend John Lapeyre living at the Rising Sun, Northern Liberties. Sd. wife Josephine Verrier to be guardian of son Peter Delaunay.
Wit: A. Farrowilh(?), I. Ribaut.

BAMENT, HANNAH. Phila. Widow of John Bament. June 30, 1809. June 2, 1813. 4.350.
Bequeaths her house in Phila. (devised to her by her former husband Samuel Snowden) to her dau. Mary wife of Peter Miercken, at her death to her two daus. Catharine and Josephine Meircken. All residue to son William Bament, whom she appoints sole exec.
Exec: Son William Bament.
Wit: Josiah Siddons, Thomas Mitchell.

TRUMAN, RICHARD. Phila. Nov 9, 1808. June 7, 1813. 4.352.
To his four children viz: Mary Sikes Truman, Isabella Bewley Truman, Abigail Truman and Thomas Sikes Truman, all his estate.
Execs: Bro. James Truman of Phila. tin plate worker and friend John Pechin of same city, collector of taxes, sd. bro. and friend to be guardians of such children as are minors.
Wit: Joseph Moulder, Peter Thomson.

DELANY, MARGARET. Widow of Sharp Delany. Sept 23, 1811. May 22, 1813. 4.354.
Estate to Richard Peters, the younger, of Phila. in trust, he to pay rents &c. to her two daus. Ann and Mary Delany, at death of sd. daus. in trust for benefit of her right heirs.
Exec: Sd. Richard Peters, the younger.
Wit: Thomas Robinson, William Graham.

BOOK 5

deESQUILBEL, PEDRO BERNARDO. Captain in the Royal Army. May 26, 1813. June 14, 1813. 5.1.
Wife Donna Manuela Castaneda, by whom he has two children, one named Manuel who is married in Lima and the other Maria de los Delores married to Don Francisco Espelius, Captain of a Frigate in the Royal Navy of Spain, now residing in Cadiz, to whom he leaves all estate. Exec. in this country Don Joseph Bruno Magdalena, formerly secretary to the Spanish Legation in the United States and to what concerns his estate in the Peninsula and other Spanish Dominions he appoints his wife and in default of her, his son-in-law Don Francisco Espelius. Owes money to John Dubarry of this city, merchant, he to settle the Baltimore business. To Mrs. Maria Dixon.
Codicil May 29, 1813. Appoints Anton's de Mendoza, an exec. also.
Wit: Bme. Renquenet, Josef Bruno Magdalena, Peter S. DuPonceau.
Execs: Don Joseph Bruno Magdalena, his wife and son-in-law Don Francisco Espelius.
Wit: Peter Stephen DuPonceau, Notary Public, Don Antonio de Mendoza, Capt. of a Frigate in the Spanish Navy, James Julian, Robert Malenfaut, Edward D. Coxe and John Francis Canonge.

WOOD, SARAH. Northern Liberties. Phila. Widow. April 24, 1813. June 17, 1813. 5.5.
Dau. Sarah Geyger, the wife of George Geyger, to have use of all estate.
Exec: Friend William Britton of Northern Liberties, lumber merchant.
Wit: R. Whitehead, John Hellings.

JOHNSON, LYDIA. Phila. Spinster. Nov 30, 1811. June 16, 1813. 5.6.
To friend Benjamin R. Morgan, Esq. To Elizabeth Smith (aunt to sd. Benjn. R. Morgan). To Lydia Beakes (dau. of Nathan Beakes living near Trenton) a silver can formerly belonged to Hannah Beakes, aunt of sd. Lydia. To friend Lydia Hollinshead, now living in Burlington (dau. of late Edmund Hollinshead, the elder, dec'd). To Atlantic Allen, a young woman that formerly lived with her and to her dau. Lydia Allen. In trust to the Treasurer of Monthly Meeting of Friends of Phila., Northern District. To cousin Anna Thomson (dau. of late Peter Thomson, the elder and cousin Hannah, his wife) sd. Anna to pay annuity to her mother, at her death to her bro. Peter, he to continue payment to his mother, sd. Hannah Thomson. To Sarah Biddle Thomson (dau. of sd. cousin Peter Thomson and his late wife Rebecca). To Hannah Thomson, Jr., also dau. of sd.

Peter and Rebecca. Releases cousin John Thomas from debt. To Dr. John D. Thomas (son of sd. John Thomas). Cousin Thomas P. Cope. To cousin Mary Cope (wife of sd. Thomas P.).
Execs: Cousins Thomas P. Coope and Peter Thomson.
Wit: Edward McCam, Benjamin C. Binder.

KUNCKLE, CHRISTIAN. Northern Liberties. Phila. Shop Keeper. Sept 26, 1793. June 22, 1813. 5.10.
Wife Catharine Kunckle to have interest of estate, she to support and educate his children namely: Mary, John, Margaret, Catharine and Ann Kunckle.
Execs: Wife Catharine, his bro. John Kunckle and friend Richard Whitehead, in case of death of execs. he appoints his friends Lawrence Sickle, Abraham Wilt and George Forepaugh.
Wit: Mahlon Bennett, John Wharton, Robert Whitehead.
Letters granted to Catharine Kunckle.

HARPER, JOHN. Phila. Gentleman. May 4, 1811. June 25, 1813. 5.12.
To wife Margaret the income of his estate. To John Harper Smith, son of John and Lohra Smith. To two grandsons Peter and William Harper, sons of Thomas Harper.
Execs: Son-in-law Thomas Harper and friend Matthew Lawler of sd. city, Esq.
Wit: Jacob Vodges, Abraham Shoemaker.

HAMILTON, WILLIAM. Woodlands, Blockley Twp. Phila. Co. Sept 9, 1811. June 11, 1813. 5.13.
To niece Margaret Hamilton. To execs. in trust for niece Rebecca O'Brien, the wife of Francis O'Brien. To Frances Hilton. To George W. Hilton. To Hagar, a woman of colour in his family. To friends Dr. Thomas Parke and William Cramond. To nephew James Hamilton.
Execs: Nephew James Hamilton, friends Dr. Thomas Parke and William Cramond.
Wit: John Vaughan, Casper Wistar, Jr., Joseph Sansom, Frederick Smyth.

REINSEIMER, MAGDALENA. Kensington. Northern Liberties. Phila. Co. June 24, 1813. July 1, 1813. 5.15.
To son Christian Reinsimer the use of the dwelling house he now lives in, at his death to her grandchildren. To dau.-in-law Mary Reinseimer, the income of estate which she (Magdalene Reinseimer) has occupied after

her death to her children namely: Charles, Jacob, Mary, Susanna, Catharine and Sarah, also any that shall be born by the present marriage of son and his present wife Mary.
Execs: John Johnston (schoolmaster) and Martin Geiger (baker).
Wit: John Reap, George Miller.

BOWEN, JOSEPH. Phila. Co. District of Southwark. Grocer. March 23, 1804. July 9, 1813. 5.17.
Estate to wife Hannah Bowen, at her death to sons John and James Bowen.
Wit: William Campbell and Jacob Carman.

FARQUHAR, GEORGE. Late of the Island of Jamaica, at present in Phila., U.S.A., Dr. of Medicine. Dec 22, 1804. July 7, 1813. 5.17.
Interest of all property to his wife Elizabeth excepting following bequeaths: annuity to his mother in Aberdeen, at death of sd. wife, to his children, namely: Geo. Wildman Farquhar, Elizabeth Widowson Farquhar and the child with which wife is now pregnant.
Execs: Sd. wife Elizabeth and bro.-in-law Samuel Yorke of Phila., if wife marries, Samuel York to act as guardian.
Wit: Joshua Lippincott, Frederick Smith, Charles Smith.
Letters granted to Elizabeth Farquhar.

SHEETZ, CHRISTIAN. Kensington. Phila. Co. June 19, 1813. July 14, 1813. 5.19.
Wife Magdalena to have income of estate in Kensington, Hanover Street, also house in Northern Liberties. Dau. Christianna estate bought of John C. Otto and others. Daus. Elizabeth and Hannah each to have half his estate bought of John Dickerson and Michael Lieb. Son Peter to have lot bought of Joseph Baldwin, also small house and lot bought of John Baldwin, should Hannah the wife of sd. son Peter out live him, she to have the income of his share, at her death to their children.
Execs: Sd. son Peter Sheetz and Henry Rihl.
Wit: John Johnson, John Gardy.

MULLEN, JANE. Phila. Widow. Oct 4, 1810. July 20, 1813. 5.20.
All estate to son William Mullen, whom she appoints sole exec.
Exec: Son William Mullen.
Wit: Thomas Mitchell, Alexr. Tod.

KER, SUSANNA. Phila. June 8, 1812. July 26, 1813. 5.21.

All estate to sister Elizabeth Ker, appointing her sole extx.
Exec: Sister Elizabeth Ker.
Wit: Hannah Willis, John Eckert, Thomas Willis.

RUTTER, JOHN JACOB. Phila. Labourer. March 12, 1810. July 28, 1813. 5.22.
To son John Jacob Rutter, one dollar. All residue to wife Catharine Rutter, at her death to nephew Jacob Rutter who now lives with him and son of the sd. John Jacob Rutter.
Execs: Sd. wife and friend Christopher Zell.
Wit: Jacob C. Stout, Christopher Zell.
Letters granted to Catharine Rutter.

DUMOUTET, JOHN BAPTISTE. A native of the Department of Cher, France, but residing for some time past in Phila. May 25, 1813. July 23, 1813. 5.23.
Stock in trade in Charleston and Phila. to be valued &c. Property in Phila. purchaed of William Shannon with other property to William Y. Birch ---- in trust for dau. Jane Dumoutet. Property purchased from Peter Neff in Frankford Co. of Phila. to sd. trustees for dau. Emma Dumoutet. Other property in Frankford to trustees for dau. Amelia Dumoutet. To sd. trustees his stock in Farmers and Mechanics Bank, stock in U.S. Loan with bonds &c. for wife Elizabeth Dumoutet. To Ann O'Brien. Property he is entitled to from France, also a certain plantation in Northumberland Co., PA, to execs. in trust, they to sell &c.
Execs: Wife Elizabeth and dau. Jane Dumoutet.
Wit: W. W. Woodward, Abm. Small, William Delany.

LOGUE, MARY. Phila. April 13, 1813. July 22, 1813. 5.27.
To children viz: Patrick, Hugh and Mary Logue, Catherine Bibbins and Rosana Uncleson. To nephew James Logue.
Execs: Friends John Ward and Peter McGawley, both of Phila.
Wit: Daniel Hitchcock, William E. Manlove.

EDWARDS, JESSE. Oxford Twp. Phila. Co. Yeoman. June 9, 1812. July 28, 1813. 5.27.
Provides for wife Hannah Edwards. His property to his children namely: John, Jesse, Thomas K., and Hannah. Property formerly belonging to and now occupied by Lawrence Seates &c. Plan of property made by Christian Lehman in year 1756, devised to bro. John Edwards and himself (Jesse Edwards). To grandchildren Maria Elenor and Catharine

Crisman, interest to begin with date of John Fesmire's Bond. Land in VA, Co. of Culpepper, purchased of Samuel Moore, which was unlawfully sold for taxes, empowers Robert Brooke to sue for same, should it be recovered, to his three sons. To four children by late wife Sarah, interest commencing with Samuel Caster's Bond. Money from mother in Nova Scotia for benefit of step bro. Nathaniel Loafborrow's children.
Execs: Friends Nathan Whitman, the elder of Bristol Twp. and Nathan Harper of Frankford and son John Edwards, when of age, until that time, friend Robert Brooke to act as exec.
Wit: Jesse Comly, Ro. Brooks, John Deprefontaine. John Edwards having attained full age, he affirmed. June 26, 1814.

KIRKNER, JACOB. Borough of Frankford. Phila. Co. March 21, 1811. July 28, 1813. 5.31.
To wife Sarah, money bequeathed her by her mother, dec'd, also estate bequeathed her by her sister Abigail Wickersham, dec'd, with annuity &c. Residue to is three children: Joseph Kirkner, Mary Harper and Martha Gillingham.
Execs: Son Joseph and son-in-law Nathan Harper.
Wit: Watson Atkinson, Nathan Shoemaker.

KINYON, STEPHEN. Phila. July 7, 1813. Aug 10, 1813. 5.32.
All estate to Elizabeth Jinnings, widow, of sd. city, whom he appoints sole extx.
Exec: Elizabeth Jinnings.
Wit: Elizabeth McBride, Hannah Hires, John Hunt, Benjamin Severne. Letters granted to Elizabeth Jinins.

JACOBS, CHARLES. Phila. Co. Mariner. June 26, 1813. Aug 16, 1813. 5.33.
All estate to friend John King, Phila. Co., innkeeper. Appointing him exec.
Exec: John King.
Wit: Elizabeth Palmer, Richard Palmer.

WATTS, JOHN. Lower Dublin Twp. Phila. Co. March 10, 1812. Aug 5, 1813. 5.34.
Provides for wife Margaret Watts. Two younger daus. Frances and Mary Watts to live with sd. wife Margaret. To dau. Rachel Bennet. To nephew John Watts.
Execs: Wife Margaret and nephew John Watts.

Wit: Joshua Jones, Amos Duffield.

LAUCK, ANN MARTHA. Phila. Widow of David Lauck. July 21, 1813. Aug 20, 1813. 5.36.
Bequeaths furniture to dau. Hannah Miller.
Exec: Friend George Smith of Germantown.
Wit: Edwin A. Atlee, Conrad Wile, John Patterson.

McCAULEY, ANDREW. Phila. April 13, 1799. Aug 23, 1813. 5.37.
To bro. Robert McCauley. To nephew David McCauley. To niece Elizabeth Jervis. To niece Sarah McConnell, whom he appoints extx.
Exec: Sarah McConnell.
Wit: M. K. Stockwell, Joseph Knox.
Letters granted to Sarah Packhorn, late Sarah McConnell.

SMITH, PETER. Germantown. Phila. Co. Blacksmith. Aug 1, 1803. Aug 21, 1813. 5.37.
House where in he dwells with lots, to his son John, he to pay to daus. Susanna and Mary. All money to sd. children.
Execs: Son John and son-in-law Jacob Keyser.
Wit: Michael Lippert, Jacob Knorr, Jr.

ADAMS, PETER. Chief Boatswains Mate U. S. Frigate President. March 7, 1809. July 27, 1813. 5.39.
All estate to friend Atcheson Thompson of Southwark, Phila. Co., whom he appoints exec.
Exec: Friend Atcheson Thompson.
Wit: Hugh Morrisson, Richard Palmer.

GARRET, MORTON. Blockley. Phila. Co. Jan 17, 1813. Aug 24, 1813. 5.39.
Wife to have use of income from estate, at her death, to his eldest son Joseph Garrot, he to have plantation &c, in Blockley, subject to payment to his bros. and sisters, including his step sister Mary Clark, dau. of wife by her former husband. Residue of estate to all his children. Guardians of minor children and execs. of will, his wife and son Joseph. Property left him by relation Andrew Garrott late of Northern Liberties, Phila., dec'd.
Execs: Wife and son Joseph.
Wit: Algermon Roberts, Joseph McAdams.

Codicil July --, 1813. Purchased land of Samuel Fulton of Phila., merchant, being land he formerly sold to Jered Ingersoll. To grandson Morton, son of son William Garrett.
Wit: Same as to will.

ALLEN, JOHN E. Phila. May 20, 1805. Aug 28, 1813. 5.42.
To Sarah Allen, if living, the sum of one guinea, she having received of him a jointure, in full of all dower. To dau. Margaret Allen, which sum lies in lands of Nuns Quarter, Co. of Down, Ireland, the interest of it, paying her mother Sarah Allen, sd. jointure, which shall be paid dau. at dath of her mother. All residue to dau. Susanna Allen who has kept house for him for some years, appointing her extx.
Exec: Dau. Susanna Allen.
Wit: Thomas Young, Robert Gordon, Wm. Graham, Robt. Ross, Christian Curry.

CONRAD, JOHN, Phila. Worsted comber. Aug 11, 1801. Sept 4, 1813. 5.43.
All estate to wife Christina Conrad, at her death to the German Roman Catholic Church called the Holy Trinity Church of Phila., to be used for schooling poor children belonging to sd. congregation.
Execs: Sd. wife and friend Frederick Hailer.
Wit: R. Whitehead, Robert Whitehead, Benjamine Brown W.*[sic]*
Letters granted to Christina Conrad.

PEARSON, JAMES Phila. House Carpenter. Aug 17, 1813. Sept 1, 1813. 5.44.
Property in Phila. to eldest son Henry Paschall Pearson. To dau. Hannah Pearson. To dau. Jane Serrill, wife of George Serrill of Darby. To dau. Anna Pearson. To dau. Susan Powers. To dau. Martha B. Pearson. To execs. in trust for son James Hart Pearson. All residue to wife Susanna Pearson at, at her death to his eldest dau. Mary Pearson, the property wherein he now lives.
Execs: Sd. dau. Mary Pearson and son-in-law George Serrill.
Wit: John James, Ebenezer Betts.

TILLYER, WILLIAM. Moreland Twp. Phila. Co. Farmer. Feb 28, 1806. Sept 6, 1813. 5.47.
To only son William Tillyer. To daus. Mary Beans, Ann Ashton, Phoebe Krewson and Sarah Finney. Plantation in tenor of Thomas Helveson to be sold, monies to his sd. four daus., son-in-law Derrick Krewson.

Execs: Son William Tillyer, sons-in-law Thomas Beans and Joseph Finney.
Wit: Christopher Vanasdalen, Joseph Vanosten, Rudolph White.

EVANS, SUSANNA. Phila. July 13, 1813. Sept 6, 1813. 5.49.
Interest of estate for support of her two sisters, Margaret and Lydia. To Martha Evans wife of bro. Edward Evans. After death of sd. sisters, to Catharine, dau. of Griffith Jones. To niece Sarah Evans and her bros. John and Thomas Evans. Residue of estate after death of sd. sisters, to nieces Catharine James, Susanna Munn, Sarah Evans and Lydia Evans.
Exec: George Williams.
Wit: Asa Elkinton, Esther Williams.

KUHN, JOHN. Phila. Shopkeeper. July 1, 1807. Sept 7, 1813. 5.50.
To wife Elizabeth, all his estate, at her death to her children: John, Magdalen and George Kern.
Execs: Sd. wife Elizabeth and her son John Kern.
Wit: Robert Burkhart, Isaac Wampole.

PETERSON, NICHOLAS. Phila. Co. Mariner. Sept 26, 1811. Sept 6, 1813. 5.51.
All estate to friend John Connor of Southwark in sd. co., cordwainer, whom he appoints exec.
Exec: Friend John Connor.
Wit: John McLinchey, James McLinchey.

TURNER, WILLIAM. Phila. Merchant. March 22, 1808. Sept 7, 1813. 5.51.
To wife Abigail all his estate, consisting of two houses and lots in Phila., plantation in Northern Liberties of Phila. Land in Northumberland Co., ground rents &c. To son Joseph Turner. To son William A. Turner. To dau. Abby Ann.
Exec: Sd. wife Abigail.
Wit: Elliston Perot, John Perot, F. H. Brinton.

DUNN, JACOB. Phila. Shopkeeper. Sept 11, 1813. Sept 15, 1813. 5.53.
All estate to wife Rachel Dunn.
Execs: Sd. wife and friend John B. Wilson.
Wit: Robt. Whitehead, Saml. L. Wilson, Ellis Stokes.

PETERS, JOSEPH. Miles Town. Starting for Great Egg Harbour. April 11, 1812. Sept 13, 1813. 5.54.
To Mary Ann Peters, at Silas Wilsons. To Sybilla P. Wilson. To Rebecca Wilson dau. of Aa. Wilson. To Sarah Wilson dau. of Aa. Wilson. To each of George Peters (dec'd) five children. The balance to his Moravian Church or some other Charitable Institution. Balance due him at River La Plata. John Shepherd has done that business, John Evans can tell where to find him.
Execs: Friends John Wilson and John Maybin.
Wit: Robert Whitehead. Jacob Peters affirmed.

KEFFER, MARTIN. Kensington. Northern Liberties. Phila. Weaver. Aug 25, 1813. Sept 20, 1813. 5.55.
Use and profits of all estate to wife Mary Keffer, at her death, property to be sold and money to his children viz: Anthony Keffer and Rachel Dolin and grandchildren viz: John Keffer, Andrew Wilkinson, William and Margaret Dolin.
Execs: Son Anthony Keffer of Kensington and bro. John Keffer of Phila.
Wit: Isaac J. Kip, Jacob Smith.

SAY, BENJAMIN. Phila. Physician. June 12, 1808. May 17, 1813. 5.56.
To wife Miriam and his children: Thomas, Benjamin, Rebecca Ann, Caroline, William Penn and Miriam Say, his property in Phila., consisting of that bought of Daniel Hunter, of George Makem, of Patrick Dougherty, of Joseph Campbell, of James Morgan. Property in which John Ferraday now dwells. Property purchased of John Kane, of Daniel Hunter. Property in which Henry Rapsom lives. Property purchased of Joseph Jordan, of Michael Kenny, of Robert Adams, of James Kane, of Abraham Moore. His country house at the Cliffs on Schuylkill adj. Grays Ferry to be kept for use of his wife. Sd. wife Miriam Say to be guardian of children.
Codicil March 18, 1813. Property in tenure of William Dorans, in tenure of John Smith. Appoints his son Benjamin to be exec. also.
Wit: John Aitken, Benjamin S. Janney.
Execs: Sd. wife and son Thomas Say, mother Rebecca Say.
Wit: John Aitken, Barnaby Barnes.

GEISSE, RACHEL. Northern Liberties. Phila. Widow of Francis Geisse. May 27, 1807. Sept 22, 1813. 5.62.
To dau. Mary Denny, now wife of Philip Buckius. To son Lawrence Shissler, a legacy devised to her, by his father Casper Shisler. At death of

sd. Mary and Lawrence, to their children. All residue of estate to her daus. Wilhelmina Geisse and Ann Geisse.
Execs: Friends Peter Deal and James Whitehead.
Wit: Hannah Eyre, Robert Whitehead, Benjn. Brown W.
Codicil Dec 3, 1809. Wearing apparel to daus. Mary Buckius, Wilhelmina now Wilhelmina Buckius and Ann Geisse.
Wit: Robert Whitehead, Elizabeth Neff.

WILSON, ALEXANDER. Now of Phila. Aug 16, 1813. Sept 25, 1813. 5.64.
To father (no name given). To nephew William Duncan. All residue to Sarah Miller.
Execs: Daniel H. Miller and George Ord of Phila.
Wit: Henry L. Coryell, Susannah Jones.

ROE, McDERMOT MICHAL M. Late of Ireland, now in Phila. Sept 19, 1813. Sept 25, 1813. 5.65.
Estate to two daus. Honour and Mary McDermot Roe, wife Ann McDermott Row and bro. Patrick.
Execs: Peter McDurmed and Peter Philips of Phila. and Patrick Benson of NY.
Wit: Charles Fanning, James McGarant, John Dolan.
Letters granted to Peter McDermott.

PAGE, ROBERT N. Phila. July 28, 1812. June 23, 1813. 5.66.
To Robert Waln of Phila. merchant. To John Wharton also of sd. city, merchant. Residue to his bros.: Lewis, Peyton R., W. B. Page, Octavus A. and Hugh Nelson Page.
Execs: Friend Robert Waln and John Wharton.
Wit: Thomas Hope, Mary Linn.

LEFEVRE, JOHN FELIX. Phila. Silversmith. Sept 7, 1813. Oct 1, 1813. 5.67.
To mother Elizabeth Cordeil. To wife Margaret Lefevre. To son Felix LeFevre, three years of age.
Execs: Rene' L. Gravelle and Lewis Desaque.
Wit: A. Baugier de la Bruyerd and Peter LeBarbier Du Plessis.

HINCKLE, JOHN. Phila. Gentleman. Sept 6, 1813. Oct 5, 1813. 5.69.
Property in Phila. adj. land late of David Kennedy Esq., dec'd, ground late of William Poyntell, dec'd, &c. to sd. execs. in trust for use of dau.

Sarah Elizabeth Jurney or Jenney. To dau. Hannah, property adj. ground lately of Isaac Harvey, Jr., ground adj. land late of Conrad Abel, dec'd.
Execs: Dau. Hannah Lauck and friend Frederick Beates of Phila., serivener.
Wit: Caspar Rehn, James Cook.

LAUDER, HANNAH. Southwark. Phila. Co. Widow. Oct 2, 1813. Oct 6, 1813. 5.72.
To son Joseph Foster all estate. If he dies under age, to five youngest children of John Ffirth viz: Hannah, Henry, Elizabeth, Taber and Mary Firth.
Execs: Son Joseph Foster and James Akin. To Elizabeth Helm.
Wit: Thomas Bigelow, Eliza Akin, Daniel Carson.

HOWARD, MARGARET. Moyamensing. Phila. Co. Widow of George Howard, late of Mountholly, NJ, Labourer, dec'd. Sept 30, 1813. Oct 6, 1813. 5.73.
Her property in Moyamensing Twp. to her three daus. namely: Sarah Burke, wife of Thomas Burke of Phila., yeoman, Elizabeth Knight, widow of John Knight, late of same city, cordwainer and Mary Knight.
Execs: Woodbridge Odlin of Phila., mariner and John Tittermary of Moyamensing, rope maker.
Wit: James Gibson, William Andrews.

MILLER, ELIZABETH. Late of Phila. Widow residing in Frankford, Phila. Co. Feb 28, 1810. Oct 7, 1813. 5.74.
To Ann Renow who has lived with her since infancy. To niece Eliza Webb, who now lives with her and is the dau. of William Webb of Charleston, South Carolina. To dau.-in-law Elizabeth Miller. Residue to grandson Charles Meredith Miller, son of sd. dau.-in-law. To John Dupuy and Charles Meredith Dupuy (sons of Daniel Dupuy of Phila. and his wife Mary).
Codicil July 25, 1813. Exec. Thomas Gillingham of Frankford to act with friend Daniel Dupuy.
Wit: Watson Atkinson, Mahlon Gillingham.
Exec: Friend sd. Daniel Dupuy.
Wit: George Snyder, Peter Thomson.
Letters granted to Thomas Gillingham.

WALN, NICHOLAS. Phila. April 8, 1811. Oct 13, 1813. 5.77.

To James Simpson. To Benjamin White of Bucks. To John Townsend. To children of H. and Mary Drinker. To children of Samuel Smith, Currier. To Monthly Meeting of Friends of Phila., Southern District, to be paid to Jesse Williams. To Jane Halfpenny. To servant Tom Mor'n. All residue to wife Sarah Waln.
Execs: Sons William and Nicholas.
Wit: John R. Lattimer of Phila., accountant and John Elliott Cresson of Phila., conveyancer, affirmed.

BAKER, CHRISTOPHER. Phila. Whitesmith. ----, 1801. Oct 16, 1813. 5.78.
Income of all estate to wife Elizabeth Baker. To grandson John Baker, son of son Samuel Baker, dec'd. At death of wife all estate to only son John R. Baker.
Execs: Wife Elizabeth and son John R. Baker.
Wit: John Stroup, Henry Schlesman.
Letters granted to surviving exec. John R. Baker.

PETERS, MARY. Phila. Widow. Nov 9, 1807. Oct 19, 1813. 5.79.
To grandson Milner Widdow Peters. To granddau. Mary Corbe Peters. To granddau. Ann Widdow Peters. Rents, issues &c. of place where he dwells to Samuel Rickey and Josiah Johnston in trust for son Isaac, at death of sd. son to the three named grandchildren.
Execs: Relations Josiah Johnson and Samuel Rickey.
Wit: James Milnor of Phila., Attorney at Law and Thomas Roberts.

WARNER, WILLIAM. Blockley. Phila. Co. Farmer. April 28, 1812. Oct 7, 1813. 5.--.
Estate to wife Nancy Warner, at her death to bro. John Warner. To sister Tacy Roberts wife of Algernon Roberts. To sister Lydia Cress, widow of John Cress. To three daus. of bro. Joseph Warner, dec'd, namely: Lydia, Mary and Rebecca Warner.
Execs: Wife Nancy, bro. John Warner and bro.-in-law Algernon Roberts.
Wit: Samuel Hains, Joseph Roberts.

OLD, THOMASIN. Phila. widow. Oct 5, 1813. Oct 23, 1813. 5.83.
To sister-in-law Elizabeth Hellings and to Sarah Cox her dau. To Patimer Goree(?). Debt owing her by nephew John Hellings, she bequeaths to exec. in trust for niece Lucetta Aitkins and to sd. John Hellings. To nephew James Hellings. To Sarah One. To Polly Miles.
Exec: Richard Willing, Esq.

Wit: Sarah Moore, James Gibson.

YOUNG, JACOB. Northern Liberties. Phila. Painter. July 21, 1808. Oct 27, 1813. 5.83.
Interest of estate to wife Maria Anna Young, at her death, to his three children namely: Maria Ann, Charles and John.
Exec: Sd. wife Maria Anna Young.
Wit: Abraham Stein, Frederick Beates.
Codicil Oct 11, 1811.
Wit: Jacob Cooper and John Goodman.

WEAVER, JOHN. Northern Liberties. Phila. Co. Physician. Feb 29, 1812. Oct 11, 1813. 5.86.
Provides for wife Anna Maria. To bro. Conrad Weaver. To nephew Dr. Joseph Stouse. At wife's death property to be sold, proceeds to children of wife's sister Esther Stouse. To two sons of late sister Barbara Luther, namely: Dr. John Luther and Martin Luther. To four children of late sister Catharine Leester, John the only one named. To sister Elizabeth Kreig. To Conrad Weaver, Jr., son of bro. Conrad and to his other children.
Execs: Wife Anna Maria, friend John Bender, lumber merchant and nephews Dr. John Luther and Dr. Joseph Stouse.
Wit: Joseph Delaplaine, Frederick Fricke, John Smith, taylor.

MITCHELL, DEBORAH. Phila. June 6, 1807. Sept 29, 1813. 5.88.
To Deborah Chloe, dau. of her former servant woman Comfort Chloe, if sd. Deborah dies under age, bequeaths to her elder sister Teany Chloe.
Execs: Bro.-in-law Isaac Parrish and sister Sarah Parish, wife of Isaac, to whom she leaves all residue of estate.
Wit: Eden Haydock, Robert Milnor.
Letters granted to Isaac Parrish.

SENDOS, DOMINIQUE CHEGARAY. Native of Bayonne in France, about 49 years of age, (son of Fabien Chegaray Sendos, dec'd) now of Phila. Sept 28, 1813. Oct 7, 1813. 5.89.
To wife Sarah Sendos, his plantation at Came near Bayonne in France, in possession of sister Elizabeth Sendos. Sd. wife to be sole extx.
Exec: Wife Sarah Sendos.
Wit: John Williams, Joseph Levy, Benjn. Nones.

KUNCKLE, JOHN. Northern Liberties. Phila. Co. Baker. Oct 7, 1813. Nov 1, 1813. 5.90.
To Susanna Kunckle and John Hurtenstein with himself were trustees named in certain Indenture, sum to be held by sd. Susanna and John for purposes mentioned sd. Indenture. Residue of estate to mother Catharine Kunckle, whom he appoints sole extx.
Exec: Mother Catharine Kunckle.
Wit: Caleb Carmalt, Jr., George Kugler, John Fisher.

RUDULPH, ESTHER. Phila. Co. Widow. May 31, 1804. Sept 27, 1813. 5.91.
Late dau. Martha. to Trustees of Fund for support of itinerant superanuated and worn out ministers of the M. E. Church in United States, their widow &c. Residue of estate to son Philip Syng Bunting. to son Charles Samuel Bunting. To dau. Elizabeth Ellis and her children, her share to trustees Caleb North and Samuel Harvey both of Phila. Considering the afflicted state of son Charles' mind, leaves his share to son Philip in trust.
Codicil ----. Son Charles Bunting's three children now living namely: Charles, Christiana and Hannah Bunting and such other child he may have, to have his share at his death.
Exec: Sd. son Philip Lyng Bunting.
Wit: Robert Whitehead, R. Whitehead, Benjamin Brown W.

KUHL, FREDERICK. Late of Phila., at present residing in Bordentown, NJ, Burlington Co. July 28, 1813. Nov 3, 1813. 5.94.
To bro. Henry Kuhl. To sister Deborah Kuhl. To cousin Samuel Hillegas. To cousin Henrietta Hillegas. To cousin Maria Hillegas.
Execs: Sd. bro. Henry. To Mrs. May Lippincot and Miss Hannah Lippincot.
Wit: Jos. Redman, Charles B. Lawrence.

FOTHERGILL, ANTHONY. M.D. ff. R. S. and member of sundry learned Societies, formerly of City of Bath, afterwards of Phila. U.S.A. late of St. Georges Place, Black Friars Road in Co. of Sussex. Sept 7, 1810. Feb 26, 1814. 5.96.
To be buried in Episcopal Church where he usually attends. I. C. Lettson of Sambroke Court, London, exec. of British Property and Messrs. John Warder and Sons of Phila., of his American Property. To cousin Revd. Thomas Bainbridge, Curate of Church at Adlethorpe, near Spillsbury, Lincolnshire, his estate at Barkstougill in Dent, Yorkshire, also house in

Northampton, on the demise of Ann Binyon as aged woman tenant. To his bro. John Bainbridge, Surgeon at Sedbergh. To cousin John Bainbridge of Sedbergh, father of sd. Thomas and John. To cousin John Drake Bainbridge, Surgeon at City of Durham, if not living, to his sister Elenor Bainbridge, late of London, now of Durham. To cousins Harry, Thomas and Frances Bainbridge (children of late uncle Harry Bainbridge of Wittongilbert near Durham). Ground rents of late William Parsons of Hollaway near Bath, England. Mr. Skurray, his agent to receive ground rents. To cousin Thomas Bainbridge, Esq., of Bedford Row, London. George Davies of London. Lieutenant Robins. Fanny Bainbridge, sister of sd. Thomas. Wife of sd. Thomas Bainbridge (name not given). Five children of late Mr. Chetham. To Granville Sharp, Esq. of Fulham, and his sister Mrs. Prowse. To male heir of late kinsman Anthony Fothergill of the name of Fothergill or to nearest female line. Kinsman Anthony Dent of Dovengill in Ravonstondale. To widow of friend Dr. W. Hawes. To friend Dr. I. C. Lettson. To friend Benjamin Dawson of Bath and his wife Jane. To Mr. Thomas Skurray, Attorney at Berkington, near Bath. To Mrs. Henrietta Fordyce at Bathwick. To Mrs. Fisher at Bathwick and Esther Fisher (her sister) Bathwick. Mrs. Bindon, Great Poultney Street and her dau. Miss Bindon. To Dr. William Moodie, Bath. To Mr. Shaw, Surgeon Dentist, Bath. To Mr. Laughley at Waterhouse, near Bath. To Dr. Birkit, Bath. To Mr. Millard, Millwright Land, Road Walcot. To Mr. Bailey, hairdresser, Bath. To Mr. Windaw, tailor, in or near Crooked Row, Bath. To Rev. Mr. Townsend, Rector of Pusey. To Mr. Robinson, Bath. To Elias Vanderhorst, American Consul, Bristol. To Mrs. Poans, late house keeper of Dr. Ronauldt, Bristol Wells. To Mr. Baynton, Surgeon, Bristol. To Dr. Woodford, near Castlerary. To remaining family of the Dents at Dovingill, Westmoorland. To remaining family of late Anthony Fothergill of Murthwaite in Ravenstondale. American property in Phila. To Jermiah Warder, bro. of John Warder. To Mr. Clifford and his daus. Mary and Sarah Clifford. To Judge Frederick Smith. To Dr. William Currie. To Dr. James. To Rev. Dr. Collin, Minister of Swedes Church. To Mr. Reubens Peale, musician. To Mrs. Chevalier and her dau. Mrs. Turner and Mrs. Turner's son and dau. To Mrs. Roberts, his old land lady. To Robert Clark, his late English domestic and his wife Ann Clark. To Alexander Moore, his late land lord. To Mr. John Capper of London. To Ann Case. To Benjamin Hawes of London. To Dr. Glentworth, Phila. To Rev. Dr. Pillmore, D.D., Phila. To Fothergill Bainbridge, son of cousin Thomas Bainbridge, if he dies under age, to male issue of late nephew Anthony Fothergill of Murthwaite,

Ravenstondale. To Mrs. Warder, wife of John Warder. To Dr. Benjamin Say. To Dr. Redman Coxe. To Dr. C. Wistar.
Wit: John Riley, watchmaker, John Hart, druggist, William Richards, Jr., watchmaker.
Codicil July 15, 1812. Ann Binyon since deceased. Mentions Matthew Bacon, Mrs. Bacon.
Wit: John Mounsey, T. H. Cook, Elizabeth Clark.

CAREY, RICHARD. ----. Nov 15, 1813. 5.113.
All estate to Mrs. Mary Shea of Island of Jamaica for use of his cousins (and daus. of his uncles and benefactors) namely: Mary Shea (dau. of Daniel Shea) and Dorothy and Mary Ann Shea, daus. of Richard Shea.
Exec: Stephen Simpson.
Wit: Joseph Williams, Cashier of Commercial Bank of PA and John Meany of sd. city, merchant, affirmed.

FITZGERALD, ROBERT. Phila. Block and Pump Maker. April 2, 1812. April 8, 1813. 5.114 of 1813.
His estate in Phila. also land formerly in Rye Twp., now of Juniatta in Cumberland Co., also property formerly of Wheatfield Twp. now of Indianna Co. &c. To wife Lydia Fitzgerald. To dau. Martha. To dau. Ann. To Elikim Garretson. To George Hoopes of Goshan in Chester Co., mason. To son John Fitzgerald.
Exec: Sd. wife Lydia.
Wit: Thomas Hood, William Hood, Robert Ross.

BUZBY, ABRAHAM. Oxford Twp. Phila. Co. Yeoman. June 17, 1810. Nov 13, 1813. 5.116.
To dau. Hannah Carpenter, late Hannah Buzby. After her death, to her two children Rebecca and Lydia Carpenter and grandson, son of son John and grandchildren, the children of Mary Howell. To dau. Agness Buzby. All residue to his seven children viz: Joseph, Agness, Abraham and Israel Buzby, Martha Freese, wife of George Freese, Thomas and Samuel Buzby. To dau. Mary Howell wife of Reading Howell.
Execs: Nephew Samuel Powell and Isaac Worrell and John H. Worrell, both of Frankford.
Wit: Nathan Harper, Watson Atkinson.

LYTHGO, THOMAS. (Formerly of Boulton Le: Moors in the Co. of Lancaster and Kingdom of Great Britton, now of Phila.). Nov 5, 1813. Nov 16, 1813. 5.118. (Nuncupative.)

Property to be sold and monies to Isaac, Hester, Anna, Jacob and Margaret Lythgo (sons and daus. of Isaac and Bettey Lythgo) and Bettey Pendlebury (dau. of Sarah Pendlebury) all of Bolton.
Execs: James Brindle and David James.
Wit: David James, James Brindle.

LONDON, PETER. Twp. of Oxford. Phila. Co. Labourer. Nov 15, 1813. Nov 22, 1813. 5.118.
All estate to friend Gardiner Fulton.
Exec: Friend John H. Worrell.
Wit: Mayberry Whitman, Rudolph Worrell.

KEEHMLE, LEONARD. Phila. March 2, 1813. Nov 22, 1813. 5.119.
To dau. Mary, the wife of Isaac Altemus. Provides for wife Peggy Keehmle, she to educate his youngest son William. At death of wife, estate to his three children: Leonard, Mary and William.
Exec: Nephew Samuel Keemle of Phila. Attorney at Law.
Wit: Abraham Stein, Robert Murphy.

WILD, FREDERICK. Southwark. Phila. Baker. Oct 15, 1813. Nov 25, 1813. 5.121.
All estate to wife Mary and his three children: Christiana Catharine, Mary and John, all minors.
Exec: Andrew Zeiss of Phila., baker.
Wit: Henry Engles, Daniel Bussier.

FERGUSON, ELIZABETH. Southwark. Phila. Co. Widow. Aug 28, 1812. Nov 29, 1813. 5.122.
All estate to dau. Elizabeth Hurst, whom she appoints sole extx.
Exec: Dau. Elizabeth Hurst.
Wit: Robert Whitehead, Maria Graff, William Strembeck.

THOMAS, LEWIS. Northern Liberties. Phila. Co. Nov 12, 1813. Nov 22, 1813. 5.123.
To mother Sarah Thomas out of money to be received from Thomas Warrick. To wife Sarah Thomas. To friend Ann Lair. All residue to be invested until children Robert, Sarah and Joseph Thomas are of age, interest to be received by sd. wife Sarah.
Execs: Bros. Israel and George Thomas.
Wit: Frederick Boley, George Worl.

JONES, ISRAEL. Phila. Merchant. Dec 17, 1802. Oct 18, 1813. 5.124.
All estate to bros. John and Isaiah Jones, sister Priscilla Hollowell and to Theodore and Harriet Jones, son and dau. of David and Ruth Jones. Codicil Oct 18, 1806. Bequeaths to Charles Jones, bro. to sd. Theodore and Harriet Jones.
Execs: Bros. John and Isaiah and bro.-in-law Thomas Hollowell.
Wit: Israel Whelen, H- de Haven.

WRAN, MARYAN. Southwark. Widow. June 22, 1807. Nov 30, 1813. 5.125.
To two daus. Rebecca Bosio Hawkins and Elizabeth Bosio Hawkins, if they die under age, to Moses Hawkins.
Exec: Friend Moses Hawkins of Phila.
Wit: Ebenezer Ferguson, John Thompson, William Smith.

CRAP, CHRISTIANA. Phila. Widow. Nov 16, 1813. Nov 29, 1813. 5.126.
Estate to execs. in trust for her two children Susannah Crap and Samuel R. Crap.
Execs: Anthony Steel, windsor chair maker and George Tryon, copper smith.
Wit: Thomas Mitchell, George L. Morris, Joseph Allen.

WEST, HANNAH. Northern Liberties. Phila. Widow. Dec 16, 1809. Dec 1, 1813. 5.127.
To daus. Ann Jenks, Sarah Bacon and Mary Starr. To grandson Samuel Bacon, her watch which was Samuel West's. To son Charles West. To friend Mary Stackhouse. To cousin Lydia Hollinshead. Property where she dwells to be sold, monies to all her grandchildren. Has advanced to grandsons Charles and David Bacon.
Execs: Cousin Samuel Noble and son-in-law Joseph Bacon.
Wit: Amos Stackhouse, Thomas Barnitt.
Codicil Aug 14, 1812. To grandson Thomas Bacon.
Wit: Hannah Pollin, Thomas Norton.

GROSSCUP or GROSSKOP, JACOB. Springfield Twp., Montgomery Co. Yeoman. Sept 11, 1811. Dec 4, 1813. 5.129.
To sons John and William Grosscup. To dau. Elizabeth Goodwin, wife of Joseph Goodwin, late Elizabeth Grosscup. To grandson Jacob Keysel, the natural son of sd. dau. Elizabeth. All residue to sd. sons John and William Grosscup and daus. Catharine McBride, wife of John McBride, late Catharine Grosscup and Mary Grosscup.

Execs: Eldest son John Grosscup and friend John Haston of Germantown Twp., Phila. Co., Esq.
Wit: John Streper, Joseph Hustan.
Codicil Dec 4, 1813.
Wit: Jacob Haas, William Stallman.

HOLLINSHEAD, CATHARINE. Northern Liberties. Phila. Widow of Capt. Samuel Hollinshead and dau. of John Sober and Elizabeth, his wife. July 4, 1807. Dec 7, 1813. 5.131.
To granddau., Catharine Sober Davenport (dau. of William Davenport and Elizabeth Sober Davenport, his wife). To friends Benjamin Say of Phila., physician, Peter Brown of sd. city, Esq., John Hart of sd. city, druggist, and Stephen Simmons of Northern Liberties, lumber merchant, in trust for sd. dau. Elizabeth Sober Davenport and her dau. Catharine Sober Davenport, after death of sd. dau. Elizabeth in trust for support of grandchildren, sd. Catharine Sober Davenport, Samuel Davenport and William Davenport, Jr. (three children of sd. William Davenport and Elizabeth his wife) and any other child they may have. To Rebecca Knox and Sarah Rice (daus. of Thomas Rice and Penelope, his wife, dec'd). To aunts Rebecca Judah and Catharine Havard.
Execs: Benjamin Say, Peter Browne, Esq., John Hart, and Stephen Simmons, they to be guardians of devisees in minority.
Wit: Thomas Norton, Stephen Maxfield, Joseph Thomas.

McDERMITT, CHARLES. Phila. Plaisterer. Oct 16, 1813. Dec 13, 1813. 5.137.
All estate to wife Elizabeth McDermott, at her death to his two children John McDermitt and James McDermitt. If sons die under age, gives to his bro.-in-law Samuel Reed and his present wife.
Execs: Bros.-in-law Samuel Reed and James Stewart.
Wit: Jos. Brebston, Nathan R. Potts.

NOTTNAGELL, LEOPOLD. Phila. Merchant. Jan 31, 1800. Dec 18, 1813. 5.138.
To wife Henrietta Nottnagel. To two sons Lewis and William Nottnagel. To bro. William and Christian Nottnagel and sister Catherine Videlange (born Nottnagel). To nephew Francis Videlange. Wife Henrietta Nottnagel formerly Henrietta Montmollin.
Execs: Stephen Dutilh and John Godfried Wachsmuth. In case of death of either exec., to be replaced by James I. Mazurie.
Wit: Clement Biddle, Frans. Munhall, Philip Taylor, Thomas Wright.

Letters granted to surviving exec. John Godfried Wachsmuth. James S. Mazurie renounced.

MOORE, SARAH. Phila. Widow of Thomas Moore, late of sd. city, gentleman, dec'd. Nov 9, 1812. Dec 21, 1813. 5.140.
Property in Phila. (late in tenure of Richard Hopkins) she gives to Arthur Howell of sd. city, currier. Property in tenure of William Boggs to Joshua Parke, now living with her, he to pay to his mother Jane Parke, if he dies without issue, same to his two sisters Ann and Susannah Parke. Property in tenure of William Levis, to her cousin John Elliott Cresson of sd. city, conveyancer. Property where she dwells to her cousin Caleb Cresson, Jr., of sd. city, merchant, he to pay to Elizabeth Lukens, (wife of Matthew Lukens and dau. of John Jones, late of Germantown, dec'd). To Mary Pusey, widow of William Pusey, at her death to her three daus. To Sarah Parker of sd. city, widow, one of the daus. of Joseph and Hannah Howell, dec'd, at death of sd. Sarah, same to Deborah Howell, one of the daus. of above named Arthur Howell, if she dies without issue to her bro. William W. Howell. To Sarah Carman, wife of James Carman, and her children. To Mary Fisher, widow of Elisha Fisher, at her death to her children. To Ann Burr, wife of William Hudson Burr of Mountholly, NJ. In trust for six children of Hugh Roberts and Hannah, his wife (lately dec'd) children of Daniel and Margaret Jones (sd. Margaret dau. of Mordecai Moore, dec'd) namely: Martha, Hannah, Margaret, Jonathan, George and Daniel Jones and Rachel Morris widow of Samuel Morris and her three children viz: Elizabeth, Thomas and Samuel Morris. Property in Southwark purchased of Job Bacon and Joseph Page to sd. John Elliott Cresson and Caleb Cresson, Jr. Property purchased of Buckridge Sims to Sarah Woolman (wife of William Woolman and dau. of late Hudson Burr, dec'd) at her death to children of sd. Sarah Woolman. Lot originally let to Joseph Jenkins she gives to Rebecca Burr, wife of Jacob Burr of NJ. To Hudson Burr, son of sd. Jacob and Rebecca. To Hannah and Sarah Burr, daus. of sd. Jacob and Rebecca. Property originally let to Samuel Wallis she gives to Rebecca Jones (wife of David Jones of sd. city, hatter, and dau. of Josiah Foster). Ground originally let to Joseph Jacob Wallis (now of the heirs of William Sheaff) she gives to sd. Jane Parke of Duck Creek, Delaware, widow, at her death to her dau. Ann Parke. Property originally let to Michael Gunkle and Charles Sing, she gives to Rachel Foster, wife of Josiah Foster, at her death to her dau. Rachel Foster, Jr., and to Hannah Hollingshead, widow of Edmund Hollingshead and dau. of sd. Rachel Foster. To Lydia Shepard (wife of Richard Shepard of Cohansey and dau. of sd. Rachel Foster). Rent

charge payable by Nathan and David Sellers. Rent charge out of lot originally let to Adam Eckart and Jacob Spicer (now of Stephen North) she gives to Sophia Wood, at her death to her nephew Daniel Woolaston. Rent charge out of ground originally let to Charles Sing (now of the heirs of Josiah Matlack dec'd) to Jacob and Rebecca Burr, at their death, to their two daus. Rent charge out of lot originally let to Jacob Door (now or late of the heirs of Philip Sydelman) also lot originally let to George Adam Fister, lot originally let to Catharine Hawning (now or late of George Sens) to Ann Morris, wid. of cousin Luke Morris, at her death to their children. Rent charge out of lots left by her uncle Caleb Emlen, dec'd, to her and her late bro. Hudson Emlen, she gives to Samuel Emlen Mifflin and Lemuel Mifflin, sons of Ann Mifflin, widow of Warner Mifflin. Rent charge out of lot originally let to James Poultney (now of Jacob Baker) also one originally let to George Fleck she gives to her cousin the sd. Ann Mifflin. Rent charge payable by Robert Blane. To execs. in trust to carry out her father's intentions relative to Public Prisons. Lot now or late in tenure of Jacob Burr to sd. John Elliott Cresson and Caleb Cresson, Jr., they paying to Elizabeth Balderson and to Samuel Hopkins and Hannah his wife, late of this city, now of Rahway, NJ, at their death to Ann and Elizabeth Hopkins, daus. of sd. Samuel and Hannah. To William Ogden and his children. Rent charge originally let to John Wickart of Frederick Breinen, out of lot originally let to Aieoronimus(?) Warner, to Elizabeth Smith and to Thomas Smith. To Mary Pryor, wife of Edmund Pryor of N. Y. City (dau. of Henry and Hannah Haydock). To Hannah Lawrence, wife of Richard Lawrence of N. Y. City (dau. of sd. Henry and Hannah Haydock). To Rebecca Barrow, wife of John Barrow (dau. of sd. Henry and Hannah Haydock). To Susanna Stockden, wife of Abraham Stockden of Burlington, NJ, at her death, to her children and her (sd. Susanna Stockden's) bro. Samuel's dau. and her bro. Thomas' two sons. To Susanna Bond, formerly Susanna Knight, a relation of her mothers. To Rebecca Price, sister of Sarah Price, dec'd, at her death, to her (sd. Rebecca's) niece Sarah Price. To Jane Parke, at her death to her sons Samuel Emlen Parke and Robert Parke and her daus. Ann and Susanna Park. To Rachel Morris widow of Samuel Morris, at her death to her three children namely: Thomas Moore Morris, Samuel and Elizabeth Morris. To friend Robert Wharton of Phila. in trust for Hannah Cuthbert, late Hannah Duer, one of the daus. of above named William Ogden, at her death to her children. To Benjamin B. Howell, son of Joseph Howell. To Sarah Emlen Moore dau. of Samuel Preston Moore and Susanna, his wife. To Rachel Lewis dau. of Joseph and Hannah Wharton. To Sarah Green and Ann Wharton, daus. of William and Mary

Green, deceased. To Henry Moore, son of Mordecai Moore, dec'd. To Mary Heston, Mary Heston, Jr., Mordecai Heston and Charles Heston. To seven children of above named Hannah Hollingshead. To children of Daniel and Margaret Jones. To two sons of above named Elizabeth Lukens. To cousin Owen Jones. To John Elliott of London, England, for children or grandchildren of Mary Rament, widow of Robert Rament, formerly a tobacconist of London. To Sarah Hoopes, who formerly lived with her, now of Chester Co. To Lydia Morris. To Henry Moore of Montgomery Co. and his six children. To Deborah Jackson (dau. of Mordecai Moore) and her three daus. Lot now let to William Martin, she gives to William Carman.
Execs: Cousins sd. Owen Jones, John Elliott Cresson and Caleb Cresson, Jr.
Wit: John Syng Dorsey, William Andrews.

MARTIN, CHARLES. Southwark. Phila. Co. Mariner. July 17, 1807. Dec 22, 1813. 5.153.
All estate to wife Sarah Martin, she to educate their children, also those by her former husband, at her death, to all their children.
Execs: Wife Sarah and friend Jehu Hollingsworth of Phila., merchant.
Wit: William Meredith. John Reed of Southwark, mariner, affirmed.

McDONOUGH, ELIZABETH. Southwark. Phila. Co. Widow. Feb 18, 1812. Dec 24, 1813. 5.154.
Execs. to employ Benjamin Lindell as undertaker. Property where she lives to be sold for benefit of her grandchildren, John, Thomas and Mary Murphy. To granddaus. Elizabeth Healy and Mary Goring. To grandson Joseph Goring. To dau. Catharine Albertus or Alburtus.
Execs: Chas. Shultz of Southwark, flour merchant and James Gibson, distiller.
Wit: Thomas William Bell, Edwin White, Edward Pepplow.

CLEMSON, JAMES. Phila. Merchant. Dec 20, 1813. Dec 24, 1813. 5.156.
To bro. Joseph Clemson and sisters Susannah Mickle, Hannah Davis Sophia Clemson, Elizabeth Clemson, Rachel Clemson and Mary Clemson and children of dec'd bro. Thomas Clemson. To his mother (no name given) an annuity. To nephews John B. Clemson, Thomas Clemson and William Clemson. To Amelia Henry. To Henry Sausman.
Execs: Bro. Joseph Clemson, Ellis Davis, Charles Bird and Jacob S. Waln.
Wit: Joseph R. Jenks, Michl. Gunkle, W. H. Dillingham.

WILSON, SAMUEL. Twp. of Bristol, PA. Yeoman. Sept 20, 1813. Dec 29, 1813. 5.158.
To son John Wilson. Two daus. Mary and Mercy Wilson to have a legacy, also free use of part of house where he lives while they are unmarried. To son Samuel Wilson, his plantation in Bristol Twp. to dau. Rebecca, in trust during her husband's life.
Execs: Son Samuel Wilson and bro. Oliver Wilson.
Wit: Jonathan Mather, Benjamin Mather, Jr.

NUTTER, MARY. Southwark, PA. Widow. June 16, 1810. Dec 30, 1813. 5.160.
Legacy to Dutch Lutheran Church called Sion. To Mary Shyer, an orphan. To Hannah Shyer, a widow. To Mary Timely. To Charlotte Hinneman, widow. To Mary Fiss, widow. To Elizabeth Reed, dau. of Francis Reed. To William Reed, son of Francis Reed. To Ann Connelly, Elizabeth Connelly, Jacob Connelly, Margaret Connelly and Geo. Connelly, children of Jacob and Ann Connelly. To Elizabeth Hennion, an orphan. Residue to Ann, wife of Jacob Connelly.
Execs: Jacob Connelly of sd. District, blacksmith and Francis Reed, Phila. Co., farmer.
Wit: Richard Penshaw, Barnet Bush.

POHT, HENRY. Kensington. Northern Liberties. Phila. Yeoman. July 31, 1813. Jan 5, 1814. 5.162.
To sons Peter, Jacob, Matthias and Henry Poht and dau. Elizabeth Pister.
Exec: Friend Jacob Beideman, Jr.
Wit: Robert Whitehead, Benjamin Huggins and L. W. Eyre.

SMITH, ELIZABETH. Phila. Widow of George Smith. June 6, 1812. Jan 5, 1814. 5.163.
To grandson George Smith. To Robert Owen Wharton. To Ruth, the dau. of Samuel and Sarah Roberts of Pikeland, Chester Co. To granddau. Elizabeth Smith. To Maria Snell, Sophia Humphrey and Sarah Burns of Phila., spinsters. To Jane Lister of same place, spinster. To sister Susanna Beatty her farm in Uwchland, Chester Co. To four grandchildren Morgan, John, Awbrey and Geo. Hoffman. To nephew Benjn. R. Morgan.
Execs: Robert Wharton, Esq. of Phila., and Benjn. R. Morgan.
Wit: William Brewer, Catharine H. Ryan and Ann Brewer.

PATTON, ROBERT. Phila. Esq. Dec 12, 1813. Jan 6, 1814. 5.164.
To wife Tace Patton. To his children namely: John C., Robert B., Cornelia, William, Mary, Henry and Catherine B. Patton.
Execs: Sd. wife Tace and friends Robert Murdock of sd. city, merchant and William Davison of same city, broker and sons sd. John C. and Robert B. Patton.
Wit: Francis C. Deimling, Peter Morgan, Jr., and William Andrews.

SWIFT, EDWARD. Moreland Twp. Phila. Co. Farmer. April 24, 1813. Jan 11, 1814. 5.166.
To five sons: Joseph Kinnersley Swift, Samuel, Edward, John and Charles Swift. To two daus. Mary and Caroline Swift. Rem. to wife Elizabeth Swift.
Codicil Dec 24, 1813. To child with which wife is pregnant.
Execs: Sd. wife Elizabeth and son Joseph K. Swift.
Wit: Edward Duffield, Elizabeth Worthington, John Boileau.

SWIFT, JOHN. Moreland Twp. Phila. Co. Farmer. Dec 27, 1813. Jan 11, 1814. 5.167.
Provides for wife Phebe. To grandsons Samuel and Edward Swift. To John Swift(?). To Charles Swift(?). Son-in-law Abraham Van Beuren. To granddau. Mary van Beuren. To sister-in-law Patience Swift. Rem. to grandchildren, the children of son Edward, dec'd.
Execs: Kinsman Edward Duffield of Moorland township and grandson Joseph K. Swift.
Wit: William Maghee, Joshua Comly.

SWIFT, PHOEBE. Dec 30, 1813. Jan 11, 1814. 5.169.
To grandchildren. To dau.-in-law Elizabeth Swift. To sister Rebecca Vansant. Phoebe Vanortsdalen, Elizabeth Worthington, Elizabeth Swift.
Exec: Edward Duffield. To negro Jude.
Wit: Sarah Brown, Edward Duffield, Joshua Comly.

KEYSER, MARY. Germantown. Phila. Co. Aug 11, 1813. Jan 13, 1814. 5.170.
To Elizabeth Roop, Ann Roop, Hannah Will and Catharine Will. To children of Lidia Roop and Sarah Will excepting Sarah Harry who does not need it. Residue to two nieces Sarah Will and Lidia Roop.
Execs: Daniel Pastorous and Jacob Roop.
Wit: Conrad Carpenter, Joseph Jacob.

JONES, DAVID. Formerly of the Parish of Lannarth, Co. of Cardigan, South Wales, Great Britain, now near Phila. in PA. Joiner. Oct 12, 1813. Jan 29, 1814. 5.171.
Estate to bro. Thomas Jones of London, joiner. To sister Magdalen Jones of London. To sisters Sarah Owens and Mary Jones of Wales.
Execs: Josiah Evans and Coleman Sellers of Phila.
Wit: John Davis, Jr., Daniel Davis, Isaac Davis, John Davis.

CLOWES, HIRAM. Germantown. Phila. Co. Dec 8, 1813. Jan 29, 1814. 5.172.
To wife Elizabeth Clowes, whom he appoints extx. Money due from Charles Redheffer.
Exec: Wife Elizabeth Clowes.
Wit: Daniel Snyder, Henry Cress.

ALBERT, HENRY. Oct 28, 1811. Jan 31, 1814. 5.173.
His teas and other articles to be sold as per memorandum in order to remit to Mr. Hawqua Hong, merchant, Canton. Leaves all to his mother (no name given).
Execs: James S. Duvall, John M. Chapron and Mark Anthony Frenaye.
Wit: P. F. Fontanges, Stephen F. Nidelet.

KOCH, JOHN. (alias Cook.) Germantown. Phila. June 18, 1807. Jan 31, 1814. 5.174.
To grandchild John Kock (alias Cook) property in Germantown, some of which joins lands of John Taylor and Caspar Haines, dec'd, also lands of Anthony Johnson, if sd. grandchild dies under age, then the children of dau. Catharine Leppard to inherit the estate. To grandchildren Daniel Leppard and Jesse Leppard. To grandchild Sarah Cannon. To three grandchildren Mary Leppard, Susanna Kolph (Kolb) and Catharine Leppard. To son-in-law Michael Leppard. To dau. Catharine Leppard.
Execs: Son-in-law Michael Leppard, dau. Catharine Leppard, grandchildren Mary Leppard, Sarah Cannon and Susanna Kolp.
Wit: William Bowman, Daniel Bowman.

CRAIG, MARGARET M. July 10, 1811. Feb 7, 1814. 5.177.
To sisters Anne and Jane Craig. To friend Mrs. Anne Backhouse. To cousins Elizabeth, Jane and Ellin Montgomery, Co. of Antrim, province of Ulster, Ireland. To friend Mrs. Sarah de St. Croix of Hommerton Hackney near London. To Mrs. I. C. Sarmients, the wife of nephew James. To niece and goddau. Mrs. Julia Barry. To friend CircÕ de

Ronceray. To Miss Elizabeth Shippen, should her sister Mrs. Wallen outlive her, the sd. Miss Shippen, annuity to continue to sd. sister. To her two sons and execs. James Craig and Nicholas Biddle, she intrusts the care of the little boy Roger Dillon Drake, as he much attached to her little son John desires they shall not be separated &c. To friend Mr. Miller. To son James. Friend young Mr. Barclay Height. To aunt Mrs. Alexander Campbell of Leith near Edinburg in Scotland. To son-in-law Nicholas Biddle, should any accident prevent his marriage with her dau., the sum still to be devoted to him and his heirs. Property where she lives to her dau. (no name given), bro. James to be allowed to select articles purchased by him &c.
Execs: Sd. son James Craig and Nicholas Biddle.
Wit: William Miller, CircÕ de Ronceray, Mary S. Chalmers. Did not mention distribution of property to little son John because his fortune will have so much longer to accumulate.

ELIOT, MARY. Croydon, Co. of Surry. Spinster. July 19, 1787. Feb 1, 1797. 5.181.
To Elizabeth Sharpe and Frances Sharpe, two daus. of John Sharpe late of the Bank of England, dec'd. To nephew John Eliot. To Thomas Sutton, the younger, of London, Gentleman. To Mary Horrod(?) (late Mary Bowman) of Croydon. To trustees of the Monthly Meetings at Croydon commonly called Quakers, at Brightelmstone Co. of Sussex, at Cirencester, Co. of Gloucester. To sister Dame Rebecca Bridger. To niece Mary Bridger. Lands &c. in America for use of cousin John Eliot Turner. Property in counties of Oxford, Gloucester, Wilts and Warwick to sd. Elizabeth and Frances Sharpe and Thomas Sutton in trust for sd. niece Mary Bridger, at her death to daus. or sons of sd. Mary. Property in or near Brighthelmstone, aforesd., Co. of Sussex to sd. Elizabeth and Frances Sharpe.
Execs: Elizabeth and Frances Sharpe and Thomas Sutton.
Wit: Edward Fisby, I. Blaksley, James Prior all of London.
Codicil July 19, 1787. To Dame Catharine Duckenfied wife of Sir Nathanel Duckenfield Bart. two Picketer of her father Jno. Warde, Esq. To Danile Clified. To Elenor Smith, wife of Edward Smith, musick man. To Susanh Galton living in Friends Meeting House in Blacklane Croydon. To Ann Hollowday living in a Poor house by the Church at Croydon. To Jane Ballame of Yorkshire her servant maid. To Danale Clifford and his wife Sarry Clifford. Jan 20, 1794 Thomas Sutton, the younger, of Parish of Saint Michael Bassishaw, London, gentleman, George Eades, Parish of Allhallows, London, coach maker and William Shallcrass (Shallcraft or

Shallcross) of Bansted, Co. of Surry, farmer, affirmed. John Eliot of London declared that he was a half nephew of Mary Eliot, late of Croydon and that he was informed that she died on or about Jan 9, 1794.

INGRAM, MARY. Widow of Joseph Ingram, late of Cheapside, London, Linen Draper. July 14, 1749*[sic]*. Feb 1, 1797. 5.189.
To dau. Frances Vandewall. Confirms settlement which sd. Joseph Ingram and she made on their dau. at the time of her marriage with Joseph Vandewall. To son Thomas Ingram, all her estate at Hoxton Parish of St. Leonard Shoreditch Co. of Middlesex, all Freehold Lands to which she is entitled by will of her late father John Bellers and her aunt Elizabeth Fettiplace in Counties of Wilts, Oxford and Berks, also lands in PA and West NJ. Estates held under the Dean and Chapter of Gloucester &c. To son Samuel Ingram £4,400. To Susannah, widow of Benjamin Clerk and Christobell Lund, wife of Benjamin Lund of Bristoll, daus. of Robert Ingram, dec'd, bro. of sd. late husband. To Ann Tarbox wife of Joseph Tarbox of Winthmore Hill.
Execs: Sons Thomas and Samuel Ingram.
Wit: John Howell, Tho. Cater, John Halfpenny. Jarvis Kendrick of London, gentleman, affirmed.

BELLERS, JOHN. Late of London, Merchant, now of Coln St. Alwins in Co. of Gloucester, Gentleman. March 3, 1724/5. Feb 1, 1797. 5.193.
To cousin Ann Bellers of Upton, Co. of Worcester. To dau. Mary, the wife of Joseph Ingram property at Greenwich, Co. of Kent, now let to Richard Walker and George Crad, weaver, and late in occupation of Philip Rutt, ground lately held by Thomas Norman, brewer and now by Capt. Medcalfe who married his widow. Lands at Little Anlue, Parish of Austin Cantls, in the Co. of Warwick and lands at Lim Hill, Parish of Letchlad, Co. of Gloucester, some of which dau. Mary and her husband Joseph Ingram have settled by deed upon their sister Theophila and her husband John Elliott, merchant, then of Falmouth, now of London. In trust to sd. dau. Theophila, wife of sd. John Elliott. To Committee of Friends workhouse. To cousin Thomas Church, things from Kensington that were sister Elizabeth Fettiplace's. To Public Libraries of London and Westminster and Oxford and Cambridge. In trust to cousin Jacob Harvey, merchant and cousin John Mucklow, silk man, all lands at Poulton, Co. of Wilts, which are not before settled on son Fettiplace Bellers, also lands at Remerton, Co. of Warwick, lands at Radcott, Co. of Oxford, lands at Lemhill, Parish of Langford, Co. of Berks, lands at Islington, Co. of Middlesex, lands in Pensilvania and West NJ, in Conne

St. Alwins aforsd. &c. Children of sister. Mason and friend John Askew to be paid what is due them by son Fettiplace Bellers.
Execs: Said cousins Jacob Harvey and John Mucklow.
Wit: Henrietta Coock, servant to Mr. Bellers, John Bellamy, Nathl. Bellamy. Aug 16, 1725. Fettiplace Bellers of the Inner Temple, London, Esq., declared he was the natural and lawful son of John Bellers late of Coln, St. Aldwin, Co. of Gloucester, dec'd, who died in April last.

SCHNEIDER, CASPER. Northern Liberties. Phila. Co. Distiller. Nov 26, 1813. Feb 7, 1814. 5.199.
Provides for wife Rachel Schneider. Mortgage Bond and Warrant of Attorny from Leonard Hocker, dec'd, to George G. Waelper &c. Also Bond and Warrant from Rachel Hocker and Samuel Clothier. Children Catharine Schneider and Elizabeth Boyd. Grandchildren Catharine Schneider, Jr., and Hannah Schneider, children of late son John Schneider, dec'd.
Execs: Two daus. Catharine Schneider and Elizabeth Boyd.
Wit: Jno. Goodman, William Binder and William Giles.

STILES, ROBERT. Phila. Bricklayer. Nov 4, 1813. Feb 12, 1814. 5.201.
All estate to wife Catharine Stiles whom he appoints extx.
Exec: wife Catharine Stiles.
Wit: Robert Whitehead, Isaac Thomas.

COX, ESTHER. Phila. Widow of John Coxe, Esq. April 14, 1808. Feb 15, 1814. 5.202.
To niece Theodosia Henrietta Coxe, wife of Richard Coxe, Esq. To niece Mary Elizabeth Sayre. To niece Esther Beman, late widow of Christopher Robeson. To Esther Hansell, dau. of Barnet and Sarah Hansell. To Eleanor Reed. To Mary Rogers, widow of William Rogers, late of Trenton, NJ. To trustees of Free School of Christ Church and St. Peters in Phila. To Female Association for relief of women and children in distress. To Theodosia, dau. of niece Mrs. Theodosia H. Coxe. Residue to daus. Rachel, wife of John Stevens, Esq., Esther wife of Matthias Barton, Esq., Mary wife of James Chesnut, Esq., Sarah, wife of Dr. John Redman Coxe, Elizabeth, wife of Horace Binney, Esq., Catharine, wife of Revd. Nathaniel Harris. To four sons of sd. dau. Catharine and her daus. Julia and Esther Stockdon. To Francis Bowes Stevens and Francis Bowes Stockton, the former, son of dau. Rachel, the latter, son of dau. Catharine.

Codicil. Revokes legacy to niece Mary Elizabeth Sayre now Mary Elizabeth Grant, wife of Revd. Thomas Grant. Signed Aug 17, 1808.
Codicil. To dau. Catharine, widow of Nathaniel Harris. Signed Feb 2, 1812.
Execs: Sons-in-law John Stevens, Matthias Barton, John Redman Coxe and Horace Binney.
Wit: Charles Chauncey, Joshua M. Wallace, Jr., I. Simon Cohen, M. B. Spring.
Letters granted to Horace Binney and Dr. John Redman Coxe.

THOMAS, MARY. Phila. Gentlewoman. Aug 25, 1813. Feb 18, 1814. 5.206.
To James Childs, son of cousin John Childs. To Hannah Lippincott, dau. of sd. John Childs. To Jane, Mary, Elizabeth, Beulah and Ann Childs,the children of sd. John Childs. To Tacy Eldridge, wife of Job Eldridge and Hannah Cooper, nieces of sd. John Childs. To Anna Davis, wife of James Davis and niece of late husband. To Rebecca McVeaugh and Elizabeth Richardson, sisters to said Anna Davis. To Hetty Hulings, the young girl who now lives with her. All residue to niece Mary Phillips, wife of Joseph Phillips of Pittsburg, Co. of Alleghany, PA.
Execs: Sd. Joseph Phillips and his wife Mary.
Wit: Robert Whitehead, Pearson Parvin.

SMITH, JAMES. Phila. Merchant. Dec 7, 1813. Feb 23, 1814. 5.207.
All estate to father William Smith of Peacock Bank, Parish of Urney, and Co. of Tyrone, Kingdom of Ireland and to sisters Jane Gillespie, Dorothy Knox, Catharine Adams, Nancy Smith and Mary Smith.
Execs: Alexander Cranston and John Knox.
Wit: John H. Brown, John Horner.

JOHNSTON, JOHN. Phila. Yeoman. Jan 31, 1810. Feb 24, 1814. 5.208.
To exec. in trust, he to pay unto Arche Allinson of Great Valley Chester Co. To Isaac Boardley (a coloured man) of Phila. To Joseph and Charles Bonsall, children of Isaac Bonsall.
Exec: Friend, Isaac Bonsall.
Wit: John Bonsall, John Hardy, Jr.

BYRNE, PATRICK. Phila. May 15, 1813. Feb 24, 1814. 5.209.
Provides for wife Ellen Byrne. To son Henry at death of wife, his property on Ridge Road Phila. Co. &c. to daus. Mary and Ellen Byrne. To Son Patrick Byrne. To step son Daniel Coleman, tract of land called

Bloomfield in Bald Eagle Twp., Centre Co., PA, to Alexander McCausland and his bro. John McCausland, all estate not before disposed of, he bequeaths to wife Ellen, son Henry an daus. Mary and Ellen.
Execs: Wife, son Henry C. Byrne and Alexander McCausland.
Wit: William L. Sonntag, Jr., Samuel Davis.

DEETZ, FREDERICK. Phila. Co. May 14, 1808. March 3, 1814. 5.210.
To grandchildren Solomon and John Deetz, sons of Fredrich Deetz and Michael and Fredrich Deetz sons of Daniel Deetz.
Execs: Peter Young, farmer and Peter Leval, merchant.
Wit: John Hoover, John Carns.
Letters granted to Peter Leval.

HUMPHREYS, HANNAH. Phila. Dec 3, 1813. March 7, 1814. 5.211.
To mother Margaret Humphreys. To sister Mary Thomas. To sister Margaret Garrigues. To nieces Jane Thomas, Margaret Mendenhall, Eliza Mendenhall and Hannah H. Garrigues.
Exec: Sd. mother Margaret Humphreys.
Wit: Joseph Crukshank, Israel Maule.

ROE, JESSE. Phila. House Carpenter. July 15, 1807. March 7, 1814. 5.212.
To daus. Martha Matilda McCurdy (wife of John McCurdy) and Anne Carothers (wife of John Carothers).
Wit: Samuel Taylor, Peter Thomson.
Letters granted to Martha Matilda McCurdy.

LAWLESS, MARY. Relict of John Sawless. Sept 5, 1805. March 4, 1814. 5.213.
To dau. Ann Shirkey and son Richard John Lawless, sd. son shall be bound apprentice bet. 14 and 15 years of age. Patrick Shirkey, husband of dau. Ann.
Exec: Robert Gordon.
Wit: Michael Cooper, I. Lithgow.

ROGIERS, HORATIO H. Soldier in U. S. Army. Dec 6, 1813. March 10, 1814. 5.215.
To friends Samuel Bardeer and Catharine his wife.
Exec: Samuel Bardeer.
Wit: Abraham Shoemaker, Henry Shoemaker.

HEATLY, CHARLES. Barrister at Law. Feb 14, 1814. Feb 22, 1814. 5.215.
To be interred in burial ground of Christ Church as near as possible to his wife. To sister-in-law Eliza Hales, if living. To Mary Welsh, his housekeeper. To Thomas Walsh, Mary Walshes son now living with him. Residue to bros. and sisters John, Henry, Mary, Martha and Lucy. If sister Henrietta or any of her children shall appear and make good their claim within two years &c. To eldest son of bro. John who shall have been educated in the College of Dublin.
Execs: Hugh Holmes and Benjamin Wilson, both of Phila., merchants.
Wit: Archd. Woodruff, Robert Dawson, Robert S. Stafford, physician.

BION, JOHN MARIE. Aged 56 years, born at Condom, Province of Gascogne in France, now Department of the Gers. lawful son of Peter Bion and Mary Roquet, formerly a merchant at Port au Prince in Island and Coast of St. Domingo, now residing in Phila., PA, U.S.A. June 20, 1811. March 12, 1814. 5.218.
Property received from his parents, he bequeaths to his sister. Property acquired by Industry he leaves to Stephen John Guier(?) his partner, residing in sd. city, appointing him sole exec., he to pay legacies to bros. Joseph and Emmanuel, both priests residing in Condom. To AmideÕ and Legrange, whom he acknowledges as his natural sons now residing at Port au Prince with their mother Elizabeth Mary Susanna LaMarre. To Jane Mary Henrietta, whom he acknowledges as his dau. and who is also dau. of sd. Elizabeth Mary Susanna LaMarre boarding with Mrs. Cartys in Phila
Exec: Stephen John Guier.
Wit: Anthony Julian Chevas and Severin Anthony Salaignac.

FULLER, ELIZABETH. District of Southwark. Widow. Sept 21, 1808. March 16, 1814. 5.220.
All property to dau. Ann Merrit, late wife of Marmaduke Merritt and to son John Fuller. To grandchildren: Archibald, John, William and Elizabeth, children of sd. son John. Mentions Deed given by Zachariah Netman and Mary, his wife, to Elizabeth Fuller.
Execs: Friends Robert McMullin and Alexander Urgerhart.
Wit: Robert Grant, James Hutchison and Tanton Mason.

VOIGT, HENRY. Phila. Chief Corner of the Mint of the U.S. Dec 8, 1813. Feb 15, 1814. 5.222.

To be buried in Kensington Burial Ground. Wife Margaretta to have absolute use of all estate. Daus. Ann and Louisa, if they marry to have the same as given to their elder sisters at such times. As long as dau. Mary shall remain with her mother and not be married to another husband, no charge shall be made. All books, drawings &c. to son Henry. Son Thomas already received his watch makers tools.
Wit: Adam Eckfeldt, G. Ehrenzeller.

JEFFERS, JAMES. Phila. Laborer. Feb 28, 1814. March 21, 1814. 5.224.
Andrew Dun is in debt to him $450, also note against Danel Jeffers and his wife, both sums he bequeaths to Alexander Marshell.
Administrators Alexander Marshill, James Kee.
Wit: James Dunlap, Hugh Miller, Andraw Kelley.

HUME, THOMAS. Roxborough Twp. Phila. Co. Labourer. Jan 24, 1814. March 21, 1814. 5.224.
To nephews Archibald, William and Charles Hoy, sons of sister Mary. To Mary Kean of Germantown, Phila. Co. Residue to Sophia Wood of Roxborough Twp.
Execs: Sophia Wood and John Holget of Roxborough Twp.
Wit: John Levering, Cornelius Holget.

FLINN, RICHARD. Phila. Co. Mariner. Now going Master of the Brig Louisa of Phila. bound to the Havana. Aug 14, 1798. March 25, 1814. 5.226.
To wife Catharine Flinn. To mother Catharine Flinn of Waterford, Co. of Waterford, Ireland.
Exec: Friend Hugh Christy, grocer.
Wit: Richd. Whitehead, Robt. Whitehead.

CHANCELLOR, WILLIAM. Phila. Merchant. Aug 19, 1812. March 30, 1814. 5.227.
To Sarah Robinson, Martha Wharton and Elizabeth Wharton, daus. of Joseph Wharton. To Samuel Coats one of the trustees of PA Hospital, for benefit of sd. Institution. All residue for benefit of wife Hannah Chancellor and children William Chancellor, Sarah Wharton Chancellor, Henry Chancellor and Wharton Chancellor.
Execs: James C. Fisher, Thomas M. Hall and Joseph D. Brown, also guardians of sd. children.
Wit: Israel Whelen and John Russell both of Phila., merchants, affirmed.

PUDVINE, JAMES. Southwark. Storekeeper. March 25, 1814. March 30, 1814. 5.228.
Provides for wife (no name given). Five children: Nancy Weiler, Marian, Eliza, Margret and James.
Execs: Samuel Black and John Weiler.
Wit: Michael Freytag, Samuel Black.

ALLISON, WILLIAM. Phila. Gentleman. March 29, 1814. April 4, 1814. 5.230.
To wife Rachel. To dau. Abigail Mitchell. All residue to granddau. Amy Allison Mitchell. At her death to friend John Sibbett, whom he appoints exec. desiring him to apply rents &c. of sd. estate for use of educating sd. granddau. during minority.
Exec: John Sibbett.
Wit: Abraham Shoemaker, Jr., John P. Ripley, Isaac W. Chadwick.

ROHR, JOHN A. Phila. Gentleman. May 17, 1813. March 28, 1814. 5.231.
To bro. John Frederick Rohr. All residue to friends Robert Whitehead, Phila. conveyancer and Samuel Badger of same city, Attorney at Law, for benefit of wife Catharine Rohr, at her death to the aforesd. John Frederick Rohr. At his death, to his daus. Maria and Elizabeth. To nephew Charles Henry Rohr.
Execs: Friends Robert Whitehead and Samuel Badger.
Wit: Barnard Gallagher, Samuel Stewart, Smith Alleson.

BRAND, MARTHA G. Phila. Jan 28, 1809. April 4, 1814. 5.233.
The house wherein she now dwells she leaves to Elizabeth Skinner, dau. of James and Mary Skinner. To Mary L. Reeves, dau. of James and Mary Skinner. To Women's Middle Meeting of Friends in Phila. All residue to sd. Elizabeth Skinner.
Execs: Friends Robert Gill, the elder and Nathan Sellers.
Wit: Robert Gill, Hannah Gill. Robert Gill renounced.

FISHER, TABITHA. Phila. Spinster. July 2, 1812. April 2, 1814. 5.234.
Property in tenure of Amos Taylor, merchant, and ground which Hannah Wharton and others by indenture conveyed to her father William Fisher, she bequeaths to sister Rebecca Fisher, at her death to nephew William Wharton Fisher. To children of bro. Samuel W. Fisher. Sister Rebecca to sole extx.
Exec: Rebecca Fisher.

Wit: Andrew Pettit, Benjamin R. Morgan.

LAWS, STEPHEN. Phila. Hackdriver. March 22, 1814. April 7, 1814. 5.235.
To wife Jane Laws. To dau. Lear. To son Wesley. To dau. Anna. Execs. to bind to trade dau. Anna and son Wesley.
Execs: Revd. Richard Allen and Richard Howell, both of Phila.
Wit: Jonathan Trusty, William Grinnell.

HAUCK, JOHN. Phila. Sept 4, 1813. April 11, 1814. 5.237.
To niece Elizabeth Clements. To nephew Peter Stout. All residue to nephew John Lohra.
Execs: Sd. John Lohra and Adam Eckfeldt.
Wit: George Kern, Jacob Fink, John Kern. Adam Eckfeldt declines to be exec.

NAW, PETER. Aged about thirty years, born at Bordeaux, Department of the Girondle, lawful and only son of late Francis Naw and Jane Joubertiere, both dec'd, now residing in U.S.A. April 8, 1814. April 14, 1814. 5.238.
Leaves to his wife (no name given) one half of his estate in St. Domingo consisting of lot in city of Cape Francois and GrimprÕ, also possessions in Phila., the other half to his friend James Felix Chasteau, whom he appoints exec.
Exec: Friend James Felix Chasteau.
Wit: Ls. Michael Baroux, Louis Vesin.

SINGLETON, SAMUEL. Phila. Mariner. Feb 5, 1814. Feb 18, 1814. 5.240.
To wife Sarah Singleton he leaves all his estate appointing her sole extx.
Exec: Wife Sarah Singleton.
Wit: William Ogle, William Thomson.

BICKERTON, ELIZABETH. District of Southwark. Phila. Widow. May 4, 1813. April 16, 1814. 5.240.
Property in Southwark to son Abel, at his death to his son George, who is to give his mother Margaret Bickerton, a living out of sd. property so long as she remains a widow. Property in sd. District to grandson Thomas Bickerton, if he dies without issue, she bequeaths same to sd. grandson George Bickerton. To Benjamin Bickerton, cedar cooper, son of Robert Bickerton. To widow of Charles Bickerton. To Robert Bickerton's

youngest dau. Mary. To widow Jackson, relict of John Jackson. To son Robert Bickerton, 67 cents. To Mary Bickerton, wife of grandson Thomas Bickerton. To Margaret Bickerton wife of son Abm. Bickerton. Grandson George Bickerton's share to be in hands of his bro. Thomas Bickerton.
Execs: Son Abraham and grandson Thomas Bickerton.
Wit: Bernard Rooney, George F. Buckhalter, John Deamer.

SIVERT, BARBARA. Phila. Widow. Aug 10, 1810. April 16, 1814. 5.242.
To Mary Winemore, Elizabeth Winemore and John Winemore, grandchildren of bro. Conrad Maag. To Frances Shetzline, wife of George Shetzline and dau. of bro. Henry Maag. To Trustees of Evangelical Reformed Church. All residue to Ann Wiley wife of Robert Wiley and granddau. of bro. Henry Maag. To John Maag of Twp. of Passyunk, farmer, grandson of bro. Henry.
Exec: Philip Peltz.
Wit: John Serritt, David Lentz.

MENTZ, ELIZABETH. Phila. Widow. March 5, 1814. April 19, 1814. 5.243.
To daus.-in-law the wives of sons George Washington Mentz and Charles Mentz and granddau. Elizabeth Mentz. All residue to sd. sons George Washington Mentz and Charles Mentz.
Exec: Sd. son George Washington Mentz.
Wit: Thomas Moyer, Frederick Beates.

MURREY, MARTHA. Southwark. Phila. Widow of John Murrey. Dec 31, 1813. April 20, 1814. 5.244.
Legacy to Sarah Preaston. Estate to Elizabeth Miller, if she dies without issue, bequeaths same to her (Martha Murrey's) bro. James Edger and sisters Catharine and Ann and the children of dec'd sister Margaret, all of the Co. of Antrim and parish of Dunain in Ireland.
Execs: William Ennis and Elizabeth Miller.
Wit: Joshua Bickham, Samuel Workman.

REAP, BARNARD. Northern Liberties. Phila. Feb 6, 1814. April 23, 1814. 5.244.
Provides for wife Susan Reap, at her death or marriage, to his children: William, Anna, Susan, Mary and Joseph Reap.
Execs: Henry Read and Joseph Abbott.
Wit: Jesse Justice, Henry Read.

Letters granted to Henry Reed and Joseph Abbet.

KREAMER, HENRY. Phila. Yeoman. March 19, 1811. April 28, 1814. 5.245.
His property to remain in hands of his wife Catharine, at her death to dau. Eliz. Magt., son Henry and the heirs of dau. Catharine (at present the wife of Philip Krahmer) she to receive interest during their minority, should she survive her children, at her death go to the heirs of above named dau. Elizabeth Margaret Schill, widow, and heirs of sd. son Henry.
Exec: Sd. wife Catharine Kreamer.
Wit: Peter Nonnater, John P. Meyers.

EASTLACK, ANN. Phila. Widow. Jan 20, 1810. ----. 5.246.
To eldest dau. of Moses Burrows. To Susan Cooper. To Betsey Betterton. To Henry Schriver's eldest dau., if she dies in her minority, sd. legacy to her mother. To Sarah Alberson. To Reuben Kemble, her late husband's sisters son. To Thomas Young's children. to Mary Stone, widow of Daniel Stone. To Phoebe Dickinson. To Betsy Hindman. To Moses Burrow's wife. To Moses Burrow' second dau. To Reuben Kembell's eldest dau. To John Fleming's eldest dau. by his first wife. To Betsey Caster. To Eleanor Hart. To Nancy Alberson. To Patrick Smith. To children of William Alberson, Moses Burrows and John Fleming. All residue to John Fleming, Sarah Alberson and Rachel Burrows.
Execs: John Hindman and Moses Burrows.
Wit: Robert Whitehead, John F. Watson.
Codicil May 24, 1810. To Hannah Shriver, dau. of friend Henry Schriver, to be kept at interest under direction of Thomas Norton until she is of age.
Wit: Robert Whitehead and Hannah Eyre.

JOHNSON, ELIAS. April 23, 1813. April 23, 1814. 5.248.
Property to be disposed of according to law for disposal of intestate estates. Dau. Christiana Johnson shall be put on equal footing with his other children.
Execs: Bro. Benjamin Johnson and friend and neighbor George Brick.
Wit: Jacob Wagner, Joseph Foster, John Enoch, John Ruan.

SCATTERGOOD, THOMAS. Northern Liberties. Phila. Tanner. Jan 16, 1813. May 4, 1814. 5.249.

Provides for wife Sarah Scattergood, at her death, to his son Joseph and dau. Rebecca Scattergood, to nephew John Scattergood, at his death to his children. To children of cousin Leoy Murrell, late of Burlington, dec'd. To children of cousin Samuel Scattergood, late of Burlington, dec'd, to niece Rebecca Savery. To David Test. To Martin Miller, his faithful journeyman. Bibles purchased of Isaac Collins and of John Bevan of England also one called Biras he gives to his wife and children Rebecca and Joseph. To execs. of uncle John Head's estate. To Sarah More. To Rebecca McConnell of Burlington.
Execs: Wife, son Joseph, bro. Joseph Bacon and bro. John Hoskins.
Wit: Thomas Norton, Northern Liberties, gentleman, and Thomas Stewardson, Phila., gentleman, affirmed.

SUMMERS, PHILIP. Norther Liberties. Phila. Nov 29, 1813. May 6, 1814. 5.251.
All estate to wife Sarah Summers, at her death to his eight children: Martin, George, Nicholas, Philip, John, Peter, Henry and Anthony Summers.
Execs: Sd. wife Sarah and two sons Martin and John Summers.
Wit: Frederick Schaumenkessel, Frederick Wolbert. For deposition of second witness, see Will Book, No. 12, Page 694.

SINGLETON, JOSEPH Y. Phila. Jan 25, 1814. May 3, 1814. 5.252.
Estate to be divided between his wife Catharine and his mother Sarah Singleton.
Execs: Bro. Samuel Singleton, Stephen Cabot, John Crowley and said wife Catharine Singleton.
Wit: William Watts Jones, George Guier, George Robinson, Edmund Bridge, Jr.
Letters granted to John Crowley.

BRADY, MARGARET. Phila. Wife of Charles Brady. Bookseller. Jan 10, 1814. May 10, 1814. 5.253.
To sons James and Charles Brady, children of sd. husband Charles Brady, both minors. Property owned by sister Eleanor Wray and herself in right of their dec'd father Michael Green.
Exec: Husband Charles Brady, empowering him to act as guardian of their sd. children.
Wit: John Frans. Soares, John Gillespy.

RIDGWAY, ELIZABETH. April 29, 1814. May 14, 1814. 5.254.

To sister Martha Ridgeway. To sister Unis Ridgeway, whom she appoints extx.
Exec: Sister Unis Ridgeway.
Wit: Pamela Ives, Edward Garrigues, Jr.

PAGE, JAMES. Northern Liberties. Phila. Sept 15, 1813. May 17, 1814. 5.254.
Income of all estate to wife Hannah Page, at her death to his three children: Amelia, Robert and Hannah Page.
Execs: Sd. wife and friend Thomas Norton.
Wit: Robert Whitehead, Nathaniel Parker.

FRY, JOHN. Germantown. Phila. Co. Storekeeper. Sept 18, 1813. May 19, 1814. 5.255.
The tenement in which he dwells with lot he bequeaths to son John. Property in Beggarstown to be held for benefit of dau. Elizabeth Derr, at her death, sd. messuage and lot in Beggarstown to her children. To granddau. Ann Hesser. To Evangelical Lutheran congregation of Germantown. To sons Jacob and John Fry. To daus. Catharine Staddelman and Eve Ashmead in trust for dau. Susanna Mason.
Execs: Sons Jacob and John Fry and sons-in-law William Staddelman and James Ashmead.
Wit: Alexander Provest, Charles I. Wister.

YOUNKER, YOST. Twp. of Oxford. Phila. Co. Yeoman. July 27, 1812. May 18, 1814. 5.---.
To wife Sarah he leaves his house hold furniture with $80 a year &c. To daus. Margaret, Elizabeth, Mary, Sarah and Martha each $350. To dau. Ann $250. Residue to sons Daniel, Joseph, Abraham, George, Charles and William.
Execs: Sd. wife Sarah and sons Daniel and Joseph.
Wit: Jacob Foulkrod, John Foulkrod.
Letters granted to Daniel Younker.

BELTZ, CROFT. Phila. Yeoman. Now a soldier in the U.S. Army. Sept 3, 1813. May 19, 1814. 5.260.
To wife Louisa and two children John and George Beltz he leaves all estate.
Exec: Sd. wife Louisa Beltz.
Wit: Abraham Shoemaker, Francis Shoemaker.
Letters granted to Louisa Greenevelt, late Louisa Beltz.

JEWELL, JOSEPH. Late of Cecil Co., MD, now of Phila. April 29, 1814. May 20, 1814. 5.261.
All estate to sister Precilla Cooper, whom he appoints sole extx.
Exec: Sister Precilla Cooper.
Wit: Samuel Ross, Philip Hersh, W. P. Chandler.

MUIR, JAMES. Late of Glasgow in Scotland, now of Phila., PA. Bookbinder. Jan 26, 1792. May 19, 1814. 5.261.
To bros. Richard and William. To his mother. To bros. John and George and to sisters Rachel, Grizzel and Elizabeth Muir.
Execs: Joseph Crukshank, printer and book seller and Robert Henderson, merchant, both of Phila.
Wit: Thomas Affleck, Thomas Lang, Thomas Stillas. Thomas Dobson of Phila., book seller and George Hyde of Phila., stationer and bookbinder, affirmed.

DEAL, SUSANNA. Relict of Peter Deal. Phila. Porter. July 27, 1812. April 26, 1814. 5.263.
All estate to her three sons: Peter, Daniel and Jacob Deal, they to be execs.
Execs: Sons Peter, Daniel and Jacob Deal.
Wit: Robert Whitehead, Martin Shuster.

GLOVER, WILLIAM. District of Southwark, PA. Mariner. Nov 5, 1812. May 24, 1814. 5.264.
All estate to wife Hester Glover, whom he appoints sole extx.
Exec: Wife Hester Glover.
Wit: John McLinchey, Richard Renshaw.

EGERT, GEORGE. Phila. March 15, 1814. May 23, 1814. 5.265.
Property in Phila., subect to a ground rent, to son George. Legacy to son Philip, out of which exec. to pay Justus Scheetz, which sd. son Philip owes to Justus Scheetz. To Sybilla Kerbach, dau. of Polly Kerbach. Stepson Matthias Upman. To children of sd. son Philip.
Execs: Son George and Frederick Bates of this city, scrivner.
Wit: Wm. Lee, Peter Abel. Frederick Bates renounced.

FALCONER, MARY. Relict of William Falconer. Phila. March 23, 1812. May 25, 1814. 5.267.
To Matthew and Hannah Brown of Pittstown, NJ, after the death of both of them, to their surviving children. To William Lane, bro. of sd.

Hannah Brown, residing near Lancaster. To Daniel H. and Charles Mandeville, children of David and Sarah Mandeville. To Catharine Scott and Mary Durlin(?) her sister. To Mary McCoy and Jehu Rees Bouller, residing at Mrs. Hoods. To Sarah Wright, Jane Ferguson, William Falconer Leiper, son of James and Sarah Leiper. To Mrs. Mead, late Mrs. Greenman and Mrs. McCadan. To Mary Brown, dau. of aforesd. Matthew and Hannah Brown. To David Mandeville of Phila. the works of Revd. Mr. Flavel. To Evangelical Society of Phila. and the Union School for education of Female children of indigent parents.
Execs: Friends Robert Ralston and David Mandeville, both of Phila.
Wit: Reinhart Smeltz, William Berrett and Robert Murphy. Robert Ralston renounced.

CLIFFORD, THOMAS. Phila. Merchant. Made and signed at Lancaster during a temporary absence of himself and family from the city on account of the yellow fever raging there. Sept 27, 1798. May 30, 1814. 5.268.
Provides for wife Sarah Clifford. To bro. John Clifford. To son John D. Clifford. To son Thomas Clifford. To dau. Mary Coltman, wife of William I. Coltman, residing in England. To daus. Anna and Sarah Clifford.
Execs: Wife Sarah Clifford, bro. John Clifford and sd. son John D. Clifford.
Wit: Richard Paxson of Phila., iron monger and Charles N. Bancker of Phila., merchant, affirmed.

HUMMELL, CASPER. Northern Liberties. Phila. Yeoman. May 17, 1814. June 1, 1814. 5.270.
Wife Magdalena Humell to have use, interest &c. of all estate for herself and his children. Oldest dau. Barbara.
Execs: Aredrw*[sic]* Leibbrandt and John Hummell.
Wit: Jacob Belsterling, Thomas Sailer. John Andrew Liebbrandt and John Hummell affirmed.

HARDY, THOMAS. Phila. Grocer. March 16, 1814. April 4, 1814. 5.271.
To wife Julia Ann Hardy all his personal property.
Execs: Sd. wife Julia Ann Hardy and friend Thomas McClean.
Wit: Thomas Maitland, B. Drum.

McCARTY, ALEXANDER. Late of Co. of Antrim in Ireland, now of Phila. Co., PA. March 11, 1814. May 24, 1814. 5.272.

Legacy to friends John Hanna and Patrick Skelly of Phila. Co. All residue to eldest child of bro. James and eldest child of bro. Daniel of the Parish of Ashlines, Co. of Antrim.
Execs: Above named John Hanna and Patrick Skelly.
Wit: Robert Whitehead, William Wilson. John Hanna sworn Mary 25, 1814.

SHALLCROSS, BETTY. Late of State of Delaware, now of Phila., PA. Feb 15, 1812. June 6, 1814. 5.273.
Her stock of the United States Insurance Company she bequeaths to sister Mary Lovering, nephew Samuel Hollingsworth, nephew Thomas G. Hollinsworth, niece Ann Maria Hollingsworth and nephew Morris C. Shallcross. Her shares in Union Insurance Company to bro. John Shallcross of Delaware State, bro. Isaac Shallcross. After death of bro. Isaac, his share to be sold, proceeds to children of sister Mary Lovering. To children of late bro. Dr. Joseph Shallcross, to wit: Eliza, Hannah and Joseph Shallcross, Jr., also to Rebecca Russell. To nephew Joseph S. Lovering. To two nieces Sarah S. Lovering and Mary Lovering.
Exec: Bro. John Shallcross.
Wit: Jehu Hollingsworth, Jr., Robert Clinton, Samuel B. Morris.

EVANS, JOHN. Phila. Merchant. March 6, 1814. June 4, 1814. 5.274.
To wife Barbara Evans the messuage and lot which they now occupy with the one adj. which he purchased of Thomas Stevens, also an annuity &c. Farm near Grays Ferry, Phila. Co., tract of land in Luzerne Co. and his interest in lot of ground in Northern Libertie, now in tenure of Frederick Baker, to be sold. He lately sold to Joseph Lownes of this city, silver smith, a stable and lot of ground in sd. city. Execs. to obtain possession of estate in Frankfort, KY, they to sell the same. To Rachel Redman, dau. of John Redman, late of Salem, NJ, his house and lot of ground in tenure of Joseph Kite, subject to annuity to sd. wife Barbara Evans, should sd. Rachel die without issue, bequeaths sd. property to John E. Redman of sd. city, merchant. To John E. Redman. To kinswomen Rebecca Potter, Sarah Day and Hannah Alexander and to their bro. Thomas Redman, Jr. To cousin Mary Shephard and to her son John E. Shephard. To kinswomen Rebecca Lawrence and Mary Redman and their bro. Dr. Thomas Redman. To kinsman Alexander Elmslie. To Nathaniel Holland, John Simmons and Joseph Price, formerly his apprentices. To late partner in trade John Elmslie of the Cape of Good Hope. To John Shephard his late apprentice. To his old journeyman Peter Birkey. To Thomas Young of this city, shopkeeper and Sarah his

wife. To Dr. Joseph Redman of Bordentown, NJ. After decease of sd. wife, the sd. messuage and lot which he now occupies, with one adj., to be sold by execs. monies from such sale bequeaths to contributors to the PA Hospital, to Phila. Dispensary, to Magdalen Society of Phila. To PA Society for promoting abolition of slavery and improving condition of the African race. To Phila. Society for establishment and support of charity schools. To kinsman Alexander Crukshank of Edinburgh, hosier and to his cousin James Crukshank and to his sister Jane Robb. To Evans John Young, son of William Young, late of this city. A large proportion of his monies is lying in England and owing to the unhappy differences existing between America and England, it may be impossible for execs. to obtain same &c.
Execs: Sd. wife Barbara Evans, friend Thomas Latimer and the sd. Alexander Elmslie and John E. Redman.
Wit: Margaret Arthur, William Andrews.

REPPERT, JOHN. Phila. Co. Northern Liberties. Blacksmith. March 6, 1812. June 7, 1814. 5.279.
All estate to wife Sarah Reppert, together with legacy left him by his father Daniel Reppert, to be paid him after death of his mother Dorothy Reppert. To son John Reppert. Wife Sarah to be sole extx.
Exec: Wife Sarah Reppert.
Wit: Jacob Ford, William Gault.

DICK, SUSANNA. Phila. Widow. June 9, 1814. June 21, 1814. 5.280.
Estate to three children: William, Susan and Elizabeth. In case of death without issue, bequeaths same to her nieces and nephew Betsy Ginder, Susan Benninghove and John Benninghove.
Execs: Friends William Nassaw, Alexander Purves and William Kemble Jr., merchants of sd. city. Mrs. Elizabeth Benninghove, widow, to have care of the persons of her sd. children during minority.
Wit: John H. Curtis, Isaac Wampole.

WOODROW, HESTER. Germantown. Widow. March 31, 1814. June 29, 1814. 5.283.
To sisters Mary Rush and Ann Stoneburner. Legacies to Rebecca Crout (dau. of John Crout) now living in the family. To John Engle, taylor (son of William Engle). All residue to her two grandchildren George Stoneburner Clemens and Charles Woodrow Clemens (sons of dec'd dau. Sarah). To Jacob Clemens the father of sd. grandchildren for their support and maintenance during their minorities.

Execs: Son-in-law Jacob Clemens and friend Francis Engle.
Wit: William Keyser, John McClune.

ADAMS, PETER. Twp. of Roxborough. Phila. Co. Miller. March 17, 1814. June 29, 1814. 5.283.
To wife Mary Adams the full yearly income of his whole estate and after her death unto his seven children namely: George Adams, Elizabeth Campbell, Peter, John, Jacob, Mary and Sarah Adams. Son George's share to be in trust.
Execs: Friend William Yardly of Phila. and sd. son John Adams.
Wit: John Gorgas, John Gominger.

PERKINS, MARY. Late of Marcus Hook, now residing in District of Southwark, Co. of Phila. Feb 2, 1814. July 5, 1814. 5.284.
To son Isaac Hendrickson.
Exec: David Landreth.
Wit: Lyndsey Munns, William Moore.

DOUGLAS, JAMES. Phila. Accountant. June 1, 1814. July 6, 1814. 5.285.
Estate to his father James Douglas living in Sintown, Co. of Roxburg in North Britain and to his bros. John, George and William Douglas and his sister Janet Douglas.
Execs: Friends Thomas Dobson of Phila., bookseller and Peter Graham of sd. city, merchant, directing them to send proceeds of his estate to James Dickson, banker in Herwick in sd. co. of Roxburgh in North Britain to be by him divided, together with his estate in Scotland.
Wit: Philip Carrigain, Charles H. Parker.

LARE, JOHN. Passyunk Twp. Phila. Co. Yeoman. Oct --, 1804. July 6, 1814. 5.286.
To wife Catharine Lare his bequeaths all his messuages, lots of ground, monies &c. for support of herself and children who are now in minority.
To his fourteen children namely: John, Elizabeth, Margaret, Godfrey, Peter, George, Henry, Jacob, Isaac, Mary, Susanna, Rebecca, William and Catharine Lare.
Execs: Wife Catharine, son-in-law George Westberger of Passyunk Twp., aforesd., yeoman, and friend John Snyder of Moyamensing Twp., yeoman.
Wit: Edward Bonsall, Jacob M. Lewis.

Codicil Aug 25, 1813. To wife Catharine lot of land purchased of Jacob Clarkson and others.
Wit: Edward Bonsall, Isaac Bonsall.

HOLMES, WILLIAM. Mariner, on board the United States Frigate Essex. Oct 10, 1812. July 11, 1814. 5.288.
All estate to Jeremiah Peck of Phila. Co., boardinghouse keeper, appointing sd. Jeremiah to be exec.
Exec: Jeremiah Peck.
Wit: Edward D. Corfield, David Woodruff.

PAINE, WILLIAM. Northern Liberties. Phila. Grocer. June 21, 1813. June 21, 1814. 5.288.
Bequeaths all estate to wife Sarah Paine, appointing her sole extx.
Exec: Wife Sarah Paine.
Wit: Robert Whitehead, John Taylor.

CLAPHAMSON, MARGARET. Twp. of Blockley. Co. of Phila. Widdow. March 20, 1812. July 16, 1814. 5.289.
Legacies to nieces Mary and Susanna Bonsall, the wives of nephews Moses and Enoch Bonsall. To Rachel the wife of grandson John Adams. To niece Ann Bonsall. To kindsman Samuel Bonsall, son of nephew Moses Bonsall. To kindswoman Lydia Roberts, dau. of niece Tacy. To grandson John Adams, bond due from Charles Quandrel, also money lent to George Roarman. To Phebe and Margret Adams, the daus. of grandson John Adams. To nephew Edward Robeson. To niece Tacy Roberts, to be divided between her daus. as she sees fit, and to her sister Lydia Cress. To nephews William, Enoch, Moses and Samuel Bonsall.
Execs: Kindsmen Moses Bonsall and Algernon Roberts.
Wit: Jacob Hoffman, Jacob Trasel.

PROUD, ROBERT. Phila. Jan 21, 1813. July 26, 1814. 5.291.
To friends Owen Jones, Miers Fisher, Dr. Thomas Parke, Joseph P. Norris, Benjamin R. Morgan, Dr. Thomas C. James, Joshua Ash, Joseph Sansom and John Elliott Cresson all of or near sd. city, all his estate in trust. Sd. trustees to take under their care his copyright to his History of PA, printed copies unsold in possession of Kimber and Conrad, printers and stationers in Phila., together with all his printed books &c. After debts are paid, residue to his relations in England, his bro. James Proud at Darlington in the Co. of Durham, sister Ann Bainbridge and sister Mary Brown in Yorkshire and sister-in-law Mary Proud, widow, at

Kelvedon in Essex and nephew Robert Bainbridge, now, he supposes in the house of John Janson and Company, merchants in London. Sd. trustees to be joint execs.
Execs: Owen Jones, Miers Fisher, Dr. Thomas Parke, Joseph P. Norris, Benjamin R. Morgan, Dr. Thomas C. James, Joshua Ash, Joseph Sansom and John Elliott Cresson.
Wit: John Thompson, James B. Thompson.
Note and Memorand: His former connexions in England being mostly dec'd, his last intercourse from thence by writing with his sister-in-law Mary Proud and her dau. Rachel at Kelvedon in Essex and with his nephew Robert Bainbridge at John Jansons and Company, merchants in London (a relation of his) R. Bainbridge is intimate with William Fry of Mildred Court, Poultry, London, in whose house bro. John Proud was so long concerned and at his death left him sd. Wm. Fry his exec. Owns property in Luzerne Co., PA. Owes to estate of Henry Chapman execs. of William Neate both of London, dec'd, since secured by mortgage on his lands &c. to Phineas Bond, Esq. Exec. to sd. Chapman. July 21, 1814. Letters granted to Joseph P. Norris and Benjamin R. Morgan, the other seven execs. renounced.

KIRKHAM, DEBORAH. Phila. Widow. April 12, 1814. July 23, 1814. 5.293.
Estate to son William and dau. Maria Kirkham, sd. daus. share to son William in trust.
Exec: Sd. son William.
Wit: Elizabeth Harding, Edward Tilghman.

EGAN, MICHAEL. Roman Catholic Bishop. Phila. July 6, 1814. ----. 5.294.
In debt to Mr. Philip Smith, incurred by him and his colleagues, the Revd. I. Rosseter and the Revd. William N. Harold on account of deficiencies in their salary during enlargement of St. Mary's Church. Desires his nephews Michael Egan and Michael Connery be educated in a suitable manner to qualify them for holy orders. If one continues in sd. vocation and not the other one, he to receive the whole estate, if both decline the Priesthood, his estate to be applied to the maintenance and education of one or more poor children for the Priesthood of Roman Catholic Church, under same conditions.
Execs: John Carrell and Thomas Hurley, Jr.
Wit: Michael Hurley, Joseph A. Wigmore.

DUBOURG, MICHAEL. Born in Bordeaux in France, Aug 1, 1761, now of Phila. Tobacconist, wishing to live and die in the Roman Catholic Apostolic Religion, being that of his forefathers. Feb 4, 1814. July 28, 1814. 5.295.
Desires to be interred in the Roman Catholic Church of St. Mary's Phila. Bequeaths to Pstor of sd. Roman Catholic Church of St. Mary's. All residue to wife Elizabeth Dubourg, whom he appoints extx.
Exec: Wife Elizabeth Dubourg.
Wit: David B. Nones, I. Solms, Benjamin Nones.

STACY, SARAH. District of Southwark. Co. of Phila. Widow. Feb 23, 1814. July 30, 1814. 5.296.
Estate to friend James Cox, teacher of a dancing school in Phila. appointing sd. James Cox as exec.
Exec: James Cox.
Wit: James Engle, Jno. Negus, Jr., Thomas S. Engle.

HELT or HILT, HENRY. Twp. of Byberry. Co. of Phila. July 31, 1805. July 30, 1814. 5.297.
His wood lot in Montgomery Co. adj. lands of Jacob Sommer and George Newell and the meadow lot left by his father situated in Byberry Twp. and adj. lands, late of Garret Vansant and Casper Roades, to be sold, proceeds from sd. sale to wife ---- and daus. Hannah, Elizabeth and Mary and to stepdau. Sarah Powell. His dwelling house and lots adj. on the new town road to be for use of his sd. wife ----. Dau. Hannah's share in trust.
Execs: Jacob Roads and Jacob Sommer.
Wit: John Worthington, Asa Worthington.
Codicil July 6, 1807. Dau. Mary's share who is intermarried with Frederick Burkelow be secured in same manner that dau. Hannah's share is directed to be.
Execs: Ezra Townsend and Jesse James of Bensalem Twp. and Bucks Co. in the room of those heretofore appointed.
Wit: Joshua Comly and Asa Worthington.

LAWSON, JOHN. Northern Liberties. Phila. Co. Mariner. June 8, 1796. Aug 2, 1814. 5.298.
To wife Rachel Lawson all his estate, appointing sd. wife extx.
Exec: Wife Rachel Lawson.

Wit: James Trimble, Isaac Howell and John Hastings. Simon Phillipson of Phila., merchant and John E. Claypoole of Phila., upholsterer, affirmed.

GREER, MARTHA. District of Southwark. Phila. Co., PA. Widow of James Greer. July 19, 1814. Aug 3, 1814. 5.300.
Desires to be buried in Mr. Potts Burying Ground. To exec. James Forsythe, grocer, her house and lot in Shipping between Persian Road and Fifth Streets to be sold as sd. James Forsythe may think most advantageous, he to pay to William and John McCreary and Margaret and Sarah McCreary, first deducting his charges. All personal property to sd. James Forsythe to be disposed of as he may think fit.
Exec: James Forsythe.
Wit: William Sweeny, Patrick Carson.

SAXTON, CHARLES. Northern Liberties. Phila., PA. Sept 20, 1812. Aug 9, 1814. 5.301.
To dauter Rhoda Small and to sons John Saxton and Richard Saxton each five shillings. To dauter Mary Saxton the whole of his personal estate. To son Peter Saxton, the income of real estate arising from lot of ground and messuage thereon erected where he (Charles Saxton) now lives, subject to ground rent payable to sd. son John Saxton, after death of sd. son Peter, execs. to rent the same for use of Mary Saxton and her heirs.
Execs: Dauter Mary Saxton and son Charles Saxton.
Wit: Lawrence Hover, Benjamin Vanleer.

BIDDLE, CLEMENT. Phila. Scrivener. April 27, 1814. July 26, 1814. 5.302.
To the widow of General Moses Hazens (if living). To wife Rebekah Biddle one half of his estate. Legacies to sons Thomas Biddle and Clement C. Biddle and to daus. Mary Cadwalader and Rebekah Chapman and to sons John G. Biddle, James C. Biddle and Edward Robert Bidle. All residue to daus. Lydia Biddle and Ann Biddle.
Execs: Wife Rebekah Biddle and sons Thomas Biddle and John G. Biddle.
Wit: Thomas Wright, Jr., John Gouge, Joseph K. Hillegas.
Letters granted to John G. Biddle and Rebekah Biddle.

CASKEY, JOHN. Phila. Aug 4, 1814. Aug 10, 1814. 5.303.

To bros. James Caskey and Samuel Caskey. To sisters Mary and Rebecca Caskey and their heirs, except their husbands. All residue to bro. John Caskey whom he appoints sole exec.
Exec: Bro. John Caskey.
Wit: James Hemphill, Samuel Arthur.

NILL, CONRADE. Twp. of Germantown. Co. of Phila. Oak Cooper. Aug 8, 1814. Aug 11, 1814. 5.304.
Money due him at Andrew Trullingers. Money in the hands of the Church wardens of the English Presbyterian Church in Germantown for the use of his wife Margaret Nill. To his five children: John, Ann, Mary, Charles and Samuel.
Exec: Friend and kinsman Earnes Jelty of Twp. aforesd., cooper.
Wit: Godfried Pope, Yost Smith.

PENNEGAR, MARGARET. Blockley Twp. Phila. Co. Single woman. Dec 6, 1811. Aug 15, 1814. 5.305.
To nephew Joseph Garrett. Exonerates her bro. Amos Pennegar from payment of the debt due by him. To nieces Mary Clark and Margaret Garrett. To sister Susanna Garrett (wife of Morton Garrett).
Execs: Sd. sister Susanna Garrett and sd. nephew Joseph Garrett.
Wit: Adam Mendenhall, Samuel Butler, Robert Brodnax.

MARSHALL, MARGARET. Phila. Widow. April 27, 1814. Aug 15, 1814. 5.306.
To dau.-in-law Sarah Hutchins Marshall. To Andrew A. Stevenson. To Elizabeth Ellison, widow. To the woman who nursed her son Isaac when an infant and who now lives in NJ and whose name she believes was then Elizabeth Rogers. To grandson Edmund Marshall property in Phila., a ground rent issuing out of a lot of ground bounded by ground granted to Patrick Byrne, by Paschall's Alley, by ground granted to Jacob Ridgeway payable by John Brazier, also lot let on ground rent to George Wilson, one other lot to Daniel Smith, one to Joseph Smith and one to Stephen Eastwick, also all her other vacant lots within Twp. of Northern Liberties, Co. of Phila. Should sd. grandson die without issue, sd. properties to be sold and proceeds to following persons to wit: John Hillman, Hannah, (late Hannah Hillman, now the wife of David Hurley), Elizabeth, (late Elizabeth Hillman, now the wife of ---- Sexton), Patience, Ann, Margaret, Mary Ann and Rachel Hillman (all children of sister Patience Hillman of NJ), nephew Thomas P. Roberts, niece Margaret M. Baker, Howard Malcolm son of nephew John Malcolm, dec'd, sister

Patience Hillman and Hannah Poole of NY. Dau.-in-law Sarah Hutchins Marshall to be guardian to sd. grandson Edmund Marshall. To sister Jane Hornor.
Execs: Humphrey Atherton, Attorney at Law, nephew Thomas P. Roberts, Howard Malcolm, grandson Edmund Marshall, dau.-in-law Sarah Hutchins Marshall.
Wit: Samuel Emery, Richard Thos. Atkins Edey.
Codicil May 26, 1814. Had omitted by mistake the name of Rebecca Hillman, dau. of sister Patience Hillman, she to receive equal share with her bros. and sisters.

SMITH, JOHN. Northern Liberties. Phila. Weaver. Feb 12, 1812. Sept 8, 1814. 5.309.
All estate to wife Mary Smith, she maintaining and educating his minor children. After death of sd. wife and youngest child arrives to age of fifteen years, division of estate to be made as follows: to friend and neighbour Geo. Kline in trust for use of dau. Elizabeth Shillingford, at her death to be divided amongst her children. To daus. Mary and Margaret. To son Joseph. To dau. Catharine. To son John.
Execs: Wife Mary Smith and friend George Kline before named.
Wit: Robert Whitehead, Joseph Lewis, John Kline.

STEPHENS, WALTER. Phila. PA. ----. Aug 22, 1814. 5.311.
Bequeaths house wherein he lives to wife ---- with all furniture and every other article belonging to him.
Wit: Joseph Vancise, Amos Comly. Isaac W. Norris, Northern Liberties, ship chandler and William Britton, Northern Liberties, lumber merchant, affirmed.

deVAQUEZ, JEAN BAPTISTE. Formerly merchant at the Cape in the Island and Coast of St. Domingo, now in the city of Phila. PA. July 3, 1805. Nov 4, 1813. 5.313.
He bequeaths to Marie Louise Carton all his property real and personal which may belong to him in whatever places the same may be, especially his half of the plantation planted with coffee at Dondon near the Cape aforesd. purchased from Madam the Viscountess of Choiseul in 1784 for joint account between the late Mr. Boucharlet and himself.
Exec: Mr. John Dubarry of sd. city, merchant.
Wit: F. Thibault, P. Tanguy, Peter LeBarbier du Plesis.
Letters granted to John Dubarry Aug 30, 1814.

RYAN, JANE. Phila. Dealer. Aug 19, 1814. Sept 1, 1814. 5.314.
To Michal Conry, cabinet maker of this city, twenty dollars in cash for a coffin made for Mr. Quinlin. To Matthias O'Conway, accountant. To Capt. Kain's wife who lives in this neighbourhood. To Jesse Thornton, who married her niece of this city. Remainder of goods &c. to be sold. Exec. to remit to Jane and John Ryan, grandchildren of James Ryan, hatter, of the town of Limerick in Ireland (lived back of the market house in year 1794) or to their children. If sd. Jane and John Ryan cannot be found after three years, sd. sum to the managers of the Roman Catholic Society, styled St. Joseph's for educating and maintaining poor orphan children.
Exec: John Smith, stone cutter and grocer of sd. city.
Wit: James Stuart, John Gartland.

McDEED, PATRICK. Phila. Labourer. Sept 11, 1814. Sept 14, 1814. 5.315.
Bequeaths to friend Thomas Cole of Phila., shoemaker, all his property real and personal.
Exec: Sd. Thomas Cole.
Wit: John Johnson, Joseph Heath.

MILLER, JACOB. Bristol Twp. Phila. Co. Sept 4, 1814. Sept 17, 1814. 5.315.
To son Daniel, all his books &c. having heretofore given him possession of his share of estate. All residue of estate to be sold, proceeds to daus. Mary, Margaret, Hannah, Susanna and Sarah. Nicholas Jones, late husband of dau. Susanna.
Execs: Son Daniel and Joseph Miller of Germantown.
Wit: Silas Wilson, Michael Showers.

MAISON, ELIZABETH. Germantown Twp. Phila. Co., PA. Widow. Sept 23, 1812. Sept 21, 1814. 5.318.
Annuity to father Jacob Strouce. To son John Maison, her messuage or tenement now occupied as a Public Tavern House and lot on Germantown and Perkiomen Turnpike Road in Germantown, also adj. land now in tenure of son Adam Maison at the valued price of four thousand dollars. Execs. to convert in to money his lot of land in Germantown Twp. aforesd., purchased of Cornelius Roop and others, devisees of John Roop, dec'd. Bequeaths one fourth thereof to son Peter Maison, one fourth part thereof to sd. son John Maison and the annual interest of one fourth to son Adam Maison and the same to son Jacob

Maison, after death of sd. sons Adam and Jacob, the principal sum to their children if any.
Execs: Sons sd. Peter and John Maison.
Wit: John Huston, William Huston.
Codicils Nov 11, 1813 and June 26, 1814. Revokes the part of will which only gives the interest to sons Jacob and Adam Maison and leaves them each their full one fourth part of the principal sum.
Wit: John Huston, John Nace.

LONGSTRETH, SUSANNA. Lower Dublin Twp. Phila. Co. Widow of Joseph Longstreth, late of Bucks Co., dec'd. April 19, 1809. Sept 21, 1814. 5.321.
To dau. Ann Hallowell, all her wearing apparel. To son Josiah Longstreth during life all that part of her plantation and tract of land in Abington Twp. in the Co. of Montgomery, commonly called *The Saw Mill Tract*, after his death gives sd. tract of land to all his lawful children if he leaves any. Execs. to sell all the rest of her estate real and personal, the monies arising from the sales, bequeaths to her five youngest children to wit: Joshua, William, Ann, Samuel and Thomas Longstreth. Directs that all money that she has paid or shall have to pay for son Wm. be accounted for in the settlement of her estate. Execs. to provide for subsistence of sd. son William, his wife and child or children.
Execs: Bro.-in-law Jesse Williams of Phila. and her son Joshua Longstreth.
Wit: Thomas Livezey, Matthew Conard.

FISHER, JAMES LOGAN. Elmwood in the Co. of Phila. Gentleman. Dec 5, 18--. Sept 21, 1814. 5.323.
Bequeathes to wife Eliza G. Fisher all his household furniture, his plate, all his bound servants subject to their indenture, his horses, carriages &c. All his monies in his house or in the banks of Phila. and generally all his personal estate except his share of the produce of the sales of real estate in state of NY which William Cooper, Esq., attorney to his father Thomas Fisher sold upon certain conditions in which bro. William Logan Fisher and nephew Joshua Fisher son of eldest bro. Joshua Fisher, dec'd, have an interest. Previous to marriage with sd. wife Eliza George, her estate in Cecil Co., MD, by indenture tripartite in which he (James Logan Fisher) was a party, was vested in a trustee to secure her a separate right in and power over it and was agreed that she should receive the rents and profits for her own use - he bequeaths to sd. wife during term of her remaining his widow until his sons Sydney George

Fisher and James Logan Fisher shall attain their lawful age of twenty one years, the whole interest, rents and profits of all his estate, each son when of age to receive one third. Appoints sd. wife so long as she continues his widow, bro. William Logan Fisher and cousin Albanus C. Logan to be the guardians of the persons and estates of sd. sons, also appoints sd. wife, bro. and cousin to be execs.
Codicil March, 1814. In distribution of that part of his estate allotted to two sons Sydney Geo. Fisher and James Logan Fisher, he wishes it fully understood as his will and intention to bequeath to them an equal proportion with any other child or children born after them.
Execs: Wife Eliza G. Fisher, bro. William Logan Fisher and cousin Albanus C. Logan.
Wit: James Smith, Hannah L. Smith, Esther Fisher.

INGS, DAVID. Late of Phila. now of Union Town in the Co. of Fayette. Jan 10, 1814. June 10, 1814. 5.326.
All estate to his wife Lucy Ann Ings during life or widowhood, should sd. wife marry, then one half of estate to dau. Sarah Ings. If wife and dau. both die without issue devises all above property to Sarah Chibnal sister of sd. wife, should she die without issue, then to the children of John Chibnall, bro. of sd. wife.
Execs: Friends Maulby John Littleboy, military storekeeper and James Wood, lace and fringe maker, both of Phila.
Wit: Thomas Hadden, William S. Neale.
Codicil May 6, 1814. He further appoints John Miller of Uniontown, in the Co. of Fayette together with Maulby John Littleboy and James Wood aforesd.
Wit: To will and codicil, Thomas Hadden, William S. Neale. Maulby John Littleboy, one of the execs. sworn Oct 24, 1814.

SHEA, LUKE. Phila. Labourer. Feb 13, 1814. April 25, 1814. 5.327.
Legacies to eldest bro. Thomas Shea near Castle Camber, in the Co. of Kilkenney, Ireland. To sister Mary Shea, alias Gaffany, wife of John Gaffany, near Castle Camber aforesd. and to bro. James Shea of the Co. of Kilkenny aforesd. Legacies to John Daly and William McEvoy. Mrs. Daly to dispose of remainder of his clothes.
Execs: John Daly, Benjamin Prentiss and Redman McManus.
Wit: Rodger Muray, John McFarland.
Letters granted to John Daly and Benjn. Prentice.

EDELMAN, ISAAC. Phila., PA. House Carpenter. Sept 3, 1814. Sept 30, 1814. 5.328.
Annuity to mother Sarah Edelman. Provides for wife Mary Edleman, after her death, all estate to his children: Francis Elizabeth Edelman, eldest son Isaac Edelman and youngest son George Washington Edelman.
Execs: Sd. wife Mary Edleman and friend George Peterman.
Wit: William Griffith, George Peterman and David Fisher.

HILLMAN, CORNELIUS. Phila. Inn Keeper. Feb 7, 1814. Sept 26, 1814. 5.329.
All his estate to his three children: Thomas, Sarah and Mary Ann Hillman, they to be placed at trades at the age of fifteen. Legacies to Martha Browne, wife of Joseph Browne and Mrs. C. Cushing, widow of the late Capt. Cushing.
Execs: George Rees, cordwainer and Jacob Smith, surgeon dentist, of the District of Southwark, Co. of Phila.
Wit: William Thomson, George Thomson and Robert Ross.

BERNER, ANDREW. Jan 29, 1813. Sept 26, 1814. 5.332.
Bequeaths unto wife Elizabeth Berner all his personal estate with all interest of moneys invested, to be paid her annually, after death of wife bequeaths unto Ludwick Berner, unto Andrew Wentz, Elizabeth Wentz and Mary Wentz, children of John and Catharine Wentz. Unto Peter Pluker, (his bro.-in-law). To Elizabeth Kerper, wife of George Kerper. To sister Barbara and to sister Agnes. As George Freas is in debt to him, directs that no demand be made of him except interest within two years after his death.
Execs: Sd. wife Elizabeth Berner and friend Charles Nice.
Wit: Francis William Bockius, George Freas.

GARWOOD, WILLIAM. District of Southwark. Co. of Phila., PA. Shipwright. Aug 12, 1814. Sept 1, 1814. 5.334.
Bequeaths all estate to wife Barbara.
Execs: Sd. wife Barbara, Thomas Pritchett of Phila., cooper and John McLeod of Co. of aforesd., rope maker.
Wit: Richard Sparks, Elias Noe. Thomas Sparks of the District of Southwark, Shot manufacturer, affirmed.

THOMSON, HANNAH. Phila. Widow of Peter Thompson the elder, late of sd. city, Conveyancer, dec'd. May 25, 1812. Oct 2, 1814. 5.335.

Bequeaths unto her dau. Anna Thomson, all her estate, appointing her sole extx.
Exec: Dau. Anna Thomson.
Wit: Charles Thomson, Peter Thomson, Jesse Thomson.

JERVIS, SARAH. Late of city of Phila., now of Southwark. Spinster. Sept 9, 1814. Oct 3, 1814. 5.336.
Execs. to sell her strip of land bounded by land held by heirs of Charles Jervis, dec'd, by land, late of David Bacon, dec'd, and by Jervis's Lane. Property in Phila. to cousin Mary wife of John Gardiner, Jr., to cousin Elizabeth Gardiner dau. of sd. John and Mary Gardiner. To cousin Mary Gardiner sister of Elizabeth Gardiner. To Richard Gardiner, bro. to sd. Elizabeth and Mary. To cousin Mary Rhoads, widow. To Samuel Rhoads, son of sd. Mary. To friend Ann Wilson, wife of John Wilson. To cousin John Evans. To cousin Ann Skyrin, wife of John Skyrin. To cousin William Drinker. To John Gardiner, Jr., in trust for benefit of cousin Samuel Jervis, after his death to his dau. Phoebe, if she dies under age, then to her mother Jane Jervis. To cousin Elizabeth Wallace living near Muncy in PA. To Joseph Wallace, son of sd. Elizabeth. To Hannah Sonntagg, wife of William Sontagg, at her death to her dau. Euphrosna Sontagg. To Matilda Williams. To Rachel Taylor dau. of John R. Taylor. To Hannah, wife of James Widdifield. To Hannah Widdifield, dau. of sd. James. To cousin Jona. Evans. To Noah Simons. To Elizabeth Moore, wife of James Moore. To Ann Miles, lot adj. ground held by the heirs of Charles Jervis, deceased, after her death to her dau. Ann Wilson. To Caroline Cook dau. of John and Rebecca Cook. Executors to purchase gold watches for the following: cousins William, Mary and Hannah Evans, Jr. To Elizabeth Skyrin, Eleanor Skyrin, Elizabeth Gardiner, Caroline Cook, Maria Cook, Hannah Widdifield wife of James Widdifield.
Execs: Cousin Jonathan Evans and his son William Evans.
Wit: John Townsend, Jr., Edward H. Bonsall.

LYON, JOHN. Phila. Botanist and Gardener. Dec 13, 1811. Oct 4, 1814. 5.339.
All money he may be possessed of, he bequeaths to James and John, the sons of late bro. David Lyon of Forfar, in the Shire of Forfar, in the Kingdom of Great Britain, dec'd. To his only surviving bro. James Lyon of Dundee in Shire aforesd. After his death to his son James and to his only surviving sister Mary, wife of Andrew Adam of Dundee, aforesd. after her death to be divided amongst her children.
Execs: Friends Thomas Dobson and David Landreth of Phila.

Wit: Judah Dobson, Wm. White.

STRUNCK, PHILIP. Meamensing. Co. of Phila. Farmer. Sept 28, 1814. Oct 5, 1814. 5.340.
Bequeaths unto his wife Catharine Strunck, born Catharine Lantsinger, his estate, real and personal appointing sd. wife sole extx.
Exec: Wife Catharine Strunck.
Wit: James Oellers, Abraham Chlows.

McCREA, JAMES. Phila. Merchant. Aug 13, 1814. Oct 6, 1814. 5.341.
By a certain Deed of Trust executed by him to William Davidson, Thomas Hale and John McCrea, he conveyed real estate therein specified, to them in trust for certain purposes, he desires that the sd. real estate should be sold after his death and the proceeds to his seven children therein named viz: Elizabeth Jackson, Jane, Mary, Hannah, Margaret, John and James McCrea. Since execution of sd. Deed of Trust he has purchased two lots of ground in Phila. from James Gibson. Recommends his son Robert McCrea to the care of his bros. and sisters.
Execs: Friend William Davidson, broker and sons John and James McCrea.
Wit: Samuel Ewing, John Davis, John Snyder, Jr.

MILLER, JOHN. Phila. Late Marble Cutter. June 18, 1813. Oct 12, 1814. 5.343.
To wife Margaret Miller he bequeaths the ground rent of the lot on which the Academy of Fine Arts now stands and the one adj., occupied as a Tavern and Livery Stable, all his books, papers &c. to be disposed of as she thinks proper. To dau. Jane M. Hickey a house and lot in Phila. To dau. Helen Miller, his farm at Tradyffrin Twp., Chester Co., with three wood lots belonging to it. To nephew John M. Wickey*[sic]*. To dau. Margaret Miller his marble house and lot stable and lot with the small house adj. stable &c. Annuity to those who may have the care of his sister Helen Miller, Mr. Thomas Irwin of NY has often got his bro. William to do it for him. To dau. Julia R. Miller, property in sd. city part of which is occupied by William Gray. To grandson John M. Dickey*[sic]* for the purpose of educating him for the Holy Ministery if he should be so inclined. To Silas E. Weir. To John Magoffin. Has a claim on lands of the late Robert Morris, State of NY.
Execs: Margaret Miller, son-in-law Revd. Ebenezer Dickey and friends Silas E. Weir, auctioneer and John Magoffin, merchant.
Wit: James Gray, James Traquair.

HALL, MARY. Borough of Lancaster in the Co. of Lancaster, PA. At present sojourning in Phila. Single Woman. Oct 13, 1814. Oct 28, 1814. 5.346.
Bequeaths legacies to sisters Jane Mercer and Elizabeth Hamilton and step sister Sarah Ann Heron. To sister Rebecca Hall all her one half part of a debt owing to her and to her sd. sister Rebecca by John Mercer, also all residue of her estate.
Execs: Said sisters Elizabeth Hamilton and Rebecca Hall.
Wit: Fanny Craig, William Andrews.

MATTERN, ANDREW. Northern Liberties. Phila. Potter. June 6, 1812. Oct 28, 1814. 5.347.
Bequeaths unto his wife Mary Mattern all his personal estate, she to have the use and income of his messuages, tenements, pot house kiln and lot of ground in Northern Liberties, Phila. including premises now in tenure of son-in-law Matthias Metzger so long as she thinks proper to carry on the pottery trade. Should sd. wife decline carrying on the said trade, sd. messuages &c. to be sold and the monies to sd. wife Mary Mattern, unto dau. Christina Metzger and to son Adam Mattern. Also gives to wife all his lots on Germantown Turnpike Road in the Co. of Phila. with buildings and to his sd. children all his lands and tenements in Co. of Northumberland, PA.
Execs: Wife Mary Mattern and Robert Whitehead of Phila.
Wit: Jacob Culp, William Allibone, Charles Smith.

KAIGHN, JOHN. Chester in the Co. of Burlington, NJ. May 11, 1812. Aug 28, 1812. 5.---.
To relations Ann Edwards, Samuel Edwards, Elizabeth Edwards, Sarah the wife of Joseph Collins and Charles Edwards real estate in Moores Town. To his friend Samuel Jones. Property in Phila. to Abigail Grover, Elizabeth Gardiner, John, Robert, Sarah, Abigail, Jr., and Charles Grover. To John Kain, Jr. To Kaighn*[sic]* son of Saml. Kaighn, dec'd, and Arabella, his wife late of Fairfax Co. in VA, he bequeaths property in state of TN and VA. To William Kaighn.
Execs: Friends John Welch, merchant and Benjamin R. Morgan, Esq., of Phila.
Wit: Josh. Matlack, David Vanderveer, William Roberts.

WILSON, JACOB. Byberry Twp. Phila. Co., PA. Sept 17, 1814. Oct 22, 1814. 5.351.

Provides for wife Rebekah Wilson, during widowhood. His property to sons Mardon, Jonathan and Jabez (last named, in his minority). Legacies to sons David, Robert and Ethan and to dau. Ann Small.
Execs: Two sons Mardon and Jonathan Wilson and friend Ezra Townsend.
Wit: Daniel Knight, Griffith Street.
Letters granted to Mardon and Jonathan Wilson.
Codicil Sept 27, 1814.
Wit: Rachel Wilson, Catharine Forrest.

BULL, JOHN. Sept 28, 1814. Oct 14, 1814. 5.354.
Bequeaths to wife Catharine Bull all his estate real and personal and after her decease to be sold and proceeds to his five children to wit: Sarah, John, Elizabeth, Abigail and Richard.
Wit: John Bennet, Phillip F. Claridge.

PHILIPS, BENJAMIN. District of Southwark. Shipwright. Sept 10, 1814. Oct 14, 1814. 5.355.
Legacies to dau. Hannah and son Benjamin. All residue of estate to his six children: Jane Gibson, Hannah Philips, Sarah Peirce, Benjamin Philips, Thomas Philips and Angelina Philips. Dau. Hannah Philips to be the guardian of his three minor children Benjamin, Thomas and Angelina.
Execs: Friends Joseph S. Lewis and Samuel N. Lewis.
Wit: Charles Penrose, Simon Kingston.

VAN DUSEN, LYDIA. Northern Liberties. Co. of Phila. (Relict of Matthew Van Dusen, late of Kensington in the Northern Liberties, dec'd. Blacksmith.) Sept 16, 1814. Oct 14, 1814. 5.356.
Her messuage or tenement in Southwark (being part of the real estate late of her dec'd father Nicholas Brehaut allotted for her share) she bequeaths to daus.: Elizabeth, Lydia and Mary Van Dusen. All remainder of her estate she bequeaths unto her five sons: Nicholas, Andrew, Matthew, John and Washington Van Dusen.
Execs: Friend John C. Browne and nephew Samuel Bonnell, also to be guardians of the persons and estate of her sd. three daus.
Wit: Franklin Eyre, George Eyre.

HOPP, GODFREY. Germantown Twp. Co. of Phila. Taylor. Dec 30, 1812. Oct 17, 1814. 5.358.

All his estate to his wife Mary. Sd. wife Mary and Jacob Kulp to be the execs.
Execs: Sd. wife Mary and Jacob Kulp.
Wit: John Dettweiler, Joseph Shriver or Schriver.

NEALE, ELIZABETH. Northern Liberties. Phila., PA. Widow of John Neale late of the city of Burlington, NJ. Sept 15, 1814. Oct 21, 1814. 5.358.
Bequeaths to execs. her estate including that part of the estate of her father situate in PA, DE, or elsewhere not yet divided, in which she is to have a share, in trust for son Standish Ford Edward, dau. Elizabeth Neale and son John. Dau. Elizabeth and son John both minors.
Execs: Friend John Hoskins and nephew John Hulme both of Burlington aforesd. also to be guardians of the persons and estate of minor children.
Wit: George Fagundus, Peter Abel, James Wiley. John Hoskins renounced.

PIPER, MICHEL. Twp. of Northern Liberties. Phila. Farmer. Nov 3, 1814. Nov 9, 1814. 5.360.
To son Jacob Piper $100. Bequeaths unto wife Rachel, use and occupation of all rest of his estate, after her decease, all sd. estate to his children namely: Jacob, George, Mary, Catharine and Dolly.
Execs: Sd. wife Rachel, Peter Deal and son Jacob Piper.
Wit: Benjn. DePrefontaine, Matthias Nunviller.

MARKER, JACOB. Northern Liberties. Phila. Gentleman. Oct 15, 1811. Nov 9, 1814. 5.361.
Wife Elizabeth to have rents, interest and profits of all estate, and after her decease bequeaths sd. estate unto his relations namely: bro. Theobald Marker and the children of dec'd bro. Peter and dec'd sister Elizabeth, who are now in Germany. If they fail to arrive in America in seven years, bequeaths to ministers, vestrymen and church wardens of German Lutheran Congregation in and near Phila. &c.
Execs: Friends John Adam Culman and Yost Hollobush of the Co. of Phila.
Wit: Abraham Stein, Fredk. Beates.

BEDFORD, JOSEPH ATKINSON. City of Phila. July 21, 1814. Nov 9, 1814. 5.362.
Bequeaths to wife Ann Bedford all the interests and profits from all real and personal estate, she to educate and support his children if any be in

their minority at the time of his decease. Bequeaths to his four children viz: Isaac, Thomas, Susanna and Sarah all the effects, real and personal remaining after death of his wife.
Execs: Sd. wife Ann Bedford and son Isaac.
Wit: Joseph Parrish, I. Horwitz, Sarah Wyatt Donavan.

NICHOLSON, WILLIAM, JR. Phila. Merchant. Oct --, 1814. Nov 15, 1814. 5.364.
Execs. to sell all estate real and personal, monies to his wife and his children.
Execs: Friends Daniel L. Miller and James Kinsey of Phila.
Wit: Clement Remington, Thomas Smith, Alexander Knight.

SMITH, PHILIP. Nice Town in Penn Twp. Co. of Phila., PA. Stocking Weaver. Nov 10, 1814. Nov 19, 1814. 5.365.
Provides for wife Catharine and his five children viz: Daniel, Michal, Catharine, Henry and Elisabeth.
Execs: Wife Catharine Smith and friends Jacob Piper and George Piper.
Wit: George Geisel, George DeBenneville.

REESE, PATIENCE. Phila. Oct 21, 1814. Nov 23, 1814. 5.366.
Legacies to nephew Benjamin Bolter. To bro. Benjamin Bolter. To nephew John Rees Bolter. To wife of sd. bro. To Mary Vance. To friend Hannah Hood.
Execs: Sd. nephew John Rees Bolter and friend Robert Murphy of Phila.
Wit: John McMullin, Daniel Smith.
Letters granted to John Rees Bolter.

COLEMAN, JOSEPH. Phila. July 6, 1813. Nov 24, 1814. 5.367.
Bros.-in-law Nathan Sellers and David Sellers. To sisters Hannah Coleman and Margaret Coleman. To bro. William Coleman.
Execs: Bro.-in-law Nathan Sellers and nephew Samuel Sellers.
Wit: David Sellers, Samuel Sellers. Nathan Sellers renounced.

GARRAUD, JACOB. Phila. PA. Taylor. May 7, 1813. Dec 22, 1814. 5.368.
He gives unto his stepson John Beaby, son of late John Beaty, $400. To the trustees of the Charity School of Saint Paul Church in Phila. To Susanna File who live with him now as house keeper he gives $400. All the remainder of his property he gives to the children of late sister Catharine Garraud and to nephew Jean Jacques Garraud, joyner, at Berne in Switzerland.

Execs: Friends Sebastian Salade of the city of Phila., fringe maker, and the aforenamed John Beaty of same place, paper hanger.
Wit: Wm. Willing, Joel Atkinson, Peter LeBarbier du Plessis.

SORBER, HENRY. Germantown Twp. Co. of Phila. Carpenter. Nov 7, 1814. Dec 31, 1814. 5.369.
Provides for wife Catherena Sorber and their children viz: Elias Sorber, Catherena Sorber, now mared*[sic]* to Waltor Cammel and Ann Sorber.
Execs: Wife Catherena and bro. Joseph Sorber.
Wit: Gottlieb Kleever, Georg Tillman.

CASTOR, HENRY. Twp. of Oxford. Co. of Phila., PA. Sept 26, 1814. Oct 13, 1814. 5.370.
Legacies to dau. Sarah and unto step son John Magargal, sd. John's legacy in hands of Allen Magargal and John Athan Magargal. Provides for wife Mary Castor. To daus.: Elizabeth Rorer, Catharine, Anna and Sarah Caster and to any child or children which may be born. Son-in-law Thomas Rorer.
Execs: Friend Jonathan Magargal and son-in-law Thomas Rorer.
Wit: Lewis Waln, Francis Waln.

MARTIN, DANIEL. Phila. Gentleman. March 21, 1814. Oct 19, 1814. 5.372.
Bequeaths all estate to wife Mary Martin, sd. wife sole extx.
Exec: Wife Mary Martin.
Wit: William Davis, John Dudgeon.

WAGANER, PHILIP. Twp. of Penn. Co. of Phila. Stocking Weaver. Jan 21, 1813. Nov 1, 1814. 5.373.
Bequeaths unto his wife Hannah Waganer. After sd. wife's decease to following persons viz: John Waganer of Kensington, sd. Co. of Phila., cordwainer, Conrad Bear, Elizabeth Dover of Northern Liberties, widow, John Shuster, oak cooper, of Penn Twp., Matthias Edle and John Edle, both of Co. of Phila., oak coopers, Molly the wife of George Guizel, (or Gisel), stocking weaver, of Penn Twp. aforesd., Caty the wife of Henry Servor, house carpenter, Margaret, the wife of Henry Bear, cordwainer, Philip Smith, stocking weaver, of sd. Penn Twp., William Rab (or Rap) oak cooper and Mary the wife of George Wile of Penn Twp. aforse., taylor.
Execs: Friends Philip Smith of Penn Twp., stocking weaver and John Wintzall, yeoman of sd. place and co., aforesd.

Wit: Joseph H. Fleming, Thomas Braman, Joshua Wollison.

SHARP, JOHN. Kensington. Phila. Co., PA. Oct 8, 1814. Nov 3, 1814. 5.375.
Bequeaths unto wife Susannah Sharp all his freehold estate within town afforsaid. After her death to his three children: John, Elizabeth and Catharine.
Execs: Wife Susannah and son John.
Wit: Roswell McGonegal, George Sharp, Matthias Coocker.

WHARTON, REBECCA. Phila. Widow. May 8, 1814. Nov 8, 1814. 5.375.
Legacies to sister Hannah Hart, Isaac Oakford, James Chamless of NJ, Elizabeth Clement, dau. of Aaron Oakford, Sarah Acton of Solom, widow, James Wharton son of Beynall Wharton, Rebecca Dickey of NJ, Benjn. White of Bucks Co., Jesse Kersey of Chester Co., Sarah Murphoy wife of Mahlan Murphoy, Ann Leeds wife of Noah Leeds, Martha Shaw wife of Samuel Shaw, George Wharton, Charles Wharton son of George Wharton, Elizabeth Oakford, widow, William Flanner of OH, Sarah Likens, widow, Jeremiah Paul and Rebecca his wife, Deborah Jackson wife of Isaac Jackson, Chamless Allen, Rebecca Thompson, Sarah Egen. Legacy to John Wistar, William Carpenter and Joseph Reeves of Salem, NJ, for poor friends and other worthy persons not under care of the guardians of the poor. To overseers of Public Schools founded by charter in town and Co. of Phila. for poor friends &c.
Execs: Isaac Oakford of Darby and Alexander Wilson of Phila.
Wit: Richard Oakford, Isaac Clement.

PATTERSON, GEORGE. Oct 30, 1814. Nov 23, 1814. 5.377.
Provides for wife Jane Patterson. To his six children viz: James Burd Patterson, William Augustus Patterson, George, Mary, Charlotte and Elisabeth Patterson.
Execs: Sd. wife Jane and eldest son James Burd Patterson.
Wit: Valentine Kerper, Frederick Kerper.

McELROY, JOHN. Northern Liberties. Co. of Phila. Dealer in Flour and Grain. Feb 7, 1808. Nov 22, 1814. 5.378.
To his wife Catharine (Kitty) McElroy he leaves all his estate, she to pay each of his children ten shillings as they come of age, wife to be sole extx.
Exec: Wife Catharine (Kitty) McElroy.
Wit: John Sneeringer, Philip Graba, Richard Folwell.

WELSH, JAMES. Southwark. Co. of Phila. Grocer. Aug 25, 1814. Nov 23, 1814. 5.379.
All estate to wife Mary Welsh, appointing her sole extx.
Exec: Wife Mary Welsh.
Wit:Thomas Mitchell, William Strenbeck.

WIGGLESWORTH, WILLIAM. Phila. Merchant. March 8, 1814. Dec 3, 1814. 5.381.
Bequeaths unto wife Ann Wigglesworth, use, income &c. of all estate. After decease of sd. wife his sister Sarah Stringer and her children to receive a legacy. All residue of estate he bequeaths to friends Joseph Williams and Mary Pfeiffer and to their children.
Execs: Sd. wife Ann and sd. Joseph Williams.
Wit: Harvey Lewis, Isaac Wampole.
Letters granted to Ann Wigglesworth.

DUFFIELD, SAMUEL. Phila., PA. Physician. Jan 19, 1813. Dec 31, 1814. 5.381.
All estate to his children viz: William, George, Elizabeth, John and Maria.
Codicid Dec 3, 1813. Legacy to Ruth Hengel an old and faithful domestic.
Execs: Dau. Maria and sons William and John.
Wit: William Cochrane, Jona. Patterson, Jona. Smith.

KEATES, GEORGE. Southwark. Phila. Co. Whipmaker. Oct 15, 1814. Dec 15, 1814. 5.383.
All estate to wife Margaret Keates, appointing sd. wife extx.
Exec: Wife Margaret Keates.
Wit: Jno. McAllister, Jr., William Bell.

CHIENE, MARGARETTA. Phila. Widow. April 18, 1814. Dec 15, 1814. 5.384.
To sister Elizabeth Nowlin, she bequeaths the income of all estate, she to pay for support of education of adopted son Eugene Brown, son of nephew John Brown and Sarah Brown until he attains age of 21 years. After death of sd. sister bequeaths all estate to sd. Eugene Brown, Thomas H. Brown, Margaretta Brown, Angelica Brown and Harriet H. Brown.
Execs: Charles G. Paleske and Peter A. Browne of sd. city, Esqrs.
Wit: John Troubat, Henry Willis. Charles G. Paleske renounced.

MENG, ELIZABETH. Widow. Dec 28, 1813. Dec 20, 1814. 5.385.
Legacy to only dau. Anna Lesher in trust. To granddau. Harriot Lesher and to her sister Anna Maria Lesher. All remainder of moveables or property to be sold and divided with residue of personal estate between her other children. William Lehman (son of eldest son William Lehman, dec'd) trustee for sd. dau. Ann Lesher. Son Joseph Lehman sole exec.
Exec: Son Joseph Lehman.
Wit: Charles Richards, Charles S. Bunting, Charles Lesher.

PAUL, JACOB. Twp. of Germantown. Phila. Co. Miller. March 6, 1806. Dec 24, 1814. 5.386.
Provides for wife Mary Paul. To son Joseph Paul his mill and plantation near the Valley Forge, Co. of Montgomery. To son Samuel Paul, his mill and plantation in Germantown Twp., Phila. Co. Legacies to his four daus. All residue to his six children: Joseph Paul, Martha Jones, Ann, Mary, Samuel and Elizabeth Paul.
Execs: Sd. wife Mary, sons Joseph and Samuel Paul and son-in-law Samuel Jones.
Wit: George Peirce, Charles Longstreth.

BOYER, JOHN. Bristol Twp. Co. of Phila. Yeoman. June 8, 1812. Dec 29, 1814. 5.388.
All estate to wife Mary and after her death unto his children and grandchildren. Children: Gabriel, Peter, John, Jacob, David, Henry, Elizabeth now the wife of William Bowman, Sarah now the wife of Jonathan Quicksall and Mary now the wife of John Dewees, Jr. Grandchildren: Mary now the wife of Thomas Norton, Rudolph Mower and John Mower, the children of late dau. Rebecca.
Execs: Two sons Gabriel and Peter Boyer.
Wit: Conrad Wilin, John Deprefontaine.

KNOX, REBECCA. Phila., PA. Spinster. Nov 4, 1814. Dec 29, 1815. 5.389.
Bequeaths unto John Prairie or Pearce the elder, of Concord Twp., Delaware Co., farmer, after his death, to his children. To uncle William Knox of Kensington, Northern Liberties, Phila. To aunt Mary Moore of Concord Twp., Delaware Co. To friend Rebecca Fletcher. To friend Hannah Nicery, sister of sd. Rebecca Fletcher.
Execs: Friends Jona. Smith, Esq., cashier of Bank of PA, and Henry Toland of Phila., merchant.
Wit: David C. Wood, James B. Wallace, Joseph S. Kennedy.

INDEX

-A-

ABBET, Joseph, 158
ABBOTT, Charlotta Clarissa, 91; Eliza Wood, 91; Elizabeth Harr, 24; Jeptha, 28; Joseph, 99, 157; Juliann, 91; Margery, 91; Mary Ann, 91; William Smith, 91
ABEL, Conrad, 133; Peter, 161, 180
ABINGTON, Susanna Penelope, 114
ACKERMAN, Elizabeth, 109
ACKLEY, David, 29, 30; Elizabeth, 29, 30; John, 30; John B., 29, 30; Martha, 30; Mary, 29, 30; Mercy, 29, 30; Mordecai, 30; Rachel, 30; Rebecca, 30; Sarah, 30; Thomas, 29, 30
ACTON, Sarah, 183
ADAM, Andrew, 176; Mary, 176
ADAMS, Catharine, 151; Edward George, 70; Elizabeth, 165; George, 165; Jacob, 165; John, 70, 165, 166; Margret, 166; Mary, 165; Peter, 128, 165; Phebe, 166; Rachel, 166; Robert, 103, 131; Sarah, 165
ADDIS, Daniel, 42, 65
ADOLPH, John, 17, 51, 80, 87, 120; Margaret, 80
AFFLECK, Thomas, 161
AFFLERBACK, Henry, 108
AITKEN, John, 131
AITKINS, Lucetta, 134
AKIN, James, 133
ALBERSON, Nancy, 158; Sarah, 158; William, 158
ALBERT, Henry, 147
ALBERTI, George F., 41
ALBERTSON, Benjamin, 43; Jonathan, 43; Susannah, 43; Thomas, 43
ALBERTUS, Catharine, 144
ALBURTUS, Catharine, 144
ALCORN, George, 93
ALDENBURGH, Rebecca, 40
ALDERFFER, Joseph, 71
ALEXANDER, Hannah, 163; John, 54; John R., 89
ALGEO, Thomas, 6
ALLEN, Atlantic, 123; Chamless, 47, 183; Christina, 36; David, 84, 85; Jane, 87; John, 36, 49, 108; John E., 129; Joseph, 140; Lydia, 123; Margaret, 129; Mary, 49, 87; Michael, 104; Mr., 50; Rachel, 47; Richard, 50, 156; Sarah, 129; Susanna, 129; William, 36
ALLESON, Smith, 155
ALLIBONE, William, 33, 178
ALLINSON, Arche, 151; Bernice, 60; James, 51, 60, 62; Mary, 38; Samuel, 38; William, 38, 61
ALLISON, Abigail, 155; John, 32; Rachel, 155; William, 35, 155
ALLOWAY, Robert, 2
ALSOP, Mr., 3
ALTEMUS, Isaac, 139; Mary, 139
AMIES, Thomas, 2
AMOUS, Nicholas, 46
ANDERSON, Elizabeth, 63; Esker, 63; James C., 70; Samuel, 23; Samuel V., 94; Thomas, 63; William, 90
ANDREWS, Elizabeth, 32; John, 32; Sophia, 32; William, 34, 57, 102, 105, 115, 133, 144, 146, 164, 178
ANNELY, William, 56
ARDMAN, Andrew, 17
ARMAT, Thomas, 116
ARMBRUSTER, Nicholas, 66
ARMSTRONG, Christopher, 33; Johanna, 55; John D., 29; Nicholas, 35; Thomas, 107
ARNELL, John, 3
ARTHUR, Margaret, 164; Samuel, 170
ASH, Abigail, 71; Caleb, 71; Charles, 71; James, 51; Joshua, 71, 166, 167; Michael W., 116; Samuel Evans, 71
ASHBRIDGE, Jane, 87; Rebeca, 93
ASHLEY, John, 27
ASHMEAD, B., 88; David, 108; Eve, 160; Jacob, 30, 59, 63, 102; James, 160; John, 71; R., 88
ASHTON, Ann, 129; Elizabeth, 103; George, 41, 103; Isaac Smallwood, 41; John, 103; Margaret C., 89; Mary, 103; Rachael, 103; Samuel, 59; Sarah, 103; Susan, 103; William, 43, 103
ASKEW, John, 150
ASTLEY, Thomas, 64
ATCHESON, David, 76; Eliza Young, 76
ATHERTON, Humphrey, 105, 171; Humprey, 104

ATKINSON, Joel, 182; Sarah, 85; Watson, 7, 85, 114, 127, 133, 138
ATLEE, Edwin A., 128
ATTMORE, Anne, 114; Caleb, 114; Mary, 114
AUSTIN, Francis, 58; Mary, 113; Susanna, 20
AXLEY, Ann, 109; Henr, 109; John, 109; Sarah, 109
AYARS, Hambleton, 76; Shepard, 76

-B-

BACHE, Anna Maria, 60; Benjamin Franklin, 59; Catharine, 59; Deborah, 59; Elizabeth Franklin, 59; Louis, 59, 60; Martha, 60; Richard, 59, 60; Sarah, 60; William, 59
BACKHOUSE, Anne, 147
BACKIUS, Charles, 112; Peter, 111
BACON, David, 140, 176; Job, 142; Joseph, 140, 159; Matthew, 138; Mrs., 138; Samuel, 99, 140
BACOT, Henry H., 56; T. W., 56; Thomas W., 56
BADGER, Samuel, 155
BAILEY, Francis, 91; Mr., 137
BAINBRIDGE, Ann, 166; Anthony, 137; Elenor, 137; Fanny, 137; Fothegill, 137; Frances, 137; Harry, 137; John, 137; John Drake, 137; Robert, 167; Thomas, 136, 137
BAINITT, Samuel, 91
BAIRD, Ann, 32; Mark, 32; Martha, 32; Sarah, 32; Susannah, 32; William, 32
BAISCH, Catharine, 111; George, 111; Jacob, 111; Joseph, 111; Margaret, 111
BAKER, Benjamin, 90; Catharine, 36, 94; Christopher, 134; Eleanor, 82; Elizabeth, 89, 134; Frederick, 89, 163; George, 36; George A., 4, 16, 94; Isbella, 90; Jacob, 81, 143; Jno. Chri., 16; John, 31, 43, 89, 134; John R., 134; Margaret, 117; Margaret M., 170; Margaretta, 121; Mary, 20; Mrs., 89; Richard, 69; Samuel, 134; Sarah, 53; Susanna, 82; Susanna Louisa, 94; William I., 117, 121
BALDERSON, Elizabeth, 143
BALDWIN, Joseph, 125
BALL, Benjamin, 18; Joseph, 18, 80; Joseph Ingles, 18; Mary, 18; Samuel, 18; William, 18; William Whyte, 18
BALLAME, Jane, 148
BAMENT, Hannah, 122; John, 122; Mary, 122
BANCKER, Charles N., 162
BANKS, Ester, 81
BANKSON, Henrietta, 105
BANTOM, Moses, 65, 66; Sarah, 66
BARCLAY, Ann, 73; Elizabeth, 99; Francis, 42; George, 42; James, 73, 100; John, 50, 100; Maria, 100; Mary, 73, 99, 100; Robert, 99, 100; Samuel, 4, 45, 56, 69; Sarah, 100; Thomas, 100; William, 73
BARDEER, Catharine, 152; Samuel, 152
BARDON, John, 48; Luke, 48; Moses, 48; Stephen, 48; Thomas, 48
BARKER, Ann, 20; Catharine, 20; Elizabeth, 20; George, 20; John, 20; Mary, 20, 21; Rebecca, 3; Thomas, 20
BARNDOLLAR, Christopher, 2; Daniel, 1; John, 2, 114
BARNES, Barnaby, 131; Thomas, 63
BARNEY, John, 7
BARNHILL, Robert, 122
BARNITT, Thomas, 140
BARNY, Patrick, 86
BAROUX, Ls. Michael, 156
BARRIERE, Peter, 55
BARROW, John, 143; Rebecca, 143
BARRY, Julia, 147; Mary, 49
BARTHOLOMEW, Edward, 51; John, 20
BARTON, Adam, 87; Esther, 150; Joseph, 76, 87; Mathias, 150; Matthias, 151; Sarah, 59
BARTRAM, Ann, 1; Ann M., 104; Anna, 104; Archibald, 1; Elizabeth, 1; George W., 1; Isaac, 22, 26; James, 104; John, 104; Mary, 104; Moses, 1; Rachel, 1; Rachel C., 104; Rebecca, 1; William, 1
BASON, Elizabeth, 26
BASSISHAW, Michael, 148
BASTIAN, George, 69
BATES, Frederick, 161; George, 161
BAYNARD, Rachel, 6
BAYNE, Robert, 94
BAYNTON, Mr., 137
BEABY, John, 181
BEAKES, Hannah, 123; Lydia,

123; Nathan, 123
BEALE, Joseph, 34, 40; Thomas, 39
BEAN, Joseph, 21; Rebecca, 21
BEANS, Benjamin, 43; Mary, 129; Susannah, 43; Thomas, 130
BEAR, Henry, 182; Margaret, 182
BEARD, Margaret, 14
BEASLY, Reuben Gacent, 51
BEATES, Barbara, 41; Catharine, 41; Conrad, 41; Frederick (Fredk.), 2, 4, 13, 14, 17, 41, 42, 49, 66, 69, 78, 81, 84, 85, 89, 106, 108, 119, 133, 135, 157, 180; Henry, 41; Mary, 41; Peter, 41; William, 41
BEATTY, Susanna, 145
BEATY, John, 181, 182
BECHTEL, Peter, 23
BECK, Paul, 64
BECKEL, George, 74; Maria Magdalen, 74
BECKER, Elizabeth, 78, 85; George, 78; Jacob, 78; John, 78; Joseph, 78, 85; Martin, 78; Mary, 78; Samuel, 78; Sarah, 78; William, 78
BECKLEY, Daniel, 108
BEDFORD, Ann, 180, 181; Isaac, 181; Joseph Atkinson, 180; Sarah, 181; Susanna, 181; Thomas, 181
BEIDEMAN, Daniel, 67; Elizabeth, 67; Jacob, 67, 145; Margaret, 67; Mary, 67
BEIDERMAN, Catharine, 79
BEIGEL, Rachel, 4
BELL, Hannah, 72; James, 108; James Forder, 72; Mary, 108; Thomas, 108, 109; Thomas William, 144; William, 184
BELLAMY, John, 150; Nathl., 150
BELLARS, Fettiplace, 150
BELLERS, Ann, 149; Fettiplace, 149; John, 149, 150; Mary, 149
BELLEVILLE, N., 25
BELSTERLING, Jacob, 116, 162
BELTZ, Croft, 160; George, 160; John, 160; Louisa, 160
BEMAN, Esther, 150
BENDER, Emericus, 117; John, 17, 135; Mary, 117
BENEZET, Anthony, 40
BENNERT, Peter, 107
BENNET, John, 179; Rachel, 127
BENNETT, Mahlon, 124
BENNINGHOVE, Catharine, 9; Elizabeth, 9, 164; Jacob, 8; John, 9, 164; Sarah, 9; Susan, 164; Susanna, 9
BENSON, Patrick, 132
BERGENDOLLAR, Anne, 29; Catharine, 29; Daniel, 29; Eliza, 29; Frederick, 29; John, 29; Nancy, 29
BERGER, George, 19, 85
BERNAL, Dn. Andre, 25
BERNANOS, Claudius, 56
BERNER, Agnes, 175; Andrew, 175; Barbara, 175; Elizabeth, 175; Ludwick, 175
BERRETT, William, 162
BERRIMIN, Jemima, 3
BERRY, Mrs., 113
BERRYMAN, Jamima, 55
BERT, Claudius Medardus Felix, 56
BETHUSEN, Ernst Christian, 94
BETLER, John, 3
BETTERTON, Betsey, 158
BETTLE, Samuel, 62, 114
BETTON, Catharine, 35, 36; Catherine, 7; John, 35; John Price, 7, 36; Mary Ann, 7; Mary Anne, 35; Samuel, 7, 35, 36
BETTS, Ebenezer, 129
BETZ, Catharine, 68; Christian, 68; Hannah, 68; John, 68
BEVAN, John, 159
BIBBINS, Catherine, 126
BICKERTON, Abel, 156; Abm., 157; Benjamin, 156; Charles, 156; Elizabeth, 156; George, 156, 157; Margaret, 156, 157; Mary, 157; Robert, 156, 157; Thomas, 156, 157; Widow, 156
BICKHAM, Abia, 47; Ann, 47, 78; Caleb, 3, 31, 47; Christiana, 78; Elizabeth, 47; George, 47; Joshua, 47, 157; Margaret, 47; Mary, 47; Thomas, 47
BICKING, John, 95
BICKLEY, Abigail, 3; Abraham, 110; Daniel, 3; Eliza, 3; Elizabeth, 110; Hannah, 110; Henry, 3, 104; Isaac, 110; Jacob, 3; Lydia, 110; Margaret, 3, 110; Mary, 3, 110; Robert, 110
BIDDIS, George, 59; John, 59; Samuel, 59, 102
BIDDLE, Ann, 47; Charles, 51; Clement, 24, 62, 63, 73, 87, 141, 169; Clement C., 169; Edward Robert, 169; George, 63; George Washington, 87; Hannah, 47; James C., 169; John, 15, 114; John C., 169;

Mary, 169; Nicholas, 88, 148; Rebecca, 87; Rebekah, 169; Thomas, 87, 88, 169; William S., 47, 48
BIEGLER, Ann, 1; Elizabeth, 1; Juliana, 1; Mary, 1; Philip, 1; Samuel P., 1
BIGELOW, Thomas, 133
BILLMEYER, Mary, 91
BINDER, Benjamin C., 124; William, 33, 150
BINDON, Miss, 137; Mrs., 137
BINGHAM, Margaret, 73
BINNEY, Elizabeth, 150; Horace, 150, 151
BINYON, Ann, 137, 138
BION, Amideé, 153; Emmanuel, 153; John Marie, 153; Joseph, 153; Legrange, 153; Mary, 153; Peter, 153
BIRCH, William Y., 46, 126
BIRD, Catharine, 55; Charles, 144; Joseph, 36, 55
BIRKEY, Peter, 163
BIRKIT, Dr., 137
BISHOP, William, 74
BISHOPBERGER, Christina, 116; George, 116; Jacob, 116; Susannah, 116
BITTERS, Charles, 51
BLACK, Samuel, 155; Susanna, 14
BLACKSON, Thomas, 49
BLACKWELL, Robert, 50
BLAIN, Charles, 49
BLAIR, Charles, 65; Elizabeth, 10; Hannah, 10; Robert, 10; William, 9
BLAKE, Ann Margaret, 102; George E., 102; Timothy, 120
BLAKEY, Joshua, 119; William, 119
BLAKSLEY, I., 148
BLANE, Robert, 143
BLAYNEY, Arthur, 102
BLEYLER, John, 80
BLIGHT, John, 19
BLODGET, Samuel G., 82; William Henry, 82
BOARDLEY, Isaac, 151
BOAT, Margaret, 46
BOCKIUS, Christopher, 90; Francis William, 175; Godfrey, 2
BODENSTEIN, Andrew, 82; Hannah, 82
BODENSTINE, Andrew, 82; Hannah, 82
BOEHM, Catherine, 55
BOGGS, William, 142
BOILEAU, John, 146
BOIREN, Margaret, 9
BOLEY, Frederick, 139
BOLLER, John, 89
BOLTER, Benjamin, 181; John Rees, 181
BOND, Phineas, 114, 167; R., 114; Susanna, 143
BONNELL, Samuel, 103, 179
BONNITT, Dowding Thornhill, 110
BONSAL, Isaac, 56
BONSALL, Ann, 166; Charles, 151; Edward, 22, 165, 166; Edward H., 176; Enoch, 166; Isaac, 62, 151, 166; John, 40, 121; Joseph, 151; Mary, 166; Moses, 166; Samuel, 166; Susanna, 166; William, 166
BONSLEY, Sarah, 112
BOOKCHOP, John George, 39
BOON, Edith, 64; Mary, 64
BORDEN, William, 119
BORREKENS, H. P., 12
BORTON, Abigail, 38; Joshua, 38; Martha, 38
BOSBY, Christian, 73
BOUCHARLET, Mr., 171
BOUGHMAN, Aaron, 118; Ann, 118; Peter, 118
BOULLER, Jehu Rees, 162
BOURKE, Thomas, 48; William, 101
BOWEN, Hannah, 125; James, 125; John, 125; Joseph, 125; Joseph E., 87; William, 120
BOWERS, Elizabeth, 19; George, 72; Jacob, 72; Jacob Lowns, 72; John, 42, 72; Joseph Thorne, 72; Mary, 72; Samuel, 44, 72; Susannah, 72; William, 72
BOWMAN, Daniel, 147; Elizabeth, 185; Mary, 148; William, 147, 185
BOYCE, Jane, 112
BOYD, Andrew, 82; Catharine, 40; Edward, 40; Elizabeth, 150; Francis, 40; Sarah, 33, 82; William, 33
BOYER, David, 185; Elizabeth, 185; Gabriel, 185; Henry, 185; Jacob, 185; John, 185; Mary, 185; Peter, 185; Rebecca, 185; Sarah, 185
BOYLE, Alexander, 6; Catharine, 6
BRADFORD, John, 60; Joseph, 60; Thomas, 42, 113; William, 60
BRADY, Catharine, 46; Charles, 159; James, 12, 46, 159; Margaret, 159; Mary, 12
BRAMAN, Thomas, 183
BRAND, Martha G., 155

BRANHAM, Christiana, 77; Ebenezer, 77; Elizabeth, 77; John, 77; Ludlow, 77; Marmaduke, 77; Mary, 77
BRANNON, Ann, 102; Elizabeth, 102; John, 102
BRARMAN, Unice, 44
BRAUTIGAM, Daniel, 49
BRAY, John, 100
BRAZIER, John, 170
BREARLEY, James, 39; Mary, 39
BRECK, Catharine Douce, 75; George, 75
BREHAUT, Lydia, 179; Nicholas, 179
BREIDENHART, George, 14
BREINEN, Frederic, 143
BREINTNALL, Thomas, 6
BRESTON, Jos., 141
BREVARD, Rebecca, 118
BREWER, Ann, 145; William, 145
BRICE, John, 96; Sarah, 96
BRICK, George, 158
BRIDGE, Edmund, 159
BRIDGER, Mary, 148; Rebecca, 148
BRIGHT, Jacob, 58; Michl., 26; Susanna, 58
BRINDLE, James, 139
BRINGHURST, Ann, 62; Deborah, 62; Edward, 62; George, 1; Isaac, 30; James, 15, 16, 62; Jonathan, 15; Joseph, 15, 16, 62; Ruth, 15, 16; Sarah Anne, 62
BRINTON, F. H., 130
BRISTOL, Jacob, 51; Sarah, 51
BRITTAIN, Francis, 110
BRITTON, William, 123, 171
BROCK, George Fite, 19; Sally, 19
BRODHEAD, Daniel, 80
BRODNAX, Robert, 170
BRODY, Michael, 69
BROOKE, Robert, 127
BROOKS, Boyer, 80; Ro., 127
BROTON, Margaret, 101
BROWN, Angelica, 184; Ann, 36, 40, 90, 103; Benjamin, 29, 49, 62; Catharine, 78; Elizabeth, 113; Eugene, 184; Hannah, 161, 162; Harriet H., 184; Hugh, 70; Jacob, 81; James, 73, 103; Jane, 31; Jehosheba, 53; Jesse, 21, 111; John, 31, 84, 98, 119, 184; John H., 151; Joseph, 70; Joseph D., 154; Josiah, 53; Lewis R., 78; Lucy, 3; Margaretta, 184; Mary, 162, 166; Matthew, 161, 162; Nancy, 32; Peter, 141; Rebecca, 21; Sarah, 39, 146, 184; Susanna, 78; Thomas H., 184; William, 36, 39, 73, 103
BROWN W., Benjamin, 136; Benjamine, 129; Benjn., 132
BROWNE, Andrew, 26; John, 73; John C., 105, 179; John Coats, 38, 39; Joseph, 175; Martha, 175; Peter, 38; Peter A., 18, 121, 184; Sarah, 38; William J., 39; William Johnson, 38
BRUCE, Samuel Laraque, 110
BRUMELL, Archer, 70
BRUNARD, Abagail, 98
BRUNER, Catharina, 97; George, 97
BRUNNER, Adam, 66; Henry, 61
BRYIN, James, 4
BRYNE, Patrick, 170
BUCHANAN, James, 49
BUCHANNEN, Rachel, 10
BUCKHALTER, George F., 157
BUCKIUS, Joseph, 95; Mary, 132; Peter, 111; Philip, 131; Wilhelmina, 132
BUDD, Joseph, 10; Mahlon, 119; Mary, 10; Rachel, 10; Rebecca, 10
BUDWELL, John, 39
BUFFINGTON, Joshua, 87
BULL, Abigail, 179; Catharine, 179; Elizabeth, 179; John, 179; Richard, 179; Sarah, 179
BUNNER, Sarah, 113
BUNTING, Ann, 18; Charles, 136; Charles S., 185; Charles Samuel, 136; Christiana, 136; Elizabeth, 20; Hannah, 136; Joseph, 117; Margaret, 18; Philip Lyng, 136; Philip S., 20; Philip Syng, 136
BUNTON, Russell Perot Moses, 50
BURCKHART, Henry, 29
BURD, Edward, 5, 16, 45, 120; Elizabeth, 16
BURDEN, Benjamin C., 69; Benjamin Chew, 69
BURILS, Eliza, 75
BURKE, Rachel, 4; Richard, 121; Sarah, 133; Thomas, 133
BURKELOW, Frederick, 168; Mary, 168
BURKERT, Elizabeth, 17; Jacob, 17; Margaret, 17; Mary, 17
BURKET, Elizabeth, 17; Jacob, 17; Margaret, 17; Mary, 17
BURKHART, Robert, 130
BURKIT, Harriet, 42; John, 42; Moses, 42

BURKLOE, Samuel, 72
BURKS, John, 94
BURNETT, Daniel, 119
BURNHETER, John, 35
BURNS, George, 14; Hugh, 103; Nicholas, 10; Sarah, 145
BURR, Ann, 142; Hannah, 142; Hudson, 142; Jacob, 142, 143; Phebe, 38; Rebecca, 142, 143; Sarah, 142; William Hudson, 142
BURROW, Moses, 158
BURROWES, William Ward, 13
BURROWS, Eden, 89; Elizabeth, 89; Harriet, 55; John, 41; Moses, 158; Rachel, 158; William, 55
BURTEN, John, 101
BURTON, Henry L., 48
BURWELL, Stephen, 94
BUSBY, Ann, 38; Benjamin, 38; Grace, 38; Jabez, 38; Mary, 38; Nathaniel, 38
BUSH, Barnet, 145; Mathias M., 104
BUSSIER, Daniel, 20, 139
BUTLER, Ann, 89; George, 89; Hannah, 89; James, 109; Martha, 89; Samuel, 170; Sarah, 89; William, 89
BUTTAM, John, 68
BUZBY, Abraham, 138; Agness, 138; Hannah, 138; Israel, 138; Joseph, 138; Martha, 138; Samuel, 138; Thomas, 138
BYRNE, Ann, 84; Ellen, 151, 152; Eloner, 2; Henry, 151, 152; Henry C., 152; James, 3; Mary, 151, 152; Patrick, 84, 151

-C-

CABOT, Stephen, 159
CADWALDER, Lambert, 107; Mary, 169; Thomas, 87, 88
CAKRIN, Mary, 84
CALDCLEUGH, Robert A., 64
CALDWELL, Andrew, 93; C., 101; Elianor, 93; Elizabeth, 93, 111, 113; James, 93; Mary, 93; Rosanna, 93; William, 79
CALLENDER, Ann, 109, 110; Edward, 109; Hannah, 109; William Pitt, 109
CAMBELL, George, 100
CAMERON, James, 22
CAMMAL, Catharine, 97
CAMMEL, Catherena, 182; Waltor, 182
CAMPBELL, Alexander, 84, 148; Charles, 36; David, 11; Elizabeth, 11, 165; Ellen, 100; George, 6, 7, 41; Hannah, 11; Helen, 7, 41; James, 11; Joseph, 4, 131; Mary, 113; Quintin, 105; Sarah, 113; Susanna, 11; William, 125
CANBY, Samuel, 95
CANELAS, Dn. Mariano Josep, 25
CANNON, Sarah, 147
CANONGE, John Francis, 123
CAPELLE, Joseph, 83; Manus, 83
CAPER, John, 137
CAR, Elizabeth, 55
CARETHORN, Hannah, 50
CAREY, Matthew, 65; Richard, 138
CARMALT, Caleb, 73, 75, 77, 136; Hannah, 55; Jonathan, 55, 119; Mary, 57; Sarah, 57; Susanna, 55; Thomas Say, 57
CARMAN, Jacob, 125; James, 142; Sarah, 142; William, 144
CARNES, Rebecca, 71
CARNS, John, 152
CAROTHERS, Anne, 152; John, 152
CARPENTER, Benjamin, 98; Conrad, 98, 146; Hannah, 138; John, 138; Lewis D., 101; Lydia, 138; Mary, 138; Rebecca, 138; Samuel, 75; William, 183
CARR, Ann M., 104; Robert, 104
CARRELL, Edwin, 84; Eleanor Ann, 84; Eliza M., 84; Elizabeth, 84; Henry Byne, 84; James M., 84; John, 167; Maria Eleanor, 84
CARRIGAIN, Philip, 165
CARROLL, Charles, 5; Harriet, 5
CARSON, Charles, 101; Daniel, 133; Patrick, 101, 169; R. D., 108; William, 53
CARTER, Eliza Catharine, 74, 85; John, 110
CARTON, Marie Louise, 171
CARTYS, Mrs., 153
CARVER, John, 60; Mary, 60; Rachel, 60
CASE, Ann, 137
CASKEY, James, 170; John, 169, 170; Joseph, 4; Mary, 170; Rebecca, 170; Samuel, 170
CASSIN, John, 42
CASTER, Betsey, 158; George, 54; Margaret, 54; Mathias, 54; Samuel, 127; William, 54
CASTOR, Henry, 182; Sarah, 182
CATER, Thomas, 149
CAUFFMAN, Catharine, 71; Charlotte, 71; Eliza, 71;

Jacob, 71; Samuel, 71
CAVILSON, Hannah, 82
CAWELL, John V., 109
CHADWICK, Isaac W., 155
CHALKLEY, Thomas, 62
CHALMERS, Mary S., 148
CHAMBERLAIN, Hannah, 37
CHAMLESS, James, 183
CHAMPEAN, James, 111
CHAMPION, Samuel C., 41
CHANCELLOR, Hannah, 154; Henry, 154; Sarah Wharton, 154; Wharton, 154; William, 154
CHANDLER, W. P., 161; William, 53
CHAPIN, Nathan, 2, 13, 33
CHAPMAN, Henry, 167; Rebekah, 169
CHAPPELL, Thomas, 43
CHAPRON, John M., 147
CHARD, George, 18
CHASTEAU, James Felix, 156
CHAUNCEY, Ch:, 99; Charles, 151; Elihu, 82
CHESNUT, James, 150
CHETHAM, Mr., 137
CHEVALIER, Mrs., 137
CHEVAS, Anthony Julian, 153
CHEW, Anna Maria, 5; Benjamin, 5; Catherine, 5; Elizabeth, 5; Harriet, 5; Henrietta, 5; Juliana, 5; Margaret, 5; Maria, 5; Mary, 5; Sarah, 5; Sophia, 5
CHIBNAL, John, 174; Sarah, 174
CHIENE, Margretta, 184
CHILDS, Ann, 151; Beulah, 151; Hannah, 151; James, 151; Jane, 151; John, 151; Mary, 151
CHLOE, Comfort, 135; Deborah, 135; Teany, 135
CHLOWS, Abraham, 177
CHRIST, Johannes, 67
CHRISTY, Hugh, 154
CHUR, Jacob, 46, 78
CHURCH, Harriet, 93; Thomas, 149
CHURCHMAN, Mord., 51; Mordecai, 53
CLAIBBORN, Joshua, 95
CLAPHAMSON, Margaret, 166
CLAPIER, Lewis, 5, 27
CLAPPER, Jacob, 106
CLARE, Rebecca, 63; William, 63
CLARIDGE, Philip F., 179; Philip I., 22
CLARK, Ann, 137; Daniel, 100; Elizabeth, 138; Isaac Smallwood, 41; Jane, 99; John, 23, 77; Joseph, 54, 55, 59; Mary, 84, 100, 128, 170; Robert, 137; Thomas, 84
CLARKSON, Jacob, 166; John, 76; Mary, 76
CLAYPOOLE, Deborah, 62; John E., 169
CLAYTON, Charles, 63
CLEAVER, Jesse, 12, 44
CLEMENS, Charles Woodrow, 164; George Stoneburner, 164; Jacob, 112, 164, 165
CLEMENT, Adelaide, 9; Elizabeth, 183; Isaac, 183; Lucy Ducasse, 9; William, 78
CLEMENTS, Elizabeth, 156
CLEMSON, Elizabeth, 144; Hannah, 144; James, 144; John B., 144; Joseph, 144; Mary, 144; Rachel, 144; Sophia, 144; Susannah, 144; Thomas, 144; William, 144
CLERK, Benjamin, 149; Susanna, 149
CLIFFORD, Anna, 25, 162; Danale, 148; John, 162; John D., 162; Mary, 120, 137, 162; Mr., 137; Sarah, 25, 137, 162; Sarry, 148; Thomas, 162
CLIFIED, Danile, 148
CLIFTON, Alfred Wharton, 48; Anna Maria, 47; Frances, 48
CLINE, Anne, 61; Barbara, 61; Joseph, 61; Mary, 61; Rebekah, 61
CLINTON, Robert, 83, 163
CLOTHIER, Samuel, 150
CLOUD, Anne, 77; Caroline, 77; Charles F., 76; Helen, 77; Susan, 77
CLOVET, Anne, 102; Joseph, 102
CLOWES, Elizabeth, 147; Hiram, 147
CLYMER, Elizabeth, 107; George, 107; Henry, 107
COATES, Daniel, 35; Samuel, 15, 16
COATS, Samuel, 105, 154
COBB, Mary, 16
COCHELL, Miriam, 119
COCHRAN, Elizabeth, 111
COCHRANE, William, 184
COCK, Samuel, 111
COCKER, Matthias, 183
COFFIN, Thomas, 98
COHEN, Abraham, 67; Deborah, 67; Esther, 67; Goodhous, 67; Jacob, 67; Jacob J., 16; Rachel, 16, 67; Rebecca, 67; Richea, 67; Richey, 67; Simon, 151
COLE, Thomas, 172

COLEMAN, Daniel, 151; Hannah, 181; Jacob, 90; John A., 14; Joseph, 181; Margaret, 89, 90, 181; William, 181
COLHOUN, Gustavus, 12; Samuel, 42; Thomas, 12
COLIN, Catharine, 117
COLLADAY, Charles, 88
COLLARD, Michael, 67
COLLIN, Rev. Dr., 137
COLLINS, Ann, 27, 104; Benjamin, 35, 104; Carolina, 34; Chalkley, 34; Eliza Laetitia, 94; Elizabeth, 34; Hannah, 104; Isaac, 159; Joseph, 178; Joshua, 34, 94, 104; Mary, 34, 104; Sarah, 104, 178; Thomas B., 34
COLLMAN, John, 42; John A., 103
COLLOM, Jonathan, 99
COLTMAN, Mary, 162; Robert, 119; William I., 162
COMING, John, 111
COMINGS, Catharine, 112
COMLY, Amos, 171; Franklin, 11; Jcob, 105; Jesse, 127; Jonathan, 105; Joseph, 2; Joshua, 11, 19, 105, 146, 168; Phebe, 2
CONAROE, Thomas, 67
CONCHY, Agnes, 107; Eleanor, 107; James, 107
CONCY, Jane, 107; Margaret, 107
CONNELLY, Ann, 145; Elizabeth, 145; George, 145; I. M., 83; Jacob, 145; John, 101; Margaret, 145
CONNER, Mary, 113
CONNERY, Michael, 167
CONNOR, John, 130; Mary, 113; Michael, 113
CONRAD, Christina, 129; John, 90, 112, 129; Matthew, 173; Michael, 16
CONRADE, John, 3; Joseph, 3
CONRY, Michal, 172
CONWAY, Bernard, 110; Harriot, 116; James O., 47
COOCK, Henrietta, 150
COOK, Caroline, 176; James, 133; John, 147, 176; Maria, 176; Rebecca, 176; T. H., 138
COOMBE, Thomas, 46
COOMBS, David, 74, 76
COOPE, Thomas P., 124
COOPER, Derick, 89; Elizabeth, 89; Hannah, 151; Jacob, 135; James, 27, 43; Mary, 83; Michael, 94, 152; Precilla, 161; Susan, 158; William, 31, 173; William E., 106
COPE, Elizabeth, 74; Mary, 124; Thomas P., 119, 124
CORCEY, Emily, 51
CORDEIL, Elizabeth, 132
CORFIELD, Edward D., 166
CORKIN, Mary, 84
CORNOGG, David, 32
CORYELL, Ann Eliza, 51; Deborah, 51; Henry L., 132; Joseph, 51; Sarah, 51; Susanna, 51
COTTMAN, Benjamin, 95; Hannah, 95; Joseph, 95; Rebecca, 95; Susanna, 95; William, 95
COUGHLING, Elizabeth, 30; Lydia, 30; Martha, 29, 30; Rebecca, 30; Samuel, 30; Thomas, 30
COULSTON, Anna, 68; Barney, 68
COULTER, John, 79; Maria Isabella, 100; Mary Jane, 100
COULTON, Margaret, 40
COUPER, Belfour, 75; Bridget, 75
COWPERTHWAITE, Jos., 39; Joseph, 39
COX, Barbary, 63; Catharine, 150; Elizabeth, 26, 150; Esther, 150; Jacob, 81; James, 26, 168; John, 13; John D., 51; John G., 51; John T., 120; Kitty, 81; Margaret, 63; Mary, 120, 150; Nicholas, 51; Rachel, 150; Ruth, 51; Sarah, 134, 150; Thomas R., 63; William, 50, 51
COXE, Edward D., 123; John Redman, 150, 151; Redman, 138; Richard, 150; Sarah, 150; Theodosia, 150; Theodosia Henrietta, 150
CRABB, William, 105
CRAD, George, 149
CRAIG, Andrew, 101; Anne, 147; Fanny, 178; James, 148; Jane, 147; John, 148; Margaret, 147; Seth, 112; William, 118
CRAMNEER, Catharine, 106
CRAMOND, Mr., 3; William, 124
CRANE, Elizabeth, 64
CRANSTON, Alexander, 151
CRAP, Christiana, 140; Samuel R., 140; Susannah, 140
CRAWFORD, James, 88
CREAM, John, 9
CRESS, Henry, 147; John, 134; Lydia, 134, 166
CRESSON, Caleb, 142, 143, 144; Eleanor, 44; Jacob Keen, 44; John Elliott, 105, 134, 142,

143, 144, 166, 167; Richard C., 44
CRESSWELL, R. C., 51
CRIBS, Richard, 87
CRISMAN, Catharine, 127; Maria Elenor, 126
CROCKER, Charlotta, 64; Thomas, 64
CROMWELL, Oliver, 120
CRONE, John, 108
CROOKE, Charles, 76
CROSBY, Elizabeth, 42; Sampson, 42
CROUT, John, 164; Rebecca, 164
CROWELL, John V., 109
CROWER, George, 7
CROWLEY, John, 159
CROZET, Christiana, 68; J.B.M., 68
CRUCKSHANK, Joseph, 27, 28
CRUKSHANK, Alexnader, 164; James, 164; Jane, 164; Joseph, 105, 152, 161
CUBIN, John, 35; Sarah, 35; William, 35
CULINE, John, 50
CULMAN, John Adam, 180
CULP, Jacob, 178
CUMMINGS, Elizabeth Rogers, 101; John, 99, 111; Mary Ann, 101; William, 101
CUMMINS, David, 99
CUMMONS, James, 8
CUNNINGHAM, Christopher, 32; John, 28; Martha, 32; Mary, 21, 82
CURFIS, Sabina, 46
CURLET, Mrs., 96
CURRIE, Ann, 104; Cornelia, 104; Isabella, 104; Margaretta, 104; William, 104, 105, 109, 137; William M., 104
CURRY, Christian, 129; Susanna, 54; William, 54
CURTES, Samuel, 42
CURTIS, John, 35; John H., 164
CUSHING, C., 175; Capt., 175
CUTBUSH, Edward, 85
CUTHBERT, Frances, 26; Hannah, 143; Jacob, 26; Jacob Peter, 26; James S., 26; John, 26
CUTHBERTSON, James, 79
CUTTERIDGE, Sarah, 98

-D-

DAGNIE, William, 31
DAHETZE, Martin, 17
DALE, Dr., 2; Margaret, 2
DALLEY, Mary, 56
DALY, John, 174; Mrs., 174
DALZELL, William, 10, 55
DANACKERK, Christian, 11
DANIEL, Thomas, 85
DANNACHER, George, 41
DANNAKER, Catharine, 11
DARRACH, James, 111
DAVENPORT, Catharine Sober, 141; Elizabeth Sober, 141; Samuel, 141; William, 141
DAVIDS, Sarah, 10
DAVIDSON, James, 31; William, 34, 177
DAVIES, Garland, 10; George, 137
DAVIS, Anna, 151; Caleb, 117; Catharine, 54; Daniel, 147; Eliza, 77; Elizabeth, 93, 108; Ellis, 144; Evan, 61; George, 117; Hannah, 144; Israel, 90; James, 151; John, 147, 177; Lydia, 117; Mary, 15; Noah, 54, 108; Richard, 93; Samson, 120; Samuel, 152; Stephen, 23, 108; William, 182
DAVISON, William, 146
DAVISSON, John, 39
DAWSON, Ann, 11; Benjamin, 137; George, 78; George B., 11; Jane, 137; Robert, 153
DAY, John K., 23, 100, 107; Michael, 87; Sarah, 163
DAYMON, Francis, 115
DE BENNEVILLE, David, 122
DE BOUGON, John Vincent Marie Robineau, 46
DE LA BRUYER, A. Baugier, 132; Anthony Baugier, 8; Margaret Baugier, 8
DE LA MATER, John, 82
DE LA ROCHE, Isabella, 101; John Goyaux, 101; Louisa, 101; Mary G., 101
DE MENDOZA, Anton, 123; Antonio, 123
DE RONCERAY, Circé, 148
DE ST. CROIX, Sarah, 147
DEAL, Daniel, 161; Jacob, 161; Peter, 132, 161, 180; Susanna, 161
DEAMER, John, 157
DEAN, Alexander, 71; Elizabeth, 100; Frances, 100; John, 100; Mary, 100; Ruthy Ann, 100; William, 100
DEATON, Brazilla, 119
DEAVS, Samuel, 55
DEBENNEVILLE, George, 181
DECATUR, Ann, 83; John V., 83; Stephen, 83
DEDECKER, Charles, 64; Mary, 65

DE ESQUILBEL, Donna Manuela Castaneda, 123; Manuel, 123; Maria de los Delores, 123; Pedro Bernardo, 123
DEETZ, Daniel, 152; Frederick, 152; Fredrich, 152; John, 152; Michael, 152; Solomon, 152
DEFORREST, George, 82; Henry, 82; John, 82; Mary, 82; Peter, 82; Sophia, 82
DEIMLING, Francis C., 146
DELANY, Ann, 122; Margaret, 122; Mary, 122; William, 126
DELAPLAINE, Joseph, 135
DELAUNAY, John, 122; Josephine Verrier, 122; Julia, 122; Peter, 122; Robert, 122
DENCKLA, Anna Maria, 51; Christian, 51; Christian Christopher, 51; Henry Augustus, 51; Maria Magdalen, 51; Paul, 51; Sarah, 51
DENNIS, Hannah, 85; Sarah, 85
DENORMANDIE, Mary, 39
DENT, Anthony, 137
DEPREFONTAINE, Benjn., 180; John, 51, 127, 185
DERR, Elizabeth, 160
DERRCHAM, Doras, 93
DESALINAS, Joseph, 25
DESAQUE, Lewis, 132
DESAUQUE, L., 101
DESCAMPS, Dominique, 55; John, 55; Sarah, 55
DESHONG, Frederick, 15
DETTWEILER, John, 180
DEVAQUEZ, Jean Baptiste, 171
DEVIS, John, 50; Sarah, 50; Thomas, 50
DEWEES, John, 185; Mary, 185
DEWEY, James, 30
DEXTER, Richard, 53; Sarah, 53
DICK, Alexander, 59; Daniel, 9; Elizabeth, 164; Hester Ann, 29; James, 59; Mary, 29; Nancy, 59; Susan, 164; Susanna, 9, 164; William, 164
DICKERSON, John, 125
DICKEY, Ebenezer, 177; John M., 177; Rebecca, 183
DICKINSON, Charles, 24; Francis, 29; Jesse, 24; Joseph, 24; Mary, 24, 96; Phoebe, 29, 158; Tabitha, 24
DICKSON, James, 165
DIETERICK, Catharine, 42, 43; Joseph, 42
DIETZ, Susan, 66
DIFFENBACK, John, 120
DILLINGHAM, W. H., 144; William H., 104
DILLON, John, 82; Rodiah, 82
DIXON, Maria, 123; Sophia, 118
DOBBIE, Johanna, 103; Margret, 103
DOBSON, Judah, 177; Thomas, 103, 161, 165, 176
DOLAN, John, 132
DOLBY, John, 77; Mary, 77
DOLIN, Margaret, 131; Rachel, 131; William, 131
DONAGAN, Thomas, 81
DONALDSON, John, 70, 101; William T., 4
DONATH, Joseph, 63
DONAVAN, Sarah Wyatt, 181
DONEHOWER, George, 117
DONEL, Con. O., 33
DONNALDSON, Edward M., 6; Eliza, 6; George, 6; Hugh, 6; John, 6; Mary, 7; Richard M., 6; Sarah, 6; Susan M., 7
DONNELL, Nathaniel, 111; Sarah, 111
DOOR, Jacob, 143
DORAN, Margaret, 108; Michael, 86; Patrick, 108
DORANS, William, 131
DORLAND, George, 24
D'ORLIE, Marie Dominick James, 46
DORSEY, Ann, 108; Dr., 108; John, 18; John S., 120; John Syng, 48, 79, 144
DOUGHERTY, George, 42; Patrick, 131
DOUGLAS, George, 165; James, 165; Janet, 165; John, 165; William, 165
DOUGLASS, Abraham, 79; Elizabeth Mary, 79; Gustavus, 79; John, 79
DOVER, Elizabeth, 182
DOWE, John, 12
DOWELL, Margaret, 16
DOWNHEIM, John, 89; Maria Magdalen, 89, 90
DOWNING, Hunt, 51; Jacob, 80; Rachel, 97
DOYLES, John, 104
DRAIDREICH, David, 70
DRAKE, Roger Dillon, 148
DRAPER, Jonathan, 79; Mary, 79
DREPREFONTAINE, John, 27
DRESHER, George, 16; Mary, 16
DRINKER, H., 134; Mary, 134; William, 1, 176
DRUM, B., 21, 162
DRUMMOND, John K., 7
DU PLESSIS, P. S. Barbear, 8; Peter LeBarbier, 132, 171,

182
DU PONCEAU, Peter Stephen, 46
DU SILVA, Manuel Anto., 39
DUANE, Deborah, 59
DUBARRY, John, 123, 171
DUBOURG, Elizabeth, 168; Michael, 168
DUBUY, Susanna, 20
DUCE, Benjamin, 110
DUCHÉ, Jacob, 113; Jane, 3; John, 3
DUCKENFIED, Catharine, 148; Nathanel, 148
DUDGEON, John, 182
DUER, Hannah, 143
DUFFIELD, Abraham, 105; Amos, 128; Edward, 146; Elizabeth, 184; George, 184; John, 184; Maria, 184; Rachel, 81; Samuel, 184; William, 184
DUFFY, Catharine, 12; Patrick, 11; Phillip, 75
DUGDALE, Thomas, 1, 12, 41, 51, 62
DUHAMEL, B., 73
DUHARST, Julien, 17
DUMAS, Francis, 51
DUMOUTET, Amelia, 126; Elizabeth, 126; Emma, 126; Jane, 126; John Baptiste, 126
DUN, Andrew, 154
DUNCAN, Margaret, 36; Margaret Brogden, 103; William, 132
DUNGAN, Amos, 117, 121
DUNLAP, Ann, 105; Charlotte, 105; Elizabeth, 105; Harriot, 105; James, 40, 154; John, 105; Mary, 105; Sarah, 105; William, 105
DUNN, Jacob, 130; James L., 51; Nathan, 101; Philip T., 78; Rachel, 130
DUNWOODY, John, 51
DUPONCEAU, Peter S., 5, 102, 123; Peter Stephen, 123
DUPUY, Charles Meredith, 133; Daniel, 15, 133; John, 133; Mary, 133
DURLIN, Mary, 162
DURNEY, Michael, 72
DUTILH, Abel Peter, 5; Catharine Magdalen, 5; Catherine Magdalen, 4; Stephen, 4, 141
DUTTON, Hannah, 106; James, 105, 106; John, 106
DUVALL, James S., 147
DUVIGNAN, Jean Baptiste, 17

-E-

EADEN, Joseph, 51
EADES, G, 148
EAGEN, Michael, 84
EAGLE, John, 98
EAKIN, Alexander, 105; Ann, 105; Eliza, 105; Henrietta Bankson, 105; Samuel, 105; William, 105
EARL, Clayton, 18
EARLE, Caleb, 65; Edward, 82, 83
EASTBURN, Caroline, 87; Elouisa, 87; Esther, 87; Rachel, 87
EASTLACK, Ann, 158
EASTON, Jonathan, 15
EASTWICK, Stephen, 170
EBERLE, Charles, 51
EBERLIN, T. T., 68
ECCLES, James, 33
ECFELDT, Adam, 5
ECKARD, Susan R., 83
ECKART, Adam, 143
ECKERT, John, 126
ECKFELDT, Adam, 90, 97, 154, 156
EDDY, Catharine, 96; Charles, 96; Esther, 96, 97; Frances, 96; George, 96; James, 96; Lewis, 96; Lucy, 96; Mary Ann, 96, 97; Phebe, 96
EDELMAN, Francis Elizabeth, 175; George Washington, 175; Isaac, 175; Mary, 175; Sarah, 175
EDENBORN, Jacob, 74; Mary, 74
EDEY, Richard Thomas Atkins, 171
EDGER, Ann, 157; Catharine, 157; James, 157; Margaret, 157; Martha, 157
EDLE, John, 182; Matthias, 182
EDWARDS, Ann, 178; Charles, 178; David, 11; Elizabeth, 178; Ezekiel, 24; Griffith, 24; Hannah, 126; Jane, 11; Jesse, 126; John, 126, 127; Margaret, 113; Samuel, 178; Sarah, 24, 127; Thomas K., 126
EGAN, Michael, 167
EGEN, Sarah, 183
EGERT, George, 161; Philip, 161
EHRENZELLER, G., 60, 154
EICKANDS, Thomas, 87
EISENRING, Andrew, 66; Christian, 66; George, 66; John, 66; Lawrence, 66
ELDER, Elizabeth, 80; Thomas, 80
ELDRIDGE, Job, 151; Tacy, 151
ELIOT, John, 148; Mary, 148

ELKINS, Ann, 27; James, 27; Joseph, 27; Mary, 27; William, 27
ELKINTON, Asa, 130
ELLIN, Elizabeth, 147; Jane, 147
ELLING, William, 47
ELLIOT, John, 149; Mary, 149
ELLIOTT, Daniel, 27, 28; Elizabeth, 27; Hannah, 27, 97; Harvey, 27; Isaac, 69; John, 25, 27, 28, 144, 149; Mary, 27; Theophila, 149
ELLIS, Elizabeth, 136; Samuel B., 75
ELLISON, Elizabeth, 170
ELMSLIE, Alexander, 71, 163, 164
ELTON, Anthony, 102; Mary, 102
EMERICK, Dewalt, 81; Frederick, 81; Henry, 81; Maria Catharina, 81; Maria Magdalena, 81
EMERY, Samuel, 171; Sarah, 22
EMLEN, Caleb, 143; George, 31; Hudson, 143; Samuel, 31
EMRY, Hannah, 8; Hetty, 8; John, 8; Julian, 8; Sally, 8; Sarah, 8; William, 8
ENGARD, Abraham, 9
ENGLE, Francis, 165; James, 29, 168; John, 164; Margaret, 111; Thomas S., 168; W. James, 29; William, 164
ENGLES, Henry, 139
ENGLISH, Charles, 51; Emily, 51
ENNIS, William, 157
ENOCH, John, 158
ENTRIKIN, Thomas, 81
ERDMAN, Charles, 97; Jacob, 74
ERWIN, Robert, 37
ESHERS, William, 8
ESLER, Elizabeth Knox, 99; George, 99; John Knox, 99; Rebecca, 99
ESPELIUS, Francisco, 123; Maria de los Delores, 123
ESTLACK, Margaret, 61
ESTY, Moses, 44
ETRIS, Catherine, 23; Elizabeth, 23; Mary, 23; Matilda, 23; Samuel, 74
EUSKILE, Henry, 97
EUSTACK, Margaret, 9; Mary, 9
EUTACHE, Daniel, 9
EVANS, Barbara, 163, 164; Charles, 24; David, 13; Edward, 130; Eliza, 90; Elizabeth, 109; Hannah, 86, 176; Issachar, 90; Jane, 13; Jenkins, 90; John, 13, 115, 130, 163, 176; John C., 15, 62; Jona., 176; Jonathan, 32, 176; Joseph 13; Josiah, 147; Lydia, 130; Margaret, 130; Martha, 130; Mary, 12, 176; Miles, 86; Rachel, 13; Robert, 12, 13, 90; Robert T., 90; Sarah, 90, 106, 130; Sarah E., 24; Susanna, 130; Thomas, 130; William, 13, 176
EVERHART, Charlotte, 38; John, 38
EWING, Amelia, 34, 88; Catharine, 88; Edward, 77; Elizabeth, 34; Hannah, 34; James S., 88; John, 34, 77, 89; Joseph, 77; Samuel, 34, 88, 89, 177; Thomas, 34; William, 34; William Elliott, 34
EYRE, Franklin, 103, 105, 179; George, 103, 179; Hannah, 23, 29, 118, 132; L. W., 145; Manuel, 118; Nathan, 82; Thomas, 67

-F-

FACKMAN, Christian F., 28
FAGUNDUS, George, 180
FAIRPOUX, John, 119
FALCONER, Mary, 24, 161; Nathan, 110; William, 24
FANNEN, Anthony, 16
FANNING, Charles, 132
FARIES, William, 102
FARQUHAR, Benajah A., 118; Elizabeth, 125; Elizabeth Widowson, 125; George, 125; Wildman, 125
FARRON, James, 44
FARROWILH, A., 122
FEARISS, Francis, 111
FEARON, James, 44
FEBIGER, Christian, 89; Mrs., 89
FEINOUE, George, 64
FELGENTREFF, Frederick, 78
FELTON, Elizabeth, 106; George, 106
FENTON, David, 8; Peter, 8
FERGUSON, Ann, 32; Ebenezer, 11, 72, 140; Elizabeth, 139; Jane, 162; William, 32
FERIS, Benjamin, 60
FERRADAY, John, 131
FERRETY, Joseph M., 25
FESMIRE, John, 127
FEST, Christopher, 116; Eliza, 116
FETTIPLACE, Elizabeth, 149
FFEACHON, Mary, 37; William, 37

FFIRTH, Elizabeth, 133; Hannah, 133; Henry, 133; John, 133; Mary, 133; Taber, 133
FFOGDEN, Elizabeth, 37; Thomas, 37
FIBLER, Daniel, 100
FIELD, Thomas S., 73
FILE, Susanna, 181
FILLAR, Jacob, 93, 96
FINK, Jacob, 156
FINNEY, Christiana, 78; Elizabeth, 113; Joseph, 130; Sarah, 129
FIRTH, Thomas, 56
FISBY, Edward, 148
FISHER, Albanus C., 174; Coleman, 37; David, 175; Elisha, 142; Eliza G., 173, 174; Elizabeth, 96; Elizabeth Powell, 30, 31; Esther, 30, 31, 137, 174; Hannah, 27, 155; Hannah Logan, 30, 53; Jabez Maud, 31; James C., 154; James Logan, 30, 31, 173, 174; John, 96, 136; Joshua, 30, 31, 173; Mary, 142; Miers, 30, 31, 47, 166, 167; Mrs., 137; Rebecca, 155; Redwood, 31; Samuel, 27; Samuel R., 15, 31; Samuel Rhoads, 37; Samuel W., 37, 155; Sydney George, 173, 174; Tabitha, 155; Thomas, 30, 31, 53, 173; William, 155; William Logan, 30, 31, 174
FISS, Mary, 145
FISTER, George Adam, 143
FITE, Anna, 19; Richard, 19
FITZGERALD, Ann, 138; Catharine, 2; John, 138; Lydia, 138; Martha, 138; Robert, 138; Thomas, 33
FITZGERLAND, Thomas, 2
FITZIMONS, Thomas, 31
FLAGG, Ann, 99; Eliza, 99; Jonathan, 99
FLANAGAN, Hannah, 68; James, 90
FLANEGAN, James, 5
FLANNER, William, 183
FLAVEL, David, 162; Ferdinand, 84
FLECK, George, 143
FLECKENSTINE, Samuel, 63
FLECKINSTINE, Samuel, 59
FLEMING, John, 158; Joseph H., 183; Robert, 6
FLETCHER, Anna, 55; Rebecca, 185
FLINN, Catharine, 154; Richard, 154
FLOWER, Enock, 77
FLOWERS, John, 3
FLOYD, John, 6
FOGDON, Thomas, 37
FOLWELL, John, 18, 100; Mary Weed, 100; Richard, 58, 183; Ruth, 100
FONTANGES, P. F., 147
FORD, Elizabeth, 84; Jacob, 164; Lawrence, 46
FORDYCE, Henrietta, 137
FOREPAUGH, George, 124
FORER, Pat., 56
FORREST, Catharine, 179; Mary, 109; Thomas, 7, 109
FORST, Abraham, 68
FORSYTHE, James, 169
FOSTER, Joseph, 133, 158; Josiah, 142; Lydia, 142; Sarah, 109
FOTHERGILL, Anthony, 136, 137
FOTTERALL, Stephen C., 55
FOULKE, Eleanor, 62; Elizabeth, 62; George, 108; John, 62
FOULKROD, Jacob, 160; John, 160
FOURNIER, John, 9
FOWLER, Maria, 74
FOX, Christian, 66; Frances, 66, 67; George, 105; Joseph, 66; Justinian, 29, 66; Michael, 97; Sibella, 22; William, 22, 80
FRALEY, Elizabeth, 40; John W., 40; Rebecca, 109
FRANCE, Abraham, 31
FRANCIS, Abby, 74; Ann, 74; Catharine, 2; Charles, 74; Dorothy, 74; Elizabeth, 2; Elizabeth Powell, 74; John, 44; John Brown, 74; Sarah, 2, 32; Thomas, 2, 33; Thomas Eg., 70; Thomas W., 70; Thomas Willing, 74
FRANK, John Elizabeth, 54; Lewis, 54; T. L. W., 62
FRANKLIN, Benjamin, 59
FRAZER, Robert, 40
FRAZIER, Ann, 64; Anne, 100; Nalbro, 64
FREAS, George, 175
FREDERICK, John George, 66
FREEMAN, John, 106
FREESE, George, 138; Martha, 138
FRENAYE, Mark Anthony, 147
FRENCH, Charles, 28; Charles C., 13; Jonathan, 74
FRENO, Paul, 16
FREYTAG, Michael, 155
FRICKE, Frederick, 135
FRICKER, Joseph, 29; Nicholas, 69

FRICKES, Frederick, 17
FRITZ, Catharine, 83; Elizabeth, 84; Jacob, 83; John, 84; Peter, 87
FRY, Catharine, 160; Elizabeth, 160; Eve, 160; Jacob, 160; John, 63, 160; John H., 93; William, 94, 167
FRYBURG, Catharine, 94; Elizabeth, 94; Hannah, 94; Jacob, 94; John, 94; John L.; Joseph, 94; Mary, 94; Sarah, 94; Susanna, 94
FRYETT, Daniel, 37
FRYHOFFER, John, 9; Wollery, 90; Woolery, 30, 111
FULLER, Ann, 153; Archibald, 153; Elizabeth, 153; John, 153; Mrs., 113; William, 153
FULTON, Gardiner, 139; Samuel, 129
FUNK, Henry, 18
FYAN, John, 55; Mrs., 55

-G-

GAFFANY, John, 174; Mary, 174
GALBRAITH, Andrews, 80; Betsey, 80; Hugh, 80; John, 81; Samuel, 80
GALLAGHAR, James, 5
GALLAGHER, Anna M., 63; Barnard, 155; Catharine, 63; John P., 63; Mary, 63; Thomas, 63
GALLAHER, James, 63, 99
GALLOWAY, John, 5; Sarah, 5
GALTON, Susanh, 148
GAMBER, John, 42; Mary, 42
GAMBLE, James, 85; John, 94
GARAUD, Jacob, 181
GARDINER, Elizabeth, 176, 178; John, 176; Mary, 176; Richard, 176
GARDNER, Catharine, 32; Henry, 32; Jacob, 32; John Jacob, 32; Mary, 40, 53; Nancy, 32; Rachael, 32, 108; Rachel, 111; Valentine, 32
GARDY, John, 125
GARRAUD, Catharine, 181; Jean Jacques, 181
GARRET, Andrew, 102; Joseph, 128; Morton, 102, 128; Samuel, 102
GARRETSON, Elikim, 138
GARRETT, Joseph, 170; Levi, 69; Margaret, 170; Morton, 129, 170; Susanna, 170; William, 129
GARRIGUES, Ab. M., 39; Abraham M., 39; Edward, 117, 160; Hannah H., 152; Margaret, 152; Samuel, 20; William, 59
GARRITSON, Hannah, 82
GARROTT, Andrew, 128
GARTLAND, John, 172
GARWOOD, Benjamin, 175; William, 175
GASKILL, Caleb, 119
GAUDIEHAND, Peter, 61
GAULT, William, 164
GAVANER, Valentine, 68
GAVIN, Thomas, 48
GAW, Gilbert, 30
GEIGER, Martin, 125
GEISE, Johannes, 87
GEISEL, George, 181
GEISSE, Ann, 132; Mary Denny, 131; Rachel, 131; Wilhelmina, 132
GEORGE, Eliza, 173; Joseph, 19; Margaret, 6, 7; Mary, 6; Mrs., 73
GERTARD, William, 117
GESNER, George, 117; Maria, 117
GEYER, Catharine, 84; Elizabeth, 83
GEYGER, George, 123; Sarah, 123
GIBBES, Philip, 110
GIBESON, Phebe, 121
GIBSON, Ann, 18; James, 5, 43, 107, 133, 135, 144, 177
GIEDOR, Josannen, 41
GIFFORD, William, 37
GILBERT, Samuel, 9
GILES, Ann, 51; Thomas, 53; William, 150
GILL, Hannah, 155; Robert, 155
GILLESPIE, Jane, 151
GILLESPY, John, 159
GILLIARD, John, 113
GILLINGHAM, Mahlon, 133; Martha, 127; Thomas, 133
GILPIN, Joshua, 31; Lydia, 31; Thomas, 31
GINDER, Betsy, 164
GISEL, George, 182; Molly, 182
GLEN, Frances, 97; James, 80; Mary, 97
GLENTWORTH, Dr., 137; Plunket F., 121
GLONINGER, Philip, 117
GLOUCESTER, John, 76
GLOVER, Hester, 161; William, 161
GOELHARDT, Ludwig, 47
GOETZ, Andrew, 97; Apollonia, 97; Barbara, 97; Catharina, 97; George, 97; Johannes, 97; John, 97; Michael, 97
GOLDEN, David, 76; Hannah, 76; John, 76

GOLDSMITH, John, 99
GOMES, Dom. Jose, 39
GOMINGER, John, 165
GOOD, Conrad, 91; Elizabeth, 1; Jacob, 1, 45
GOODMAN, ---, 80; George Michael, 119; John, 135, 150
GOODWIN, Elizabeth, 140; George, 34; Joseph, 140; Mrs., 32; Thomas, 32
GORDON, Abigail, 23; Ann, 6; Catharine, 6; Clarise, 2; David, 2; Elisha, 2, 13, 33; Elizabeth, 2, 33; Enoch, 23; Henry, 6; James, 6; John, 6; Mordecai L., 23, 104; Rebecca, 13; Robert, 2, 129, 152; Sarah, 2; Thomas, 2
GOREE, Patimer, 134
GORGAS, George, 25; John, 23, 165; Joseph, 121
GORING, Joseph, 144; Mary, 144
GOSNER, George, 94
GOSTLING, George, 51; Nathaniel, 51
GOUGE, John, 169
GOUGH, Edward, 67; Jesse, 67
GOVETT, Sarah, 113
GRABA, Philip, 183
GRAFELY, Christopher, 15
GRAFF, Charles, 14; Frederick, 14; George, 117; Jacob, 14; Maria, 139; Mary, 14
GRAHAM, Dav., 78; Peter, 165; Robert H., 115; Robert W., 115; William, 6, 122, 129
GRAMER, Catharina, 91
GRANT, Margaret, 11; Mary Elizabeth, 151; Robert, 21, 153; Thomas, 151
GRASSLER, Anna Sophia, 1
GRATZ, Simon, 85
GRAVELLE, Rene' L., 132
GRAVENSTINE, I. N., 65; Peter, 62
GRAY, Elizabeth, 57; George, 15; James, 177; Kitty, 57; Nathan, 81; Patima, 70; Sarah, 57; William, 57, 177
GREAVES, Caspar, 83; Mary, 83
GREBLE, George, 66; Jacob, 66; Rebecca, 66; William, 66
GREEMAN, Anna, 98; Barsheba, 98; David, 99; James, 99; Jolianna, 99; Mary, 98; Mrs., 162; Thomas, 98; William, 99
GREEN, Ann, 143; Ashbel, 24; Jane, 100; Mary, 143; Michael, 159; Robert, 21; Robert M., 60; Robert S., 60; Sarah, 96, 97, 143; William, 143
GREENAY, Sarah, 70
GREENE, Myles, 53
GREENER, John, 111; Mary, 111
GREENEVELT, Louisa, 160
GREER, James, 169; Martha, 169
GREINER, John, 36, 46, 103, 111; Sarah, 67
GRIFFING, Joseph Carson, 108
GRIFFITH, George, 3; John, 38; William, 175; William V., 99
GRIFFITHS, Elizabeth, 93; Samuel Powel, 93; William, 68
GRIFFITTS, Samuel P., 7
GRIFITH, Samuel, 99
GRIM, Peter, 36
GRINNELL, William, 156
GROSSCUP, Catharine, 140; Elizabeth, 140; Jacob, 140; John, 140, 141; Mary, 140; William, 140
GROSSKOP, Jacob, 140
GROVER, Abigail, 178; Charles, 178; Elizabeth, 178; John, 178; Martha, 9; Robert, 178; Sarah, 178
GROVES, Daniel, 46
GRUB, Samuel, 112
GUIER, George, 159; Stephen John, 153
GUIZEL, George, 182; Molly, 182
GUNKLE, Michael, 142; Michl., 144
GURNEY, Francis, 15, 50, 83; Henry, 118; Mary, 83
GUSTIS, Absolom, 76
GUYER, Casper, 35
GUYON, John, 9

-H-

HAAS, Frederick, 66, 81; Jacob, 16, 141
HADDEN, Thomas, 174
HAFFLINE, Frederick, 71
HAGA, Frederick, 89; Godfrey, 68, 89; Mrs., 89
HAGUE, Michael, 83
HAILER, Frederick, 129
HAINES, Amos, 38; Ann, 11; Anna Catharine, 10; Caspar, 147; Catharine, 11; Hannah, 97; Jane, 24; John, 11; Margaret, 10, 11; Mary, 10, 38; Richard, 38; Samuel, 134
HALBERSTADT, George, 77
HALE, Thomas, 101, 177
HALES, Eliza, 153
HALFPENNY, Jane, 134; John, 149
HALL, Catharine Hannah, 88; David, 18; Elizabeth, 14; John, 82, 88; Martha, 60;

Mary, 178; Rebecca, 178; Samuel Scotten, 40; Sarah, 88; Thomas, 40; Thomas M., 154; White, 99
HALLOWEL, Ann, 173
HALLOWELL, Agnes, 109; William, 95
HALZEL, Philip, 24
HALZELL, Philip, 44
HAM, James, 56
HAMILL, James, 21
HAMILTON, Elizabeth, 178; James, 103, 124; Margaret, 124; Mary, 117; William, 124
HAMMEL, James, 82
HAMMER, Louis, 47
HAMMETT, Samuel, 42
HAMMITT, Frances, 33
HAMPTON, Alexr., 60; Priscilla, 41
HANCHMAN, John, 79
HAND, Hannah, 102; Nathan, 102
HANNA, John, 163
HANSELL, Barnet, 150; Esther, 150; Jacob, 2, 51; Mary, 2; Sarah, 150
HANSMAN, Christopher, 74; Daniel, 74
HARBESON, Benjamin Cottman, 95; Susanna, 95
HARDEN, Charles, 53; Elizabeth, 53
HARDING, Elizabeth, 167
HARDY, John, 151; Julia Ann, 162; Peggy, 96; Thomas, 162
HARE, Ann, 45, 102; Charles Willing, 45; Charlotte, 45; Elizabeth, 102; George, 102; Hannah, 102; James, 45; Jane, 102; John Powel, 45; Margaret, 45; Martha, 45; Mary, 102; Richard, 45; Robert, 45, 82, 102; Sidney, 102; William, 102
HARKER, Joseph, 47
HARLAN, Alice, 27
HARLAND, Sarah, 83
HARMER, Lewis, 8
HAROLD, William N., 167
HARPER, James, 79; John, 124; Margaret, 124; Mary, 127; Nathan, 92, 127, 138; Patrick, 86; Peter, 124; Thomas, 79, 124; William, 124
HARR, Elizabeth, 23
HARRIS, Abigail, 112; Catharine, 150, 151; Elizabeth, 17; George, 112; Hannah, 112; Jesse, 112; Mary, 112; Nathaniel, 150, 151; Rebecca, 112; Samuel, 112; Sarah, 112; Thomas, 112; William, 112
HARRISON, George, 74; James, 40, 93; Jane, 55; Joseph, 96; Peyton, 100; Richard, 30; Robert, 13; Ruth, 13; Sarah, 96; Sophia, 74; William, 16
HARRY, Sarah, 146
HART, Eleanor, 158; Esther, 67; Hannah, 104, 183; John, 138, 141; Samuel D., 67
HARTLE, George, 110
HARTLEY, Michael, 27
HARTLY, John M., 49
HARTMAN, Henry, 31
HARTSHORN, William, 45
HARTSHORNE, Sarah, 40
HARVARD, Catharine, 141
HARVEY, Isaac, 51, 133; Jacob, 149, 150; Job, 51; Margaret, 111; Samuel, 136; Thomas, 111
HARWOOD, Elizabeth Franklin, 59
HASTINGS, John, 169; Rebecca, 50
HASTON, John, 141
HATFIELD, Nathan, 61
HATHAWAY, Caleb, 76
HAUCK, John, 156
HAVENSTRITE, Jacob, 72; Samuel, 72
HAVLIND, Cornelius, 12
HAWES, Benjamin, 137; W., 137
HAWKINS, Elizabeth Bosio, 140; Moses, 140; Rebecca Bosio, 140
HAWNING, Catharine, 143
HAWTHORN, Daniel, 85; Mary, 61; Thomas P., 85
HAY, Edward, 115
HAYDOCK, Ann, 40; Eden, 10, 40, 97, 135; Hannah, 143; Henry, 143; Rebecca, 143; Robert, 40; Samuel, 40; Susan, 40
HAZENS, Moses, 169
HEAD, John, 159
HEALY, Elizabeth, 144
HEATH, Joseph, 172
HEATLY, Charles, 153; Henrietta, 153; Henry, 153; John, 153; Lucy, 153; Martha, 153; Mary, 153
HEBER, Johannes L., 91
HEFFERNAN, John, 35; Mary, 35
HEIBERGER, George, 108
HEIGHT, Barclay, 148
HEILEY, Casper, 20
HEILING, John, 71
HEINISSEN, Jacob, 10
HEISLER, Mary, 121; Peter, 69; William, 121
HELLINGS, Elizabeth, 134;

James, 134; John, 33, 123, 134
HELM, Ann, 89; Christian, 89; Elizabeth, 89, 133; John, 89
HELMS, Job, 117; Mary, 117
HELMUTH, John K., 51
HELT, Elizabeth, 168; Hannah, 168; Henry, 168; Mary, 168
HELVESON, Thomas, 129
HEMERY, John, 22
HEMPHILL, James, 170; Joseph, 19
HENDERSON, Ann, 8; Robert, 161
HENDRICKS, James, 3
HENDRICKSON, Isaac, 165
HENDRY, James, 69; Sarah, 69, 118
HENDY, James, 110
HENGEL, Ruth, 184
HENKELS, Daniel, 108
HENNION, Elizabeth, 145
HENRY, Alexander, 78; Amelia, 144; Caleb Bickham, 47
HEPBURN, James, 75
HEREN, John, 94
HERENSTAD, Catharine, 101
HERNEISEN, Ann Margaret, 102; Anna Maria, 102; George, 102; Jacob, 102
HERNSTAD, Joseph, 101
HERON, Sarah Ann, 178
HERRITAGE, Josiah, 28
HERSY, Philip, 161
HERTZOG, Andrew, 58; Barbara, 58; Eve, 22; Joseph, 58; Michel, 43; Peter, 25, 58; Rachel, 58; Rebecca, 58; Susan, 58; Walter, 22
HESS, George, 15
HESSER, Ann, 160
HESTON, Abraham, 19; Charles, 144; Mary, 144; Mordecai, 144
HEVELAND, John, 24; Stephen, 24
HEWSON, John, 18, 87; Thomas, 23; Thomas L., 41
HEY, Augustus, 11
HEYDRICK, Abraham, 16; Susanna, 16
HEYL, Elizabeth, 40; George, 49; John, 8, 40, 41; Mary, 40; Philip, 40; William, 96
HICKEY, Jane M., 177
HIESLER, William, 45
HIFFERNAN, John, 35; Mary, 35
HIGBEE, Elizabeth, 97; Virginia, 97
HIGGINS, Francis, 46, 57, 108; Hannah, 108; Jemima, 99
HILBORN, Ruth, 50
HILBOURN, Mary, 113
HILL, Catharine, 12; Elizabeth, 12; Hannah, 12; Henry, 31; John, 115, 117; Jonathan, 12; Margaret, 19, 115; Mary, 12; Moses, 12; Rachel, 12; Richard, 19, 115; William, 117
HILLEGAS, Henrietta, 136; Joseph K., 169; Maria, 136; Samuel, 136
HILLIS, David, 92
HILLMAN, Ann, 170; Cornelius, 175; Elizabeth, 170; Hannah, 170; John, 170; Margaret, 170; Mary Ann, 170, 175; Patience, 170, 171; Rachel, 170; Rebecca, 171; Sarah, 175; Thomas, 175
HILT, Elizabeth, 168; Hannah, 168; Henry, 168; Mary, 168
HILTON, Frances, 124; George W., 124
HILYARD, Kezia, 61; Martha, 61
HINCKLE, John, 132
HINCKLES, Daniel, 108
HINDMAN, Betsy, 158; John, 158
HINDSILLWOOD, John, 79
HINKLE, Hannah, 133; John, 117
HINNEMAN, Charlotte, 145
HINTER, Elizabeth, 30; George, 30; Isabella, 30; Mary, 30; Sarah, 30
HIRE, George, 75
HIREBONE, William, 80
HIRES, Hannah, 127
HITCHCOCK, Daniel, 12, 126
HOCKER, Leonard, 150; Rachel, 150
HODGDON, Elizabeth, 22
HOFFMAN, Ann, 78; Awbrey, 145; Catharine, 78; Daniel, 78; Frederick, 78; Jacob, 166; John, 78, 145; Mary, 78; Morgan, 145; Sebastian, 3; Susanna, 78, 79; Valentine, 78
HOFFNER, Anna Maria, 66; Eliza, 66; George, 66; Henry, 66; Maria, 66; William, 66
HOGAN, Denis, 19
HOLAHAN, Amos, 60; David, 60; Hannah, 60; Phoebe, 60
HOLDERNESSE, John F., 54
HOLGATE, jacob, 15
HOLGET, Cornelius, 154; John, 92, 154
HOLKER, John, 31
HOLLABUSH, Yost, 14
HOLLAND, Nathaniel, 91, 163
HOLLINGSHEAD, Edmund, 123, 142; Hannah, 142, 144; Lydia, 123
HOLLINGSWORTH, Ann Maria, 163;

Jehu, 83, 144, 163; Samuel, 163; Thomas G., 163
HOLLINSHEAD, Catharine, 141; Lydia, 140; Samuel, 141
HOLLOBUSH, Yost, 180
HOLLOWDAY, Ann, 148
HOLLOWELL, Priscilla, 140; Thomas, 140
HOLMES, George, 101; Hugh, 153; William, 166
HOLSTON, George, 19
HONG, Hawqua, 147
HOOD, Hannah, 181; Thomas, 138; William, 138
HOODS, Mrs., 162
HOOK, Catharine, 87; Christina Susannah, 87; Elizabeth, 87; Hester, 87; John, 58, 87; Margaret, 87; Mary, 58, 87; William, 87
HOOP, Adam, 99; David, 99; Margaret, 99; Mary, 99; Robert, 99
HOOPER, Henry, 94; Sarah, 94
HOOPES, George, 138; Sarah, 144
HOOPS, David, 100; Mary, 112; Sarah, 112
HOOVER, John, 152
HOPE, Thomas, 132
HOPKINS, Ann, 143; Elizabeth, 143; Hannah, 143; Matthew, 53; Richard, 142; Samuel, 143
HOPP, Godfrey, 179; Mary, 180
HOPPER, Isaac T., 37
HORNER, John, 19, 151
HORNKETH, Jeremiah, 97
HORNOR, Jane, 171
HORROD, Mary, 148
HORTZ, Peter, 29
HORWITZ, I., 181
HOSKIN, Thomas, 44, 120
HOSKINS, John, 159, 180
HOUGH, Mary, 18; Thomas, 18, 31
HOULTON, David, 53; Jemima, 53; John, 53; Mary, 53; Sarah, 53; Thomas, 53; William, 53
HOUPT, Jacob, 56
HOUSTON, Paul, 3; Sidney Jane, 112; Thomas Washington, 4
HOVER, Lawrence, 169
HOW, Jeffery, 27
HOWARD, Elizabeth, 133; George, 133; John, 103; John Eager, 5; Margaret, 5, 133; Mary, 133; Rebecca, 113; Sarah, 133
HOWELL, Ann, 107; Arthur, 142; Benjamin B., 143; Deborah, 142; Hannah, 142; Isaac, 169; James, 57; John, 149; Joseph, 142, 143; Lemuel, 119; Maria Meredith, 107; Mary, 138; Reading, 138; Richard, 156; Sarah, 98; William W., 142
HOWEY, James, 106
HOY, Archibald, 154; Charles, 154; Mary, 154; William, 154
HOYLAND, John, 15
HOZEY, Isaac, 3
HUBLEY, Bernard, 14; Elizabeth, 14; Elizabeth Rich, 14; Eve, 14; George Washington, 14; James Sample, 14; John Adams, 14; Mary Magdalen, 14; Tamar Sarah Ann, 14
HUCKEL, Joseph, 73
HUDDELL, Joseph, 7, 75
HUFFNAGLE, John, 4
HUGG, Jacob, 79
HUGGINS, Benjamin, 145
HUGHES, Daniel, 121; Elizabeth, 89; Mary, 121; William, 121
HUIGES, John J., 90
HULBY, William, 23
HULINGS, Hetty, 151; Micahol, 18; Mrs., 100; William E., 100
HULME, John, 180
HULSECAMP, Catharine, 83; Garret, 83; Mary, 83
HUME, Thomas, 154
HUMMELL, Barbara, 162; Casper, 162; John, 162; Magdalena, 162
HUMPHREY, Sophia, 145
HUMPHREYS, Andrew Y., 5; Assheton Y., 5; Hannah, 152; James, 5; James Y., 5; Lodowick Sprogell, 5; Margaret, 152; Martha Y., 6; Mary York, 6; Mary Yorke, 5; Susanna Y., 5, 6; Thomas Y., 5
HUMPHRIES, Hannah, 117
HUNT, John, 127
HUNTER, Daniel, 131; Rachel, 87
HUNTSMAN, Hezekiah, 23
HURLEY, David, 170; Hannah, 170; Michael, 167; Thomas, 167
HURST, Ann, 83; Elizabeth, 139
HURTENSTEIN, John, 136
HUSBAND, Lydia, 96
HUSTAN, Joseph, 141
HUSTON, John, 15, 76, 173; Matthew, 51; William, 15, 58, 173
HUTCHINSON, Elizabeth, 119; James, 103; John, 51, 88, 116, 120; Mahlon, 118; Nancy C., 119; R., 93; Sarah, 103; Sidney E., 93; Thomas, 119
HUTCHISON, James, 153

HUTT, Elijah, 51; Jonathan, 51; Lucy, 51; Mary, 51; Rebecca, 51; Tabitha, 51
HUTTON, Ann, 60; John, 60
HYDE, Catharine, 67; George, 161

-I-
INGELS, George, 90
INGERSOLL, Jared, 80; Jered, 129
INGLIS, Joseph L., 18
INGRAM, Christobell, 149; Frances, 149; Joseph, 149; Mary, 149; Robert, 149; Samuel, 149; Susannah, 149; Theophila, 149; Thomas, 149
INGS, David, 174; Lucy Ann, 174; Sarah, 174
IRELAND, Alphonso, 98; George, 33
IRWIN, James, 116; Margaret, 110; Thomas, 177
ISRAEL, Catharine Douce, 75; Charles Hutchinson, 75; Israel, 51; Joseph, 75; Mary Cammack, 75; Mary Reading, 75; William Hewitt, 75
IVES, John, 120; Pamela, 61, 160; Pamelia, 120

-J-
JACKSON, Alfred E., 70; Ann, 22; Caroline, 70; Christian, 78; Deborah, 144, 183; Edith, 28; Eliza, 70; Elizabeth, 70, 177; Hannah, 28; Harriet, 70; Harriot, 45; Henry, 28, 70; Holliday, 18; Isaac, 28, 183; James, 22; Jane, 18; John, 28, 110, 157; Joseph, 28; Mary, 28; Nancy, 28; Samuel, 70; Thomas, 28; Widow, 157; William, 22
JACOB, Joseph, 146
JACOBS, Chapman, 9; Charles, 127; Israel, 16; James, 9; Joseph Dwight, 9; Samuel H., 28
JAMES, Catharine, 130; David, 139; Dr., 137; James, 74; Jesse, 168; John, 129; Otto, 75; Thomas C., 93, 166, 167; Thomas Chalkley, 62
JAMISON, Samuel, 89
JANNEY, Benjamin, 64; Elizabeth, 64; George Fox, 64; Israel Pennock, 64; Lewis, 64; Mary, 64; Say, 64
JANNNEY, Benjamin S., 131
JANUARY, Widow, 111
JARRETT, David, 50; Lydia, 20; Mary, 20; Rebecca, 50
JASPER, James, 82; Susanna, 82
JAUDON, Daniel, 4
JAUDRAU, John, 9
JEFFERS, Daniel, 154; James, 154
JELTY, Earnes, 170
JENDER, Susannah, 54
JENKINS, Joseph, 142
JENKS, Ann, 140; Joseph R., 144
JENNER, Edward, 51
JENNEY, Sarah Elizabeth, 133
JERVIS, Charles, 176; Elizabeth, 1, 128; Jane, 176; Lucy, 97; Phoebe, 176; Samuel, 176; Sarah, 1, 176
JEWELL, Joseph, 161
JININS, Elizabeth, 127
JINNINGS, Elizabeth, 127
JOHNS, Joseph, 77; Mary, 49; Matthew, 49; Thomas, 49
JOHNSON, Abraham, 77; Anthony, 55, 147; Benjamin, 8, 51, 158; Christiana, 158; Eleanor, 69; Elias, 158; Elizabeth Jones, 77; Francis, 81; Hannah, 10, 29, 40; Isaac, 60; Jane, 69; John, 81, 93, 106, 125, 172; Joseph, 77; Joseph Morris, 77; Josiah, 30; Justus, 55; Lawrence, 60; Lydia, 123; M., 46; Magdalen, 77; Maria, 54; Mary, 77; Moses, 69; Rachel, 114; Robert, 106; Samuel, 71, 92, 98; Stephen, 46; Susannah, 54; Wenyfred, 106
JOHNSTON, Adam, 107; Alexander, 64; Ann, 89; Capt., 89; David J., 36; Eleanor, 107; Hannah, 111; John, 36, 84, 125, 151; Josiah, 134
JONES, Abraham, 72; Absalom, 22, 50, 57; Absolom, 81; Ann, 19; Benjamin, 10, 17; Blathwaite, 3; Caroline, 11; Catharine, 19, 130; Charles, 140; Daniel, 142, 144; David, 19, 140, 142, 147; Deborah, 92; Elizabeth, 39, 102; Emly, 11; George, 142; Gibbs, 3; Griffith, 130; Hannah, 142; Harriet, 140; Horatis Gates, 92; Isaiah, 140; Israel, 140; Jacob Comly, 11; James, 19, 22, 117; Jane, 19; Jesse, 11; John, 93, 96, 140, 142; Jonathan, 142; Joshua, 121, 128; Kitte Ann, 11; Lewis, 19; Loyd, 96; Magdalen, 147;

Margaret, 142, 144; Martha, 89, 142, 185; Mary, 3, 11, 104, 147; Mrs., 113; Nathan, 19, 104; Nicholas, 172; Owen, 31, 144, 166, 167; Priscilla, 140; Rebecca, 31, 96; Ruth, 140; Samuel, 122, 178, 185; Sarah, 55, 147; Sebina, 22; Susanna, 172; Susannah, 132; Theodore, 140; Thomas, 19, 147; Valentine, 109; William Watts, 159
JORDAN, Ann, 90; Hannah, 90; Isbella, 90; Jeremiah, 90; John, 51, 68, 89, 90, 120; Joseph, 90, 131; Lydia Cooper, 90; Mary, 90; Samuel, 90; William Ross, 90
JOSEPH, Jacob, 110
JOSIAH, Eliza, 83; James, 83
JOUBERTIERE, Jane, 156
JOURS, Susan, 111
JUDAH, Rebecca, 141
JULIAN, James, 123
JURNEY, Sarah Elizabeth, 133
JUSTICE, Jesse, 157

-K-

KAIGHN, Arabella, 178; John, 178; Samuel, 178; William, 178
KAIN, Capt., 172; John, 178
KAMMERER, Joseph R., 94; Mary, 94, 104
KANE, James, 131; John, 131
KARR, James, 17; Rachel, 17
KEAN, Daniel, 84; Eliza, 84; Jacob, 4; John, 84; Mary, 154; Neal, 84; Sarah, 84
KEATES, George, 184; Margaret, 184
KEATS, Mrs., 6
KECK, Christian G., 94
KEE, James, 154
KEEHMLE, Leonard, 139; Mary, 139; Peggy, 139; William, 139
KEEMLE, Samuel, 139
KEEN, Eleanor, 44; Jacob, 24, 44; John, 44; Joseph, 69; Mercy, 44
KEENE, Sarah, 47
KEFFER, Anthony, 131; John, 131; Martin, 131; Rachel, 131
KEHR, Johan G., 71; John George, 66
KEICHLER, Ann, 27; George, 27
KEIM, George D. B., 80
KEITH, Capt., 51
KELLER, Adam, 103; Mary, 103
KELLEY, Andraw, 154
KELLY, Laurce., 48; Lawr., 48
KEMBELL, Reuben, 158
KEMBLE, Reuben, 158; William, 164
KEMPE, G., 50
KENDERDINE, Christiana, 30
KENDRICK, Jarvis, 149
KENNARD, Asbury, 99; George, 99; Henry, 99; Jacob, 51; John Westly, 99; Mary, 51, 99; Richard Tilghman, 99; William, 99
KENNEDY, Andrew, 54, 65; Anthony, 82; David, 17, 132; Eleanor, 65; Eliza, 65; Elizabeth, 65; Francis, 17; Geo. Washington, 17, 65; H. H., 32; James, 17; Joseph S., 185; Mary, 65; Robert, 17, 30, 65; Susan, 65
KENNY, Michael, 131
KENTON, James C., 65
KEPLE, Adam, 113; Catharine, 113
KEPPELE, Catharine, 111; Mary Ann, 111; Michael, 111
KER, Elizabeth, 126; Susanna, 125
KERBACH, Polly, 161; Sybilla, 161
KERN, George, 156; John, 156
KERPER, Elizabeth, 175; Frederick, 183; George, 175; Valentine, 183
KERR, James, 17; Rachel, 17, 18
KERSEY, Jesse, 183
KERWOOD, G., 37
KESLER, Adam, 33; Catharine, 33; Daniel, 33; Eve, 33; Frederick, 33; Martin, 33; Mary, 33; Susan, 33
KESLOR, Rachel, 36
KETLAND, Elizabeth, 47; Kitty, 47; Thomas, 47
KEWTAN, Nelly, 102
KEYSEL, Jacob, 140
KEYSER, Abraham, 12, 98, 121; Andrew, 57; Ann, 57; Anna, 121; Barbara, 91; Catherine, 57; Charles, 121; Daniel, 57; Elizabeth, 121; Frederick, 112; Jacob, 121, 128; John, 121; Libert, 91; Mary, 12, 121, 146; Michael, 57; Peter, 107, 112; William, 45, 91, 112, 121, 165
KIER, Cathrine, 43
KIES, Dorrothy, 91
KILBY, Jennet, 75; Turpin, 75
KILLEHER, Johannes, 112
KILLHOWER, Adam, 112; Catharine, 112; Elizabeth,

112; Martin, 112; Michael, 112; Nancy, 112; Sarah, 112
KIMBER, Emmers, 95; Emmor, 15; Joshua, 15
KING, Charles, 88; John, 127; William, 72, 107
KINGSTON, Simon, 50, 179
KINNEMAN, Susan, 77
KINSEY, James, 181
KINTZNG, Abraham, 80
KINYON, Stephen, 127
KIP, Isaac J., 131
KIRK, Robert, 45; Sarah, 45
KIRKHAM, Charles, 22, 89; Deborah, 22, 167; Maria, 89, 167; William, 167
KIRKNER, Jacob, 127; Joseph, 114, 127; Martha, 127; Mary, 114, 127; Sarah, 127
KIRKPATRICK, Mary, 31
KISER, Peter, 92
KISSICK, John, 75
KITCHEN, Andrew Boyd, 82
KITE, Abi, 116; Benjamin, 116; Joseph, 163; Rebecca, 116
KITTERIDGE, Francis, 42; Lucy, 42
KLEEVER, Gottlieb, 182
KLINE, George, 36, 171; John, 171
KLING, Elizabeth, 36, 84; George A., 36; George Philip, 36; John, 36, 84; Mary Ann, 36, 37; Sopha Charlotte, 36
KLINGEL, George, 34
KNIGHT, Alexander, 181; Daniel, 179; Elizabeth, 133; John, 133; Jonathan, 90, 121; Martha, 114; Mary, 133; Thomas, 2
KNOR, George, 11
KNORR, Ann, 98; Elizabeth, 98; Francis, 98; George, 27, 98; Jacob, 92, 128; Jacob K., 98; Susanna, 98
KNOX, Dorothy, 151; Elizabeth, 99; John, 99, 151; Joseph, 128; Rebecca, 141, 185; William, 185
KOCH, John, 147
KOCK, John, 147
KOLB, Susanna, 147
KOLP, Barbara, 58; Isaac, 58; Susanna, 147
KOLPH, Susanna, 147
KRAFFT, Michael, 49
KRAHMER, Catharine, 158; Philip, 158
KREAMER, Catharine, 158; Eliz. Magt., 158; Henry, 158
KREBS, George, 98
KREIG, Elizabeth, 135
KREWSON, Derrick, 129; Phoebe, 129
KUGLER, George, 136
KUHL, Catharine, 119; Conrad, 12; Deborah, 136; Frederick, 51, 85, 119, 136; Henry, 12, 114, 136
KUHN, Adam, 41; Daniel, 12; Elizabeth, 130; George, 130; John, 130; Magdalen, 130; Margaret, 12
KULP, Isaac, 51; Jacob, 180
KUNCKLE, Ann, 124; Catharine, 124, 136; Christian, 124; John, 124, 136; Margaret, 124; Mary, 124; Susanna, 136
KURSUS, Sabina, 8

-L-

LAFFERTY, Mary, 55
LAFORCADE, Auguste, 61
LAIR, Ann, 139
LAIRD, Elizabeth, 73; James, 73; Margaret, 73
LAMARRE, Elizabeth Mary Susanna, 153; Jane Mary Henrietta, 153
LAMBERT, Peter, 56
LAMESIERE, Peter, 61
LAND, Mary, 108
LANDRETH, David, 165, 176
LANE, Edward, 88; Hannah, 92; James, 92; William, 161
LANG, Thomas, 161
LANGE, Joachim, 45
LANGSTROTH, George, 53; Huson, 53; Mary, 53
LAPEYRE, John, 122
LARANER, Frances, 118; Hannah, 118; John, 118; William, 118
LARDNER, Lynford, 43
LARE, Catharine, 165, 166; Elizabeth, 165; George, 165; Godfrey, 165; Henry, 165; Isaac, 165; Jacob, 165; John, 115, 165; Margaret, 165; Mary, 165; Peter, 165; Rebecca, 165; Susanna, 165; William, 165
LARGE, Dorothy, 35; Ebenezer, 35; James, 35; John Baldwin, 35; Sarah, 35
LARREW, John, 114
LASHER, Barbara, 25; Francis, 25; Jacob, 25
LASKEY, Catharine, 40; Ed, 40; Elizabeth, 40; Harriet, 40; John, 40; Mary, 40; Rebecca, 40; Sarah, 40
LATIMER, Thomas, 164

LATTIMER, John R., 134
LAUCK, Ann Martha, 128; Anna Martha, 12; David, 12; Hannah, 12, 133; John, 12; Joseph, 12; Margaret, 12; Mary, 12; William, 12
LAUDER, Hannah, 133
LAUGHLEY, Mr., 137
LAW, Samuel, 3
LAWERSWYLER, Eliza, 26; Jacob W., 26
LAWLER, Matthew, 124
LAWLESS, Ann, 152; Mary, 152; Richard John, 152
LAWRENCE, Anna, 68; Charles B., 136; Elizabeth, 63; George Washington, 68; Hannah, 143; John, 63; Lawrence, 68; Mary, 68, 117; Rebecca, 163; Richard, 143; Samuel, 63; Thomas, 63; William, 54, 68
LAWS, Anna, 156; Jane, 156; Lear, 156; Stephen, 156; Wesley, 156
LAWSON, Ann, 10; Elizabeth, 10, 108; John, 10, 168; Lavinia, 10; Mary Ann, 108; Rachel, 10, 168
LE MARQUIS DE CAXAUX, Monsieur, 46
LEA, Sarah, 16
LEAGUE, John, 115
LEAMING, Rebecca, 113; Thomas F., 25, 113
LEBONE, Mary, 70
LECKLER, George E., 94
LEE, Alexander, 85; William, 64, 79, 161
LEEACH, Sarah, 53
LEECH, Isaac, 95; Richard F., 30
LEEDOM, Sarah, 105; William, 36
LEEDS, Ann, 183; Noah, 183
LEES, Maria Magdalen, 74; Peter, 74
LEESTER, Catharine, 135; John, 135
LEFAVRE, N., 47
LEFEVRE, Felix, 132; John Felix, 132; Mary, 132
LEGERS, Catharine, 116
LEHMAN, Christian, 126; Joseph, 185; Lewis, 59; Samuel, 33; William, 185
LEHR, Henry, 51
LEIB, Susan, 65
LEIBBRANDT, Aredrw, 162
LEIBERT, Barbara, 91; John, 91; Mary, 91; Peter, 91; William, 91
LEINAU, Andrew, 26
LEIPER, James, 162; James G. S., 7; Sarah, 162; Thomas, 7; William Falconer, 162
LEISZ, Catharine, 54; Dorothea, 54; Elizabeth, 54; George, 54; Henry, 54; Jacob, 54; John Elizabeth, 54; Maria, 54; Susanna, 54
LEMMIRE, H. E., 48
LEMOINE, Augustin, 61
LENOX, David, 59, 60; Tacey, 47
LENTZ, David, 157; Jacob, 17
LEPPARD, Catharine, 147; Daniel, 147; Jesse, 147; Mary, 147; Michael, 147
LESHER, Anna, 185; Anna Maria, 7, 185; Catherine, 7; Charles, 185; Harriot, 185; John, 10
LETTSON, I. C., 136, 137
LEVAL, Peter, 152
LEVERING, Aaron, 92; Charles, 92; Deborah, 92; John, 154; Nathan, 92; Sarah, 92; Susannah, 92; Thomas, 92
LEVIS, William, 118, 142
LEVY, Henrietta Maria, 83; Joseph, 135; Martha, 83; Martha Mary Ann, 83; Mary, 83; Moses, 83; Samson, 88
LEWIS, Daid, 96; David, 97; Ellis, 96; Francis, 93, 97; Harvey, 184; Jacob M., 165; John, 97; Joseph, 68, 171; Joseph S., 77, 93, 114, 179; Lawrance, 97; Lawrence, 97; Mary, 68, 97; Nathaniel, 97; Phebe, 96, 97; Rachel, 143; Robert, 96, 97; Ruth, 96; Samuel N., 179; Sarah, 96; Wharton, 35
LEWTHWAIT, William, 70
LEX, Peter, 2
LIDDON, Abraham, 26; Isabella, 26
LIEB, Michael, 125
LIEBBRANDT, John Andrew, 162
LIGERS, Catharine, 116
LIKENS, Sarah, 183
LILLY, Jemmy, 109
LIMEBURNER, John, 77; Philip, 106
LINCOLN, Mr., 46
LINDELL, Benjamin, 144
LINDMUTH, Christopher, 55; John, 55
LINDSAY, William, 45
LINN, Mary, 132
LINNINGTON, Esther, 121; Maria, 121; Mary, 121, 122; Sarah, 121, 122

LINTON, Jeremiah, 68
LIPPARD, Michael, 92
LIPPERT, Michael, 128
LIPPINCLOTT, Jesse, 38; John, 38; Joshua, 38; Seth, 38; Wallace, 38
LIPPINCOTT, Aquilla, 38; Caleb, 38; Grace, 38; Hannah, 136, 151; Joshua, 38, 125; Mary, 38; May, 136; Nathaniel, 38
LISLE, John, 72
LISTER, Jane, 145
LITHGOW, I., 152
LITTLEBOY, Maulby John, 174
LIVEZEY, Anthony, 78; John, 78; Nathan, 78; Thomas, 173
LIVINGSTON, Mary, 34
LLOYD, Priscilla, 51; Robert, 118; William, 118
LOAFBORROW, Nathaniel, 127
LOCKE, Eliza, 90
LOCKMAN, George, 98; Susanna, 78
LOESER, Christopher, 106
LOGAN, Debby, 109; Dr., 109; Elizabeth, 56; Samuel, 42; Sarah, 31; Thomas, 56; William, 31, 173
LOGUE, Catherine, 126; Hugh, 126; James, 126; John, 12; Mary, 126; Patrick, 126; Rosana, 126; Timothy, 17
LOHRA, John, 156; Peter, 12, 55
LOLLER, Alexander, 93, 96; Hannah, 93, 96; Maria, 96; Mary, 93; Peter, 93, 96; Thomas, 93, 96
LON, David, 176; James, 176; John, 176; Mary, 176
LONDON, Peter, 139
LONG, Ann, 61; Anne, 61; Bridget, 46; Christopher, 46; Eliza, 65; Hannah, 68; Jacob, 116; James, 46; John, 10, 36, 40, 51, 69; Kennedy, 65; Kezia, 61, 120; Lettice, 61; Lydia, 61; Myra, 50; Rachel, 61; Silas, 61; William, 46, 61
LONGRETH, Cristoff, 99
LONGSTRETCH, Isaac T., 51; Susanna, 173
LONGSTRETH, Ann, 173; Charles, 185; Joshua, 173; Josiah, 173; Samuel, 173; Thomas, 173; William, 173
LONSTRETH, Joshua, 95
LORA, Harriott, 30
LORAIN, Elizabeth Shewell, 21; John, 22; Lydia, 22
LOTT, Elizabeth, 97; Henry, 11, 97; Mary, 97; Samuel, 97
LOVE, Rebecca, 114
LOVELL, Peter, 82
LOVERING, Joseph S., 163; Mary, 163; Sarah S., 163
LOWE, John, 39
LOWNES, Caleb, 34; David, 34; Edward, 34; George, 34; Jane, 13; John, 34; Joseph, 163; Margaret, 34
LOXLEY, G. W., 101
LOYD, John, 75; Joseph, 75; Mary, 75; Philip, 75; Rebecca, 75; William, 75
LUDLAM, George, 50
LUKENS, Charles, 5; Elizabeth, 142, 144; Hannah, 20; Martha, 20; Matthew, 142; Newbery, 93; Sarah, 93
LUND, Benjamin, 149; Christobell, 149
LUNHOFF, John K., 110
LUTHER, Barbara, 135; John, 135; Martin, 135
LYBRAND, George, 71
LYLE, Alexander, 99; Elizabeth, 55; William, 55, 66
LYMAN, Anna, 51; Frances, 51; Helen Maria, 51; Jerudshia, 51; Martha, 51; William, 51, 52, 53
LYND, James, 114
LYNDAL, Benjamin, 76
LYONS, Benjamin, 85; Moses, 85; Rachel, 67, 85; Rebecca, 85; Sarah, 85; Solomon, 85; Zaligman, 85
LYRINGREN, Joachim, 68
LYTHGO, Anna, 139; Bettey, 139; Hester, 139; Isaac, 139; Jacob, 139; Margaret, 139; Thomas, 138

-M-

MAAG, Conrad, 157; Henry, 157; John, 157; Mary, 55
MAC GAULLEY, Peter, 90
MCADAMS, Joseph, 128
MCALLISTER, Alexander, 102; Jno., 184; John, 65, 82
MCALPIN, James, 65
MCANNALL, William, 65
MCARA, John, 107
MCBARSON, Mitchal, 110
MCBRIDE, Catharine, 140; Elizabeth, 127; John, 140
MCCABE, Hannah, 20
MCCADAN, Mrs., 162
MCCALL, Catharine, 93; George Clymer, 107; Richard, 82; William, 35; William Coleman,

107
MCCALLA, Alexander, 30; John, 30; William, 30, 61
MCCAM, Edward, 124
MCCARTAR, John, 108
MCCARTY, Alexander, 162; Daniel, 163; Felix, 72; James, 163
MCCAULEY, Andrew, 128; David, 128; Robert, 128
MCCAUSLAND, Alexander, 152
MCCAWLEY, James, 30
MCCLAKIN, Nancy, 84
MCCLAN, Mary, 63
MCCLARY, Samuel, 106
MCCLEAN, Thomas, 162
MCCLENACHAN, Anne, 88; Blair, 5, 88; Mary, 88; Robert, 88
MCCLINTUCK, Eliza, 87; Joseph, 87; Mary, 87; Thomas, 87
MCCLUNE, John, 165
MCCLURG, Samuel, 45
MCCLURY, Samuel, 106
MCCOLLOCH, John, 107
MCCOLLOH, Hannah, 87
MCCONNELL, Andrew, 84; Rebecca, 159; Sarah, 128
MCCOY, Mary, 162
MCCRAVEY, Hector, 67
MCCREA, Elizabeth, 177; Hannah, 177; James, 177; Jane, 177; John, 177; Margaret, 177; Mary, 177; Robert, 177
MCCREALES, John, 25
MCCREALS, John, 25
MCCREARY, John, 169; Margaret, 169; Sarah, 169; William, 169
MCCULLOCH, James, 76; John, 76, 107; Sarah, 47
MCCULLY, Henery, 33
MCCURDY, Hugh, 24; James, 28; John, 24, 25, 152; Martha Matilda, 152; Mary, 24, 28; Robert, 24
MCCURRACH, Ann Isabella, 43; Isabella, 43; James, 43; James Grant, 43; Margaret, 43
MCCUTCHEON, Samuel, 71
MCDANIEL, Catherine C., 56
MCDEED, Patrick, 172
MCDERMITT, Charles, 141; Elizabeth, 141; James, 141; John, 141
MCDERMOTT, Peter, 132
MCDONOUGH, Elizabeth, 144
MCDOUGLAS, Eliza, 50; John, 50; Samuel, 50
MCDOWELL, Ann, 24; Sarah Evans, 24; William, 24
MCDURMED, Peter, 132
MCELROY, Catharine, 183; John, 183; Kitty, 183
MCEUEN, Henry, 45
MCEVOY, William, 174
MCFADEN, William, 39
MCFAGERTY, ---, 72
MCFALL, Daniel, 4; Mary, 4
MCFARLAND, George, 57; John, 174
MCFARLANE, John, 77
MACFERRAN, Samuel, 116
MCGANDY, Daniel, 44; Henry, 44; Margaret, 44; Patrick, 44
MCGARANT, James, 132
MCGAWLEY, Peter, 126
MCGINNIS, Neil, 108
MCGLATHERY, George, 72
MCGONEGAL, Roswell, 183
MCGRATH, James, 93
MCGREGGOR, Sarah, 71
MCGUIRE, Mary, 3, 4
MCHARTLY, John, 74
MCHENRY, Nicholas, 72
MCILHENNEY, Moses, 21; William, 60
MCILVAINE, John, 64; Joseph, 118; Mary, 16
MCKEAN, Ann, 80; Robert, 80
MCKENZEY, Alexander, 73; Elizabeth, 73; James, 73; Margaret, 73; Thomas, 73
MCKENZIE, Mary Cammack, 75
MACKIE, T. Lowery, 43; Thomas, 43
MCKIM, John, 31
MCKINLEY, James, 39; John, 98
MCKINZEY, Mary, 73
MCKINZIE, William, 109
MCKNIGHT, Anna, 83; George, 115; Mary, 83; Priscilla, 83; Stephen D., 83
MCKOWEN, Grace, 4; Mary, 4; Robert, 4
MCLENEHY, Jame, 56
MCLEOD, Jane, 37; John, 175
MCLINCHEY, James, 130; John, 130, 161
MCMANUS, Benjamin, 174; Redman, 174
MCMULLEN, Daniel, 98; Robert, 75
MCMULLIN, Catharine, 6; Daniel, 6; John, 181; Robert, 153
MCMURTIE, Ann, 43
MCMURTRIE, Henry, 43
MCNEMEA, Anna, 87
MCNEVAN, Malcom, 82
MACPHERSON, Widow, 111
MCSHANE, Francis, 22
MCVAUGH, James, 67; Rebecca, 151
MCVEAUGH, Alice, 13; Daniel,

81, 117; Eleanor, 13; Mary, 13; Rachel, 13; Ruth, 13
MADDEN, Stacy, 1
MADDOCK, Caroline, 24; Elizabeth Harr, 24; Emma, 24; Ezekiel, 24; Jane, 24; Phoebe, 24; Randall Malon, 24; Sarah, 24; Sarah Moore, 24; William, 24; William L., 24
MAFFAT, Spencer, 93
MAFFETT, Robert, 39
MAGARGAL, Allen, 182; John, 182
MAGDALENA, Josef Bruno, 123; Joseph Bruno, 123
MAGHEE, William, 146
MAGIE, Robert, 39
MAGNER, Mary, 46
MAGOFFIN, John, 177
MAGUIRE, Hugh, 110; Philip, 110
MAHER, Eleanor, 84
MAISON, Adam, 172, 173; Elizabeth, 172; Jacob, 172, 173; John, 172, 173; Peter, 172, 173
MAITLAND, John, 44; Thomas, 162
MAJOR, William, 111
MAKEM, George, 131
MAKEMSON, James, 87
MAKNEW, Thomas, 79
MALCOLM, Howard, 170, 171; John, 170
MALENFANT, J. R., 56
MALENFAUT, Robert, 123
MALLET, Francis, 34
MALONE, John S., 72; Mari Ann, 72; Mary, 72; Patrick, 72; Rebecca, 72; William H., 72
MANDEVILLE, Charles, 162; Daniel H., 162; David, 24, 162; Sarah, 162
MANLOVE, William E., 126
MANN, William, 14, 32
MANNA, Sarah, 106
MANNON, Elizabeth, 117
MARISON, James, 9
MARKER, Andrew, 10; Elizabeth, 10, 180; Jacob, 180; Peter, 180; Theobald, 180
MARKLE, Jacob, 58
MARKOE, Francis, 100
MARNY, Jacob, 87
MARPLE, Ann, 121; Christena, 121; Edward, 121; Jesse, 121; John, 121; Joseph, 121; Joshua, 121; Phebe, 121; Sarah, 121; Thomas, 121
MARQUEDANT, Barbara, 14; Charles, 14, 56
MARSAHALL, Sarah Hutchins, 104
MARSHALL, Amos, 41; Armitt, 109; Charles, 104, 114; Christopher, 24; Edmund, 170, 171; Elizabeth, 104, 112; Francis, 63; Isaac, 170; Isaac R., 104; Jonathan, 2; Joseph, 2; Margaret, 105, 109, 170; Mary, 41; Nathan, 2; Patience, 114; Richard, 109; Sarah H., 105; Sarah Hutchins, 170, 171; Thomas, 2, 109
MARSHELL, Alexander, 154
MARSHILL, Alexander, 154
MARTIN, Benjamin, 109; Catharine Magdalen, 5; Charles, 144; Daniel, 182; George, 95; James, 97; John, 26; Mary, 182; Robert, 25; Sarah, 144; William, 144
MASON, Benjamin, 31; Christian, 91; Christopher, 91; Susanna, 160; Tanton, 153; Widow, 35
MASSEY, Ann, 36; Charles, 36; Col., 100; John, 36; Thomas, 36
MASTER, William, 93
MASTERS, Thomas, 62
MATHER, Benjamin, 145; Jonathan, 145
MATHISON, Niel, 76
MATLACK, John, 38; Josh., 178; Josiah, 143
MATTERN, Adam, 178; Andrew, 178; Mary, 178
MATTHEWS, James, 88, 98; Julia Ann, 84; Lucy, 44; Mary, 88; Sarah, 96
MATTHIAS, Abel, 108; Catharine, 6
MATTSON, Jacob, 104
MAUGE, Agnes, 17
MAULE, Israel, 152
MAXFIELD, Stephen, 141
MAXWELL, Sarah, 11; William, 11
MAY, Adam, 42, 69
MAYBIN, John, 26, 131
MAYO, John, 31
MAZURIE, James I., 141; James S., 142
MEAD, Mary, 98; Mrs., 162
MEANY, John, 27, 138
MEARS, Benjamin, 113
MECHLIN, Jacob, 54; Samuel, 46, 51, 54, 58
MECKLIN, Samuel, 8
MEDCALF, Abraham, 53; Jemima, 53
MEDCALFE, Capt., 149
MEGERGEY, Jacob, 106; Sary, 106
MELIZET, Francis, 17
MELONE, James, 50; Mary, 50

MENBURN, Mary, 100
MENDENHALL, Adam, 170; Margaret, 152
MENDINHALL, Adam, 119
MENG, Anna, 185; Christopher, 98; Elizabeth, 98, 185; Mary Davis, 98; Melchoir, 98
MENTZ, Charles, 157; Elizabeth, 157; George Washington, 157
MERCER, Jane, 178; John, 178
MEREDITH, David, 61; Elizabeth, 53; Jonathan, 61; Samuel, 107; William, 61, 89, 144
MERRIT, Ann, 153; Marmaduke, 153
MERVIN, Catharine, 68; Samuel, 68
MERVINE, Catharine, 76; George, 76; Hannah, 76; Samuel, 76
METZGER, Christina, 178; Matthias, 178
MEYER, John, 95
MEYERS, Elizabeth, 94; Jacob, 19; John P., 158
MICKLE, Susannah, 144
MIDDLETON, Jane Allen, 85; Joseph, 85; William, 85
MIERCKEN, Catharine, 122; Josephine, 122; Mary, 122; Peter, 122
MIFFLIN, Ann, 143; Caspar, 120; Charles, 120; Clementina, 120; Elizabeth, 74, 120; John, 120; Lemuel, 143; Lydia, 96; Mary, 96; Samuel Emlen, 143; Sarah, 35, 120; Warner, 143
MILES, Ann, 176; Elizabeth, 95; Joseph, 95; Polly, 134; Thomas, 81
MILLARD, Dr., 137; Thomas, 57; William, 79
MILLER, Andrew, 69; Ann, 69; Anna Barbara, 120; Barbara, 69, 120; Catharine, 120; Charles Meredith, 133; D. H., 74; Daniel, 172; Daniel H., 132; Daniel L., 181; Elizabeth, 133, 157; Frederick, 69; George, 4, 91, 125; Hannah, 128, 172; Helen, 177; Henry, 12, 69; Hester Ann, 28; Hugh, 154; Jacob, 118, 172; Jane M., 177; John, 69, 174, 177; John George, 120; John Jacob, 120; Joseph, 91, 172; Julia R., 177; Margaret, 172, 177; Martin, 159; Mary, 29, 91, 172; Mordecai, 45; Mr., 148; Samuel, 91; Sarah, 132, 172; Sebastian, 35; Susanna, 172; William, 148, 177
MILNOR, James, 51, 134; Robert, 135
MILTMAN, Rebecca, 58
MINNICK, Ann Eliza, 119; Beulah, 119
MITCHEL, James, 2; Mary, 2; Randal, 111
MITCHELL, ---, 49; Abigail, 155; Amy Allison, 155; Deborah, 135; James, 115; John, 111; Mary, 57, 111, 113; T., 10, 11; Thomas, 50, 73, 75, 77, 83, 96, 99, 109, 119, 122, 125, 140, 184; William, 43, 100
MODE, Elizabeth, 111; Henry, 111; Mary, 111; Pachens, 111
MOFFETT, James, 35
MOLLOY, Nicholas, 86
MONAGHAN, Henry, 110
MONGES, J. A., 63; Ja. A., 101; John A., 20
MONTELIUS, William, 85
MONTGOMERY, Alex., 108; Elizabeth, 147; Ellin, 147; Jane, 147; Thomas, 73, 80; William, 83
MONTMOLLIN, Henrietta, 141
MOODIE, William, 137
MOODY, Margaret, 26; Sarah, 26
MOORE, Abraham, 131; Alexander, 137; Andrew, 76; Deborah, 144; Elizabeth, 76, 176; Hannah, 76; Henry, 144; James, 176; Joseph, 24, 101; Major, 50; Margaret, 142; Mary, 50, 185; Miliah Martha, 51; Mordecai, 142, 144; Samuel, 21, 127; Samuel Preston, 143; Sarah, 135, 142; Susanna, 143; Thomas, 48, 142; William, 110, 165
MORE, Sarah, 159
MORELY, Jh., 102
MORGAN, Benjamin, 65; Benjamin R., 41, 123, 156, 166, 167, 178; Benjn. R., 145; George W., 65; James, 131; Peter, 146; Rachel, 77; Ruth, 77; Thomas, 65; Thomas W., 35
MORHAINE, Joseph, 105
MOR'N, Tom, 134
MORRELL, Abraham, 88; Benjamin, 88; James, 88; John, 22, 88; John W., 88; Richard, 88; Robert, 88; Thomas, 88
MORRIS, Ann, 74, 143; Anthony, 91; Benjamin W., 91; Casper W., 91; Catharine W., 91;

Deborah, 3; Elizabeth, 142, 143; Ezekiel, 108; George, 75; George L., 140; Isaac, 3; Isaac W., 4, 91, 114; Isaac Wistar, 27, 28; Israel W., 91; John, 76, 92, 119; Joseph, 82; Luke, 143; Luke W., 91; Lydia, 144; Rachel, 142, 143; Robert, 177; Samuel, 91, 142, 143; Samuel B., 163; Thomas, 26, 142; Thomas Moore, 143
MORRISON, John, 100
MORRISSON, Hugh, 128
MORT, John, 70; Joseph, 70
MORTON, Benjamin, 4; Fanny, 108, 109; James, 95; John, 62, 95, 109; Margaret, 95; Mary Ann, 109; Phebe, 96; Samuel, 96
MOSER, Jacob, 67
MOSES, Philip, 16; Sarah, 16
MOTT, Edward, 118; James, 98
MOULDER, Joseph, 122
MOUNSEY, John, 138
MOWER, John, 185; Rudolph, 185
MOYER, Thomas, 157
MOYLAN, Anna Maria, 79; Isabella, 79, 100; Jasper, 79; Julia, 79
MOYT, Casper, 63
MUCKLOW, John, 149, 150
MUIR, Elizabeth, 161; George, 161; Grizzel, 161; James, 161; John, 161; Rachel, 161; Richard, 161; William, 161
MULLEN, Jane, 125; William, 125
MUMBURN, Mary, 100
MUMFORD, John, 42; Thomas, 42
MUNHALL, Frans., 141
MUNN, Susanna, 130
MUNNS, Lyndsey, 165
MURAY, Rodger, 174
MURDOCK, Emeline, 97; Harriot, 97; Mary, 56; Mary Dalley, 56; Robert, 50, 97, 146; William, 56
MURGATROYD, Mary, 25; Sarah P., 25; Thomas, 25
MURPHOY, Mahlan, 183; Sarah, 183
MURPHY, Ann, 102; Eleanor, 107; John, 107, 144; Laetitia, 107; Mary, 144; Rebecca, 107; Robert, 139, 162, 181; Sarah, 107; Thomas, 144; William, 102
MURRAY, Alexander, 54; Ann, 54; James S., 22; John, 3; Michael, 119; Sarah B., 22
MURRELL, Leoy, 159
MURREY, Martha, 157
MURRY, John, 42
MYER, George, 78; Jacob, 23
MYERS, Jacob, 85
MYNICK, Rachael, 103

-N-

NACE, Alice, 35; Jacob, 35; John, 35, 173; Martin, 35; Peter, 35
NAILER, Elizabeth, 84
NAMIE, James John, 59
NASSAU, William, 9
NASSAW, William, 164
NAW, Francis, 156; Peter, 156
NAYLOR, Joseph, 20
NEALE, Elizabeth, 180; John, 19, 180; Michael, 19; William S., 174
NEATE, William, 167
NEEDLES, Elizabeth, 87
NEFF, Elizabeth, 132; Peter, 126; Rudolph, 68
NEGRO, Aubah, 110; Betty, 109; Betty Grace, 109; Bob, 110; Castledose, 110; Celia, 101; Chloe, 113; David, 5; Fenders, 95; George, 5; Hagar, 124; Harry, 5, 62; Jesse, 5; Joanna, 109; Joe, 109; John, 109; Jude, 146; Kitty, 109; Lemon, 109; Lucy, 109; Mary Lemon, 109; Moses, 48; Newton, 109; Peter, 109; Phebe, 109; Philenah, 109; Primus, 109; Prince, 109; Robert, 18, 48; Rose, 110; Sabinet, 109; Sammy, 109; Sarah, 5; Sarah Lemon, 109; Sary, 109; Syrus, 108; Tibbat Rose, 110; Tom, 109; Violet, 109; York, 110
NEGUS, John, 168
NEILL, Lewis, 78
NELSON, Acksah, 99; Elizabeth Beth, 99; Elizabeth Knox, 99; George, 99
NERBACK, Jacob, 58; Mary, 58
NETMAN, Mary, 153; Zachariah, 153
NEUFFERIN, Charlotta, 91
NEWBOLD, Deborah, 85; Joshua, 85; Samuel, 85
NEWBOULD, Margaret, 50; Mikel, 50
NEWBY, James, 36
NEWCOMB, B., 28; Bayse, 105
NEWELL, George, 168; William, 82
NEWKIRK, Garret, 22
NEWLAN, Cyrus, 96; Mary, 96

NEWMAN, Lucy, 49; Mary, 49
NEWPORT, James, 55; Mrs., 55
NEWTON, Thomas, 64
NICE, Charles, 35, 175
NICERY, Hannah, 185
NICHOLSON, Samuel, 28; William, 181
NICKLIN, Juliana, 5; Philip, 5
NIDELET, Stephen F., 147
NIGHTINGALE, Hannah, 95
NILL, Ann, 170; Charles, 170; Conrade, 170; John, 170; Margaret, 170; Mary, 170; Samuel, 170
NIPPES, Abraham, 108; Anna Maria, 108; Charles, 108; Daniel, 108; Louisa, 108
NISBET, Ann, 13; John, 13
NOBLE, Elizabeth, 77; Samuel, 140; William, 77
NOE, Elias, 175
NONES, Benjamin (Benjn.), 135, 168; David B., 168
NONNATER, Peter, 158
NORBECK, Daniel, 20
NORKEY, John, 7; Mary, 7
NORMAN, John, 108; Joseph, 37, 93, 96; Susanna, 108; Thomas, 149
NORQUE, Eliza, 7; John, 7; Mary, 7
NORRIS, George, 53; Isaac, 51; Isaac W., 171; Joseph P., 166, 167
NORTH, Caleb, 136; Jane, 44; Joseph, 44; Lydia, 44; Mary, 44; Stephen, 143
NORTHROP, John, 81; Mary, 81; Sarah, 81
NORTON, Mary, 185; Thomas, 51, 67, 106, 115, 140, 141, 158, 159, 160, 185
NOTTNAGEL, Leopold, 5
NOTTNAGELL, Catherine, 141; Christian, 141; Henrietta, 141; Leopold, 141; Lewis, 141; William, 141
NOWLIN, Elizabeth, 184
NUGENT, Richard, 48
NUNGESSER, Catharine, 95; John, 95
NUNVILLER, Matthias, 180
NUTTER, Mary, 145
NUTTLE, Robert E., 87
NUTZ, John, 57

-O-

OAKFORD, Aaron, 183; Elizabeth, 183; Isaac, 183; Richard, 183
OAT, Jesse, 51
O'BRIEN, Ann, 126; Francis, 124; Rebecca, 124
O'CONNOR, Maria, 46
O'CONWAY, Matthias, 172
ODENHEIMER, John, 76
ODLIN, Woodbridge, 133
OELLERS, James, 83, 177
OGDEN, Elizabeth, 61; Jesse, 98; Sarah, 120; William, 143
OGLE, William, 156
OLD, Thomasin, 134
OLDDEN, James, 18; Thomas Hough, 18
OLDEN, Elizabeth, 18; Mary Hough, 18
OLIVER, John, 13; John G., 54; Maria, 13; William, 54
ONE, Sarah, 134
O'NEILL, Henry, 65
ORANGE, Elizabeth, 100
ORD, George, 132
ORLANDY, Mary, 9; Paul, 9
ORR, James, 22, 115; Mary, 115; Robert, 65, 115; Thomas, 43, 44; William, 22, 115
OSIUS, Christopher, 19
OTTO, Daniel, 72; John C., 33, 41, 72, 125
OVERINGTON, John, 37; Mary, 37; Sarah, 37; Thomas, 37; William, 37
OWENS, Sarah, 147
OWLSON, Andrew, 72
OX, Lidia, 91
OXLEY, Ann, 110; Jane, 110; John, 110; Nathaniel, 110; William, 110
OZUM, Davis, 25

-P-

PACKHORN, Sarah, 128
PAGE, Amelia, 160; David, 106; Elizabeth, 106; Hannah, 106, 160; Hugh Nelson, 132; James, 160; John, 106; Joseph, 142; Lewis, 132; Mary, 8; Octavus A., 132; Peyton R., 132; Robert, 160; Robert N., 132; W. B., 132
PAINE, Sarah, 166; William, 166
PAINTER, George, 119; Jacob, 2, 36
PALESKE, Charles G., 184
PALMER, Ann, 80; Anthony A., 82; Asher, 80; Elizabeth, 29, 80, 127; John, 33; John Jones, 29; Jonathan, 80; Phoebe Jones, 29; Richard, 29, 60, 75, 127, 128; Thomas, 80; William, 29, 80; William Thomas, 29
PANCOAST, David, 59; Samuel,

34, 78; Sarah, 59
PAR J DA HAZA, Charles, 48
PARHAM, Widow, 3
PARKE, Ann, 142, 143; Hannah, 59; I., 110; James Pemberton, 59; Jane, 142, 143; Joshua, 142; Robert, 143; Samuel Emlen, 143; Susanna, 143; Susannah, 142; Thomas, 37, 59, 124, 166, 167
PARKER, Alexander, 77; Charles H., 165; Deborah, 56; Joseph, 56; Mary, 71; Nathaniel, 160; Robert, 104; Sarah, 142
PARKINSON, Sarah, 99
PARRENNE, Elizabeth, 83
PARRISH, Isaac, 77, 135; Jos., 104; Joseph, 77, 181; Samuel, 77; Sarah, 77, 97, 135
PARRY, Isaac, 69; John, 88; Jonathan, 2; Rebecca, 2; Susanna, 2
PARSONS, Charles, 48; William, 137
PARVIN, Pearson, 151
PASTOROUS, David, 146
PATERSON, Stephen, 9
PATRICK, Rebecca, 54
PATTERSON, Charlotte, 183; Elisabeth, 183; George, 183; James Burd, 183; Jane, 183; John, 128; Jona., 184; Mary, 183; William Augustus, 183
PATTON, Catherine B., 146; Cornelia, 146; Henry, 146; John C., 146; Mary, 146; Robert, 146; Robert B., 146; Tace, 146; William, 146
PAUL, Ann, 185; David, 108; Elizabeth, 185; Hannah, 114; Jacob, 185; Jeremiah, 116, 183; Joseph, 185; Madam, 9; Martha, 185; Mary, 9, 185; Rebecca, 183; Samuel, 185; Thomas, 114
PAWLING, George H., 115
PAXSON, Joseph W., 119; Mahlon, 119; Richard, 162; Sarah, 119; Timothy, 34
PEALE, James, 119; Reubens, 137
PEARCE, Anna G., 83; Anna Gertrude, 83; Emma, 83; Henry, 83; John, 185; Margaret, 83; Mathew, 83
PEARSON, Alice, 71; Anna, 129; Benjamin, 71, 87; David, 51, 62; Hannah, 129; Henry, 129; James, 129; James Hart, 129; Jane, 129; Martha B., 129; Mary, 62, 129; Susan, 129; Susanna, 129; William, 62
PEART, Ann, 83; William, 83
PECHIN, John, 122
PECK, Jeremiah, 166; Michael, 67
PEE, Thomas D., 57
PEEBLES, Ann, 57; John, 57
PEIFFER, Christian, 66
PEIRCE, Caleb, 101; George, 185; Sarah, 179
PELTZ, Mary, 55; Philip, 22, 55, 73, 157
PEMBER, Edward, 21; Margaret, 21
PEMBERTON, Hannah, 58, 59; James, 96; John, 59; Lewis, 97; Phebe, 96
PENDLEBURY, Bettey, 139; Sarah, 139
PENN, John, 5; William, 31
PENNEGAR, Amos, 170; Margaret, 170
PENNOCK, Abraham Liddon, 26
PENROSE, Cesar, 95; Charles, 179; Jonathan, 42, 99; Samuel, 99; Thomas, 3
PENSHAW, Richard, 145
PEPPER, Esther, 111
PEPPLOW, Edward, 144
PERCIVAL, Jonathan, 36
PERKIN, John, 121
PERKINS, Mary, 165
PEROT, Elliston, 59, 130; John, 25
PETER, Joseph, 26
PETERMAN, George, 175
PETERS, Ann Widdow, 134; George, 41, 131; Jacob, 131; Joseph, 23, 131; Margaret, 73; Mary, 134; Mary Ann, 131; Mary Corbe, 134; Michael, 31; Milner Widdow, 134; Richard, 122; William, 31
PETERSON, Nicholas, 130
PETIT, Jonathan, 104
PETTIT, Andrew, 156
PFEIFFER, Mary, 184
PFLAUME, Francis, 61
PHILIPS, Angelina, 179; Anna, 93; Benjamin, 179; Clement, 93; Elizabeth, 93; Emmeline, 93; Hannah, 179; Jane, 179; John, 93; Levy, 67; Marthat, 102; Peter, 132; Sarah, 179; Sophia, 5; Thomas, 179; William, 93
PHILLIPS, Goodhous, 67; Isaac B., 67, 68; James, 16; John, 1, 110; Joseph, 151; Mary, 151; Rebecca, 16
PHILLIPSON, Simon, 169
PHIPPS, Isaac, 55; Llewellyn,

55; Thomas, 55
PICANDS, James, 63; Rebecca, 63; Samuel, 63; Thomas, 63
PICHANDS, James, 63; Rebecca, 63; Samuel, 63; Thomas, 63
PIERCE, Caleb, 27
PIERSON, Ann, 113; Clarissa, 113; Daniel, 113; Dr., 113; Elisha, 113; John, 113
PIESCH, Abraham, 51
PILE, Rebecca, 65; Samuel, 65
PILES, Samuel, 3
PILLMORE, Dr., 137
PINE, Lazarus, 38; Mr., 114
PINKERTON, Eliza, 71; John, 54, 71; Lydia, 71; Rebecca, 71; Sarah, 71
PINTARD, Thomas, 8
PINYARD, Margaret, 111
PIPER, Catharine, 180; Dolly, 180; George, 180, 181; Jaco, 181; Jacob, 180; Mary, 180; Michel, 180; Rachel, 180
PITT, Richard, 109
PLEASANTS, Mary, 37, 59; Samuel, 59
PLECKER, Peter, 16
PLUKER, Peter, 175
POANS, Mrs., 137
POHT, Elizabeth, 145; Henry, 145; Jacob, 145; Matthias, 145; Peter, 145
POLE, Edward, 58, 112
POLGREEN, James, 110
POLLIN, Hannah, 140
POOL, Hannah, 104
POOLE, Hannah, 171
POPE, Godfried, 170
PORCH, Isaac Smallwood, 41; John, 41
PORCOL, Mary, 97
PORTER, Alexander, 105; Betty, 37; Catharine, 74, 85; Cyrus, 57; Margaret, 53; Thomas C., 85; Thomas Clarke, 74; William, 37
POSTER, Elizabeth, 145
POTTER, Rebecca, 163; William W., 6
POTTS, George C., 6, 26; Joshua, 19; Mr., 169; Nathan R., 82, 141; Rebecca, 118; Sarah, 118
POULTNEY, James, 143
POWELL, Eliza, 70; Samuel, 138; Sarah, 168
POWERS, Susan, 129
POYNTELL, Ann, 64; George, 64; John E., 64; Rebecca, 64; Sarah, 64; William, 64, 105, 132
PRAIRIE, John, 185
PRATCHET, Ann, 70
PREASTON, Sarah, 157
PRENTICE, Benjn., 174; Elizabeth, 13; Harriot, 13; Thomas, 44
PRENTISS, Benjamin, 174
PRESTON, James, 45; Sarah, 45
PRICE, Edward, 52, 53; Elisha G., 65; Joseph, 53, 163; Lennephy, 53; Mary Dalley, 56; Rachel, 53; Rebecca, 96, 143; Samuel, 11; Sarah, 143
PRICHETT, Abraham Kintzing, 32; Anna Elizabeth, 32; John, 32; Josephine, 32
PRIOR, James, 148
PRITCHETT, Abraham Kintzing, 32; Thomas, 175
PROUD, James, 166; John, 167; Mary, 166, 167; Rachel, 167; Robert, 166
PROVEST, Alexander, 160
PROWSE, Mrs., 137
PRUANCE, Prince, 21
PRYOR, Edmund, 143; Mary, 143; Thomas W., 78
PUDVINE, Eliza, 155; James, 155; Margret, 155; Marian, 155; Nancy Weiler, 155
PUGH, Ann, 67; Edward, 67; Henry W., 1; Sarah, 67; Susan, 67
PULLINGER, Jacob, 107
PUNNETT, Henry Walter, 110
PURVES, Alexander, 164
PUSEY, Mary, 142; William, 142

-Q-

QUANDREL, Charles, 166
QUICKSALL, Jonathan, 185; Sarah, 185
QUIGLEY, Ann, 78; James, 78
QUINLIN, Mr., 172
QUINTER, Hannah, 81
QUIRK, Margaret, 79

-R-

RAB, William, 182
RAGUET, Catherine S., 56
RALSTON, Mary Ann, 90; Rebecca C., 90; Robert, 24, 59, 60, 99, 162
RALTON, Robert, 80
RAMAGE, Adam, 103
RAMENT, Mary, 144; Robert, 144
RANDOLPH, Betty, 37; Joseph, 27, 57, 81
RANKIN, Patrick, 32; Susannah, 32
RAP, William, 182

RAPINE, Joseph, 66
RAPP, Joseph, 109
RAPSOM, Henry, 131
RASER, Bernard, 8; Catherine, 8; George, 8, 41; John, 8; John B., 41; Mary, 8, 40, 41; Thomas, 8, 41; William, 8, 41
RAYBOLD, Ann Maria, 84; Jacob, 84; Joshua, 94; Sarah, 84; Susannah, 36; Thomas, 84
RAYFIELD, John, 81
READ, Dr., 26; Henry, 157, 158; James, 83; John, 83, 107; Margaret, 26; Rebecca, 26; William, 110
REAKIRT, John, 17
REAP, Anna, 157; Barnard, 157; John, 125; Joseph, 157; Mary, 157; Susan, 157; William, 157
REAVER, Bastian, 80; Catharine, 79; Henry, 79; Jacob, 79; Margaret, 80; Mary, 79; Philip, 79; Ulrich, 79
REDHEFFER, Charles, 147
REDMAN, Anna, 119; Elizabeth, 111; John, 113, 163; John E., 163, 164; Jos., 136; Joseph, 164; Mary, 163; Nancy, 113; Rachel, 163; Thomas, 163
REDNOR, Frederick, 102
REED, Eleanor, 150; Elizabeth, 110, 145; Francis, 145; George, 32; George Moody, 110; John, 144; Robert, 110; Samuel, 141; Susanna, 92; William, 145
REES, Alexander, 89; Ann, 89; Charles, 49; Elizabeth, 49; Elizabeth Helm, 89; George, 49, 89, 175; Sarah, 49
REESE, Jacob, 78; Mary, 78; Patience, 181
REESSE, Martin, 38
REEVE, Peter, 30
REEVES, Joseph, 183; Mary L., 155
REHN, Caspar, 133
REID, Allexis Caspard Michael, 56; Anne, 56; George, 56; George Bert, 56; Isabella Eliza, 56; William Moultrie, 56
REIDER, Ann, 64; Elizabeth, 64; William, 64
REIGART, Adam, 121; Em, 117; Magaretta, 121; Maria C., 117; Mary, 89, 117; Susanna, 121
REIGER, Charles, 88; Jacob, 88; Leonhard, 88; Margaretha, 88; Rudy, 88
REIGERT, Ann, 121; Henrietta, 121; Margaretta, 121; Maria, 121; Philip Wager, 121; Susanna, 121
REILLY, Luke, 110
REINSEIMER, Catharine, 125; Charles, 125; Christian, 124; Jacob, 125; Magdalena, 124; Magdalene, 124; Mary, 124, 125; Sarah, 125; Susanna, 125
RELF, Samuel, 64; Sarah, 64
REMINGTON, Clement, 13, 181
RENOW, Ann, 133
RENQUENET, Bme., 123
RENSHAW, Richard (Rich.), 4, 9, 21, 45, 50, 69, 71, 74, 161
REPPERT, Daniel, 164; Dorothy, 164; John, 164; Sarah, 164
REX, Catharine, 95; Daniel, 95
REYNOLDS, Dn. Juan, 25; Francis, 90
RHEA, Molly, 25
RHOADS, Elizabeth, 37; Mary, 37, 176; Samuel, 37, 176; Sarah, 37, 59
RIBAUT, I., 122
RIBER, Alexis Prosper, 8
RICE, Charlotte, 39; John, 2, 4, 39; Maria, 2, 4; Penelope, 141; Rebecca, 39, 141; Robert, 4; Sarah, 141; Thomas, 39, 141
RICHARDS, Benjamin, 65; Charles, 185; Mary, 80; Samuel, 80, 90, 112, 113; William, 65, 138
RICHARDSON, Elizabeth, 151; Joseph, 3
RICHE, George, 17
RICHERTS, Catharine, 107
RICHTER, Christina, 23; George, 23; John, 23
RICKER, John, 66
RICKEY, Samuel, 134
RIDDLE, John, 29
RIDGEWAY, Jacob, 170
RIDGWAY, Elizabeth, 159; Joseph, 1; Martha, 160; Thomas J., 59; Unis, 160
RIELY, John, 46
RIFFERT, Philip, 26; Ursula, 26
RIGGER, Conrad, 96
RIGHTLY, John, 77
RIHL, Henry, 125
RILEY, Catharine, 46; Elizabeth, 46; John, 23, 46, 138; Margaret, 46; Mary, 46; William, 46
RINEHART, Adam, 22
RIPLEY, John P., 68, 155
RISBERGER, Gust., 69

RITTENHOUSE, Abraham, 58; Barbara, 58; Daniel, 58; Enoch, 58; Henry, 58; Isaac, 58; Jacob, 58; John, 58; Margaret, 58, 94; Martin, 58; Mary, 58; Nicholas, 58; Samuel, 58; Susanna, 58; William, 58
RIVA, Joaquin, 25
ROADES, Casper, 168
ROADS, Jacob, 168
ROARMAN, George, 166
ROBB, James, 45; Jane, 164
ROBERTS, Abby, 27; Algermon, 128; Algernon, 134, 166; Algeron, 92; Catharine, 97; Charles, 18; Eliza, 92; Esther M., 97; Frances, 90; Grover, 9; Hannah, 142; Hugh, 142; Israel, 51, 58; James, 27; Jane, 13; Jesse, 7, 92; Job, 106; John, 31, 92; Jonathan, 91, 92; Joseph, 59, 134; Luis, 21; Lydia, 166; Martha, 51; Mary, 9; Morris, 92; Mrs., 113, 137; Nathan, 58; Rachael, 92; Rachel, 113; Robert, 32, 92; Ruth, 145; Samuel, 92, 145; Sarah, 27, 121, 145; Tacy, 134, 166; Thomas, 134; Thomas P., 170, 171; William, 178
ROBERTSON, Ann, 11; James, 11, 20; Margaretta, 20; Margaretta Jane, 11
ROBESON, Christopher, 150; Edward, 166; John, 73; Peter, 34; Rudeman, 54
ROBINSON, Anne, 114; Capt., 23; George, 159; James, 114, 115; Lewis, 22, 23; Mary, 114; Mr., 137; Samuel, 110; Sarah, 154; Thomas, 122; William, 3
RODES, Mark, 79
ROE, Ann McDermott, 132; Anna, 87; Anne, 152; David, 87; Elias Humphries, 87; Hannah, 87; Honour, 132; Jesse, 152; Joanna, 87; Martha Matilda, 152; Mary McDermot, 132; McDermot Michal M., 132; Patrick, 132; Samuel, 87; Uriah, 87
ROGERS, Elizabeth, 100, 170; Mary, 108, 150; Thomas, 101; William, 150
ROGIERS, Horatio, 152
ROHR, Catharine, 155; Charles Henry, 155; Elizabeth, 155; Henry, 89; John A., 155; John Frederick, 155; Maria, 155; Mary, 89
ROLAND, George William, 51; Henry, 51; Magdalen Elizabeth, 51; William, 51, 83
ROLPH, I., 65
RONAULDT, Dr., 137
ROONEY, Bernard, 157
ROOP, Ann, 146; Cornelius, 172; Elizabeth, 146; Jacob, 146; John, 16, 172; Lidia, 146
ROQUET, Mary, 153
RORER, Thomas, 182
ROSS, Catharine, 59; David, 55; Henry, 82; James, 95; John, 55; Marcia, 55; Robert, 90, 129, 138, 175; Samuel, 161; Thomas, 34
ROSSETER, Dominick T., 89; Eliza, 27; I., 167; John, 27
ROTHENWALDER, Esther, 94; Nicholas, 94
ROUSH, John, 44
ROWAN, James, 45; Joseph, 45
ROWLAND, Ruth, 13
ROWLER, Edward, 50
ROWLETT, John, 24; Louisa, 24; Mary, 24; Sarah Ann, 24
RUALL, Hannah, 27; John, 27; Joseph, 27; Mary, 27; Sarah, 27
RUAN, John, 158
RUDULPH, Esther, 136; Martha, 136
RUE, Margaret, 100; Richard, 100
RUHLE, Catharine, 92; John Sigmund, 92; Margaret, 92; Susanna, 92; William, 92
RULON, Abel, 85; Nathaniel, 85
RUMSEY, Hannah, 76; Rachel, 76
RUNDLE, Richard, 25
RUSH, Ann, 13; Barbara, 13, 94; Benjamin, 27, 48, 78, 120; Castharine, 94; James, 120; John, 120; Julia, 120; Lewis, 26; Mary, 13, 164; Richard, 120; Samuel, 120; William, 13, 80, 86, 120
RUSHMAN, Catharine, 83
RUSSEL, Stephen, 79
RUSSELL, John, 154
RUTH, Elizabeth, 70; Mary, 70
RUTT, Philip, 149
RUTTER, Catharine, 126; Elizabeth, 4; George, 11; Jacob, 126; Jane, 4; John, 4; John Jacob, 126; Maria, 4; Robert, 4; Sarah, 4; William, 4
RYAN, Catharine H., 145; James,

172; Jane, 172; John, 172

-S-

SABAL, Simon Augustin, 9
SACAZE, Andre, 17
SAGER, Michael, 66
SAILER, Thomas, 162
ST. JOHN, Catharine, 119; Thomas, 119
SALADE, Sebastian, 182
SALAIGNAC, Severin Anthony, 153
SALLET, Francois, 17
SALTAR, Elizabeth, 43; Francis, 43; George, 43; George G., 43; John, 43; Lucy, 43; Margret, 43; Maria, 43
SAMMS, Mary, 60; Thomas, 60
SANDERS, Phebe, 22
SANSOM, Joseph, 124, 166, 167; Samuel, 18; William, 13
SAPLEY, Sarah, 33
SARMIENTS, I. C., 147; James, 147
SATERTHWAITE, Abel, 65
SATTERBACH, John, 86
SAULMIER, John, 55
SAUNDERS, Francis, 50
SAUSMAN, Henry, 144
SAVERY, Rebecca, 159; Thomas, 51, 84
SAWER, Betsy, 113; James, 27, 32, 109, 113, 120
SAWYER, Charles, 87; Hanna, 87; Jane Allen, 87; Joseph, 87; Joseph Allen, 87; Margaret, 87
SAXTON, Charles, 169; John, 169; Mary, 169; Peter, 169; Rhoda, 169; Richard, 169
SAY, Benjamin, 74, 131, 138, 141; Caroline, 131; Miriam, 131; Rebecca Ann, 131; Thomas, 131; William Penn, 131
SAYRE, Mary Elizabeth, 150, 151
SCAROT, Elizabeth, 103; James, 103
SCATTERGOOD, John, 159; Joseph, 159; Rebecca, 159; Samuel, 159; Sarah, 159; Thomas, 158
SCHABER, Frederick, 46
SCHAFFER, Adam, 36; Charles, 26
SCHAUMENKESSEL, Frederick, 159
SCHEETZ, Justus, 161; Philip, 66
SCHELL, Henry, 77
SCHILL, Elizabeth Margaret, 158
SCHINCKLE, Elizabeth, 14; John, 14; Maria, 14; Perie, 14
SCHIVELY, George, 6
SCHLATTER, Elizabeth, 76; Esther, 75; Rachel, 76; William, 76
SCHLESMAN, Henry, 134
SCHLINTZ, George, 78
SCHMIDT, Frederick, 94; Godfrey, 94; Jacob, 94; John Frederick, 94
SCHNEIDER, Casper, 150; Catharine, 23, 71, 150; Catherine, 62; Christian, 71; Daniel, 23; David, 62; Elizabeth, 23; George, 23, 62; Hannah, 150; Hannes, 71; Jacob, 71; John, 23, 150; Ludwick, 62; Margaret, 23, 62; Mary, 23; Rachel, 150; Susanna, 23
SCHOENHEIT, Tobias, 13, 14, 119
SCHOLFIELD, Abraham, 105; Jonathan, 105; Rebecca, 105
SCHOTEEN, Jane, 13
SCHOTT, Eleanor, 65
SCHOTTEN, Stephen, 13
SCHRACKS, Henry, 77
SCHREIBER, Peter, 74
SCHREINER, Amelia, 73; Catharine, 73; Christopher, 73; Elizabeth, 73; Harriet, 73; Jacob, 73; Joseph H., 73; Maria, 73; William, 73
SCHRIVER, Henry, 158; Joseph, 180
SCHULTZ, Charles, 20; Conrad, 16
SCHUTZ, Barbara, 41; Frederick, 41
SCHWARTZ, Philip, 23; Susanna, 23
SCHWEPPENHIESER, Nicholas, 66
SCOLES, Francis, 28; Martha, 28
SCOTT, Andrew, 82; Anna, 53; Catharine, 162; David, 49; Elizabeth, 31; Fanny, 53; George, 53; Jane, 53; John, 53; Jonathan, 85; Joseph, 53; Lydia, 53; Mary, 53; Mary Ann, 49; Mary Houlton, 53
SCOTTEN, Ann, 40; Jane, 39; Lucy, 39; Samuel, 39, 40; Sarah, 39; William, 39, 40
SEELIG, Mary, 117
SEES, George, 38
SEGAR, Elizabeth, 17; John, 17
SEGUIN, Andrew, 43
SEILLARD, ---, 17
SELICK, Elizabeth, 115; Hannah, 115; John, 115; Joseph, 115; Louisa, 115; Sarah, 115
SELLARS, David, 143; Nathan, 143
SELLERS, Ann Evans, 71;

Coleman, 77, 147; David, 181; George, 71; Nathan, 27, 59, 155, 181; Samuel, 181
SEMPLE, Matthew, 25
SENDOS, Dominique Chegaray, 135; Elizabeth, 135; Fabien Chegaray, 135; Sarah, 135
SENIX, Arcadia, 64
SENS, George, 143
SERGEANT, Thomas, 34
SERMON, Jane, 10; Joseph, 10
SERRILL, George, 129; Jane, 129
SERRITT, John, 157
SERVOR, Caty, 182; Henry, 182
SEVERENE, William, 1
SEVERN, Benjamin, 1
SEVERNE, Benjamin, 127
SEXTON, Elizabeth, 170
SEYMAN, Apollonia, 97
SHAFFER, John L., 116; Margaret, 62
SHALEROFF, John, 99
SHALLCRAFT, William, 148, 149
SHALLCRASS, William, 148
SHALLCROSS, Ann, 78; Benjamin, 114; Betty, 163; Eliza, 163; Hannah, 114; Isaac, 163; John, 78, 114, 163; Joseph, 78, 163; Leonard, 114; Martha, 114; Mary, 78, 114; Morric C., 163; Priscilla, 78; Rachel, 114; Sarah, 114; Thomas, 114; William, 114
SHANKLAND, Charles, 111; Joseph, 111; William, 111
SHANNON, William, 126
SHARP, Catharine, 183; Edward, 43, 44; Elizabeth, 183; George, 183; Granville, 137; John, 183; Susannah, 183
SHARPE, Elizabeth, 148; Franceds, 148; John, 148
SHARPNECK, Matilda, 11
SHAW, Elizabeth, 80; James M., 102; John Auldham, 47; Martha, 183; Mary, 47; Mr., 137; Samuel, 47, 183; Samuel Burgess, 47; Spence, 47; Thomas, 47
SHEA, Daniel, 138; Dorothy, 138; George, 71; James, 174; Luke, 174; Mary, 138, 174; Mary Ann, 138; Richard, 138; Thomas, 174
SHEAFF, William, 142
SHEALS, And., 12
SHEAR, Frederick, 96
SHEARER, Elizabeth, 81; Jacob, 81; John, 81; Sarah, 81
SHED, Mary, 6
SHEED, Isabella, 116; Mary, 116; William, 116
SHEEDS, George, 76
SHEER, George, 20
SHEETS, Christian, 81
SHEETZ, Catharine, 87; Christian, 96, 125; Christianna, 125; Daniel, 87; Elizabeth, 125; George, 87; Hannah, 125; John, 87; Magdalena, 125; Mary, 87; Peter, 96, 125; Samuel, 87
SHELL, Jacob, 66; Rosanna, 66
SHEPARD, Lydia, 142; Richard, 142
SHEPHARD, John, 163; John E., 163; Mary, 163
SHEPHERD, John, 131
SHEPPARD, Catharine, 63; Clement, 30; Thomas, 26
SHERARD, Robert, 65
SHETTSLINE, Barbara, 73; Catharine, 73; Elizabeth, 73; George, 73; John, 73; Michael, 73; Samuel, 73
SHETZLINE, Adam, 97; Frances, 157; George, 157
SHEWELL, Elizabeth, 21, 110; Mary, 122; Robert, 110; Sarah, 121; Stephen, 110; Thomas, 121, 122
SHILLINGFORD, Elizabeth, 171
SHINCKLE, Frederick, 14; Jacob, 14; Salome, 14; Susana, 14; William, 14
SHINKLE, John, 67; Maria, 67
SHINN, Samuel, 72; Susan, 90
SHIPLEY, John, 106; William, 15
SHIPPEN, Dr., 67; Edward, 16; Elizabeth, 16, 74, 148
SHIPS, Isaiah, 9
SHIRKEY, Ann, 152; Patrick, 152
SHIRLEY, Thomas, 50, 66
SHISSLER, Casper, 131; Lawrence, 131, 132
SHITZ, Ann, 15; Barbara, 15; Catharine, 15; Daniel, 15; Elizabeth, 15; George, 15; Henry, 15; Jacob, 15; John, 15; Margaret, 15; Mary, 15; Michael, 15; Sarah, 15; Susanna, 15; Ulrick, 15
SHIVELY, George, 6
SHOBER, Blathwaite I., 64; Samuel, 3; Samuel Lieberhichn, 3; Susanna Budd, 3
SHOEMAKER, Abraham, 9, 22, 27, 42, 124, 152, 155, 160; Benjamin, 14, 118; Daniel, 75; Elizabeth, 118; Francis, 160; Henry, 152; Isaac, 50;

Jesse, 72; Jonathan, 50; Nathan, 127; Samuel, 1, 20, 113
SHORMAN, Ann, 70
SHOWERS, Michael, 172
SHREEVE, Caleb, 73
SHRIVER, Hannah, 158; Henry, 158; Joseph, 180
SHUFFLEBOTTOM, William, 51
SHUGE, William, 110
SHULTZ, Abraham, 16; Charles, 144; Regina, 16
SHUSTER, John, 182; Martin, 161
SHYER, Hannah, 145; Mary, 145
SIBADAY, John, 96; Mary, 96
SIBBETT, John, 155
SICKLE, Lawrence, 124; Richard, 124
SIDDONS, Jane, 38; Josiah, 122
SIDES, William, 8
SILECK, John, 115
SIMES, James, 119; Jane, 119; Samuel, 119
SIMMONS, Catherine, 56; Catherine O., 56; John, 163; John B., 56; Stephen, 141; William S., 56
SIMON, David, 98; Elizabeth, 98; John Bernard, 98; Mary, 98; Mary Margaret, 98
SIMONS, John, 65; Noah, 176
SIMPSON, David, 50; Hannah, 50; James, 3, 50, 134; John, 3, 50; Peter, 50; Ruth, 50; Stephen, 138
SIMS, Buckridge, 142; Joseph, 77; Walter, 108
SING, Charles, 142, 143
SINGLETON, Catharine, 159; Joseph Y., 159; Samuel, 156, 159; Sarah, 156, 159
SINK, Lawrence, 10, 73
SIVERT, Barbara, 157
SKELLY, Patrick, 163
SKERRETT, James, 57
SKILLAN, Ella, 67
SKINNER, Elizabeth, 155; James, 155; Mary, 155; Mary L., 155
SKURRAY, Mr., 137; Thomas, 137
SKYRIN, Ann, 176; Eleanor, 176; Elizabeth, 176; John, 176
SLINGLOFF, Joseph, 78, 116
SLOAN, Mary, 108
SLOCUM, Charles M., 104; Emiline, 104; Marshall C., 104
SLONE, Elijah, 79; Elizabeth, 79; Mary, 79; Solomon, 79
SMALL, Abraham (Abm.), 46, 126; Ann, 179; Rhoda, 169
SMALLWOOD, Elizabeth, 49; Isaac, 41; Manlie, 41; Martha, 75; Peter, 41; Priscilla, 41; Thomas, 49
SMECK, Catharine, 84
SMELTZ, Reinhart, 162
SMITH, Amy, 121; Ann, 57, 80; Ann Caroline, 80; Anthony, 80; Catharine, 6, 89, 113, 171, 181; Caty, 94; Charles, 125, 178; Charles E., 56, 57; Charles T., 101; Christian, 66; Clifford, 93; Daniel, 170, 181; Deborah, 56; Dockeray, 54, 65; Ed, 148; Eleanor, 111; Elenor, 148; Elisabeth, 181; Elizabeth, 1, 80, 100, 113, 116, 123, 143, 145; Frances, 21, 115; Francis G., 96; Francis Gurney, 96; Frederick, 1, 2, 6, 71, 95, 100, 125, 137; George, 1, 128, 145; Godfrey, 1; Griszell, 56, 57; Hannah L., 174; Hannah W., 121; Henry, 181; Hetty, 94; Hugh, 56, 91; Jacob, 1, 45, 100, 131, 175; James, 121, 151, 174; James B., 107; James S., 25, 113; Jane, 151; John, 1, 3, 12, 27, 71, 98, 100, 124, 128, 131, 135, 171, 172; John D., 51; John H., 42; John Harper, 124; John R., 80; John S., 50; Jona., 184, 185; Jonathan Bayard, 80; Joseph, 116, 170, 171; Joseph B., 21, 22, 115; Lewis, 83; Lojra, 124; Lydia, 113; Margaret, 56, 58, 171; Margery, 56, 91; Mary, 27, 80, 91, 111, 115, 128, 151, 171; Mary W., 56; Michal, 181; Nancy, 151; Nathan A., 57; Newberry, 57, 61; Patrick, 158; Peter, 58, 128; Philip, 86, 167, 181, 182; R., 107; Rachel, 22, 115; Ralph, 91, 107; Ralph H., 91; Rebecca, 80; Richard, 114; Richard E., 80; Sally, 94; Samuel, 113, 115, 134; Samuel Beddome, 21; Samuel H., 80; Sarah, 116; Stafford, 80; Susan, 100; Susan Bayard, 80; Susanna, 1, 2, 57, 128; Thomas, 20, 37, 50, 56, 57, 143, 181; Thomas L., 113; Valentine, 1; William, 5, 140, 151; William Allen, 57; William L., 80; William Moore, 63; William T., 80; Yost, 170

SMYTH, Frederick, 124
SNEERINGER, John, 183
SNELL, Maria, 145; Matthias, 107
SNIDER, Casper, 106; John, 107
SNOWDEN, Charles, 4; Gilbert T., 4; Hannah, 122; Isaac, 4; Joseph, 32; Leonard, 20, 31; Mary, 4; Nathaniel R., 4; Samuel F., 4; Sarah, 4; William, 4
SNYDER, Christian, 12; Daniel, 147; George, 42, 133; John, 165, 177; Margaret, 12; Philip, 42
SOARES, John Frans., 159
SOBER, Catharine, 141; Elizabeth, 141; John, 141
SOLMS, I., 168; Joseph, 56
SOLN, Richard Pruen, 51
SOMERS, Rachel, 112
SOMMER, Jacob, 105, 168
SONNTAG, William L., 152
SONNTAGG, Euphrosna, 176; Hannah, 176; William, 176
SORBER, Ann, 182; Catherena, 182; Elias, 32, 182; Henry, 32, 182; Joseph, 182
SOUDER, Charles, 93, 96
SOULDIER, John M., 9
SPARKS, Elizabeth, 28; Richard, 175; Robert, 28, 41; Simon, 74; Thomas, 175
SPEEL, Catharine, 106; Elizabeth, 106; John, 106; John L., 106; Juliana, 106; Maria, 106; Sophia, 106; Thos. Jefferson M., 106
SPEER, Sarah, 56
SPENCER, Jane, 33; John, 16, 33
SPICER, Jacob, 143
SPICKENNAGEL, W., 83
SPOHN, William, 73
SPRING, M. B., 151
SPRINGER, John, 116
SPROUL, George, 96
STACKHOUS, Susanna, 2
STACKHOUSE, Amos, 140; Elizabeth, 40; Mary, 140
STACY, Sarah, 168
STADDELMAN, Catharine, 160; William, 160
STAFFORD, Robert S., 153; Sarah, 97
STALL, Elizabeth, 27; Samuel, 27
STALLMAN, William, 141
STANTON, Priamus, 31
STAR, Mary, 140
STEBBRY, Dorothy, 91
STEEL, Anthony, 75, 140; Elizabeth, 83; John, 55, 84; Joseph, 113; Mary, 83
STEIGERIN, Maria, 91
STEIN, Abraham, 13, 49, 85, 119, 135, 139, 180
STEINMETZ, ---, 8
STEPHENS, Walter, 171
STERR, George, 118
STERRET, Augusta, 47; Rebecca, 47
STEVENS, Francis Bowes, 150; John, 114, 150, 151; Mary, 4; Rachel, 150; Reuben, 118; Thomas, 163
STEVENSON, Andrew A., 105, 170; William, 33, 77
STEWARD, Charles, 108; Hannah, 108; James, 90; Jane, 6; Mary, 90
STEWARDSON, Thomas, 51, 60, 62, 159
STEWART, Alexander, 79; Charles, 61; Charles S., 93; James, 10, 90, 141; Moses, 11, 72; Robert, 16; Samuel, 155; Thomas, 10, 38
STIER, Jacob, 7, 8; Maria, 7
STILES, Catharine, 150; Edward, 3; Robert, 150
STILLAS, Thomas, 161
STINE, Catharine, 14; John, 14
STOCK, Philip, 6
STOCKDEN, Abraham, 143; Samuel, 143; Susanna, 143; Thomas, 143
STOCKDON, Esther, 150; Julia, 150
STOCKER, John C., 113; Margaret, 113
STOCKTON, Francis Bowes, 150
STOCKWELL, M. K., 128
STODDART, John, 90
STOKES, Ellis, 130; James, 33; Samuel, 38; Sarah, 40; Thomas, 38
STOLL, Adam, 103
STONE, Daniel, 158; Mary, 158
STONEBURNER, Ann, 164
STORK, Mary, 33
STORY, Thomas, 60
STOUSE, Esther, 135; Joseph, 135
STOUT, Ann, 18; Jacob C., 126; Peter, 156
STRAHAN, Charles, 65; George, 65; John, 65; Joseph, 65; Margaret, 65; Mary, 65; Paul, 65
STREEPER, John, 95
STREET, Griffith, 179; Jane, 109; John, 63; Robert, 104;

Samuel Scotten, 40
STREMBECK, William, 139
STRENBECK, William, 184
STREPER, John, 141
STRICKER, John, 64
STRICKLER, Isaac, 80
STRINGER, Sarah, 184
STRONG, Agness, 47; Matthew, 47
STROUCE, Jacob, 172
STROUP, John, 134
STRUNCK, Catharine, 177; Philip, 177
STUART, Elizabeth, 26; James, 118, 172; Sarah, 26
STUNTZ, Catharine, 46; Frederick, 46; Heinrich Philip, 46
SULGER, Jacob, 68
SULLENDER, Elizabeth, 36; Jacob, 36; Peter, 36; Sarah Ann, 36; Wilhelmina, 36
SUMMERS, Andrew, 3; Anthony, 159; George, 159; Henry, 159; Jacob, 90; John, 159; Martin, 68, 159; Mary, 68; Nicholas, 159; Peter, 159; Philip, 159; Sarah, 159
SUTER, Daniel, 6; Susan, 58
SUTHERLAND, Daniel, 76
SUTTON, Benjamin, 3; John, 110; Mary, 79; Thomas, 148
SWAINE, Anna, 98; John, 74
SWAN, Jane Isabella, 100
SWANN, Thomas, 58
SWARTS, Peter, 19
SWARTZ, Ann, 23; Daniel, 23; George, 23; Joseph, 23; Sarah, 23; Susana, 23
SWARZ, George, 19
SWEENY, Elizabeth, 6; William, 169
SWIFT, Caroline, 146; Charles, 146; Edward, 75, 146; Elizabeth, 146; John, 146; Joseph K., 146; Joseph Kinnersley, 146; Mary, 146; Patience, 146; Phebe, 146; Samuel, 146
SYBERT, Casper, 116
SYDELMAN, Philip, 143
SYME, Martha Hoop, 100
SYNG, Philip, 120

-T-

TAGGART, Thomas, 17
TANGUY, P., 171
TANNER, Benjamin, 6
TAPSICO, Jacob, 21
TARBOX, Ann, 149; Joseph, 149
TAWS, Cathrine, 43; James, 43
TAYLER, William, 64
TAYLOR, Amos, 155; Ann Loxley, 101; Elizabeth Williams, 101; George, 106; Jacob, 87; James, 25; Jane, 25; John, 10, 25, 147, 166; John R., 176; Joseph, 107; Maria, 25; Mary Ann, 101; Phebe, 81; Philip, 141; Rachel, 176; Robert, 36; Samuel, 44, 54, 152; Stephen, 28
TEAR, Philip, 115
TEST, David, 159
TEW, Edward, 3
THACKARA, William, 32
THATCHER, Andrew, 24
THAUWORTH, Johanna, 38
THIBAULT, F., 171
THOMAS, Anna, 111; Barbara A., 87; Daniel, 13, 55; Edward A., 87; Elizabeth, 29, 95; Enoch, 82, 93; Ezekiel C., 87; George, 117, 139; Hannah A., 87; Isaac, 150; Isachar, 87; Israel, 139; Jacob, 2, 116; Jane, 87, 152; Jesse, 73, 119; John, 106, 124; John D., 124; Joseph, 95, 139, 141; Letitia, 87; Lewis, 139; Martin, 44; Mary, 151, 152; Rebecca, 44, 95, 117; Richard P., 29; Richard S., 87; Robert, 87, 139; Samuel, 93, 96; Sarah, 95, 139; Susanah, 117
THOMPSON, Atcheson, 128; James B., 35, 167; Jane, 87; John, 140, 167; Lydia, 95; Nevil, 95; Peter, 1, 101; Rebecca, 183
THOMSON, Anna, 123, 176; Atcheson, 75; Charles, 87, 176; George, 175; Hannah, 116, 123, 175; Jacob, 14; Jesse, 176; Peter, 12, 13, 14, 15, 30, 32, 33, 35, 41, 44, 51, 62, 69, 87, 103, 110, 114, 122, 123, 124, 133, 152, 175, 176; Rebecca, 123, 124; Ripon Edward, 103; Sarah, 55; Sarah Biddle, 123; William, 156, 175; Zane W., 112
THORNE, John Ulysses, 110
THORNTON, Jane, 102; Jesse, 172; Joseph, 102
THUM, Charles, 49; Eliza, 49; Elizabeth, 49; George, 49; Jacob, 49; John, 49; Mary Ann, 49; Sarah, 49
THUNN, Catharine, 7; Elizabeth, 7
TIERS, Cornelius, 46

TILGHMAN, Anna Maria, 43; Edward, 5, 167; Elizabeth, 5; Mary, 5; William, 5, 74
TILLMAN, George, 182
TILLY, Mary, 54, 65; Peter, 54
TILLYER, Ann, 129; Mary, 129; Phoebe, 129; Sarah, 129; William, 129, 130
TIMELY, Mary, 145
TIMINGS, Thomas, 11, 44, 61
TIMMEL, Jacob, 8
TITTERMARY, John, 133; Richard, 77
TOD, Alexander (Alexr.), 125; Mary, 6; William H., 6, 64, 100
TODD, Elisha, 21; Feby, 21; Hester, 21; William H., 103
TODMAN, William, 37
TOLAND, Henry, 185
TOLBERT, Hannah, 30; John, 30
TOLLAND, Henry, 88
TOMKINS, Hannah Y., 19; Isaac, 19, 20; Jacob, 19; Joseph Y., 19; Sarah, 19
TOMLIN, Samuel, 28
TOMLINSON, Jemima, 60; Jesse, 60; John, 114; Martha Worthington, 114; Sarah, 60
TOMPSON, Peter, 106
TOOD, Philes, 21
TOWNSEND, Charles, 53, 60; Elizabeth, 116; Ezra, 2, 168, 179; Hannah, 53; John, 37, 53, 87, 134, 176; Joseph, 113; Noe, 116; Rev. Mr., 137; Sarah, 116
TRAIN, John, 64
TRAQUAIR, Adam, 49; Ann, 49; James, 48, 49, 177; Thomas, 49
TRASEL, Jacob, 166
TRAVIS, Patrick, 108
TREAS, John, 42
TREMNER, Francis, 8
TRIMBLE, James, 169
TRIP, Adam, 40
TRIVITT, Thomas, 70
TROUBAT, John, 184
TROUT, John, 68; Susanna, 58
TRULLINGERS, Andrew, 170
TRUMAN, Abigail, 122; Isabella Bewley, 122; James, 68, 122; Mary Sikes, 122; Richard, 122; Thomas Sikes, 122
TRUMP, John, 95
TRUSTY, Jonathan, 21, 51, 111, 156
TRUXTON, Mary Ann, 108; William, 7
TRYON, George, 140
TUCKER, Abner, 57; Benjamin, 60; Elizabeth, 48; Johanna Maria, 58
TUNIS, Richard, 51
TUNISH, Richard, 53
TURNER, Abby Ann, 130; Abigail, 130; Daniel, 105; Eliza, 60; Francis, 28; Joanna, 87; John, 3; John Eliot, 148; Joseph, 60, 130; Mrs., 137; William, 72, 130; William A., 130
TUSTON, Eliza, 87; Israel, 87; Joseph, 87; Septimus, 87; Susannah, 87; Thomas, 87; William, 87
TUTVILER, John, 16
TWADDELL, John, 113
TYSON, Deborah, 62; Hannah, 44; Isaac, 101

-U-

UHLEN, John, 57
UNBEHERT, Valenten, 106
UNCLESON, Rosana, 126
UNROD, Ann, 112; Catharine, 112; Elizabeth, 112; Jacob, 112; Mary, 112; Sarah, 112; Susan, 112
UNSWORTH, John, 60; Mary, 60
UPMAN, Matthias, 161
UPTON, Elizabeth, 37; Thomas, 37
URGERHART, Alexander, 153
URQUHART, Alexander, 35

-V-

VACTOR, John, 117; Patience, 117
VALERIO, Dn. Francisco, 25
VAN BEUREN, Abraham, 146; Mary, 146
VAN DUSEN, Andrew, 179; Elizabeth, 179; John, 179; Lydia, 179; Mary, 179; Matthew, 179; Nicholas, 179; Washington, 179
VAN DYKE, Dirrick, 99
VAN LASHET, Christian, 109
VAN PHUL, William, 31
VAN TRUMP, Elizabeth, 79
VAN WINKEL, Jacob, 35
VANASDALEN, Christopher, 130
VANCE, Mary, 181
VANCISE, Joseph, 171
VANCLEVE, John W., 39
VANDENBERG, Matthew, 39
VANDERHORST, Elias, 137
VANDERSLICE, Daniel, 1; Jacob, 8
VANDERVEER, David, 178

VANDEWALL, Frances, 149; Joseph, 149
VANDIKE, Aron, 99; Christena, 99; David, 99; Elenor, 99; Nelley, 99; William, 99
VANDUSEN, Andrew, 103; Eliza, 103; John, 103; Lydia, 103; Mary, 103; Matthew, 103; Nicholas, 103; Washington, 103
VANGESIL, Gertrude, 55
VANHORN, Barnard, 100; Pamella, 100
VANLEER, Benjamin, 169
VANLIER, George, 118
VANORTSDALEN, Phoebe, 146
VANOSTEN, Joseph, 130
VANSANT, Garret, 168; Rebecca, 146
VANSISE, Jane, 86
VAUGHAN, John, 6, 124
VEACOCK, Samuel S., 32
VEARSON, Alex., 39
VESIN, Louis, 156
VIDELANGE, Catherine, 141; Francis, 141
VODGES, Jacob, 124
VOGELS, Gerard, 3
VOIGT, Ann, 154; Henry, 153, 154; Louisa, 154; Margaretta, 154; Mary, 154; Thomas, 154
VOLLMER, Frederick, 58, 112
VOSTAIN, Fournier, 5
VREDENBURGH, Ester, 22; Isaac, 22

-W-

WACHSMUTH, John Godfried, 141, 142
WAELPER, George G., 150
WAGANER, Hannah, 182; John, 182; Philip, 182
WAGER, Amy, 121; Ann, 80; Elizabeth, 117, 121; George, 121; Hannah, 116, 121; Hannah S., 121; Henrietta, 117; John William, 117; Juliana, 121; Juliana Elizabeth, 89; Julianna, 117; Margaret, 117; Margaretta, 121; Maria, 121; Mrs., 89; Peter, 80, 116, 117, 121; Philip, 89, 116, 117, 121; Philip S., 121; Philip Stein, 117; Sarah, 117, 121; Sophia, 121; Sophia Maria, 117; William S., 121; William Stein, 117
WAGNER, Catharine, 11; Jacob, 158; John, 64; Peter, 14, 42, 71, 81
WALAHAN, Jacob, 57
WALKER, Beulah, 118; Elizabeth, 119; Elizabeth Finney, 100; Emanuel, 118; John V. L., 118; Joseph, 118, 119; Lewis, 92; Margaret, 99; Richard, 149; Samuel, 41, 118, 119
WALLACE, Elizabeth, 176; James B., 185; John B., 32, 42; Joseph, 176; Joshua M., 151; Joshua Maddox, 51; Margaret, 29; Robert, 21, 82; Wesley William, 29; William, 29
WALLEN, Catharine, 74; Hope, 61; Kezia, 61; Lettice, 61; Mrs., 148; Rachel, 61; Sarah, 61
WALLIS, John, 36; Joseph Jacob, 142; Samuel, 142
WALN, Francis, 182; Jacob S., 47, 144; Lewis, 182; Nicholas, 10, 15, 43, 134; Nichollas, 133; Phebe, 97; Robert, 31, 32, 51, 97, 132; Sarah, 134; William, 10, 134
WALSCH, Thomas, 153
WALSH, Anna Maria, 79; Robert, 79
WALSHES, Mary, 153
WALTER, Hannah, 118; John, 20; John Peter, 118; Joseph S., 69; Peter, 118; Sophia, 118
WALTERS, John, 20
WALTMAN, Catharine, 57; Eve, 57; Margaret, 57; Mary Ann, 57; Michael, 57; Samuel, 57; William, 57
WALTON, Enoch, 13; Hannah, 114; Patience, 13; Silas, 2
WAMPOLE, Isaac, 8, 9, 11, 12, 26, 36, 37, 40, 44, 46, 49, 51, 68, 71, 72, 79, 89, 94, 97, 98, 102, 106, 113, 120, 130, 164, 184
WARD, John, 126
WARDE, John, 148
WARDER, Ann, 69; Jeremiah, 51; Jermiah, 137; John, 69, 137, 138; Miriam, 47; Mrs., 138
WARNER, Aieronimus, 143; Frederick, 30; Heronimus, 29, 87; John, 30, 72, 74, 134; John Chr., 78; Joseph, 134; Lydia, 134; Margarett, 30; Mary, 134; Nancy, 134; Prudence, 102; Rebecca, 134; William, 134
WARNOCK, John, 63
WARRICK, Thomas, 139
WARRINGTON, John, 113
WASHINGTON, Thomas, 3
WASLEY, Amelia, 105, 106

WATERMAN, Hannah, 90; Jesse, 95; Susanna, 95; Thomas, 90, 111
WATERS, William, 48
WATSON, Anne, 71; Charles, 71; David, 29; Elizabeth, 29; Hannah, 29; Isaac, 71; John, 29; John F., 158; Joseph, 29, 71; Josiah, 29; Martha, 29; Mary, 29; Sarah, 29; Thomas, 29; Tolbert, 30; Washington, 29; William, 29
WATT, Samuel, 66
WATTS, Frances, 127; John, 118, 127; Margaret, 118, 127; Mary, 127; Rachel, 127
WAY, William, 32
WEAVER, Anna, 121; Anna Maria, 135; Barbara, 135; Catharine, 51, 135; Conrad, 54, 135; David, 51; Dorothea, 54; Elizabeth, 135; Hannah, 51; Henry, 51; John, 51, 135; Mary, 51; Matthew, 98; Thomas, 51; Walter Roble, 103; Wilhelmina, 51
WEBB, Eliza, 133; Reynold, 104; Samuel P., 104; William, 133
WEBSTER, Benjamin, 43; Sarah, 43
WECKERLY, Conrad, 102
WEEKS, Samuel, 38
WEGMAN, Margaret, 117
WEILER, John, 155
WEIR, Silas E., 30, 177
WELCH, John, 178
WELLS, George, 48; John, 48; John S., 100; Lydia, 53; Sidney, 112
WELSH, Ephraim, 98; James, 184; John, 39, 51; Johna A., 98; Lydia, 51; Mary, 98, 153, 184; Rachael, 98
WENNER, Alice, 53
WENTZ, Andrew, 175; Catharine, 175; Elizabeth, 175; John, 7, 175; Maria, 7; Mary, 175
WEREBROOK, Elizabeth, 42
WERTMULLER, Adolph Ulrick, 68; Elizabeth, 68, 69
WEST, Ann, 28, 140; Betsy, 113; Cabel Davis, 117; Charles, 140; Esther, 117; Francis, 64; George, 119; Hannah, 140; Isaiah, 28; James, 113; Job, 28; Joel, 117; Joseph, 28; Maria Louisa, 82; Mary, 140; Rebecca, 117; Samuel, 140; Sarah, 28, 117, 140; Thomas, 117; William, 19
WESTBERGER, George, 165
WESTCOTT, George, 51
WESTPHAL, Charles W., 8
WETHERHEAD, Alexander, 81; Catharine, 81; Ester, 81; Margaret, 81
WETHERILL, Christopher, 9; Samuel, 1
WEVERS, Margaret, 8
WHARTON, Ann, 96, 97, 143; Beynall, 183; Charles, 3, 31, 183; Edmund, 104; Elizabeth, 154; Elizabeth F., 104; Franklin, 48; George, 183; Hannah, 143, 155; Isaac, 3; James, 183; John, 124, 132; Joseph, 3, 77, 143, 154; Margaret, 104; Martha, 154; Rachel, 143; Rebecca, 104, 183; Robert, 15, 143, 145; Robert Owen, 145; Sarah, 104, 154; Thomas, 96; Washington, 48
WHEELER, Charles, 40; Enoch, 40; Samuel, 20, 66
WHELEN, Israel, 140, 154
WHIT, Edwin, 144
WHITAKER, James, 81
WHITALL, Benjamin, 28
WHITBY, George, 65; Jane, 65; Robert, 65; William, 65
WHITE, Benjamin, 134; Benjn., 183; John, 21; Mary, 69, 89, 101, 113; Rudolph, 130; Samuel, 8; Sarah, 69; Thomas H., 47; William, 177
WHITEHEAD, James, 132; R., 5, 10, 12, 23, 24, 36, 66, 77, 94, 106, 123, 129, 136; Richard, 47, 124, 154; Robert, 3, 23, 25, 29, 43, 44, 47, 62, 66, 67, 77, 87, 107, 108, 116, 118, 124, 129, 130, 131, 132, 136, 139, 145, 150, 151, 154, 155, 158, 160, 161, 163, 166, 171, 178; W. Robert, 49
WHITEHILL, James, 78
WHITEMAN, Michael, 105
WHITESIDES, Alexander, 5
WHITMAN, Mayberry, 139; Nathan, 127
WHITTLE, Ann, 45, 46; Robert, 45
WHITTON, Abednego T., 95
WICKAM, Anastacia, 86; Eleanor, 86; James, 85, 86; Margaretta, 86
WICKART, John, 143
WICKERSHAM, Abigail, 127
WICKEY, John M., 177
WICKHAM, Michael, 86; Nicholas,

86
WIDDIFIELD, Hannah, 176; James, 176; William, 61
WIDDIS, Charles, 71
WIGGLESWORTH, Ann, 184; Sarah, 184; William, 184
WIGHTINBURG, Michael, 116
WIGMORE, Joseph A., 47, 167
WILCOCKS, James Smith, 39; John, 51; Mary, 5; Richard, 51
WILCOX, Mary, 111
WILD, Christiana Catharine, 139; Frederick, 139; John, 139; Mary, 139
WILE, Catharine, 99; Conrad, 128; George, 182; Mary, 182
WILES, Daniel, 110
WILEY, Ann, 157; Elizabeth, 73; James, 180; Robert, 157
WILIN, Conrad, 185
WILKES, Luveazer, 94
WILKINS, Elizabeth, 79; Jane, 79; John, 79; Thomas, 79
WILKINSON, Andrew, 131; John, 43; Rebecca, 39
WILL, Catharine, 146; Hannah, 146; Sarah, 146
WILLARD, George, 27
WILLETT, John S., 22, 23; Rachael, 22, 23
WILLIAM, Thomas, 20
WILLIAMS, Ann, 109; Benjamin, 17, 73; Christiana, 72; Daniel, 109; David, 115; Eliza, 33; Elizabeth Rogers, 101; Ennion, 57; Esther, 130; George, 51, 130; Hannah, 20; James, 101; Jesse, 51, 134, 173; John, 16, 33, 135; Joseph, 138, 184; Luke, 109; Margareta, 16; Martha, 7; Mary, 33; Matilda, 176; Olivia, 101; Peter, 16; Samuel H., 81; Sarah, 33; Solomon, 16; Thomas, 80; Thomas D., 72; William Jones, 47
WILLIAMSON, Jesse, 99; Joseph, 99; Peggy, 117
WILLING, Byrd, 70; Eliza, 70; Frances, 70; Hare, 70; James, 70; Richard, 66, 70, 134; Thomas M., 45; Thomas Mayne, 45; William, 182
WILLIS, Hannah, 126; Henry, 184; John, 74; Jonathan, 18, 47; Thomas, 126
WILLS, Hannah, 17; James, 40; Michael, 92
WILLSON, William, 114
WILMER, Lambert, 80
WILSON, Aa., 131; Alexander, 47, 95, 132, 183; Alice, 70; Ann, 176, 179; Ann Pratchett, 70; Benjamin, 153; David, 10, 70, 72, 89, 179; Elizabeth, 89, 115; Emma, 111; Ethan, 179; George, 101, 170; Isaac, 40; Jabez, 179; Jacob, 178; Jesse, 2; John, 28, 53, 59, 131, 145, 176; John B., 130; Jonathan, 179; Joseph, 19, 115; Mardon, 179; Maria, 26; Mary, 17, 101, 145; Mercy, 145; Oliver, 145; Philip, 89; Rachel, 179; Rebecca, 131, 145; Rebekah, 179; Robert, 179; Saml. L., 130; Samuel, 145; Sarah, 131; Silas, 131, 172; Sybilla, 26; Sybilla P., 131; Thomas, 28; William, 17, 76, 163
WILT, Abraham, 124; Andrew, 58; Christian, 58; Juliana, 58; Rachel, 58; Rebecca, 58
WINDAW, Mr., 137
WINDERGAST, Margaret, 59
WINEMORE, Elizabeth, 74, 157; Henry, 74; Jacob, 74; John, 74, 157; Mary, 157; Philip, 74
WINEY, Jacob, 26
WINNEMORE, Philip, 74
WINTERS, Robert, 102
WINTON, Mary, 46
WINTZALL, John, 182
WIRTZ, Christian, 116; Mary, 116
WISLEY, Margaret, 72
WISSINBANKS, Joseph, 21
WISTAR, C., 138; Caspar, 107; Casper, 124; John, 183; Richard, 108; Sarah, 91; Thomas, 26, 115
WISTER, Charles L., 160
WITHERSIP, Agnes, 107; Alexander, 107
WITMAN, Nathan, 105; Newberry, 105; Stephen, 105
WOGLOM, Benjamin, 89
WOLBERT, Frederick, 17, 159
WOLFE, Mary, 16
WOLFF, Aaron, 38
WOLLISON, Joshua, 183
WONTER, John, 17
WONTERS, Jacob, 17
WOOD, Andrew, 92; Ann, 92, 116; David C., 185; Elizabeth, 92; George, 92; Hannah, 92; Henry, 63; James, 174; John, 92; Mary, 63, 92; Michael,

92; Samson, 110; Sarah, 123; Sophia, 143, 154; William, 46
WOODFORD, Dr., 137
WOODHOUSE, Elizabeth, 103
WOODROW, Elizabeth, 70; Hester, 164; Susannah, 70
WOODRUFF, Archd., 153; David, 166
WOODWARD, Deborah, 42; Elizabeth, 42; Jacob, 42; Mary, 42; Sarah, 42; W. W., 111, 126
WOOLASTON, Daniel, 143
WOOLMAN, Sarah, 142; William, 142
WOOLSEY, Samuel, 104
WORK, George, 139
WORKMAN, J., 10; Samuel, 157; William, 3
WORRALL, William, 64
WORRELL, Isaac, 138; John H., 138, 139; Rudolph, 139
WORRILL, Hannah, 10; Nathan, 10; Rachel, 10
WORTH, Mary, 109; Sarah, 108, 109
WORTHINGTON, Asa, 114, 168; Benjamin, 114; Elizabeth, 146; Enos, 114; James, 114, 115; John, 114, 168; Joshua, 114; Mahlon, 114
WRAN, Elizabeth Bosio, 140; Maryan, 140; Rebecca Bosio, 140
WRAY, Eleanor, 159; William, 110
WRIGHT, Elenor, 117; Eleoner, 81; Elizabeth, 81, 117; Enoch, 117, 118; Esther, 118; George, 117; Hannah, 5; Hiram, 117; John, 5, 16, 98, 118; Joseph, 118; Mary, 117; Morgan, 117; Phebe, 117; Rachel, 117, 118; Rebecca, 118; Sarah, 5, 117, 118, 162; Thomas, 73, 118, 141, 169; William, 77, 81, 117, 118
WROTMAN, Joachim, 68
WUNDER, Sebastian, 107
WYNARD, Ann, 78

-Y-

YAGEL, Christopher, 17
YARD, James, 17
YARDLEY, William, 13, 34
YARDLY, William, 165
YARNALL, Amos, 51; Eli, 51; Ellis, 10, 27; Matilda, 51
YARNELL, Ellis, 26
YATES, Ann, 116; Catharine, 116; Harriot, 116
YEAGER, John, 42
YEAKLE, Abraham, 16; Anna, 16; Casper, 16; Christopher, 16; Mary, 16; Regina, 16; Susanna, 16
YEATES, James, 105; Mary, 114; William, 114
YETTER, Charles, 36, 78
YORK, Mary, 10
YORKE, Samuel, 6, 125
YOUNG, Charles, 135; Evans John, 164; Jacob, 135; James, 87; Johanna, 23; John, 135; Maria, 25; Maria Ann, 135; Maria Anna, 135; Peter, 152; Samuel, 36, 37, 74, 76; Sarah, 164; Thomas, 91, 129, 158, 163; William, 164
YOUNGKORTH, Frederick, 32
YOUNKER, Abraham, 160; Ann, 160; Charles, 160; Daniel, 160; Elizabeth, 160; George, 160; Joseph, 160; Margaret, 160; Martha, 160; Mary, 160; Sarah, 160; William, 160; Yost, 160

-Z-

ZANE, Isaac, 59, 77; John, 59; Sarah, 59
ZEISS, Andrew, 139
ZELERE, John Lar, 119
ZELL, Christopher, 126
ZELLER, Johann, 88
ZERNS, Catharine, 32

Other books by F. Edward Wright:

Abstracts of Bucks County, Pennsylvania Wills, 1685-1785

Abstracts of Cumberland County, Pennsylvania Wills, 1750-1785

Abstracts of Cumberland County, Pennsylvania Wills, 1785-1825

Abstracts of Philadelphia County Wills, 1726-1747

Abstracts of Philadelphia County Wills, 1748-1763

Abstracts of Philadelphia County Wills, 1763-1784

Abstracts of Philadelphia County Wills, 1777-1790

Abstracts of Philadelphia County Wills, 1790-1802

Abstracts of Philadelphia County Wills, 1802-1809

Abstracts of Philadelphia County Wills, 1810-1815

Abstracts of Philadelphia County Wills, 1815-1819

Abstracts of Philadelphia County Wills, 1820-1825

Abstracts of Philadelphia County, Pennsylvania Wills, 1682-1726

Abstracts of South Central Pennsylvania Newspapers, Volume 1, 1785-1790

Abstracts of South Central Pennsylvania Newspapers, Volume 3, 1796-1800

Abstracts of the Newspapers of Georgetown and the Federal City, 1789-99

Abstracts of York County, Pennsylvania Wills, 1749-1819

Bucks County, Pennsylvania Church Records of the 17th and 18th Centuries Volume 2: Quaker Records: Falls and Middletown Monthly Meetings
Anna Miller Watring and F. Edward Wright

Caroline County, Maryland Marriages, Births and Deaths, 1850-1880

Citizens of the Eastern Shore of Maryland, 1659-1750

Cumberland County, Pennsylvania Church Records of the 18th Century

Delaware Newspaper Abstracts, Volume 1: 1786-1795

Early Charles County, Maryland Settlers, 1658-1745
Marlene Strawser Bates and F. Edward Wright

Early Church Records of Alexandria City and Fairfax County, Virginia
F. Edward Wright and Wesley E. Pippenger

Early Church Records of New Castle County, Delaware, Volume 1, 1701-1800

Frederick County Militia in the War of 1812
Sallie A. Mallick and F. Edward Wright

Inhabitants of Baltimore County, 1692-1763

Land Records of Sussex County, Delaware, 1769-1782

Land Records of Sussex County, Delaware, 1782-1789
Elaine Hastings Mason and F. Edward Wright

Marriage Licenses of Washington, District of Columbia, 1811-1830

Marriages and Deaths from the Newspapers of Allegany and Washington Counties, Maryland, 1820-1830

Marriages and Deaths from The York Recorder, 1821-1830

Marriages and Deaths in the Newspapers of Frederick and Montgomery Counties, Maryland, 1820-1830

Marriages and Deaths in the Newspapers of Lancaster County, Pennsylvania, 1821-1830

Marriages and Deaths in the Newspapers of Lancaster County, Pennsylvania, 1831-1840

Marriages and Deaths of Cumberland County, [Pennsylvania], 1821-1830

Maryland Calendar of Wills Volume 9: 1744-1749

Maryland Calendar of Wills Volume 10: 1748-1753

Maryland Calendar of Wills Volume 11: 1753-1760

Maryland Calendar of Wills Volume 12: 1759-1764

Maryland Calendar of Wills Volume 13: 1764-1767

Maryland Calendar of Wills Volume 14: 1767-1772

Maryland Calendar of Wills Volume 15: 1772-1774

Maryland Calendar of Wills Volume 16: 1774-1777

Maryland Eastern Shore Newspaper Abstracts, Volume 1: 1790-1805

Maryland Eastern Shore Newspaper Abstracts, Volume 2: 1806-1812

Maryland Eastern Shore Newspaper Abstracts, Volume 3: 1813-1818

Maryland Eastern Shore Newspaper Abstracts, Volume 4: 1819-1824

Maryland Eastern Shore Newspaper Abstracts, Volume 5: Northern Counties, 1825-1829
F. Edward Wright and Irma Harper

Maryland Eastern Shore Newspaper Abstracts, Volume 6: Southern Counties, 1825-1829

Maryland Eastern Shore Newspaper Abstracts, Volume 7: Northern Counties, 1830-1834
Irma Harper and F. Edward Wright

Maryland Eastern Shore Newspaper Abstracts, Volume 8: Southern Counties, 1830-1834

Maryland Militia in the Revolutionary War
S. Eugene Clements and F. Edward Wright

Newspaper Abstracts of Allegany and Washington Counties, 1811-1815

Newspaper Abstracts of Cecil and Harford Counties, [Maryland], 1822-1830

Newspaper Abstracts of Frederick County, [Maryland], 1816-1819

Newspaper Abstracts of Frederick County, 1811-1815

Sketches of Maryland Eastern Shoremen

Tax List of Chester County, Pennsylvania 1768

Tax List of York County, Pennsylvania 1779

Washington County Church Records of the 18th Century, 1768-1800

Western Maryland Newspaper Abstracts, Volume 1: 1786-1798

Western Maryland Newspaper Abstracts, Volume 2: 1799-1805

Western Maryland Newspaper Abstracts, Volume 3: 1806-1810

Wills of Chester County, Pennsylvania, 1766-1778